"*Career Pathways in Adult Education* is a well-timed resource... wealth of information and expertise for current and future practitioners. I recommend... required read for those exploring alternative career paths."
  –**Anthony C. Adkisson, PhD.**, *Principal Technical Assistant Consultant, American Institutes for Research*

"*Career Pathways in Adult Education* is a long-awaited resource answering the question, 'What can I do with a degree in adult education?' This excellent book is well conceptualized, drawing from research and practitioner experiences to provide an expansive portrait of possible careers. A complementary resource for the Foundations of Adult Education."
  –**Mary V. Alfred, PhD.**, *Professor Emerita, Texas A&M University*

"*Career Pathways in Adult Education* will be valuable to those learning about the field of adult education for the first time as well as those seeking to transfer their adult education experiences and skills to a different segment of the field."
  –**Ronald M. Cervero, PhD.**, *Professor and Deputy Director, Health Professions Education, Uniformed Services University of the Health Sciences*

"This book thoughtfully details a wide-ranging exploration of adult education opportunities for professionals to enhance their skills and careers. The authors provide a toolbox of expertise to build a foundation for instructional and administrative success in adult education. A must-read for anyone striving to impact lifelong learners!"
  –**Kelly Mobray**, *Director of Adult Education, Salina Public Schools*

Career Pathways in Adult Education

Career Pathways in Adult Education showcases the wide-ranging possibilities for a satisfying career in the field of adult education.

Along with practical advice for launching and advancing a career in adult education, this book includes personal stories and insights from adult education professionals which focus on the research, practices, programs, and services within multiple industries. Divided into two parts, the book begins by examining transferable skills that adult educators need to be successful in any adult education career. Chapters in the second part focus on specific career opportunities for those with adult education backgrounds, including discussions around career lifecycle from entry to advancement, career development, and future trends. Written by active practitioners in adult education, chapters are designed to be practical, informative, and thought-provoking regarding career entry, progression, development, and advancement.

A truly one-of-a-kind text, *Career Pathways in Adult Education* is the ideal companion for students and professionals looking to transition into adult education as well as graduate program administrators who wish to share the importance of their programs.

Catherine H. Monaghan is Associate Professor Emeritus of Adult, Professional, and Higher Education at Cleveland State University, USA.

E. Paulette Isaac-Savage is Professor of Adult Education at the University of Missouri–St. Louis and is President of the American Association for Adult and Continuing Education (AAACE), USA.

Paul G. Putman is President and CEO of the Tree Research and Education Endowment Fund (TREE Fund), USA.

American Association for Adult and Continuing Education Co-Publications

Adult Learning in a Migration Society
Edited by Chad Hoggan and Tetyana Hoggan-Kloubert

Equitable Adult Learning
Four Transformative Organizations Serving Diverse Communities
Edited by Bob Hughes, Deanna Iceman Sands and Ted Kalmus

Career Pathways in Adult Education
Perspectives and Opportunities
Edited by Catherine H. Monaghan, E. Paulette Isaac-Savage, and Paul G. Putman

Career Pathways in Adult Education

Perspectives and Opportunities

Edited by
Catherine H. Monaghan, E. Paulette Isaac-Savage
and Paul G. Putman

NEW YORK AND LONDON

Designed cover image: Veronica Moses, Illustrator and Artist

First published 2024
by Routledge
605 Third Avenue, New York, NY 10158

and by Routledge
4 Park Square, Milton Park, Abingdon, Oxon OX14 4RN

Routledge is an imprint of the Taylor & Francis Group, an informa business

© 2024 selection and editorial matter, Catherine H. Monaghan, E. Paulette Isaac-Savage, and Paul G. Putman; individual chapters, the contributors

The right of Catherine H. Monaghan, E. Paulette Isaac-Savage, and Paul G. Putman to be identified as the authors of the editorial material, and of the authors for their individual chapters, has been asserted in accordance with sections 77 and 78 of the Copyright, Designs and Patents Act 1988.

All rights reserved. No part of this book may be reprinted or reproduced or utilised in any form or by any electronic, mechanical, or other means, now known or hereafter invented, including photocopying and recording, or in any information storage or retrieval system, without permission in writing from the publishers.

Trademark notice: Product or corporate names may be trademarks or registered trademarks, and are used only for identification and explanation without intent to infringe.

Library of Congress Cataloging-in-Publication Data
Names: Monaghan, Catherine H., editor. | Isaac-Savage, E. Paulette, editor. | Putman, Paul G., editor.
Title: Career pathways in adult education : perspectives and opportunities / edited by Catherine H. Monaghan, E. Paulette Isaac-Savage, and Paul G. Putman.
Description: New York : Routledge, 2024. |
Series: American Association for Adult and Continuing Education |
Includes bibliographical references and index.
Identifiers: LCCN 2023033428 | ISBN 9781032195261 (hbk) |
ISBN 9781032195278 (pbk) | ISBN 9781003259602 (ebk)
Subjects: LCSH: Adult education. | Adult learning.
Classification: LCC LC5215 .C276 2024 | DDC 374--dc23/eng/20230914
LC record available at https://lccn.loc.gov/2023033428

ISBN: 978-1-032-19526-1 (hbk)
ISBN: 978-1-032-19527-8 (pbk)
ISBN: 978-1-003-25960-2 (ebk)

DOI: 10.4324/9781003259602

Typeset in Galliard
by Taylor & Francis Books

Contents

List of Illustrations	ix
Foreword	xi
Preface	xiv
Acknowledgements	xvi
About the Editors	xvii
List of contributors	xviii

Introduction: A Career in Adult Education   1
E. PAULETTE ISAAC-SAVAGE, PAUL G. PUTMAN AND CATHERINE H. MONAGHAN

PART I
Primary Skills of an Adult Educator   9

1 Overview of the Field of Adult Education   11
KAYON MURRAY-JOHNSON AND JOVITA M. ROSS-GORDON

2 Practical Skills for Teaching Adults   24
WENDY M. GREEN AND ALEXANDER HOFFMAN

3 Facilitation Skills   34
CASANDRA BLASSINGAME

4 Program Planning Skills   42
CHRISTY M. RHODES AND STEVEN W. SCHMIDT

5 Assessment, Evaluation, and Educational Research Skills   49
LILIAN H. HILL

6 Technology Skills   59
MICHAEL D. PORTERFIELD

PART II
Practitioners' Voices   69

7 Adult Basic Education/English as a Second Language/Family Literacy   71
STEPHANIE W. COLLINS

8	Adult Environmental Education WENDY GRISWOLD	81
9	Community-Based Adult Education HLEZIPHI NAOMIE NYANUNGO	91
10	Consulting CATHRYN A. HENNES	100
11	Corporate Training, Global Learning, and Talent Management MURRAY WINLAND AND CATHERINE H. MONAGHAN	109
12	Correctional Education ROSARY-JOYCE KENNEDY	118
13	Cultural Institutions and Museum Education CLAIRE ALDENHUYSEN	128
14	Careers in Diversity, Equity, and Inclusion IAN C. BARRETT	137
15	Health Professions Education MICHAEL L. ROWLAND	146
16	Military Education ROYCE ANN COLLINS AND JAMES B. MARTIN	156
17	The Nonprofit Sector PAUL G. PUTMAN	164
18	Online Learning and Instructional Design CARYN LANZO AND MICHAEL D. PORTERFIELD	174
19	Policy Leadership in Adult Education Reform ELIZABETH A. ROUMELL, ALEXIS T. CHEREWKA AND AARON J. REYNA	184
20	Professional Development within the K-12 Setting CHRISTINA MEECHA	195
21	Professional Organizations SHAWNA L. STRICKLAND	204
22	Religious Education TRAMMELL L. BRISTOL	214
23	Workforce Development Careers YVONNE HUNTER-JOHNSON	222
	Conclusion: Creating a Career in Adult Education PAUL G. PUTMAN, E. PAULETTE ISAAC-SAVAGE AND CATHERINE H. MONAGHAN	232
	Appendix	240
	Index	242

Illustrations

Figures

1.1	Houle's Pyramid of Leadership: Adult educator roles and recommended preparation	15
4.1	ADDIE model (updated)	44
5.1	Logic model for case study	54
16.1	Pay raises based on time in position	157

Tables

5.1	Distinguishing between assessment and evaluation	50
5.2	Request for proposals	51
9.1	Opportunities in community education	97
19.1	Practitioner KSAs	187
19.2	Field-related organizations	189
19.3	Policy process KSAs	190
19.4	Policy research and analysis KSAs	191

Foreword

As a part of the ongoing mission of the American Association for Adult and Continuing Education's (AAACE) unwavering commitment to providing innovative and imaginative approaches to issues, research, programs, and opportunities, this publication, *Career Pathways in Adult Education: Perspectives and Opportunities*, offers a unique overview, and provides possibilities for thought and introspection about what, how, and why one enters and/or might enter the field of adult education. For those of us who have entered the field as researchers, scholars, and practitioners, we are quite adept at being able to describe what we do now. And if you had asked us before we entered the various positions and sectors described in this publication, we would try to define the term, tell you what we did, who we served, and even tell you why we have chosen our positions or roles. We would often use other career titles to describe the services we provide to adults in a particular setting. We used career descriptors like teacher, counselor, researcher, program or instructional designer, as well as a host of other job titles, to describe what we do and who we serve. While these are excellent descriptions of what we do, they fail to identify adult education as a professional career pathway that one chooses to enter, not by happenstance, but intentionally.

For over 50 years, researchers, scholars, practitioners, and adult educators have sought to position adult education as a discipline, field of practice and research, and professional organization. For instance, Clark (1958), situates adult education as being marginal to other disciplines and programs; Lindeman (1921/1961) and others focused on the meaning of adult education; Knowles (1970) used the term andragogy to describe the field of adult education as the art and science of teaching; Mezirow (1991), and others, expanded on the definition by providing perspective transformation as a theoretical framework to describe the changes in attitude, thoughts, and perspectives that adults undergo; Stubblefield and Keane (1994), Neufeldt and McGee (1990), Ross-Gordon et al. (2017), and others chronicled the history of adult education; Freire (1970), Hayes and Colin III (1994), Hayes and Flannery (1995), Peterson (1996), Guy (1999), Sheared and Sissel (2001), and Sheared et al. (2010), along with others, situated adult education in an epistemological sociocultural, political, and historical framework. This publication reframes and provides adult educators with language and multiple opportunities or sectors one might pursue as a career in adult education. The authors in this edition describe the multiple and varied pathways in which practitioners and scholars can intentionally pursue adult education practices as a distinct career choice.

According to Dictionary.com, ("Career Definition & Meaning"), careers are defined in three ways, as a:

Noun:
1. an occupation or profession, especially one requiring special training, followed as one's lifework: *He sought a career as a lawyer.*
2. a person's progress or general course of action through life or through a phase of life, as in some profession or undertaking: *His career as a soldier ended with the armistice...*

Verb:
3. to run or move rapidly along; go at full speed.

Adjective:
4. having or following a career; professional: a career diplomat.

Unlike other careers, adult education is one that most people enter, often by happenstance and not because of one saying that "When I grow up I want to become an adult educator." In fact, many of us, as the editors and authors in this publication share, did not even know that a career in adult education was even possible. By describing adult education and those who enter it as a professional career pathway, Monaghan, Isaac-Savage, and Putman seek to provide adult educators with language, theories, and practices that include a set of unique competences required to enter and serve adult populations.

Monaghan, Isaac-Savage, and Putman, along with this impressive list of authors representing a variety of sectors, provide us with reasons why it is so important to name one's world, to take control of the narrative that defines and shapes our world, while at the same time describing the adult education career pathway.

Through *Career Pathways in Adult Education*, the editors and authors: (a) focus attention upon adult education as a discipline, field of research and practice, and profession; and (b) situate and center the research, practices, programs, and services within and across multiple organizational and institutional, corporate, local, national, and international professional and governmental sectors.

As a young child, if anyone asked what I wanted to do, I said, "I want to be a teacher"; as a teenager, and during my high school days, I said, "I want to become a counselor," and during my undergraduate and college days, I said, "I want to be a school counselor." After graduate school, I became an alcoholism counselor, and then a social worker at Headstart. And then one day, I saw an ad for a position titled Adult Education Consultant. After a quick research effort, and locating a book written in the 1950s, I discovered a reference to adult education and its role in the military. In spite of my limited understanding, I was offered the position at Northern Illinois University. It is there that I officially learned, obtained a doctorate in adult education, and became an adult educator. Had I read or been introduced to a book on careers in adult education, how much easier my path might have been.

I would like to thank the editors and the contributing authors for their hard work and insight into this endeavor. I believe *Career Pathways in Adult Education* will be essential reading for those interested in and concerned about adult and continuing education as a profession, a field of practice; and a career chosen with an understanding of its impact on people, communities, and policies and practices that can positively influence and change lives.

I would also like to thank the Publications Committee for their work in developing this series and all my predecessors in the AAACE who have played a role in creating this series with Routledge.

Vanessa Sheared
Immediate Past President, AAACE (2022–2023)

References

Clark, B. (1958). *Marginality in adult education*. The Center for the Study of Liberal Education for Adult Education.
Freire, P. (1970). *Pedagogy of the oppressed*. Continuum.

Guy, T. C. (Ed.) (1999). *Providing culturally relevant adult education: A challenge for the twentyfirst century*. Jossey Bass.

Hayes, E., and Colin III, S. A. J. (Eds.) (1994). *Confronting racism and sexism*. Jossey-Bass.

Hayes, E., & Flannery, D. D. (1995). Adult women's learning in higher education: A critical review of the scholarship. *Initiatives*, 57(1), 29–40.

Knowles, M. S. (1970). *The modern practice of adult education: Andragogy versus pedagogy*. Association Press.

Lindeman, E. C. (1921/1961). *The meaning of adult education*. Harvest House.

Mezirow, J. (1991). *Transformative dimensions of adult learning*. Jossey-Bass.

Neufeldt, H. G., & McGee, L. (1990). *Education of the African American adult: An historical overview*. Contributions in Afro American and African Studies (Contemporary Black Poets). Praeger Publications.

Peterson, E. A. (1996). *Freedom road: Adult education of African Americans*. Kreiger Publishing.

Ross-Gordon, J. M., Rose, A. D., & Kasworm, C. (2017). *Professional foundations of adult and continuing education*. Wiley.

Sheared, V., Johnson-Bailey, J., ColinIII, S. A. J., Peterson, E., & Brookfield, S. D. (Eds.) (2010). *The handbook of race and adult education*. Jossey-Bass.

Sheared, V., & Sissel, P. A. (eds.) (2001). *Making space: Merging theory and practice in adult education*. Bergin and Garvey.

Stubblefield, H. W., & Keane, P. (1994). *Adult education in the American experience from the colonial period to the present*. Jossey-Bass.

Preface

This book was written for all those who found their way to being an adult educator before they knew there was an entire field devoted to what they were doing. It is also for those who know that they love helping adults grow and develop but are not sure where their talents would be best utilized.

Cate

The idea for this book started in 2000 when I entered my doctoral program and thought, "there are so many directions that I could go in a career in adult education: where is a book that I can read to figure out what I want to do?" This continued as I became a faculty member and started advising students. Twenty years later, I took Toni Morrison's advice from a speech she gave in 1981 at the annual Ohio Arts Council meeting in Cincinnati: "If you find a book you really want to read and it hasn't been written yet, then you must write it." With my two co-editors we created a book written by practitioners for practitioners across a wide variety of domains of the field of adult education.

The easy part of this adventure was asking two colleagues to co-edit this book with me. Paulette and I met through a professional organization when we co-edited the Commission of Professors of Adult Education (CPAE) newsletter. We knew right from the start that we were kindred spirits when it comes to writing and scholarship. I met Paul when he was a doctoral student and our mutual love of research and writing started a journey through a dissertation and co-teaching a doctoral class where we created a community of practice (CoP) that lasted 4 years, resulting in several conference presentations and publications. I could not have found two better co-editors to accompany me on this 3-year expedition.

It was quite an undertaking to find practitioners to share their stories and career advice, but it was well worth it. We searched for these practitioners through networking and LinkedIn, our former students, and colleagues. They have been very generous in giving of their time and insights to help current and future adult educators to move forward on their own voyage of discovery to find their passions and contribute to this vital endeavor, especially in today's world where it is important for all adults to be lifelong learners. We also intentionally chose contributors who were diverse across many dimensions.

I am grateful for the learners that I have had the privilege to meet along my own path as an adult educator; they always inspired and challenged me. I am also indebted to two extraordinary mentors, Dr. Ron Cervero and Dr. Ferris Anthony. And as always, I appreciate all the communities of practice that I have been part of during my life journey, even before I could put a name to it. And finally, I want to thank the Cleveland State University Academic Writing Group, for providing a weekly space to work on this book.

Paulette

When I began my doctoral program, I had a practitioner-oriented focus. I wanted to serve as an educational consultant to religious organizations. So, at that time, I was well aware of some aspects of the practitioner side but did not realize the wide range of possibilities in the field. As a faculty member I have met students and colleagues who have expanded my knowledge of the opportunities, but this book has taken it to another level.

When Cate first approached me about co-editing a book on adult education careers, I could not say, "No." Years ago, I had the pleasure of serving as co-editor with Cate for the CPAE newsletter of the American Association for Adult and Continuing Education (AAACE). Most recently, we published a book chapter in an award-winning book. We work well together and value creating quality publications on significant topics. Also, I saw this book as a great opportunity to remind some and inform others of the wide breadth of careers that the field of adult education has to offer. Hopefully, this book will help others in recognizing their adult education calling and provide resources to help them along in their journey.

Although I had not met Paul before, I knew if Cate invited him to be part of this project, he possessed skills that would be invaluable for our endeavor. We went from being co-editors to becoming friends. It was a pleasure working with Paul and Cate.

Paul

Readers with a degree in adult education, especially those with doctoral degrees, know that when an advisor or dissertation chair calls with a request, the correct answer is almost always "Yes." Luckily, in this case, for me it was an easy and enthusiastic response. I was fortuitously paired with Cate for my dissertation journey years ago and over time we have balanced each other well through various writing, research, and teaching projects. Cate had talked about this book idea for a long time, and when she called and asked if I would be interested in co-editing this book, I jumped at the opportunity to collaborate on a new and important project and test my editing skills to see if it might be something I enjoyed.

I had never met Paulette before but was somewhat familiar with her research and confident that Cate does not involve someone in projects on a whim. I anticipated that good things would come from this trio of editors. As I learned more about each of them and their expertise, I can now acknowledge that I was a bit intimidated working with these two scholars and had a fair amount of imposter syndrome. Over the past few years, and so many weekly meetings, my respect for them both has only grown, and I consider myself so lucky to have been invited to get to know them better through this collaboration. We have developed a wonderful working rhythm, each with our own quirks and specializations.

Many thanks to the original community of practice that Cate and I started in the fall of 2012, and all who helped inspire this journey, and to my husband Eric for supporting me throughout this and all of my endeavors.

Acknowledgements

We would like to thank AAACE and Routledge for recognizing the importance of this text and committing to its publication and our editorial team of Emmie Shand and Mari Zajac. Additional thanks to Katie Finnegan for copyediting along with Miranda B. and Eletha T. for their contributions to this project. Finally, we would like to thank Veronica Moses for the outstanding art that she created for our cover.

As editors, we have been honored and privileged to collaborate with outstanding contributing authors who generously shared their insights, advice, and expertise throughout this book. After nearly every chapter we would say out loud, "Wow, now I want to work in _____." We are excited to share this book with our readers and hope that it provides inspiration for their own career adventure in adult education.

Catherine H. Monaghan, Cleveland, OH
E. Paulette Isaac-Savage, St. Louis, MO
Paul G. Putman, Cleveland, OH

About the Editors

Catherine H. Monaghan is Associate Professor Emeritus at Cleveland State University in the graduate program of Adult, Professional, and Higher Education. She received the university's Distinguished Teaching Award. Her PhD is from the University of Georgia. As a consultant she mentors and provides faculty development in universities around the U.S. In addition, she continues to teach online classes for adult education programs at various universities while mentoring students at both the master's and doctoral level. Her scholarship is focused on faculty development, teaching and learning in higher education, communities of practice, critical human resource development, white privilege, critical management studies, as well as diversity and social justice initiatives. Cate has published extensively over the years in journals and book chapters. She has presented and offered faculty workshops nationally and internationally in Canada, England, Ireland, Scotland, South Africa, and Wales.

E. Paulette Isaac-Savage obtained an EdD from the University of Georgia and is Professor of Adult Education at the University of Missouri–St. Louis. She has numerous publications related to adult religious education, African American learners, and health education. She serves on the editorial review board for various journals including *Adult Education Quarterly*, *New Horizons in Adult and Human Resource Development*, and *Dialogues in Social Justice: An Adult Education Journal*. She has held executive board memberships on the Commission of Professors of Adult Education, the Adult Education Research Conference, and the American Association for Adult and Continuing Education (AAACE). Paulette currently serves as President of AAACE. She was inducted into the International Adult and Continuing Education Hall of Fame in 2019 and is a regular blood donor with the American Red Cross.

Paul G. Putman currently serves as the President and CEO of the Tree Research and Education Endowment Fund (TREE Fund). TREE Fund's mission is to identify and fund programs that support the discovery and dissemination of new knowledge in arboriculture and urban forestry. Prior to the TREE Fund, Paul worked at the Cleveland Foundation (the world's first and one of the largest community foundations) in multiple grantmaking and fundraising roles. Previously, Paul was at Cleveland State University (CSU), managing the Center for Leadership and Service. He also earned his PhD in Urban Education from CSU with a specialization in leadership and lifelong learning. Paul has published multiple book chapters, journal articles, and reviews. He taught in the Diversity Management master's program at CSU and also at Baldwin Wallace University on leadership in philanthropy and grant proposal writing.

Contributors

Claire Aldenhuysen (all-den-high-zen) is currently a grants administrator for a small nonprofit. She holds a bachelor's degree in Religious Studies from California State University Chico, a master's degree in Museology from the University of Washington, and a double master's degree in Executive Development for Public Service and Adult & Community Education from Ball State University. She has over a decade of experience in the nonprofit field and has held a variety of positions in a number of museums, community art centers, and social service organizations. When she's not in the office, you might find her at the local farmer's market, trying a new restaurant, trimming her roses, or planning a trip abroad. She is a California transplant happily living somewhere in the Midwest amidst the corn, soybeans, potholes, and snow.

Ian C. Barrett, EdD, is Executive Vice President and Chief Human Resources Officer for Kaleida Health in Buffalo, New York. His work includes human resource management, human resource development, and diversity, equity, and inclusion. He earned a doctorate in Adult Education and a bachelor's in Business Administration from the University of Georgia, and an MBA from the University of North Carolina at Chapel Hill. He is a life member of the NAACP and Alpha Phi Alpha Fraternity, Inc., and a graduate of Leadership Galveston Texas and the Urban League of Southwest Ohio's African American Leadership Development Program.

Casandra Blassingame is Executive Director of Community Women Against Hardship and Principal and Founder of Edusync International, Inc. She is an adult educator, facilitator, executive, association, and workforce professional with 25 years of experience in higher and continuing education. She is a graduate of Talladega College with a Bachelor of Arts degree in Computer Science. She earned her Master of Education in Adult and Higher Education from the University of Missouri–St. Louis, where she is also a doctoral candidate. Her research interests are equity and social justice and strengthening continuing and technical education policy, programs, and student outcomes to address the skills gap in the global workforce. She has three sons and four grandchildren and currently resides in Northern Virginia.

Trammell L. Bristol, DEd, is Director of Christian Education at a local church in a community outside of Philadelphia, Pennsylvania. She has served in this capacity for over 15 years. She holds a DEd from the Pennsylvania State University in Adult Education. She has worked in state government as an adult educator for 16 years developing training programs for staff and evaluating the quality of services and programs in New Jersey. She loves to connect with learners and inspire them to learn and grow.

Alexis T. Cherewka, PhD, is a senior technical advisor at World Education. She has a dual-title PhD in Lifelong Learning and Adult Education and Comparative and International

Education from Penn State University. Her research interests are in how adult education policies and adult educators shape adult learning opportunities, and ultimately ameliorate or increase educational and economic inequities. She has published on adult education topics in peer-reviewed journals such as *Adult Education Quarterly* and *Comparative Education Review*, and has co-authored a Migration Policy Institute policy report on adult education policy.

Royce Ann Collins is Professor of Adult Learning and Leadership at Kansas State University, and has a PhD in Adult and Continuing Education. She has over 30 years' experience as a faculty member and administrator in adult education programs. During her Kansas State University career, she has taught military students in the field of adult education for almost two decades.

Stephanie W. Collins was born in Kansas City, Missouri. She is a graduate of the University of Missouri-St. Louis (UMSL) with an MEd in Adult and Higher Education and a BSBA in Management and Organizational Behavior. She is pursuing a doctoral degree from UMSL in adult education, workforce development, and distance learning and technology. Stephanie Collins is an accomplished adult education practitioner with 20 years of experience, including university, community college, public school districts, and the private sector. She is currently Program Coordinator for the St. Charles School District Adult and Community Education program in St. Charles, Missouri.

Wendy M. Green, PhD, is an associate professor at Cleveland State University in the Levin College of Public Affairs and Education. She specializes in adult learning and development, health professions education, organizational culture, and diversity. Dr. Green's research focuses on the development of people across contexts. Prior research has examined how social identity-based affinity groups facilitate the development of group members in for-profit and university settings. Her most recent research is focused on how learners in clinical placements navigated changes in their educational experiences as a result of the widespread closure of universities and healthcare settings during the COVID-19 pandemic.

Wendy Griswold, PhD, is an associate professor in the Department of Leadership at the University of Memphis. She teaches graduate courses in the Higher and Adult Education Program. Her research interests include community education/participatory action research, education for sustainability, and contemplative education.

Cathryn A. Hennes, MEd, is the owner of GO2Learning LLC. As an education consultant, she engages with clients in all industries where the client is implementing new or upgraded software solutions for their employees. Cathryn works with various client teams (subject matter experts, lines of business, executives, employees) to develop technical documentation and training programs. She has a BA in English with a Professional Writing Certificate, an MEd in Adult Learning & Development, and an MEd in Education Technology with an Online Teaching Certificate (all earned from CSU). She helps companies to help their employees have better work lives.

Lilian H. Hill, PhD, is Professor Emerita of Adult Education at the University of Southern Mississippi. Dr. Hill served on the assessment committees of two universities and her administrative roles involved assessment, evaluation, and accreditation responsibilities. She published *Assessment, Evaluation, and Accountability in Adult Education* in 2020. She is co-editor of *Adult Learning* and a member of the executive committee of the American Association for Adult and Continuing Education. She was inducted into the International Adult and Continuing Education Hall of Fame in 2018 and recognized with the Career Achievement Award by the Commission of Professors of Adult Education in 2021.

Alexander Hoffman, PharmD, MEd, is Associate Professor of Pharmacy Practice at Northeast Ohio Medical University and a board-certified primary care pharmacist at the Cleveland Clinic. His scholarly interests include chronic disease management, learner and faculty mentorship, professional identity formation, transformative learning models, and the application of graphic medicine as a teaching method.

Yvonne Hunter-Johnson, PhD, received her PhD in Adult Education with an emphasis on human resource development and research and evaluation from the University of South Florida. Currently, she is an associate professor at Southern Illinois University (Carbondale) in the Department of Workforce Education and Development. Dr. Hunter-Johnson's research interests include (a) adult learners and learning (veterans and international students), (b) career transition (veteran and international students), (c) transfer of training, (d) learning organizations, (e) motivation to learn, and (f) employability and support systems in higher education

Rosary-Joyce Kennedy, PhD, has served as an adult basic education and literacy practitioner for over 20 years as a tutor, teacher, researcher, and administrator. She is originally from Cleveland, Ohio, where she earned her bachelor's, master's, and Doctor of Philosophy from Cleveland State University. Dr. Kennedy has worked with various types of adult learners including adult basic education and literacy educators, single teen parents, English language learners, the justice involved, and restored citizens in diverse settings from community colleges, nonprofits, and prisons. Though she has a wealth of experience in adult education, she embraces growth, change, and learning across the lifespan.

Caryn Lanzo is Director of the Center for eLearning at Cleveland State University (CSU). She also teaches as an adjunct lecturer. Caryn earned both her undergraduate (BBA) and graduate (MEd in Adult Learning) degrees at CSU. She considers herself a lifelong learner and an advocate for online learning.

James B. Martin is Dean Emeritus at the U.S. Army Command and General Staff College, the largest military leadership institution in the western world. He has a PhD in American History. He concurrently served as the Chief Academic Officer for Army University and as a senior accreditor for the Department of Defense's Joint Staff and the Higher Learning Commission.

Christina Meecha is a special education coordinator, currently for grades K-4. While working in this area she is engaged with creating varied professional development and collaboration for all personnel that fall within student services. Student services includes principals, intervention specialists, counselors, school social workers, school psychologists, regular education teachers, and special education assistants. She has a master's in Adult Learning and Development from Cleveland State University. She also has a License in Educational Leadership and Administration from Bowling Green University.

Kayon Murray-Johnson, PhD, is an adult educator whose expertise spans teaching, training, and instructional design. Her current scholarship surrounds critical dialogues on race, ethnicity and racism, faculty development, and culturally responsive teaching approaches. This work has yielded national award recognition from the POD network and the Multicultural Education SIG of the American Educational Research Association. As a core part of her professional outreach, Kayon enjoys serving diverse journals and organizations within the field of adult education. She teaches in the adult education program at the University of Rhode Island and was named the 2021 recipient of that institution's teaching excellence award.

Hleziphi (Naomie) Nyanungo, PhD, is an educator and academic administrator. Her research areas of interest include community organizing, organizational behavior, and critical pedagogies. She currently works as an educational developer supporting teaching and learning in academic contexts.

Michael D. Porterfield, PhD, is currently Educational Technology Manager at McKendree University. In this role he manages the learning management system, oversees instructional technology implementation, assists faculty with online course design including accessibility, and conducts faculty professional development. He has taught part-time adult education and educational technology courses for many schools in the U.S., especially at the University of Missouri-St. Louis (UMSL) where he also worked as a senior instructional designer for nearly 10 years. In 2019, he received the Chancellor's Award for Excellence to a Part-time Faculty Member at UMSL. He is a member of Phi Kappa Phi.

Aaron J. Reyna obtained his EdD in Education Policy from Florida State University. He is a program manager at UnidosUS. His research interests include adult and higher education policy, college access, and workforce education. His professional experiences include the K-12 setting, higher education, veterans' affairs, and adult education and literacy.

Christy M. Rhodes, PhD, is Associate Professor of Adult Education in the Department of Interdisciplinary Professions at East Carolina University. She was a teacher and program planner for English literacy classes in Tampa, Florida, where she completed her PhD in Curriculum and Instruction at the University of South Florida. Her research is centered on culturally inclusive teaching and the integration of immigrants into non-traditional immigrant-receiving areas.

Jovita M. Ross-Gordon, EdD is a distinguished Professor Emeritus of Adult, Professional and Community Education at Texas State University where she received the Graduate College Outstanding Mentor Award. Her research and writing have focused on adult/higher education and equity as related to race, gender, and (dis)ability. She is a co-recipient of the AAACE Cyril A. Houle Award and a member of the International Adult and Continuing Education Hall of Fame.

Elizabeth A. Roumell, PhD, is Associate Professor of Educational Administration and Human Resource Development at Texas A&M University in College Station, Texas, USA. Dr. Roumell teaches graduate courses in Adult Learning, Educational Research, and Human Resource Development. Her areas of research focus include adult and workforce education policy, international and comparative education, adult and e-learning, and "the future of work." She serves as Executive Director for the Texas Center for the Advancement of Literacy & Learning and was co-editor of the book, *Advancing the Global Agenda for Human Rights, Vulnerable Populations, and Environmental Sustainability: Adult Education as Strategic Partner*.

Michael L. Rowland, PhD, recently retired from his position as Association Dean for Faculty and Professional Development at the University of Kentucky College of Medicine, Lexington, Kentucky. He has been involved in health professions educational programs for over 25 years and has held numerous leadership positions in national health professions organizations. He has frequently published in numerous healthcare and adult education journals.

Steven W. Schmidt, PhD, is Professor of Adult Education and the Adult Education Program Coordinator in the Department of Interdisciplinary Professions at East Carolina University, in Greenville, North Carolina. He holds PhD and MS degrees in Adult Education from the University of Wisconsin–Milwaukee and a Bachelor of Business Administration degree from the University of Wisconsin–Whitewater. His major areas of research and writing activity include workplace learning, cultural competence, and online teaching and learning.

Shawna L. Strickland (she/her pronouns), PhD, CAE, is an association professional and registered respiratory therapist. After over a decade in clinical care, she transitioned into higher education, serving as faculty and in program administration. She transitioned into the association space in 2013 and currently serves as Associate Executive Director, Programs, at the American Epilepsy Society, where she focuses on effective association practice, clinical activities, research, and quality continuing education. In addition, Dr. Strickland is an adjunct faculty member at Rush University, teaching courses in leadership and adult education in the College of Health Sciences' Doctorate of Health Sciences program.

Murray Winland has 30 years of experience in corporate learning – more than half at the executive level. Before retirement, he was Vice President of Global Learning at Arise Virtual Solutions and Director of Learning at eBay, Progressive Insurance, Cardinal Health, and Nationwide Insurance. Murray also taught at Cleveland State University, Otterbein College, and the Ohio State University. He holds a Master of Education degree in Adult Learning & Development from Cleveland State University and was recognized as the 2014 distinguished alumnus from their College of Education and Human Services. Murray also holds a Bachelor of Business Administration degree from Ohio University.

Introduction

A Career in Adult Education

E. Paulette Isaac-Savage, Paul G. Putman and Catherine H. Monaghan

Are you looking for a career in the exciting field of adult education? Have you ever wondered about careers in the big tent called adult education? Do you want to learn more about the competencies and skills needed? Are you trying to figure out what you want to do or looking to make a career move? Are you an advisor or faculty member advising students about careers in adult education? If you answered yes to any of these questions, then this book is for you.

This book provides an overview of careers in the field of adult education and includes the distinctive skills and qualifications required for various roles, as well as current trends. Along with practical advice for launching and advancing a career in adult education, this book includes personal stories and insights from adult education professionals. If you are a student or a professional looking to transition into adult education, this book will provide you with the information and inspiration you need to succeed in this rewarding and dynamic field.

We want to be clear from the onset: this career book is not all encompassing. We present a plethora of careers; this is the tip of the iceberg. Careers in higher education, including faculty careers, are not discussed here because there are already various resources available, which we provide in the resource appendix. We have selected 17 careers within the field. However, there are numerous others that could have been explored: educator in the National Park System, union educator, an educator in an agricultural extension program, for example. The chapters are designed to provide the reader with essential information to understand a particular career in adult education.

A handbook in adult and continuing education (Rocco et al., 2021) is published every 10 years with a focus on theories and issues in the field. In the latest edition, the editors argue that adult education is moving through a turbulent time. Researchers have noted that administrators and faculty in adult education programs must concern themselves with funding (Fenwick, 2010; Yelich Biniecki & Schmidt, 2021), plus engage in a heightened degree of "accountability and evidence of program effectiveness" (Mizzi et al., 2021, p. 2). These issues are true within all careers in adult education.

The number of faculty positions for those with a PhD or EdD in adult education continues to decline (Hill & Isaac-Savage, 2022). Although adult education is a multi-billion-dollar endeavor across the globe (Statistica Research Department, 2022), there has never been a book that focused solely on careers in adult education. Our aim was to design a book that exposes readers to practical skills and their application needed as adult educators. Adult educators strive to challenge the norms and develop individuals into lifelong learners in every sphere. We also wanted to highlight the voices of practitioners as they discuss their careers and experiences, and provide advice on the competencies needed for success in their areas within the field.

During our years as faculty members in adult education preparing students at the master's and doctoral levels, we were unable to find a book that helped students to discover the vast prospects that exist in the field of adult education. Most textbooks and programs at the master's or doctoral level usually discuss a limited range of career possibilities for those who want to practice in the field, usually centering on positions in higher education. Yet, individuals with adult education degrees are making a crucial difference engaging in areas of adult education far beyond higher education. However, various areas of adult education often go undiscussed or slide under the radar because faculty themselves may not be aware of the full range of career options. In addition, there is too little cross-pollination between researchers and practitioners. Finally, as you will discover in the career stories of the practitioners, they were often initially unaware of research in a field known as adult education. We wanted to help faculty, students, and the general public understand the possibilities, through chapters written by those who are practitioners in various adult education spaces with a graduate degree in adult education.

We also hope that this book will enable graduate program administrators to learn about and present a more robust case for the importance of their programs both to the administrators at their colleges and universities and when recruiting new students. Understanding the wide range of feasible careers would (a) help them to develop relevant electives for their programs, (b) provide career guidance for current and prospective students, and (c) provide them with a worthwhile marketing tool.

Organization of this Book

This book is divided into two parts. The first part presents key competencies for those working in the field of adult education. The second part examines career opportunities from day-to-day perspectives of practitioners and is geared to those who are interested in pursuing careers outside of higher education. It contains chapters ranging from corporate training to nonprofits, military education, adult basic education, correctional education, community education, policy, health care, philanthropy, diversity initiatives, and more.

Part I

In Part I, each chapter is designed to give practical advice on the primary competencies needed across all adult education careers. Murray-Johnson and Ross-Gordon (Chapter 1) provide a very broad-brush introduction to the field of adult education. The authors define adult education and the concept of the adult learner, as well as provide outstanding examples of the informal, nonformal, and formal contexts where adult education occurs. Green and Hoffman (Chapter 2) explore practical skills for teaching adults. They discuss core principles that ground effective adult learning experiences and illustrates the connection of theoretical approaches with the development and facilitation of effective adult-focused activities. Using a vignette, the authors clarify how teaching would change to match three different core adult education learning principles of self-directed, transformational, and experiential learning. Blassingame (Chapter 3) presents the competency of facilitation, which is so important for adult educators. She focuses on skills that are essential for successful facilitation including basic strategies and best practices. The approaches covered are asset-based, affirmative, and skilled facilitation. Rhodes and Schmidt (Chapter 4) discuss the dynamics and skills needed for program planning. They provide an overview of the important models used in adult education settings. Hill (Chapter 5) details assessment and program evaluation skills needed to appraise and improve adult education. She also provides a case study of two Requests for Proposals (RFP) that are often used by organizations to fill a short-term need for evaluation and feedback. Porterfield (Chapter 6) offers examples and a method to guide the use of technology in creating adult education offerings.

Part II

The contributing authors in this part are those who are currently working in the areas they address or who are recent practitioners. To simplify Part II, careers are presented in alphabetical order. We invite readers to explore this book in a nonlinear fashion, similar to careers which often develop organically. Readers may discover chapters that are interesting to them or whose topics are unfamiliar. These chapters cover a brief overview of the authors' careers followed by practical advice on relevant competencies and information about how to be successful in pursuing a career in a particular adult education area. We have also provided callout boxes within the chapters to highlight stories or important points.

In this text, astute readers will note that various chapters in Part II of this book present careers that can occur within multiple sectors. As an example, the community education chapter (Chapter 9) makes connections to several other careers, including in health professions education (Chapter 15) and workforce development (Chapter 23) which can take place in the nonprofit sector, as well as be performed by a consultant. In this introduction, we provide a brief synopsis of the chapters categorized in terms of the three major contexts of adult learning: informal, formal, and nonformal. Murray-Johnson and Ross-Gordon (Chapter 1) provide a more in-depth explanation of these environments.

Informal Adult Education. The first context is informal learning; this is learning that occurs through daily activities that lead to learning experiences and are usually driven by the learner's interests in engaging in the educational activity (Coombs & Ahmed, 1974). Four of the chapters in Part II fall under this category. Griswold (Chapter 8) shares her journey and career in adult environmental education. The need for adult educators to engage in the work of environmental education is increasing. She discusses career competencies and opportunities in this area. Nyanungo (Chapter 9) helps us understand careers in community-based education. She makes an important career point that community educators need to help employers understand the need for a community education focus when there may not be an obvious connection. Aldenhuysen (Chapter 13) discusses careers in cultural institutions and museum education. These adult education careers can be a good fit for someone who is artistic, creative, and looking for a career where there are a variety of opportunities, sometimes all in one job. As she points out, many of us remember going on school field trips to museums as children; we may not be aware that adults are also an important education audience for these institutions. Putman (Chapter 17) reviews the opportunities for adult educators in the nonprofit arena. The adult learners who attend educational events may be potential or current donors. He provides a look at the various career possibilities within nonprofit organizations as well as resources to help readers who seek such a career.

Formal Adult Education. Again, drawing on Coombs and Ahmed (1974), the authors in Chapter 1 define the second context as formal adult education encompassing the characteristics of the K-12 and the higher education system. Four chapters might be grouped under this umbrella. Rowland (Chapter 15) considers the careers available in the health professions area. He examines career paths available to those who are not primary healthcare professionals such as physicians or nurses but who would like to pursue a career educating others about health and wellness. Collins and Martin (Chapter 16) open the world of military education to the reader. The military as an entity is responsible for educating the largest number of adults through their various programs, especially in leadership training. They provide all that you might need to pursue a career in the military, either as an enlisted person or a civilian. Lanzo and Porterfield (Chapter 18) take the reader inside the world of online training and professional development. Online training sits both within the formal educational system and outside of it, in professional development. Meecha (Chapter 20) explores the plethora of adult education careers that exist within the K-12 educational setting. There are multiple roles for adult educators in this environment including instructional technology coordinator, family liaison, behavioral specialist, English as a second language coordinator, gifted coordinator, dyslexia coordinator, as well as diversity and social emotional needs coach. While these roles may involve the education of students, peers and parents also need to be educated. Therefore, the principles of adult education are instrumental in educating adults within this arena.

Nonformal Adult Education. The final environment or context is nonformal adult education. Per Murray-Johnson and Ross-Gordon (Chapter 1), Coombs and Ahmed (1974) "defined nonformal education as 'organized systematic, education activity carried on outside the framework of the formal system to provide selected types of learning to particular subgroups in the population'" (p. 8). Nine of the 17 chapters fall under this category. Webb Collins (Chapter 7) examines careers in adult basic education, including English as a second language and family literacy. Winland and Monaghan (Chapter 11) consider the careers in corporate training, global learning, and talent management. Hennes (Chapter 10) provides career advice for working as a consultant. Kennedy (Chapter 12) shares with the reader the careers available in the correctional systems. Barrett (Chapter 14) reveals the careers and competencies required of adult educators who want to work in diversity, equity, and inclusion. Strickland (Chapter 21) describes the value of contributing to the nonformal learning of adults within professional organizations. In Chapter 22, Bristol discusses the types of careers that are possible in the field of adult religious education. Then in Chapter 23, Hunter-Johnson introduces the reader to workforce development careers.

And last, but not least, Roumell, Cherewka, and Reyna (Chapter 19) discuss career pathways in one of the most critical areas of adult education, policy. Policy in adult education is a fundamental component that drives the education of adults in numerous areas. This includes the local, state, and federal levels. However, policy is often viewed as esoteric and outside the parameters of the work of educating adults. Yet, careers in this area are of vital importance to ensuring all adults have access to the education that they need.

Career Questions Answered

Our contributing authors have answered important career questions. What does an adult educator do in this area? What was your career path? What are the typical degrees held by individuals in this branch of adult education? What competencies or knowledge, skills, and abilities (KSAs) are required for this career? How do you "sell" an adult education degree as a competitive advantage? What professional associations should I become involved in and investigate if I want to pursue this field? Where are jobs for specific careers listed?

We have also asked them to marry theory and practice so that the reader can better understand the terminology and knowledge that would be needed. Furthermore, they answered several questions including:

- How does the knowledge from your adult education program enhance your ability to do your job?
- What adult education theories are relevant to this career?
- Are there any recommended readings that you would suggest?
- What are terms that are specific to this branch of adult education?
- What success tips would you give someone who is seeking to work in this career area?

Finally, the authors addressed the future of adult education within their areas.

Career Model of Adult Education

An anonymous reviewer wondered whether there was a career model that might fit the professional trajectory of an adult educator. There is no research identifying a specific adult education career model. However, after careful consideration and research into various career models, the editors decided that the following model might be helpful for readers based on the characteristics of adult learning.

The Protean model views careers as a calling, an expression of your self-identity and values. The use of the protean metaphor is based on the Greek god Proteus, who was known for the ability to change shape and adapt. Hall et al. (1996) developed this model based on the individual's need to define and direct their own career, based not on a predetermined path or society's definition of career success, but as rooted in the individual's identity. McDonald and Hite (2023) discuss the concept of career development. They state, "while some work primarily to make ends meet, given the choice ... people tend to seek out occupations that enhance a sense of self" (p. 1). Additionally, over the lifespan an individual's self-identity can change. As you will see in the discussions of the contributing authors' stories of their careers, few took a linear path to becoming an adult educator. In addition, many were adult educators long before they had a name for their calling.

> I see myself more as an adult educator with a specialization in community education, rather than a community educator. For me, this is an important distinction in that community education does not define my role but refers to my specific skill set, professional interests, and orientation to my work.
>
> (see Nyanungo, Chapter 9)

The key elements of creating a successful career according to this model are (a) self-directed activities (Knowles et al., 2020), which occur when the individual seeks to acquire the necessary competencies through a self-charted path of

- Formal degrees
- Micro-learning certificates
- Experiences (Kolb & Kolb, 2005)
- Mentoring opportunities (Coffman et al., 2016; Kriner et al., 2015; Monaghan, 2011)

(b) combined with both internal and external career strategies

- Internal
  - Moving within an organization, both horizontally and vertically
- External
  - Moving across organizations
  - Moving across career fields

Every career path is unique; they are seldom perfectly linear, and many are circuitous.

"The implicit assumption is that a self-directed, or protean, career actor is more likely to cross career boundaries" (Briscoe & Hall, 2006, p. 1) and have a very distinct career over the course of their lifetime (Buchner, 2012; Redondo et al., 2021). In fact, you may have noticed that as individuals we often evolve in ways that impact how we see ourselves and therefore strive to self-direct our careers. This was noted by most of our contributing authors.

Conclusion

This text is not designed to be an exhaustive exploration of every career possibility for professionals with training in adult education. Our goal was to compile a book, not an encyclopedia. We have done our best to provide resources, both within the conclusion and in the appendix, including suggestions for faculty members who might utilize this book in a course for further independent exploration of the careers presented.

As we look back over the chapters that our contributors generously wrote, we were struck by three common themes across all careers in the field of adult education. First, adult educators are enthusiastic about changing the world through education in their sphere of influence. Second, they are resourceful; from developing their careers to obtaining what they need to provide educational experiences. But most important is their dedication to adult learners. Our fervent hope is that this book might inspire those who read it to consider a career in adult education that elicits their absolute best.

References

Briscoe, J. P., & Hall, D. T. (2006). Special section on boundaryless and protean careers: Next steps in conceptualizing and measuring boundaryless and protean careers. *Journal of Vocational Behavior, 69*(1), 1–3. https://doi.org/10.1177/0170840611435600

Buchner, M. (2012). *Career adjustment: The role of the protean career attitude and emotional intelligence in career adjustment.* Lambert Academic Publishing.

Coffman, K. A., Adkisson, A. C., Putman, P. G., Kriner, B. A., & Monaghan, C. H. (2016). Waiting for the expert to arrive: Using a community of practice to develop the scholarly identity of doctoral students. *International Journal of Teaching and Learning in Higher Education, 28*(1), 30–37.

Coombs, P. H., & Ahmed, M. (1974). *Attacking rural poverty: How nonformal education can help.* John Hopkins University Press.

Fenwick, T. (2010). Accountability practices in adult education: Insights from actor-network theory. *Studies in the Education of Adults, 42*(2), 170–185.

Hall, D. T., & Associates. (1996). *The career is dead–long live the career: A relational approach to careers.* Jossey-Bass.

Hill, L. H., & Isaac-Savage, E. P. (2022). Doors slam shut: Adult education program closures. *New Directions for Adult & Continuing Education, 2022*(173–174), 67–79. https://doi.org/10.1002/ace.20453

Knowles, M. S., Holton (III), E. F., Swanson, R. A., & Robinson, P. A. (2020). *The adult learner: The definitive classic in adult education and human resource development* (9th ed.). Routledge.

Kolb, A. Y., & Kolb, D. A. (2005). Learning styles and learning spaces: Enhancing experiential learning in higher education. *Academy of Management Learning and Education, 4*(2), 193–212.

Kriner, B. A., Coffman, K. A., Adkisson, A. C., Putman, P. G., & Monaghan, C. H. (2015). From students to scholars: The transformative power of communities of practice. *Adult Learning, 26*(2), 73–80. https://doi.org/10.1177/1045159515573021

McDonald, K. S., & Hite, L. M. (2023). *Career development: A human resources development perspective* (2nd ed.). Routledge.

Mizzi, R. C., Rocco, T. S., Smith, M. C., Merriweather, L. R., & Hawley, J. D. (2021). Advancing adult and continuing education through critical conversations and diverse perspectives. In T. S. Rocco, M. C. Smith, R. C. Mizzi, L. R. Merriweather, & J. D. Hawley (Eds.), *The handbook of adult and continuing education* (2020 ed., pp. 140–149). Stylus.

Monaghan, C. H. (2011). Communities of practice: A learning strategy for professional development. *Journal of Management Education, 35*(3), 428–453. https://doi.org/10.1177/1052562910387536

Redondo, R., Sparrow, P., & Hernández-Lechuga, G. (2021). The effect of protean careers on talent retention: Examining the relationship between protean career orientation, organizational commitment, job satisfaction and intention to quit for talented workers. *International Journal of Human Resource Management, 32*(9), 2046–2069. https://doi.org/10.1080/09585192.2019.1579247

Rocco, T. S., Smith, M. C., Mizzi, R. C., Merriweather, L. R., & Hawley, J. D. (Eds.). (2021). *The handbook of adult and continuing education* (2020 ed.). Stylus.

Statistica Research Department. (2022). *Market size of the global workplace training industry from 2009 to 2020, by region.* www.statista.com/statistics/1232500/size-of-the-workplace-training-market-north-america-and-rest-of-the-world

Yelich Biniecki, S., & Schmidt, S. (2021). Organization and administration of adult and continuing education. In T. S. Rocco, M. C. Smith, R. C. Mizzi, L. R. Merriweather, & J. D. Hawley (Eds.), *The handbook of adult and continuing education* (2020 ed., pp. 140–149). Stylus.

Part I

Primary Skills of an Adult Educator

Chapter 1

Overview of the Field of Adult Education

Kayon Murray-Johnson and Jovita M. Ross-Gordon

As will be apparent from this chapter and the remainder of the book, adult education is a broad field with opportunities to serve adult learners directly and indirectly in many different settings. We introduce a number of those contexts in this chapter, and we discuss historical and contemporary roles, functions, professional development of adult educators, and issues facing adult educators today.

Who Is an Adult Learner?

Just as the term adult has varied meanings in society in general, so too is the case within the field of adult education. Merriam and Brockett (2007) go beyond chronological age in defining adult education by referring to adult learners' social roles as "activities intentionally designed for the purpose of bringing about *learning among those whose age, social roles, or self-perception, define them as adults*" (p. 8, italics added). Similarly, Merriam and Bierema (2014) discuss "how an adult's life situation typically differs from that of a child and what implications this has for learning" (p. 11). For instance, the social roles of work and family living are often used in conjunction with a chronological age of 24 or 25 to distinguish adult learners in higher education from 18–24-year-olds—typically considered to be *traditional-age* learners. Adult development is another way of understanding how adults differ from children. Adult development has been considered from many perspectives, including cognitive, psychological, psychosocial, sociocultural, and integrative perspectives (Merriam & Baumgartner, 2020).

What is Adult Education?

Experiences within adult/higher education, workplace training, English as a Second Language (ESL), or adult secondary education/GED programs frequently shape how individuals conceive of adult education. Such conceptions of adult education align well with Verner's (1964) definition:

> a relationship between an educational agent and a learner in which the agent selects, arranges, and continuously directs a sequence of progressive tasks that provide systematic experiences to achieve learning for people whose participation in such activities is subsidiary and supplemental to a primary productive role in society. (p. 32)

However, many experts in the field have defined adult education more broadly. For instance, Eduard Lindeman, writing as early as 1926, stated: "The whole of life is learning, therefore education can have no endings. This new venture is called adult education—not because it is confined to adults but because adulthood, maturity, defines its limits" (p. 6). Broad definitions of adult education include the following by Cyril Houle (1972):

DOI: 10.4324/9781003259602-3

> Adult education is the process by which men and women (alone, in groups, or in institutional settings) seek to improve themselves or their society by increasing their skill, knowledge, or sensitiveness; or it is any process by which individuals, groups, or institutions try to help men and women improve in those ways. (p. 32)

Notably, this definition stresses the *process* of adult education, whatever form it might take, whether or not it involves a facilitator, and wherever it occurs.

Forms of Adult Education

Some chapters in this book will take a more focused look at settings and contexts of adult education that relate to specific careers in the field. However, a relatively simple triarchic framework has often been used to organize the broad sectors of the field, dividing it into formal, nonformal, and informal categories. Frequently cited for applying these terms to adult education are Coombs and Ahmed (1974). They began their discussion by focusing on informal education:

> Informal education as used here is the lifelong process by which every person acquires and accumulates knowledge, skills, attitudes, and insights from daily experiences and exposure to the environment—at home, at work, at play; from the example and attitudes of family and friends; from travel, reading newspapers and books; or by listening to the radio or viewing film or television. (p. 8)

Coombs and Ahmed contrasted formal education as "the highly institutionalized, chronologically graded and hierarchically structured 'education system,' spanning lower primary school and the upper reaches of the university," while they defined nonformal education as "organized systematic, education activity carried on outside the framework of the formal system to provide selected types of learning to particular subgroups in the population, adults as well as children" (p. 8). In thinking of careers in adult education, you may imagine them only in terms of formal and nonformal education, where the role of a professional educator may be more obvious. But adult educators also play important roles in supporting the informal education of adult learners.

Common Settings of Adult Education

It is not possible to discuss all settings where an adult educator might find a career in this space. Rather, we introduce a number of settings where adult educators have played an important role in working with adult learners, some of which will be addressed by the chapters to follow, organizing our discussion within the framework of formal, nonformal, and informal adult education just introduced.

The formal adult education category encompasses a wide range of diploma, certificate, and degree-related activities sponsored by "schooling" organizations often serving children, youth, or emerging adults as their primary audience. Much of publicly funded adult education is aligned with this category, including adult foundational education (adult basic and secondary education, ESL programs serving adults, and correctional education) (Chapters 7 and 12, this volume; Belzer & Kim, 2021). Most postsecondary education also fits this category, including certificate, associate degree, and transfer programs offered by community colleges; diploma and certificate programs offered by vocational-technical schools; and certificate and degree programs offered by two-year and four-year colleges and universities (Bergman, 2020).

More squarely situated in the realm of nonformal adult education are programs such as workplace training and development (Chapter 23, this volume; Scully-Ross & Vidal de Col, 2021); training programs for volunteers in governmental and non-governmental organizations; military education (Chapter 16); and many continuing professional education programs (Coady, 2021). Adult education activities sponsored by health-oriented, faith-based, and cultural organizations are in many cases nonformal in design, while at other times they are more informal (Chapters 15, 22, and 13).

Situated most clearly in the informal education or informal learning category is adult education of a more organic nature, whether self-guided or led by members of the community. This includes adult education associated with self-help groups and various contemporary social movements (e.g., voters rights, Black Lives Matter, disability rights, environmental justice, #MeToo) (Chapters 8 and 14, this volume; Ross-Gordon & Procknow, 2021; Walker & Butterwick, 2021).

Roles Played by Adult Educators

One of the earliest authors to discuss roles of adult educators was Houle (1956), who described a pyramid of leadership within adult education, which still has reasonable applicability today. At the base of Houle's pyramid were individuals who acted as adult educators on a voluntary basis across an array of settings. At the next level, he placed individuals whose paid work included adult education along with other primary duties, in settings such as libraries, museums, the armed services, and K-16 educational institutions. At the apex of the pyramid, he placed "those who have a primary concern for adult education and basic career expectations in that field" (p. 133). Here he included those who direct or coordinate adult education activities in a variety of settings, along with scholars of adult education.

The roles most individuals think of when asked to describe an adult educator are roles involving direct interaction with individual adult learners, with teaching roles foremost. Not surprisingly, many sources have focused on the teacher/trainer role (Brookfield, 2015). But the role of instructor is not the only role played by adult educators.

Other roles involving direct interaction with individual learners include those of mentor, coach, and adviser or academic counselor. *Mentoring* is a role played by many adult educators across numerous contexts, although few have a professional title that includes the term (Alston & Hansman, 2020). Mentoring is typically viewed as a developmental relationship providing potential benefits for both mentor and mentees. A closely related role is that of *coaching*, which most often occurs "in the context of dyadic, or one-on-one, interactions" (Ellinger & Kim, 2014, p. 130). While the coaching role shares characteristics with mentoring, "it is typically distinguished by its focus on collaboratively helping individuals achieve present and future goals they have set for themselves" (Ross-Gordon et al. 2017, p. 87). The *advising* role, on the other hand, is often viewed as a prescriptive role aimed at helping adult learners to navigate educational systems. If viewed within a more developmental framework, it may be assumed that goals will be jointly established by the advisor and advisee (Polson, 1994).

Aside from roles interacting with individual learners, Houle (1956) and others have also pointed to the leadership roles played by many holding primary responsibilities for adult education programs. Darkenwald and Merriam (1982) indicated the most common role of professional adult educators across a wide variety of organizations and agencies was that of the *program developer/administrator*, who typically wears hats involving both instructional/program development and managerial functions such as program assessment. Accordingly, next to teaching, program developer/development was the professional role/function most frequently addressed by a dedicated chapter in the seven handbooks of adult and continuing education published by the American Association of Adult Education and its predecessors between 1948 and 2010 (Ross-Gordon et al., 2017). Additional contemporary roles of adult educators providing indirect services to individual adult learners include organizational consultants (see Chapter 10) and diversity, equity, and inclusion specialists (see Chapter 14).

Core Skills Needed by Adult Educators

The core skills needed by adult educators are closely related to their roles, although some skills are transferable across roles and across formal, nonformal, and informal contexts. For instance, those engaged in teaching or training of adults minimally need to be skilled in curriculum and instructional design as well as in facilitation and evaluation of adult learning (Hill, 2021). Numerous sources have focused on helping instructors and trainers develop these skills (Brookfield, 2015; Chalofsky et al., 2014). Increasingly, adult educators must exhibit effective instructional strategies in online and blended environments as well as those relying on face-to-face instruction (Baldwin & Conceição, 2021). They must also be skilled in facilitating what may be challenging classroom conversations (Manglitz et al., 2014; Murray-Johnson & Ross-Gordon, 2018). Where staffing limitations mean there are no individuals tasked with advising and counseling of adults, instructors also need to possess basic skills in those areas.

Another skill set essential for many adult educators relates to program leadership, management, design, and evaluation. Daffron and Caffarella (2021) have observed that program planning is a dynamic and interactive process, influenced by many contextual variables including the various audiences who have an interest in a particular educational program or will be impacted by its implementation. Thus, adult educators must be skilled both in surveying the landscape to identify educational needs of the community and in conducting more formal needs assessments.

Monaghan (2010) has differentiated managerial skills (e.g., financing programs, marketing, and hiring) from leadership skills (e.g., question framing, reflection, abstraction, and learning). At the same time, Biniecki and Schmidt (2021) observe that the roles of administrator and leader often intersect, and in many cases may be played by the same person within an organization. They suggest that effective administrators must skillfully manage people, resources, and processes, simultaneously balancing concerns for people with concerns for resources and production, while also planning for and managing change.

Preparation for Work as an Adult Educator

One way to understand preparation is through the prism of Houle's (1956) pyramid of leadership within adult education, presented earlier in this chapter and depicted in Figure 1.1. For the many volunteers at the base of Houle's pyramid, without whom many foundational adult education programs would be unsustainable, Houle suggested role-specific preparation would be sufficient. For paid professionals whose duties include but are not primarily adult education, Houle suggested both pre-service and in-service professional education opportunities. For those whose primary roles focused on adult education, Houle recommended graduate-level study in adult education.

Douglah and Moss (1969) offered differentiated recommendations for professional preparation of adult educators by focusing on the professional's direct involvement with the content or knowledge base of the field. For those engaged as scholars of adult education, they recommended doctoral-level preparation in ACE. For full-time adult education practitioners, they suggested preparation in adult education at either the master's or doctoral level, depending on responsibilities. For those providing instruction to adults on a part-time basis, they suggested pre-service or in-service training or, where feasible, coursework or an academic minor in adult

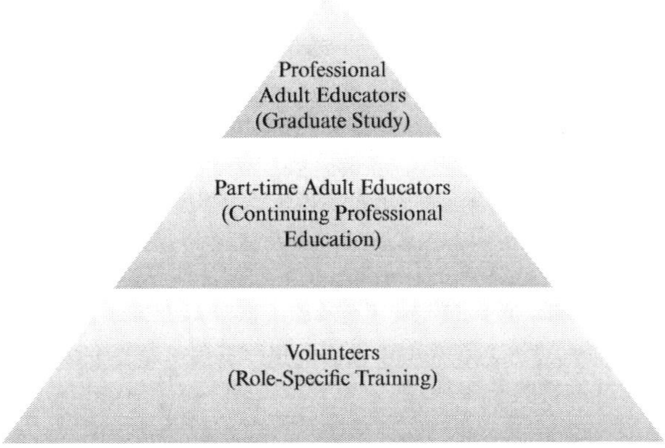

Figure 1.1 Houle's Pyramid of Leadership: Adult educator roles and recommended preparation
Note: Based on Houle (1956). Professional education for educators of adults. *Adult Education, 6*(3), 131–150.

education; such individuals might logically pursue academic degrees in the content areas they teach. Other authors have written more recently about the importance of professional development for those adult educators who do not possess degrees in the field (King & Lawler, 2003). Throughout Part II of this book, authors have included specific recommendations for preparation for the various roles discussed.

Issues Adult Educators Are Likely to Encounter

As we have learned up to this point in the chapter, adult education remains situated in a variety of contexts. Regardless of context, however, adult educators will likely be faced with one or more of the following core issues that can either bolster or threaten their engagement efforts: power, access, persistence and program completion, and the constant of change. These issues, interwoven with potential opportunities they may hold, are discussed next.

Power

When we consider power issues, we ask: Who gets to make decisions? Who gets to participate? How might that shape outcomes—for whom? Power dynamics remain "omnipresent in educational, organizational and social movement settings" (Brookfield, 2006, p. 21).

But how might adult educators be mindful of the power we possess and of its dynamics at work? Power may be inherent in a position one may hold, in one's positionalities (e.g., race, class, or gender in contexts with a long history of related discrimination), in others' perceptions, and in a host of other personal, professional, and contextual influences. For example, an individual may hold power based on a formal position, giving them the right to make demands and obtain compliance (legitimate power); on others' perception of their level of worthiness that can earn them respect (referent power); or based on high levels of skill, knowledge, and information (expert power). Individuals may also possess *reward power*—the ability to compensate others based on compliance—or conversely *coercive power*—the ability to punish, mainly through deprivation of a reward (French & Raven, 1959). As adult educators navigate relationships, power can be wielded to produce either positive or negative change. We spotlight program planning and classroom settings as examples of how power dynamics might operate.

Program Planner: Participant

A program planner who does not heed participant insights is likely yielding power negatively to the detriment of the program. Daffron and Caffarella (2021) assert a need to acknowledge power and to ensure all program stakeholders are heard. Discerning how important power and interests are remains one of their key principles—before, during, and after utilizing the interactive planning model for building effective programs. Sork's (2000) three components of program planning are also useful places to consider how power might work: (a) technical (organizing, budgeting, assessment, recruitment), (b) social and political, and (c) ethical (critical considerations of what may be right or wrong to do in context). Still, adult educators involved in planning and policy making need a careful balance between ensuring all stakeholder voices are heard and remaining practical about the potential challenges of having too many voices involved.

Educator: Learner – and Vice-Versa?

By the time they enter varied postsecondary education settings, many adult and young adult learners see a "chasm between themselves and those with expertise" (Frego, 2006, p. 47)—the instructor is the expert. Such a perception reinforces the legitimate power inherent in an educator's position. But adult educators can become the "bridge" over that chasm, encouraging equitable participation, building relationships, and using collaborative teaching strategies. Thankfully, adult learning theories have embodied the "guide on the side" rather than "sage on the stage" approach to teaching and learning with a view to encouraging democratic classroom spaces (Brookfield, 2015).

Adult educators are also encouraged to look out for "who talks, when and why" as well as questions of how learners or instructors use self-discipline or silence to control others, e.g., historically minoritized groups. Related questions might be: how does our practice of power enhance or deflate learners' motivation and sense of belonging? Or, how might our activities and assessments (and the power to choose those) reflect participants' learning preferences?

That power is a complex undergirding dynamic also suggests that it may not always work in a single direction—that is, from educator to learner. Brookfield (2006) asserts that learners hold power as well. Our own experiences in a higher education context have taught us of the power learners have, as it concerns educator evaluations for example. As women of the African Diaspora passionate about racial equity issues, we have been made aware of how materials aimed at helping learners grow in their understanding could be misconstrued and evaluated as a tool for personal discomfort and negativity. Questions arise then about choice, openness, and honesty relative to justice-oriented learning outcomes and/or about the broader institutional context—the kind that may or may not affirm a critical approach to teaching. How authentic can one (really) be? Adult educators must navigate classroom power dynamics carefully; such dynamics are often framed by larger social contexts that have historically privileged some and restricted others to the margins.

Access, Persistence, and Completion

Many adult learners face varied challenges as they seek to access, persist in, and complete their programs (Bergman, 2020). One seminal framework in our field, discussed next, is particularly helpful for illustrating the core types of challenges adults may face.

Concerning barriers to participation, Cross (1981) outlined three categories: situational, institutional, and dispositional. Situational barriers remain consistent within literature that examines adult learner persistence and retention. Cross describes them as barriers "arising from one's situation in life at a given time, such as job and home responsibilities" (p. 98). Factors like finances, time, home and work responsibilities, and childcare are also commonly cited. In fact, Hannon (2018) declares that "cost is the main barrier facing many adults who pursue postsecondary credentials. As costs have increased, state and federal financial aid has not kept up" (p. 3).

According to Blumenstyk (2018), "many of the barriers that face adult learners rest in institutions themselves and are in their power to remove" (p. 25). Institutional barriers refer to those systems, structures, or practices that discourage or impede a learner's ability to participate—for example, scheduling of programs and courses for part-time learners that are better suited to full-time status. Administrative "red tape" might also be considered an institutional barrier. When support systems and processes are unclear for adult learners, they are less likely to stay and to complete their studies (see, e.g., Pearson, 2019). Cross's dispositional barriers surround perceptions of self as a learner. Practical examples of factors affecting learner perceptions include perceived self-efficacy (level of uncertainty concerning academic ability), past experience in school, and perceptions of age as a limitation. Since context is key to understanding adult learners and programs, Cross's (1981) barriers will always need to be examined. That said, barriers to participation and access have also been layered by discrimination of historically marginalized groups—for example, women, racial minorities, and adults with disabilities to name a few.

A wide cross section of support mechanisms has been discussed for adult learner success, ranging from administrative and instructional support to career pathway support (see e.g., Merriam & Baumgartner, 2020; Pearson, 2019). Many of these mechanisms include drawing on learners' prior learning experiences, providing safe, affirming environments with multiple opportunities for collaboration, and helping learners achieve their goals by way of creative programming. Pearson (2019) shares some useful reflection questions for stakeholders that serve adult learners:

> Does the student have a plan for completion? How will the student afford studies? Does the student understand all of the support available? Does the student understand [program] opportunities? Does the student have confidence that can overcome the barriers to completion? Has the student started to build a network of supporters? (p. 18)

Inadequacy of program funding also compounds the issue of access, persistence, and completion as it lessens resources critical to learner support. In the United States, many postsecondary education programs have faced enrollment declines for the past few years (Flaherty, 2020). Calls for more robust funding relative to adult literacy programs and some postsecondary initiatives (e.g., through scholarships and grants) have been heard in the field for decades.

The Constant of Change

We have so far established that adult education aims to understand its structures, participants, and activities within a sociocultural context. Given our current national and global landscape, issues related to both diversity and change are glaring, and work in tandem with each other. We now discuss three broad areas experiencing an onslaught of change and outline how these changes might impact adults and the organizations that serve them.

Large-Scale Transitions in Technology

Large-scale expansion in uses of technology normalized remote opportunities for work and earning; much of this occurred rapidly in the context of the COVID-19 pandemic. Ninety percent of American adults said the internet was essential or important to them during the pandemic; 40% used technology in new ways (McClain et al., 2021). Such findings are reflected in multiple adult education settings; indeed, significant increases in technology use have been trending nationally and globally for the past decade. In a U.S. postsecondary context between Fall 2012 and Fall 2018, online course enrollment increased by 29%; in 2018–2019 alone, about 79% of all colleges offered either online courses or entire online degrees (National Center for Educational Statistics, 2021).

Massive Open Online Courses or MOOCs are also major contributors to the expansion of technology-based learning. Digital badging and other short-term course certification opportunities have become commonplace. Social media platforms continue to hold meaningful opportunities for informal learning, as do mobile apps. Twitter, Instagram, and vlogging platforms have spaces for short responses and reflections on content. All of this is framed by adults now having increased flexibility, completely remote or hybrid employment and training environments with expanded use of videoconferencing and digital collaboration platforms.

Large-scale expansion in technology use has brought a plethora of possibilities for improving teaching and learning in varied ways. Educators must consider the level of scaffolding necessary for adult learners to be successful, or how they might choose tools that are the most accessible, functional, and meaningful relative to learning goals. In addition, educators facilitating synchronously need to present materials in small(er) chunks with as much active learning as possible to avoid Zoom fatigue. Scholars in the field and beyond have expressed concern about misinformation and media as a threat to democracy and diversity (e.g., Merriam & Grace, 2011). Digital media literacy and information literacy may need to become part and parcel of teaching adults, as one way of guarding against misinformation in an era where almost everyone can create online content easily. Adult educators might consider how to utilize open access resources more intentionally for reduced cost to the learner. And adult educators may wrestle with questions like these: how might we consistently facilitate "deep learning" and creativity online (Murray-Johnson et al., 2021)? What are the virtual reality possibilities that may provide important learning solutions, but remain largely untapped in several adult education settings (e.g., Dyer et al., 2018)? From program planning to assessment stages, how might flexibility be optimized for adult learners in this era?

Emerging Justice Concerns, Demographic Shifts, and an Age of Trauma

In *Preparing Adult Educators for Social Justice*, Isaac-Savage and Merriweather (2021) spotlight racial justice as a critical category of social justice and share a compelling overview of the ways in which marginalized groups, and in particular, African Americans, have been discriminated against over time. Pointing to a range of scholarship, they highlight that although adult education has "intertwined with justice" over time, it has fallen somewhat short of consistently "naming" racial justice. These authors encourage us to move beyond advocacy to intentional action. They suggest action steps including building capacity for the facilitation of critical dialogue and emotional risk taking, developing and requiring diverse programs on race and racism, and establishing racial justice centers.

We encourage ourselves and our readers to embrace Isaac-Savage and Merriweather's (2021) recommendations, and we do so with a sense of extreme urgency. As we write, over 200 mass shootings in the United States have occurred in under 200 days—one of the most recent was racially motivated with the murder of 10 African Americans at a grocery store. In addition, the significant expansion of the Black Lives Matter (BLM) movement and global outcry that ensued because of the killing of George Floyd and several other individuals of Color within the past several years serves as a grim reminder that race remains the jagged edge of American life. In 2020 alone, 61.8% of all hate crimes were committed against those who were *racially* minoritized; approximately 56% of those targeted were Black or African American (U.S. Department of Justice, 2021).

In addition, some adult educators have continued to earmark equity disparities relative to gender, sexuality, class, and (dis)ability over time (see Merriam & Baumgartner, 2020, for a useful overview). Rocco (2005) termed those with disabilities "the invisible people" in the field of adult education, and later argued for the use of critical disability theory as a way of understanding the issues related to ableism and disability in working and learning spaces. Recent calls have been made for the use of Universal Design for Learning (UDL) in the field as a best practice tool for inclusive instruction (Ross-Gordon & Procknow, 2021). Opportunities remain for stakeholders in the field to examine the power they may hold as a member of a majority group. Perhaps we might pause for a short fill-in-the-blank reflective exercise here. As a reader, in what ways might my majority position as a member of (race/gender/class etc. category) influence the adult education environment or learning space that I hope to work in? The continued challenge (and potential opportunity), however, seems to be moving beyond individual micro reflection and advocacy to purposeful, united action at the macro level.

Examples of core national (U.S.) justice concerns are mere reflections of larger global trends and challenges. Among the emerging justice issues that face those who serve adults everywhere and that they must plan around are:

- Climate change and environmental justice concerns for a more sustainable world (e.g., Griswold, 2017, and Chapter 8, this volume)
- Food justice movements that might improve quality of life for economically disenfranchised groups (e.g., Levkoe, 2006)
- Demographic shifts and a significant refugee crisis, created in part by the challenges of war, in-fighting and/or violence (e.g., Ukraine, the Tigray Region in Ethiopia and within other continents)
- The COVID-19 pandemic and diverse impacts on adults, learning, and education (see, e.g., Boeren et al., 2020; James &Thériault, 2020)

Finally, multiple issues of equity, access, and justice discussed here, by their very nature also unearth a trauma-filled national and global environment. A timely publication from the Adult Higher Education Alliance book series recently probed how trauma informs, shapes, and challenges policy, andragogy, and interactions; who faces it; and how adult learning spaces might prevent or perpetuate trauma (Douglass et al., 2022). Since trauma has a direct effect on our capacity to learn and retain information, advocates of a trauma-informed approach to adult education have contended that it is critical to the success of today's adult learner (Gross, 2019). We urge stakeholders in adult education and those seeking career opportunities in the field to follow suit. The time is now as mental health challenges across our communities are at an all-time high and global unrest layered with justice concerns continue to point us to evidence of collective trauma.

Diverse Perspectives and a Shifting Society

Since education remains a microcosm of society, learner perspectives are likely to reflect diversity within the broader social landscape—a landscape that we have learned is ever-changing. The difference in this moment, however, seems to be that the shift is taking place in the context of a tremendously divisive climate. A Pew Research Global report, for example, noted that although countries with "advanced economies" like the United States embraced the idea of diversity, most have seen inevitable conflicts between partisan and racial/ethnic groups (Silver et al., 2021). In the case of the United States, the report concluded that of perceived political and ethnic conflict, "no public is more divided than Americans" (p. 13). The co-editors of the most recent *Handbook of Adult and Continuing Education* concur: "American society appears more divisive and fractured than at any time since the Vietnam war and civil rights movement" (Mizzi et al., 2021, p. 2).

So, what might current and aspiring adult educators do? We have a golden opportunity to respond by shaping a sustainable future, or recoil and risk losing it. The *Handbook* authors note that for diversity to be a strength, skillful pedagogy must be employed to encourage civil dialogue and to avoid further perpetuating incivility within and beyond our learning spaces (Mizzi et al., 2021). As author-practitioners, we are advocates of targeting instructional design, curriculum development, and teaching practices within frameworks that spotlight both cognitive and affective domains that are intentional in articulating power dynamics and equity concerns, and that are solutions based. Adult education as a field has been rich in its possession of meaningful seminal and emerging approaches to this end. Those who serve adult learners may consider Freire's (1970) critical theory that advocates reading beyond the word to reading the "world," Murray-Johnson and Ross-Gordon's (2018) framework for difficult dialogues —and a host of justice-centered pedagogies explored by Ramdeholl and Jeremic (2021). Foundational concepts essential to a dialogic approach also include Stephen Brookfield's work on discussion, and a call by Manglitz et al. (2014) for developing emotive capacity. Finally, facilitating intentional links between learners and the communities they serve as part of the learning process is key.

Conclusion

Trends discussed in this chapter highlight recurring issues reported in the field over time (e.g., factors affecting adult persistence and success, social justice concerns, and the potential of technology-based learning). But today's adult learner is situated within a context laden with a unique confluence of sociocultural and political factors—a context that threatens as much peril (if all stakeholders are not intentional in shaping positive outcomes) as it does possibility. We believe that while fierce challenges persist, both conceptual/theoretical and practical solutions to them exist in the field as a result of time-tested principles that frame adult education, as well as its growing emphasis on critical and equity-based frameworks in this era.

The field of adult education remains dynamic and, for those seeking careers in it, opportunities are abundant for individuals with open minds, creativity, spirit, and commitment to socially just and inclusive adult education for all. Beyond formal educational spaces dedicated to foundational and postsecondary education, a wide array of nonformal and informal environments exist (e.g., training, mentoring, coaching, and organizational development in corporate, governmental, health, and nonprofit settings; community-based activism and programs; design of media and learning apps). Some working in these contexts practice adult education, although they may not explicitly wear its label and may play a number of non-instructor roles. But our work in whatever learning context we find ourselves must now be holistic—rooted in and impacting both cognitive and affective domains of the adults we serve. The success of that approach in the current moment can only be limited by a siloed approach and a lack of varied types of capital and resources needed to sustain practice.

References

Alston, G. D., & Hansman, C. A. (2020). Mentoring, learning, and leadership in adult and continuing education. *New Directions for Adult and Continuing Education, 2020*(167–168).

Baldwin, C. K., & Conceição, S. C. O. (2021). Becoming effective online facilitators. *New Directions for Adult and Continuing Education, 2021*(169), 111–117. https://doi.org/10.1002/ace.20419

Belzer, K., & Kim, J. (2021). The cost of a dollars and cents rationale for adult basic education policy. In T. S. Rocco, M. C. Smith, R. C. Mizzi, L. R. Merriweather, & J. D. Hawley (Eds.), *The handbook of adult and continuing education* (2020 ed., pp. 189–196). Stylus.

Bergman, M. (2020). Adult learners in higher education. In T. S. Rocco, M. C. Smith, R. C. Mizzi, L. R. Merriweather, & J. D. Hawley (Eds.), *The handbook of adult and continuing education* (2020 ed., pp. 266–274). Stylus.

Biniecki, S., & Schmidt, S. (2021). Organization and administration of adult and continuing education programs. In T. S. Rocco, M. C. Smith, R. C. Mizzi, L. R. Merriweather, & J. D. Hawley (Eds.), *The handbook of adult and continuing education* (2020 ed., pp. 119–128). Stylus.

Blumenstyk, F. M. (2018). *The adult student: The population higher education—and the nation—cannot afford to ignore*. Chronicle of Higher Education. Inc.

Boeren, E., Roumell, E. A., & Roessger, K. M. (2020). COVID-19 and the future of adult education: An editorial. *Adult Education Quarterly, 70*(3), 201–204.

Brookfield, S. D. (2006). Authenticity and power. *New Directions for Adult and Continuing Education, 2006*(111), 5–16. https://doi.org/10.1002/ace.223

Brookfield, S. D. (2015). *The skillful teachers: On technique, trust, and responsiveness in the classroom* (3rd ed.). Jossey-Bass.

Chalofsky, N., Rocco, T. S., & Morris, M. L. (Eds.). (2014). *Handbook of human resource development*. Wiley & Sons.

Coady, M. (2021). Continuing professional education. In T. S. Rocco, M. C. Smith, R. C. Mizzi, L. R. Merriweather, & J. D. Hawley (Eds.), *The handbook of adult and continuing education* (2020 ed., pp. 257–266). Stylus.

Coombs, P. H., & Ahmed, M. (1974). *Attacking rural poverty: How nonformal education can help*. John Hopkins University Press.

Cross, K. P. (1981). *Adults as learners: Increasing participation and facilitating learning*. Jossey-Bass.

Daffron, S. R., & Caffarella, R. S. (2021). *Planning programs for adult learners: A practical guide* (4th ed.). Jossey-Bass.

Darkenwald, G. S., & Merriam, S. G. (1982). *Adult education: Foundations of practice*. Harper & Row.

Douglah, M. A., & Moss, G. M. (1969). Adult education as a field of study and its implications for the preparation of adult educators. *Adult Education Quarterly, 19*(2), 127–134.

Douglass, L. L, Threlkeld, A. & Merriweather, L. R. (Eds.). (2022). *Trauma in adult and higher education: Conversations and critical reflections*. Information Age Publishers.

Dyer, E., Swartzlander, B. J., & Gugliucci, M. R. (2018). Using virtual reality in medical education to teach empathy. *Journal of the Medical Library Association: JMLA, 106*(4), 498.

Ellinger, A., & Kim, S. (2014). Coaching and human resource development: Examining relevant theories, coaching genres, and scales to advance research and practice. *Advances in Developing Human Resources, 16*(2), 127–138. https://doi.org/10.1177/1523422313520472

Flaherty, C. (2020, October 27). *Teachers education continues to suffer death by a thousand cuts*. Inside Higher Ed. www.insidehighered.com/news/2020/10/28/teachers-education-programs-continue-suffer-death-thousand-cuts

Frego, K. (2006). Authenticity and relationships with students. *New Directions for Adult and Continuing Education, 2006*(111), 41–50. https://doi.org/10.1002/ace.226

Freire, P. (1970). *Pedagogy of the oppressed*. Seabury Press.

French, J. R. P., & Raven, B. (1959). The basis of social power. In D. Cartwright (Ed.), *Studies in social power* (pp. 529–569). University of Michigan Press.

Griswold, W. (2017). Sustainability, ecojustice, and adult education. *New Directions for Adult and Continuing Education, 2017*(153), 7–15. https://doi.org/10.1002/ace.20217

Gross, K. (2019). *Trauma impacts adult learners: Here's why*. The Council for Adult and Experiential Learning. www.cael.org/news-and-resources/trauma-impacts-adult-learners-heres-why

Hannon, K. (2018, June 5). The cost of going back to school as an adult. *The New York Times*. www.nytimes.com/2018/06/05/education/learning/financial-aid-adult-learners.html

Hill, L. H. (2021). Assessment and evaluation in adult and continuing education. In T. S. Rocco, M. C. Smith, R. C. Mizzi, L. R. Merriweather, & J. D. Hawley (Eds.), *The handbook of adult and continuing education* (2020 ed., pp. 140–149). Stylus.

Houle, C. (1956). Adult education: Professional education for educators of adults. *Adult Education, 6*(3), 131–150.

Houle, C. O. (1972). *The design of education*. Jossey-Bass.

Isaac-Savage, E. P., & Merriweather, L. R. (2021). Preparing adult educators for racial justice. *New Directions for Adult and Continuing Education, 2021*(170), 109–118. https://doi.org/10.1002/ace.20430

James, N., & Thériault, V. (2020). Adult education in times of the COVID-19 pandemic: Inequalities, changes, and resilience. *Studies in the Education of Adults, 52*(2), 129–133.

King, K. P., & Lawler, P. A. (Eds.) (2003). New perspectives on designing and implementing professional development of teachers of adults. *New Directions for Adult and Continuing Education, 2003*(98). https://doi.org/10.1002/ace.93

Levkoe, C. Z. (2006). Learning democracy through food justice movements. *Agriculture and Human Values, 23*(1), 89–98.

Lindeman, E. C. (1926). *The meaning of adult education*. New Republic.

McClain, C., Vogels, E., Perrin, A., Sechopoulos, S., & Raine, L. (2021, September 1). *The internet and the pandemic*. Pew Research Center. www.pewresearch.org/internet/2021/09/01/the-internet-and-the-pandemic

Manglitz, E., Guy, T. C., & Merriweather, L. R. (2014). Knowledge and emotions in cross-racial dialogues: Challenges and opportunities for adult educators committed to racial justice in educational settings. *Adult Learning, 25*(3), 111–118.

Merriam, S. B., & Baumgartner, L. M. (2020). *Learning in adulthood* (4th ed). Jossey-Bass.

Merriam, S. B., & Bierema, L. L. (2014). *Adult learning: Linking theory and practice*. Jossey-Bass.

Merriam, S. B., & Brockett, R. G. (2007). *The profession and practice of adult education: An introduction*. Wiley.

Merriam, S. B., & Grace, A. P. (Eds.). (2011). *The Jossey-Bass reader on contemporary issues in adult education*. Jossey-Bass.

Mizzi, R. C., Rocco, T. S., Smith, M. C., Merriweather, L. R., & Hawley, J. D. (2021). Introduction: Advancing adult and continuing education through critical conversations and diverse perspectives. In T. S. Rocco, M. C. Smith, R. C. Mizzi, L. R. Merriweather, & J. D. Hawley (Eds.), *The handbook of adult and continuing education* (2020 ed., pp. 1–8). Stylus.

Monaghan, C. H. (2010). Working against the grain: White privilege in human resource development. *New Directions for Adult and Continuing Education, 2010*(125), 53–63. https://doi.org/10.1002/ace.362

Murray-Johnson, K., & Ross-Gordon, J. M. (2018). Everything is about balance: Graduate faculty and the navigation of difficult discourses on race. *Adult Education Quarterly, 68*(2), 137–156. https://doi.org/10.1002/ace.20412

Murray-Johnson, K., Munro, A., & Popoola, R. (2021). Immersive deep learning activities online. *New Directions for Adult and Continuing Education, 2021*(169), 35–49. https://doi.org/10.1002/ace.20412

National Center for Educational Statistics. (2021, February 17). *Distance education in college: What do we know from IPEDS?* [Blog post]. https://nces.ed.gov/blogs/nces/post/distance-education-in-college-what-do-we-know-from-ipeds

Pearson, W. (2019). Persistence of adult students. *The Journal of Continuing Higher Education, 67*(1), 13–23. https://doi.org/10.1080/07377363.2019.1627166

Polson, C. J. (1994). Developmental advising for nontraditional students. *Adult Learning, 6*(1), 21–22.

Ramdeholl, D., & Jeremic, R. (2021). Activism in/and struggle: Teaching for a different world. In T. S. Rocco, M. C. Smith, R. C. Mizzi, L. R. Merriweather, & J. D. Hawley(Eds.), *The handbook of adult and continuing education* (2020 ed., pp. 171–190). Stylus.

Rocco, T. S. (2005). *From disability studies to critical race theory: Working towards critical disability theory*. Adult Education Research Conference. https://newprairiepress.org/aerc/2005/papers/17

Ross-Gordon, J. M., & Procknow, G. (2021). Adult education and disability. In T. S. Rocco, M. C. Smith, R. C. Mizzi, L. R. Merriweather, & J. D. Hawley (Eds.), *The handbook of adult and continuing education* (2020 ed., pp. 392–400). Stylus.

Ross-Gordon, J. M., Rose, A., & Kasworm, C. (2017). *Foundations of adult and continuing education.* Jossey-Bass.

Scully-Ross. E., & Vidal de Col, X. (2021). Workforce development: Past, present, and future. In T. S. Rocco, M. C. Smith, R. C. Mizzi, L. R. Merriweather, & J. D. Hawley (Eds.), *The handbook of adult and continuing education* (2020 ed., pp. 223–231). Stylus.

Silver, C., Fetterholf, J., Connaughton, A., Sechopoulos, S., & Raine, L. (2021, October 13). *Diversity and division in advanced economies.* Pew Research Center. www.pewresearch.org/global/2021/10/13/diversity-and-division-in-advanced-economies

Sork, T. J. (2000). Planning educational programs. In A. L. Wilson & E. R. Hayes (Eds.), *Handbook of adult and continuing education* (pp. 171–190). Jossey-Bass.

U.S. Department of Justice. (2021). *2020 FBI Hate Crime Statistics.* www.justice.gov/crs/highlights/2020-hate-crimes-statistics

Verner, C. (1964). *Adult education.* Center for Applied Research in Education.

Walker, J., & Butterwick, S. (2021) Education to change the world: Learning within and through social movements. In T. S. Rocco, M. C. Smith, R. C. Mizzi, L. R. Merriweather, & J. D. Hawley (Eds.), *The handbook of adult and continuing education* (2020 ed., pp. 322–329). Stylus.

Chapter 2

Practical Skills for Teaching Adults

Wendy M. Green and Alexander Hoffman

Adult education is a broad umbrella that has included remediation of literacy and basic numeracy skills, lifelong learning, and corrections education (Rocco et al., 2020). We have seen the expansion of topic areas that include international education, environmental education, labor education, health professions education, consulting, corporate training, and community education. Rose (2020) argues that the nomenclature utilized in the field is confusing as adult education can refer to any of these areas, which on the surface may appear disconnected. However, the expanse of the field is both beneficial and troublesome; the expansion of the definition of adult education is beneficial because we can consider the variety of areas where our theoretical understandings can inform practice, but it can also be confusing to newcomers since the umbrella of adult education includes a nebulous group of professions and interest areas that appear to have few obvious connections.

To highlight the diverse and multitudinous paths that one can use to come to adult education as a profession or as a field of scholarship, the authors offer their own unique personal experiences as examples. Wendy Green's progression began in the area of social services.

> I have worked as an adult educator across settings that have included residential treatment facilities, jails, and vocational training centers. I fully transitioned to adult education when I became the director of adult education for the Seminole Tribe of Florida. Aiming to improve my understanding of adult education and practice, I enrolled in a master's program in human resources development where I was introduced to the scholarship of adult education. After ten years in the field, I enrolled in a PhD program in teaching, learning, and curriculum with a focus on adult contexts. While a graduate student, a key experience was co-developing and evaluating curricula for a global health leadership program designed to develop leadership skills for mid-career physicians and nurses. This experience positioned me to work in the area of health professions education. In 2014, I started as a faculty member at Cleveland State University with a focus on adult education and health professions education.

Alexander Hoffman's trajectory was more immediate.

> In contrast to Dr. Green's experience as an adult educator, which developed over time, my entrance into adult education came as an immediate professional obligation as an entry-level healthcare worker. The training of the next generation of pharmacists is part of the professional oath of pharmacists (American Pharmacists Association, 2021), which is administered to all those graduating from Doctor of Pharmacy programs in the United States. This obligation is similar to other healthcare professions, especially those where experiential learning plays a key role in the educational process. During my residency

DOI: 10.4324/9781003259602-4

training, I underwent a teaching certificate program at an affiliated university, which introduced me to basic concepts of adult education, which I used to develop basic teaching skills. Immediately after completing my residency, supervisors required me to take learners in introductory experiential education experiences. As I advanced in my career, I was able to obtain a position that would let me continue my clinical work, continue teaching in the field, and start teaching in the classroom. As I worked in the classroom, I, like many educators, found myself repeating the techniques with which I was taught, and found myself unsatisfied with the results of my work. This desire to improve my skill set as an educator led me to pursue a master's in health professions education, which highlighted the need for me to reevaluate the theoretical principles of my teaching and the methods by which I taught.

Despite the contrasting entryways, professions, and interest areas, every educator has at least one major connecting factor – the adult learner. Adult educators recognize that adults engage in learning activities for numerous reasons (Merriam & Baumgartner, 2020). Perhaps one person engages in higher education to advance their career whereas others engage in community-based programming to enhance their personal lives. Despite the variety of interests, there are core principles that ground effective adult learning experiences. In this chapter, we take a broad approach to how we conceptualize adult education. We discuss facilitating teaching and learning activities by focusing on the integration of content with theoretical approaches that are appropriate for adult learners. We review ways educators can create effective learning environments and how learner-centered lenses affect teaching. Finally, we discuss the need for adult educators to practice lifelong learning and continual self-improvement.

Educator Competencies for Adult Learners

Adult educators may undertake educational roles due to expertise in their professional roles. For example, a high-performing sales representative may find herself teaching novice sales representatives or an accomplished writer may find himself teaching community-based writing classes. These educators may vary in their understanding of effective educational practices. It is not uncommon for educators to have substantial professional training but lack formal training in adult education. Their practice may begin as a process of replicating approaches they observed as learners as they have not developed an empirically grounded understanding of approaches and techniques that foster better outcomes. Educators who have a well-developed understanding of practical approaches to teaching and learning are shown to be effective, and make better decisions when designing and executing educational activities. The next section illustrates practices that strengthen the development of learning activities and foster positive learning environments that result in better outcomes.

Cultivating Effective Learning Environments

Regardless of the context, creating an appropriate environment for learning is a key component of facilitating an effective learning space. Adult educators recognize adult learners are entering learning environments with numerous educational experiences (Merriam & Baumgartner, 2020). These experiences are varied; some learners will be fully engaged and draw on positive experiences, whereas others may recall difficulties in prior situations. Educators should acknowledge the variety of prior learning experiences and foster a positive environment that is welcoming, personable, and provides psychological safety for participants. Educators can develop an orientation of authenticity and approachability by exhibiting empathy and respect for learners while creating conditions that promote learner cohesion (Brookfield, 2015). They can help the group establish shared goals and guide learners in the identification of parameters for success. Additionally, adult learning environments should be settings where diversity, inclusion, and equity are foregrounded and valued. Finally, learners should be encouraged to move out of their comfort zones and be supported when they do.

Authentic and Credible Educators

Brookfield (2015) argues that educators who are perceived as authentic and credible have more success in the classroom. Authentic educators position themselves as an ally in the learning space and, according to Brookfield, act in accordance with their stated values, are clear with course and assignment expectations, and are responsive to learner questions and concerns. Educators recognize they are role models in the learning environment and that how they engage their learners informs how learners engage with each other. Instructors exhibit credibility through subject matter fluency and by having prior experiences in the field. Educator credibility and authenticity are particularly salient for adult learners who are returning to formal learning environments.

Psychologically Safe Environments

A critical area of consideration for adult educators is the development of psychologically safe environments (Brookfield, 2015). Learning environments are considered psychologically safe when learners have a perception that they are allowed to step out of their comfort zones and stretch their understanding and application of concepts without the fear of embarrassment, shame, or retribution. Psychological safety also means learners are comfortable engaging in learning activities that require them to take risks or expose vulnerabilities while trying out new ideas and wrestling with course materials. Adult educators can create psychologically safe environments by cultivating a sincere interest in the well-being of learners, setting clear parameters that include expectations for engagement, and encouraging learners who respond to questions or prompts. This is particularly salient as it applies to issues of diversity and equity.

Diversity and Equity

Another essential aspect of psychologically safe learning environments is they are inclusive and recognize and value the identities and experiences of all learners. This approach not only recognizes an individual's identities in terms of race, ethnicity, gender, and sexual orientation, but expands the umbrella of how diversity is understood. For example, Bolitzer et al. (2016) argue that the understanding of diversity should be grounded in the intersectionality of learner identities, as well as recognizing the variety of lived experiences. Additionally, the application of critical perspectives helps learners link historical experiences with societal constructs and the positionality of all group members. Respecting and integrating a variety of lived experiences broadens the understanding of both educators and learners alike. In order to create more inclusive learning spaces, adult educators can expand their course materials and assignments. For example, an adult educator who is teaching a community-based literature and writing class could ensure their texts are representative of the contexts in which they teach, or that the authors represent a variety of social identities and experiences. Educators may also provide a variety of avenues for learning that moves beyond class papers.

Educators can draw on a variety of strategies that promote effective learning environments. Those who approach their practice as a learning partner and view themselves as a part of the group can cultivate an environment that has a flattened hierarchical structure and one that values learners' experiences and perspectives. Through the incorporation of mindful strategies, these actions can promote a learning environment that is psychologically safe, meaning it is one that encourages and supports learner participation and is boundary stretching (Brookfield, 2015). Finally, foregrounding aspects of diversity and equity shows the learner population that the educator values all identities and experiences in the learning environment.

Theory-Informed Instruction for Adult Learners: Concepts and Practice

Adult education is an arena of extremes and can happen in a myriad of settings. Learners may be completing remedial education or an advanced course of study. They may be completing coursework as part of an advanced degree program or for professional or personal reasons. The variations in learner populations, the needs of adult learners, and the available learning theories can overwhelm the novice adult educator. In this section, we identify three theoretical approaches to adult learning that are commonly utilized in adult education and which offer meaningfully different approaches to instruction. We will describe a theory and will use a vignette to illustrate how the use of that theory shifts the design of instruction and shapes the learning environment.

First, begin by considering the material (content) that is being taught. Answer the following questions as you review the material: What are the desired outcomes that I hope to attain through the teaching? What do I expect learners to be able to do after the learning is complete? As you consider these questions, evaluate your answers from a lens of alignment with programmatic and learner goals. Educators should analyze content based on available scaffolding and support. For example, does the instruction focus on materials that are new to the learner or does it build on previously learned material? Desired outcomes may be formulated as goals, objectives, or a vision of the learner at the end of the instruction and can be developed independently by educators or in conjunction with learners.

Educators should consider the needs and characteristics of their learners. What are the learner's needs? What are the learner's perceptions of their own needs? Adult learners often desire teaching that has relevance to their current work and can be immediately put into practice. They also expect teaching to be up to date and relevant to their lived experience. Educators should consider whether the learners have any developmental concerns and, in order to ensure that instruction is optimized for every learner, frameworks such as the Universal Design for Learning can be implemented (CAST, 2018). Finally, educators should consider the learning environment. Adult learners have specific requirements for learning environments compared to young learners. Adults desire freedom and flexibility, often desire explicit standards for the learning environment, and desire learner-centered engagement (Knowles, 1970). Learners expect a learning environment where all members are respectful and relationships between learners and educators are positive and equitable.

Building Instruction Centered in Adult-Oriented Learning Theory

In order for teaching to have the greatest impact, it must be embedded in theoretical concepts specifically tailored to adult learners. As discussed previously, the adult learner is not a "blank slate" and comes to the learning environment with a wealth of life experiences and specific expectations for their learning. Therefore, any teaching method must be embedded in a theory that respects and understands that background. In this section, we briefly discuss three major areas of learning theory that educators may draw from as they create instructional plans: self-directed learning, transformational learning, and experiential learning. In order to clarify how these theories will affect the way educators approach material, we will use the following illustrative vignette:

You are a member of a nonprofit organization that looks to reduce food inequity in urban areas. You have partnered with the local food bank and library consortium to develop educational activities to help address food inequity. Most of the identified participants in your program have a high school education or lower and all will attend classes at a local library branch.

Self-Directed Learning. Self-directed learning describes a process in which learners take the initiative for their learning (Grow, 1994). This work can be done with or without the help of others. Learners are responsible for diagnosing their learning needs, formulating their learning goals, identifying the resources needed for learning, choosing and implementing appropriate strategies for learning, and evaluating their learning outcomes. Self-directed learning can take place inside and outside of formal teaching environments and has become more prevalent as more learners have gained access to advanced technology.

Because self-directed learning is inherently driven by the learner, including it in instructional models can be challenging. Grow's (1994) Staged Self-Directed Learning (SSDL) model gives educators working in formal settings a framework for how self-directed learning can be implemented in their programs. Grow argues that learners in the SSDL model fall into one of four categories, moving from dependent learning (where a learner has low self-direction and needs an educator to tell them what to do) to a self-directed learner (where the learner is both willing and able to plan, execute, and evaluate their own learning). Educators may select from the following exercises based on the learner's self-directedness:

1. Stage 1: Dependent learner – coaching with immediate feedback, lectures
2. Stage 2: Interested learner – inspiring lecture with guided discussion, goal-setting and learning strategies, applying basics in stimulating ways
3. Stage 3: Involved learner – discussion facilitated by an educator who participates as an equal, seminars, group projects where the learners work closely with the instructor on real problems, critical thinking
4. Stage 4: Self-directed learner – internship, dissertation, individual work or self-directed study group, discovery learning where the instructor acts as an expert facilitator

If we evaluate our vignette through the lens of self-directed learning, our goal as instructors is to move learners through Grow's (1994) stages, from dependent learner to self-directed learner. We may start with introductions to healthy food available at the food bank through a short presentation, and then try to get learners invested by getting them to interact with the ingredients just discussed by trying foods made with them. As learners move through stages, we might offer sessions like menu planning or cooking classes where the learner participates while the instructor guides the session. Once the learner has reached self-directed learning, the instructor moves into a facilitator role, allowing learners to explore areas that are of specific interest to them, or by helping them introduce foods and ingredients to others in their community.

Experiential Learning. Experience is a fundamental way that adults learn, and life experience has been called "the adult learner's living textbook" (Lindeman, 1961, p. 7). However, experiencing something does not necessarily lead to learning. Experiential learning occurs when carefully chosen experiences are supported by reflection, critical analysis, and synthesis (Association for Experiential Education, 2022). Frameworks for experiential learning include the following steps:

1   Having a tangible experience
2   Reflecting on and analyzing that experience
3   Connecting the experience to "real life"
4   Applying what was learned during the experience

Many models of experiential education are cyclical in nature (Jarvis, 2010; Kolb, 2014), indicating that the process of experiential learning is lifelong. The goal of the educator in experiential learning is to expose learners to experiences that will be interesting and compelling to them while encouraging later stages of the process through questioning, coaching, or mentoring. If we consider our vignette from the perspective of experiential learning, we may have learners follow a recipe that includes new foods that are available to them at the food bank, prepare the food, and then share it with others. Learners might be asked to identify ways to modify meals they cook to incorporate new food items. Problem-based learning strategies such as this are common in experiential learning and help to serve as the core experience that learners can then build upon. As educators, we might then have learners reflect on how the process worked and whether they would be able to do similar cooking at home. We might also have learners engage in service learning, volunteerism, or internships with local charity groups to learn more about their work while encouraging reflection, analysis, and application.

Transformational Learning. Transformational learning focuses on creating fundamental changes in the way learners see themselves and the world in which they live. As Kegan (2000) notes, transformational learning does not expand a learner's previously constructed cognitive framework, but rather changes the foundations of that framework. Transformational learning can either be individualized (where the goal is a personal change in perspective) or emancipatory (where the goal is radical, social, or systems change). Both forms of transformational learning rely on experience, reflection, and action based on that reflection.

In individualized transformational learning, the goal of the educator is to stimulate changes in worldview on an independent level, relying on an initiating experience often called a "disorienting dilemma," which can take many forms (Mezirow, 2009). From an individual perspective, learners are asked to reflect on their worldviews and habits of mind and to examine how these perceptions influence their current experiences. In contrast, for emancipatory transformational learning, the goal of the educator is to lead learners through the process of conscientization, where they gradually become more aware of how societal forces intersect with experiences and opportunities. Freire (2018) argues that it is essential for learners to analyze their experiences from a broader framework and become a part of a movement for social change. This form of transformational learning relies on the educator to engage with learners on a human level and as a partner in the learning experience (Freire, 2000). Educators engage with learners through dialogue and critical reflection.

Returning to our vignette, if our goal is to teach through the lens of transformational learning, focused on shifting individuals' worldviews, we might create an activity that allows learners to understand how familial and cultural experiences of food influence their current habits. When focusing on individual transformation, an educator might employ writing prompts and journaling. Learners could be asked to share reflections and future steps with respect to meal planning and ingredient substitution to utilize available foods. The small group would provide and receive feedback on reflection and plans. When focused on developing conscientization, educators would engage learners in dialogue. Educators would provide introductory information and questions to begin the discussion, but learners would be asked to share and relate their experiences with food, food access, and the foodbank. Learners would be asked to connect their experiences with structural issues based on community experiences, for example, economic segregation or racism. Learners could consider how locations of supermarkets are determined by economic status and what foods are available in different neighborhoods. The adult educator could facilitate a field trip in which learners compare supermarkets in higher-income neighborhoods and lower-income neighborhoods while paying close attention to the availability of fresh fruits and vegetables. Learners might be requested to develop a strategy to engage with city officials to advocate for policies that are more equitable. For example, they might consider ways of creating more access to fresh foods through the development of community gardens and approach city officials for land, funds, and expertise to begin the project. They might be asked to identify other communities where there are movements focused on equity issues and community gardens and encouraged to develop networks where expertise could be shared.

Applying Adult Learning Theories: Action Steps

In the prior section, we provided an overview of how specific learning theories can guide an educator's design of learning environments. We used a vignette to illustrate how three commonly used adult-centric learning theories can facilitate learning and explained how the role of the educator and the course activities shift based on the theoretical grounding of the activity. A key component to creating effective learning environments is considering the desired outcomes and identifying activities that will facilitate the outcome. For example, if you are trying to facilitate a shift in thinking, lecture-based activities would not be most effective. Perspective shifts are more likely to happen when learners are asked to identify pre-existing belief systems, to consider how these beliefs are or are not beneficial to what they are trying to achieve, and to consider alternative paths. Incorporating time for group discussion and reflection will provide learners with the space and support to think through new ideas.

Centering What Works: Instruction and Lifelong Learning

In this final section, we address areas where alternate frameworks may support adult educators and adult learners, address educational myths, and argue for the need for educators to engage in lifelong learning.

Diversity, Equity, and Inclusion: Moving from Cultural Competence to Critical Consciousness

Adult educators have a fundamental calling to address the needs of an increasingly diverse society and address education inadequacy and disparities that adult learners may have experienced in their formative years. Indeed, social justice is embedded in much of adult education programming. To address these concerns, international societies and authors have called for an increase in cultural competency among adult educators (Mayfield, 2020). Despite coming from a children's mental health context, Cross et al. (1989) have provided the most often cited definition of cultural competency in medicine, which they frame as "a set of congruent behaviors, attitudes, and policies that come together in a system, agency or among professionals and enable that system, agency or those professions to work effectively in cross-cultural situations" (p. 13). Although we value the framework of cultural competency, we acknowledge critiques of the concepts and argue that the framework of critical consciousness adds a more nuanced and expansive way of understanding issues of diversity, equity, and inclusion. For example, Kumagai and Lypson (2009) argue that the use of competencies in health professions education may be surrounded by a view that culture is fixed. Additionally, when educators use a menu approach to teaching about cultures, there is a risk of essentializing groups or reinforcing stereotypes. Teaching about cultural attributes or associations without embedding historical context and understanding of how these contexts relate to current experiences diminishes the learners' ability to develop a broader understanding of intersectionality, positionality, and power dynamics within society. When learners complete training and are viewed as culturally competent, it is assumed that their learning objectives are achieved and no further engagement is needed. Using the critical consciousness framework focuses on the development of an orientation toward understanding "different ways of knowing" (Kumagai & Lypson, 2009, p. 783). This approach interweaves critical thinking and critical theory (Freire, 2018) and requires learners to develop a situational understanding that recognizes individuals do not exist within a vacuum but live and operate in systems that, for some, are inherently unjust. The development of a critical consciousness requires learners to "recognize differences in power and privilege and that inequities are embedded in social relationships" (Kumagai & Lypson, 2009, p. 783).

Fostering the Development of Critical Consciousness: Action Steps

Adult educators are in positions to help learners develop an orientation toward critical consciousness, enabling them to understand individuals' lived experiences within specific contexts, in our case the United States (e.g., Green et al., 2020). Instructional strategies might include having learners critically review group experiences within the United States and to trace how policies have marginalized groups and have resulted in unequal outcomes. Learners could extend the discussion by examining how structural forces have marginalized communities and have affected their ability to access healthcare, housing, and education. This approach requires learners to connect individuals' lived experiences to broader structural issues and provides a more nuanced understanding rather than teaching cultural characteristics from a static and encapsulated perspective where one develops a body of facts and is thus competent (Kumagai & Lypson, 2009).

Adult Educators as Lifelong Learners

As the world changes, educators cannot afford to stand still. Innovative technologies, platforms, and politics will drive the need for constant growth and change. Adult educators must be able to continuously improve their own skills to meet the needs of adult learners. One of the challenges faced by adult educators is the prevalence of educational literature and experience in shared public spaces, on social media, and through popular discourse. Learners and educators may have developed cognitive frameworks or adopted neuromyths about education or learning which are neither supported by theoretical approaches nor by research (Torrijos-Muelas et al., 2021).

Avoiding Concept Bloat and Practices Uninformed by Educational Theory

This potential for ideologic "concept bloat" is evident when lay media widely and uncritically accepts a theoretical framework. A salient example is Dweck's (2016) work on mindset theory, which posits that a person's implicit assumptions of their intelligence, abilities, and talent have an outsized effect on their perception of success and failure and that all people fall on a continuum between a fixed mindset and a growth mindset. Dweck argues that people with a fixed mindset perceive attributes in themselves and others as inherent to that person (e.g., they are intelligent or gifted), whereas people with a growth mindset perceive attributes as capable of improvement with effort, persistence, and additional learning. This theory has been widely implemented in education, with success noted specifically in young children. However, Dweck's mindset theory has metamorphosed into something quite different in the common understanding, where it has been conflated with open-mindedness, praising, and rewarding effort over outcomes. It has become a mantra or slogan without the associated risk-taking, hard work needed to grow, and acknowledgment of societal forces and experiences that shape individual opportunities. Social media gives us a useful anecdotal example of the "concept bloat" of growth mindset; a simple search for #growthmindset on Twitter or LinkedIn will show thousands of posts where the concept is erroneously or dubiously applied. Additional examples of concept bloat are the broader use of GRIT or learning styles. When an educational theory is diluted by a surface understanding of the theoretical concepts, a lack of broader consideration for contextual factors, and haphazard application, learners and educators may struggle in their learning goals and may not achieve learning outcomes. Additionally, schools, organizations, or higher education institutions may allocate valuable and scarce resources to approaches that are not effective. These assumptions persist despite this lack of evidence.

Educators as Lifelong Learners: Action Steps

We encourage adult educators to adopt self-directed learning principles to drive their growth as educators. Reflecting on one's own learning needs and on one's own work as an educator is foundational; as famed educator Myles Horton once noted, "You only learn from the experiences that you learn from" (Pbriggsiam, 2013). Reflection on one's skills and learning needs is essential and should be augmented with peer and learner feedback. In addition, we argue that formative assessment and feedback from colleagues can help educators understand if the theoretical and methodological decisions made while designing instruction have an appropriate impact. Adult educators who complete evaluations of their own work create avenues for reflecting on the technical, methodological, theoretical, as well as other aspects of their teaching which can develop a fertile ground for future growth. Analyzing learner reflections during coursework using Brookfield's Critical Incident Questionnaire (Brookfield, 2015) or the muddiest point formative feedback method (Mosteller, 1989) can provide immediate insights into instruction effectiveness.

We have warned about the risk of "concept bloat" and recommend educators evaluate new theories and methods for their theoretical underpinnings. Neuromyths like grit, right versus left brain activities, and generational differences in learning have consumed a large portion of popular attention and educator energy but have not routinely demonstrated educational outcomes. Despite this lack of evidence, these concepts continue to be taught in educational settings (Torrijos-Muelas et al., 2021). Dedicating time to review the empirical evidence that supports or fails to support these ideas can minimize wasting resources on activities that are not effective.

Conclusion

Adult education is a growing field held together at its center by the unique needs of adult learners, which include the development of methods and spaces that are safe, rigorous, and practicable. While there are many ways to teach adults, instructors can more readily achieve their personal and programmatic goals by developing materials and methods that are centered in adult learning theory. Adult educators should be aware that instructors and learners can come to adult education experiences with cognitive frameworks built upon concepts or theories that may not serve their purposes. Educators should reflect on their own experiences in a process of continual evaluation and self-improvement, so that they may best help learners develop their own skills.

References

American Pharmacists Association. (2021). *Oath of a pharmacist.* www.pharmacist.com/About/Oath-of-a-Pharmacist

Association for Experiential Education. (2022). *What is experiential education?* www.aee.org/what-is-experiential-education

Bolitzer, L. A., Castillo-Montoya, M., & Williams, L. A. (2016). Pursuing equity through diversity: Perspectives and propositions for teaching and learning in higher education. In L. P. Davis (Ed.), *Race, equity, and the learning environment: The global relevance of critical and inclusive pedagogies in higher education* (pp. 23–43). Stylus Publishing.

Brookfield, S. D. (2015). *The skillful teacher: On technique, trust, and responsiveness in the classroom.* John Wiley & Sons.

CAST (2018). *Universal Design for Learning Guidelines version 2.2.* http://udlguidelines.cast.org

Cross, T., Bazron, B., Dennis, K., & Isaacs, M. (1989). *Towards a culturally competent system of care, Volume I.* Georgetown University Child Development Center, CASSP Technical Assistance Center.

Dweck, C. S. (2016). *Mindset: The new psychology of success.* Ballantine Books.

Fenwick, T. (2003). *Learning through experience: Troubling orthodoxies and intersecting questions.* Krieger.

Freire, P. (2000). *Pedagogy of freedom: Ethics, democracy, and civic courage.* Rowman & Littlefield Publishers.

Freire, P. (2018). *Pedagogy of the oppressed* (50th anniversary ed.). Bloomsbury Publishing.

Gagne R. M., Briggs L. J., & Wager W. W. (1992). *Principles of instructional design.* Harcourt Brace Jovanovich.

Green, W. M., Tripp, H., & Hoffman, A. (2020). Integrating critical consciousness in Health Professions Education through leadership education and mentoring. *New Directions for Adult and Continuing Education, 2020*(167–168), 71–81.

Grow, G. (1994). In defense of the staged self-directed learning model. *Adult Education Quarterly, 44*(2), 109–114.

Jarvis, P. (2010). *Adult education and lifelong learning: Theory and practice.* Routledge.

Kegan, R. (2000). What "form" transforms? A constructive-developmental perspective on transformational learning. In J. Mezirow & Associates (Eds.), *Learning as transformation: Critical perspectives on a theory in progress* (pp. 35–70). Jossey-Bass.

Kirschner, P. A. (2017). Stop propagating the learning styles myth. *Computers & Education, 106,* 166–171.

Knowles, M. S. (1970). *The modern practice of adult education. Andragogy versus pedagogy.* Prentice-Hall.

Kolb, D. A. (2014). *Experiential learning: Experience as the source of learning and development* (2nd ed.). Pearson Education.

Kumagai, A. K., & Lypson, M. L. (2009). Beyond cultural competence: Critical consciousness, social justice, and multicultural education. *Academic Medicine, 84*(6), 782–787.

Lindeman, E. C. (1961). *The meaning of adult education in the United States.* Harvest House.

Mayfield, V. (2020). *Cultural competence now: 56 exercises to help educators understand and challenge bias, racism, and privilege.* Hawker Brownlow Education.

Merriam, S. B., & Baumgartner, L. M. (2020). *Learning in adulthood: A comprehensive guide.* John Wiley & Sons.

Mezirow, J. (2009). Transformative learning theory. In J. Mezirow, E. Taylor, & Associates (Eds.), *Transformative learning in practice* (pp. 18–32). Jossey-Bass.

Mosteller, F. (1989). The 'muddiest point in the lecture' as a feedback device. *On Teaching and Learning: The Journal of the Harvard-Danforth Center, 3,* 10–21.

Pbriggsiam (2013). *Myles Horton – radical hillbilly – a wisdom teacher for activism and civic engagement.* [Video]. YouTube. www.youtube.com/watch?v=qSwW0zc-QBQ&t=499s

Rocco, T. S., Smith, M. C., Mizzi, R. C., Merriweather, L. R., & Hawley, J. D. (Eds.). (2020). *The handbook of adult and continuing education.* Stylus Publishing.

Rose, A. D. (2020). *History of adult and continuing education.* In T. Rocco, M. C. Smith, R. C. Mizzi, L. R. Merriweather, & J. D. Hawley (Eds.), *The handbook of adult and continuing education* (pp. 22–30). Stylus Publishing.

Torrijos-Muelas, M., González-Víllora, S., & Bodoque-Osma, A. R. (2021). The persistence of neuromyths in the educational settings: A systematic review. *Frontiers in Psychology, 11,* 3658.

Chapter 3

Facilitation Skills

Casandra Blassingame

Facilitation skills are useful in interacting with learners to help them achieve their learning goals. This chapter focuses on skills that are important to being a successful facilitator, including basic strategies and best practices. The approaches covered are asset-based, affirmative, and skilled facilitation. From theory to practice, discover skills that are critical to successful and effective learning events, how to engage learners in the activities of navigating complicated business challenges, arriving at solutions and/or consensus, and ultimately achieving the learning outcomes. These outcomes are set at the beginning of the learning event or mutually agreed upon between the learner, group, and the facilitator. The chapter will also provide you with a cadre of techniques that assist you in homing in and expanding your capacity to successfully lead learners to achieve the tangible assets they sought for immediate application to real-world opportunities.

My Intentional Journey

There are countless paths individuals can find themselves on to reach the crossroads of adult education. I have encountered classmates and colleagues alike who were in careers completely detached from education altogether: executive administration, financial services, engineering, healthcare, manufacturing, and the list goes on. I hope that by sharing my intentional journey, you are informed and enlightened on how to chart your trajectory or understand how your path has been charted and why you are here. Humor me as I take you on a journey that includes purpose and the ability to show up with great agency. Let the facilitation begin!

I have approached my career with great intentions. A traditional college student whose major changed three times. From psychology to mathematics after being inspired by the insurance industry to become an actuary. I was challenged by that and saw an opportunity to engage in an industry and profession that was male dominated. When I engaged in my mathematical studies during my undergraduate schooling, I was ecstatic to discover that I was good at it. I was completely inspired by my professor's ability to guide me to success in an area where I had not previously been identified as strong. My high school transcripts tell of the harrowing experiences I had with math. I just did not get it. Through reflection, I realized that it was not me or my ability. All learners, in my opinion, are able. It was the stark contrast of instructional methods used by my teachers and professors.

Now inspired to become a math teachers for high school students who were just as lost and defeated by this subject as I was, I completed all my mathematics coursework to satisfy degree requirements except one. I finally enrolled in calculus three and my first reaction was complete and utter shock. With the absence of numbers prevalent, my understanding and interest faded very quickly. I was overcome with fear and panic to change my major once more without losing too many credits or time. The final change yielded the decision to major in computer

DOI: 10.4324/9781003259602-5

science. My rationale was that technology was growing to be the blueprint for how we exchange information, learn, engage, and collaborate in the future. I was not completely sold on this idea, but it sounded like it made sense, so I went along with the program I set for myself. At least I would always have a job. I still wanted to teach and figured I could marry my computer science degree with a degree in education. As time passed and the desire remained, it was indeed a match.

Career exploration was a critical activity that began to form when I was in high school. I enrolled in a class and joined a co-curricular club called the Distributive Education Clubs of America (DECA). DECA participants learned how to provide the best customer service and engage in teamwork, inventory, sales, and the mechanics of the retail industry. My first job assignment was as a sales associate. The informal training I received on the job allowed me to apply what I learned in the classroom. It heightened the experience for me, and I demonstrated the ability to learn more advanced functions and train new sales associates. Despite other internship opportunities over the course of my undergraduate experience, I was interested in training others.

Through other relevant experiences, including a management position, I decided I wanted to pursue a career in teaching. I applied for an instructor position to teach a food safety certification course. I had a strong desire to be in the classroom and was confident that I could teach just about anything. I just needed to get my foot in the door. The universe conspired and I got an interview. Needless to say, I was not hired to teach the food safety course. The reason they granted me an interview was because of the degree I earned in computer science. Remember that? I was offered a full-time position as an instructor. My thoughts were on point and my plan was enacted. It was 1997 and I was on my way to a career in education that started in the career and technical space.

Initially, I thought I would have a career in K-12 education. I found myself teaching adults and engaging in a phenomenon, which for me – at that time – had no name. However, there was a common theme attributed to the learners. They were non-traditional and had returned to school for a variety of reasons: career advancement; family life transitions such as death, divorce, or marriage; or having more leisure time plus the desire to acquire more knowledge. Other reasons could include resuming their education due to disruption or competing responsibilities. Nonetheless, they were here and ready to achieve.

I learned a great deal about myself and what I call the career that chose me. The seed that planted the desire to not teach, but to facilitate learning, had been planted years prior through successful experiences in various workspaces and as a student in college. The seed manifested into my path to share the experience of learning with others. I thought I wanted to be a teacher. But what that year taught me is that it was exactly what I did not want to be.

Teachers deliver content or information dump on their students for them to commit to memory and regurgitate in an exam at a later date. Sounds awful, does it not? It can be painful for an adult learner or one who learns best using andragogical methods (Knowles et al., 2020). Facilitators provide content but then take it a step further and help the student learn by understanding the process behind the content. We use experiential techniques and engage the learner to make the content relative, relevant, and tangible for immediate application.

In 1998, I transitioned from a career and technical school to a traditional community college and was hired as an adjunct faculty member in a continuing education department extension site. With a new lease on life as an educator, I transitioned my thought process about what I was doing and decided that I would no longer be a teacher, but a facilitator of knowledge! The previous year was spent with adults who were on different paths, different levels of understanding, and who had embarked on a journey to use their prior knowledge and experiences to gain new skills. From that point forward, I did not expect anything less from my audience. No matter who, what, or where.

In 2001, after 3 years of teaching adults, I enrolled in graduate school and earned a Master of Education in Adult Education from the University of Missouri–St. Louis. I found myself mirrored in my learners with an opportunity to impact the facilitation of learning in my classroom. I had the desire to grow, obtain knowledge, and increase my skills, and I had children to support. I was my real-life example of an adult learner. At this point in my career, with the desire, experience, and drive coupled with formal education that helped me put a framework around the work I was doing, I was becoming an expert at facilitating learning.

My career in adult education has spanned 25 years, specifically in continuing education and training (CE/T) along with professional studies. Although I enjoyed learning environments, I was drawn to administration to influence the faculty of the adult learners to become skilled facilitators of learning. I moved from meager beginnings as an adjunct faculty to an instructor, program coordinator, program director, director of continuing education, assistant dean, executive director, vice president, chief academic officer, and accreditation body president and CEO. The transition would bring a combination of classroom facilitation for learners, faculty, staff, and stakeholders.

Now I am in a position where I oversee the landscape of the CE/T industry through standards development and accreditation. Traditional continuing and extension education has expanded and evolved into what I call the CE/T Ecosystem. This includes learning and development, corporate training, association education, professional industry training, education entrepreneurs, workforce development, and apprenticeships. Similar to your philosophy of adult education, your area of specialization within the CE/T Ecosystem can help determine the theoretical framework you will use to facilitate learning. Undoubtedly, the theoretical framework that resonates with you will influence and inform your practical skills in facilitating learning. A good facilitator has a great understanding of applicable frameworks that could be used to ensure learner success.

Facilitation

Merriam (2008) captured it best when she offered her explanation of the complexity of adult learning theory, positing that the phenomenon could not be captured in one explanation. Adult education reflects an ever-changing mosaic where old pieces are rearranged, and new pieces are added. It could not be truer in 2023. Her examination of the complexity of the phenomenon was truly predictive of how multifaceted, rich, and complex facilitating adults has become. It has been my experience that this viewpoint is an embodiment of the needs of the adult learner and is exponentiated in today's climate of racial and socioeconomic disparities.

Facilitation Theory

Through individual complexities, what motivates one adult to learn can greatly differ from what motivates another. Adult learning theories are predicated on adults learning differently from children. Researchers have developed adult learning theories that provide a foundation that can align learners with a learning need. While there is no single theory that has identified how adults learn best, there are learning theories that can align with being or becoming a good facilitator to help adults learn.

Facilitation theory, sometimes called facilitative teaching, is a humanistic approach to learning developed by Carl Rogers (Kirschenbaum & Henderson, 1990). Rogers' theory identifies the educator's role as the most important aspect of the learning process. The educator may be a subject matter expert and, yes, there is information to transmit. But the educator must find the balance between their ability to teach and their ability to facilitate the content by establishing trust and relationships and creating an environment for engagement with the learner. It is a very fine line; however, a distinction must be made between theories of facilitation and theories of teaching. Chapter 2 discusses in detail the theory and practice of learning and teaching.

The practical meaning of facilitation theory is that "the facilitation of significant learning rests upon certain attitudinal qualities that exist in the personal relationship between facilitator and learner" (Kirschenbaum & Henderson, 1990, p. 305). The first quality is realness in the facilitator of learning. Be genuine, simply who you are, no fronts or facades. Meet the learner where they are on a person-to-person basis. The second quality is prizing, accepting, and trust. Place value on the learner, their feelings, and opinions. The basic thrust of showing that you care. The facilitator's ability to do this shows confidence and trust in the learner as a human being. Finally, empathetic understanding. Learners feel appreciated when they are understood as they are, not evaluated or judged, just understood. Empathy establishes a more personal relationship with the learner.

This theory may resonate and influence your desire or passion to become an expert facilitator. Or, just to learn something new. We believe what we believe, and we know what we know. My advice is to examine and explore different methods that inform the use of facilitation theory in diverse learning environments.

Facilitation of Varied Learning Events Techniques

Assessing your facilitator style or what approach you most effectively use is as critical as framing your philosophy of education. To identify one's style, the total atmosphere created by the educator's view on learning and their approach to teaching must be examined (Galbraith, 2004). The two most known approaches to teaching styles are teacher-centered and learner-centered approaches. Facilitation is aligned with the learner-centered approach. It focuses on the individual learner (or group) rather than on a body of information (Galbraith, 2004).

Carl Rogers' theory of facilitation (Kirschenbaum & Henderson, 1990) sees the educator as the facilitator of learning. In this human-centric approach to learning, the facilitation of learning happens through the developed relationship with the learner. Presenting as your authentic self, showing care toward your learners, and the ability to be authentic are qualities Rogers deemed necessary for the facilitation of learning to be successful. Regardless of the content, your effectiveness as a facilitator is dependent on your abilities and desire to do this work. Facilitating learning is a very personal act.

Facilitation Methods

When working with individual learners or groups, you must clearly define your role as a facilitator to be effective and for the participants to achieve the desired outcomes. The facilitation method you use will depend on the learning needs or needs of the group. It can be dictated by the industry you are engaging in as well. In addition, all approaches to facilitation are based on some core values (Schwarz, 2005). While there are multiple facilitator methods, the focus in this section will be on the skilled and affirmative approaches.

Skilled Facilitator Approach

The skilled facilitator approach clearly defines the facilitator role as a substantively neutral person who is not a group member and works for the entire group (Schwarz, 2005). Schwarz further characterizes skilled facilitation as being of two types: basic and developmental. In basic facilitation, through the lending of his or her process skills, the facilitator helps solve a substantive problem. In developmental facilitation, the facilitator not only helps the group solve a substantive problem, but they also learn to improve their processes as well.

For example, one of my experiences included facilitating the development of a strategic plan. There are multifaceted nuances involved in this process, so it is critical to the success of the process that matters are communicated and established. Facilitators need to set core values that provide a foundation for the process and serve as a guide throughout the process. You also want to establish ground rules to quickly identify dysfunctional behavior and develop successful group norms. Not only do core values and ground rules provide an operational framework for the group, but they also guide you as the facilitator.

Establishing a relationship with group members is the first order of business. Everyone involved needs to have a clear understanding of the roles and the desired outcomes. The establishment of the ground rules makes room for productive collaboration, allowing group members to honestly share their points of view, gain some consensus, and develop the appropriate course of action.

After researching the organization, concluding interviews with stakeholders and group members, and collecting and analyzing data, it can be shared with the group, so they begin to brainstorm, dialogue, and make decisions void of internal or external pressures. Information sharing, commitment to the process, small group dialogue, breakout presentations, and evaluating priorities all ensue while balancing the characteristics and behaviors of the group members, as well as myself as the facilitator.

The skilled facilitator approach does not have different sets of rules for the facilitator and group members (Schwarz, 2005). As the facilitator, using the very tools you are providing the group allows you to demonstrate the process. Your commitment to be consistent not only further establishes your credibility, but also creates a more profound sense of trust and teaches the group to govern themselves more effectively. Modeling the behaviors established in the core values and ground rules will lead to the group's ability to become self-facilitating and ultimately self-sufficient. They can also be confident that they can continue the work long after you are gone and achieve the desired outcomes.

Affirmative Facilitation Approach

Affirmative facilitation is located within the field of organization development (OD), a subset of organizational behavior (Troxel, 2005). It rests on the fundamental belief that the keys to the transformation of a community or organization are already present within the system in question rather than external to it (p. 592). There is a common phrase that we hear all the time, "think outside of the box." It sends you on a search to find tools to help you solve a problem, right? When the COVID-19 pandemic shut down the physically engaging world of work and socialization and closed the doors behind us, we were forced to "think inside of the box." Thinking inside the box turns you inward to look at the tools you already possess. The keys to transformation inherently reside in the people who are brought together to form the community or organization.

Asset-Based Approach

The asset-based approach runs parallel to the foundations of affirmative facilitation. It is based on the assumption that by providing opportunities and encouragement, individuals can use their skills and talents to achieve a better quality of life and achieve self-sufficiency. The driving question for an affirmative facilitator is, "How do I ask questions that lead this group to discover their own power?" (Troxel, 2005). As the facilitator, you must rely on their experiences, or lack of experience, to aid in the discovery of that power and ability to change their lives and for the betterment of the community or organization.

Through a series of needs assessments to determine regional workforce needs, I coordinated and facilitated a workforce development program for recipients of Temporary Assistance for Needy Families (TANF) that was designed to equip them with the skills necessary to gain entry-level employment. The program began as a 5-week course teaching Microsoft Office that included building a cover letter and resume. During the 5-week course, I continuously evaluated the program against the desired outcomes. This started as a very teacher-centered information dump in a very short time that, in the end, did not serve the learners well. I did not feel that I was accomplishing the mission, and the learners did not feel like their best interests were considered. In short, they felt this was just another dangling carrot leading them to the road to nowhere. It was frustrating, to say the least.

The challenges were difficult for a learner: absorbing Microsoft Word or how to write a cover letter or resume without basic writing skills; absorbing Microsoft Excel without basic math skills; and Access, oh forget it! That is a challenge for anyone. What are they supposed to do with that cover letter and resume? How do they balance all this transition with family obligations? Fortunately, the leadership gave me their full attention when presenting the program evaluation summary and we could exercise great agility to immediately improve the program.

The program's growth and expansion were supported from a 5-week program to a 12-week program. The new program consisted of a series of workshops to include, basic writing, basic math, job skills where they could acquire knowledge through role play and further facilitation, life skills where they could relate real-life situations and figure out how to integrate their goals into plans, and a 4-week externship in an office environment. Microsoft Access was removed from the schedule but offered as a bonus for those who were interested. Adding the additional courses to an already project-based course of learning allowed them to gain new experience, affirm their experience in the classroom, and bring them to a moment where they realized they could pursue educational goals.

My role transitioned from a teacher who dumped information due to poor program structure (designed with the best intentions) and time constraints to a facilitator of learning using projects and relevant situational experiences to facilitate learning to some incredible people. Most of the graduates of this program went on to not only find gainful employment but to pursue their education beyond the non-credit program where they began. Affirmative facilitation allows the members of a community or organization to say yes to their situation and embrace it as the basis on which their future will be built (Troxel, 2005).

Competencies and Strategies for Success

The competencies needed to be a great facilitator are as complex as the adult learner.

- A strong foundational knowledge base of adult learning theory, philosophies, and frameworks is important.
- Sound knowledge and understanding of facilitation techniques and when to use them for optimal success.
- The ability to coach and work with groups.
- The ability to assess behavior, including understanding and mitigating resistance.
- Active listening.
- Use of activities and technology.
- The ability to be genuine and respectful.
- In addition, a great sense of openness, flexibility, creativity, a spirit of innovation, and a fearlessness to care and get personal.

Be prepared by understanding the organization's needs, the assignment, the objectives, and the deliverables, establishing and nurturing the relationship with the group or the individual learner to gain trust and expectations for deliverables. This initial engagement is critical to becoming that trusted thought partner in assisting communities in achieving their desired outcomes.

Create a safe space for receiving the deliverable content. The learner must feel safe and valued, like their experiences and prior knowledge matter. We must manage the various characters in the learning setting, mitigating casualties and being prepared to have tough conversations. Be an honest, genuine, solutions-based, and perpetual seeker of knowledge and understanding.

Communicate clearly and intentionally. Again, learners are complex, and complexity brings varying levels of difference in how learners receive instruction and information. How we engage, what we hear, and how we process information and receive messaging produce diverse results. Respect and appreciate diverse thinking and respond accordingly and appropriately. Always seek to minimize misunderstanding and optimize the opportunity for achieving the outcomes by listening attentively. Use techniques like paraphrasing, empathizing, or restating the question, and be fully present. Rosenberg (2003, p. 127) posits that empathy lies in our ability to be present. Hearing and understanding their needs provides another opportunity to strengthen the partnership.

You also need to know that this is not a one-size-fits-all approach to preparing yourself as a professional. The field of facilitation is so broad and there are as many methods as there are contributors. This applies to both group facilitation, as well as facilitation of individual learners. The Eight Ps of Effective Facilitation Planning and Preparation are: Perspective, Purpose, People, Product, Place, Process, Practice, and Personal Preparation (Bracken, 2005). This is a great framework for where you can begin to home in on ways to become a skilled and effective facilitator. The rest is up to you.

Career Opportunities

The need for facilitators of adult learning is more critical now than ever. Adult learners are being served in both informal and formal settings within the CE/T Ecosystem. The learning theories used in each of these areas of the CE/T Ecosystem should be customized, to the learner, the industry needs, and the environment. The very nature of continuing education is to be nimble and responsive to learner and industry needs alike. With the number of adult learners seeking credentials, either short- or long term, there is a significant need for adult educators who are skilled in facilitating learning.

The latest disruption to our global community has paved the way for how we all do business today. Given our current climate of hybrid and remote opportunities, people have become more entrepreneurial and are taking advantage of contractual prospects and filling a need within organizations. Virtual facilitators are in the enviable role of helping people learn new ways of collaborating (Schuman, 2005). This outsourcing of the learning function has created a very smart response to collaboration and learning while significantly reducing costs.

Believe me when I tell you: there is an association for everything. A good place to start seeking career opportunities as a facilitator is within the association industry. Associations develop educational programming designed to fill an unmet need for industry professionals and have a significant need for professionals who have experience with non-traditional students. They offer webinars, online courses, in-person courses, conferences, and seminars and have a significant need for skilled facilitators with an adult education background.

The weakened talent pipeline has caused the workforce development sector (see Chapter 23) to respond to the rapidly growing population of adults who need to learn, re-skill, or upskill to service employers in their regions. The implementation of education departments on the state and federal level is focused on hiring educators who can appeal to the whole person and facilitate learning for a jobseeker with previous workplace or learning experience. Positions can be found in workforce boards, independent training organizations, and community colleges.

Conclusion

The non-traditional learner of yesterday has become the traditional learner of today. Experiences, prior knowledge, preferences, philosophies, socioeconomic status, and other situational states influence what path a learner chooses to take, what a learner chooses to learn, and how the learner wants to learn. As the world of education and work continues to evolve, so do the needs of the learner. In today's climate, the role of the facilitator is more important than ever.

The role of the adult educator may include transmitting information through lectures, demonstrating new skills, assisting the learner in planning learning activities, facilitating a discovery learning process, directing the learner to other resources, leading the learner through a series of trial-and-error experiences, and several other possible methods of facilitating learning (Galbraith, 2004). Developing your philosophy on education is essential to assisting adult learners in achieving their learning goals. Elias and Merriam (2005) believe that theory without practice leads to empty idealism, and that action without philosophical reflection leads to mindless activism.

Developing a clearly defined or framed philosophy of education brings clarity to your guiding principles as an adult educator that will inform the journey on which you engage your learners. It brings a greater understanding and the ability to problem solve, think critically, and focus on the outcomes that have meaning and applicability. Through your philosophy of education, you become the vehicle to facilitate a relationship between the learner and the world in which they become self-directed with the ability to apply the knowledge they have gained.

As you begin or travel along on your journey in the profession, you may find that you identify with one philosophy. You might straddle the fence and identify with two or more. With an adult learner population that has exponentiated in size over the last 25 years, you will find that the experiences of adults have also diversified in both positive and negative ways. Your philosophy will be challenged in ways you never thought you could imagine. Flexibility is essential as you grow and become a better facilitator of adult learning.

References

Bracken, J. (2005). Eight Ps of effective facilitation planning and preparation. In S. Schuman (Ed.), *The IAF handbook of group facilitation: Best practices from the leading organization in facilitation* (pp. 58–69). Jossey-Bass.

Elias, J. L., & Merriam, S. B. (2005). *Philosophical foundations of adult education*. Krieger.

Galbraith, M. W. (2004). *Adult learning methods: A guide for effective instruction* (3rd ed.). Krieger Publishing Company.

Kirschenbaum, H., & Henderson, V. L. (1990). *The Carl Rogers reader*. Constable.

Knowles, M. S., Holton (III), E. F., Swanson, R. A., & Robinson, P. A. (2020). *The adult learner: The definitive classic in adult education and human resource development* (9th ed.). Routledge.

Merriam, S. B. (2008). Adult learning theory for the twenty-first century. *New Directions for Adult and Continuing Education, 119*, 93–98. https://doi.org/10.1002/ace.309

Rosenberg, M. B. (2003). *Nonviolent communication: A language of life* (2nd ed.). Puddle Dancer Press.

Schuman, S. (Ed.) (2005). *The IAF handbook of group facilitation: Best practices from the leading organization in facilitation*. Jossey-Bass.

Schwarz, R. (2005). The skilled facilitator approach. In S. Schuman (Ed.), *The IAF handbook of group facilitation: Best practices from the leading organization in facilitation* (pp. 21–34). Jossey-Bass.

Troxel, J. (2005). Affirmative facilitation: An asset-based approach to process consultation. In S. Schuman (Ed.), *The IAF handbook of group facilitation: Best practices from the leading organization in facilitation* (pp. 591–608). Jossey-Bass.

Chapter 4

Program Planning Skills

Christy M. Rhodes and Steven W. Schmidt

Anyone who has attended an educational program, whether that program is a nonformal program in the workplace, a formal program in a school or college, or an informal program, such as a knitting class sponsored by a community-based organization, has experienced the work of an educational program planner. Program planners are the individuals who develop educational programs, and the work they do can run the gamut in many ways. Educational programs may consist of a single course or a series of courses; they may be courses that can be completed in a few hours or ones that take weeks or months to complete; they may be conducted face to face, online, or via some sort of hybrid method; they may include very detailed structures or be loosely structured. Some programs, especially those of a formal nature, may lead to credentials, such as degrees or certifications. There is a wide variety in the type of educational programs developed for adult learners. As such, there is a great need for educational program planners in diverse types of organizations.

Educational programs for adult learners are being created all the time. Consider the many reasons why new educational programs are developed. Evolutions in society bring about interest in learning about new topics every day. Changes in the workplace continuously result in new processes and procedures that employees must be taught in order to remain current in their jobs. Careers that were not in existence 5 or 10 years ago mean that colleges and universities must develop degree programs and credentials to qualify workers for these careers. Consider a few examples:

- The COVID-19 pandemic resulted in many different types of community-based education programs that focused on keeping people safe in all aspects of their daily lives. Community-based educational program planners sprang into action, in a race against time, to develop educational programs to meet the needs of those in their communities.
- Globalization has meant that many businesses now operate in locations around the world. Workers in one country may interact with, or be on teams with, colleagues who may live and work anywhere in the world. Workplace-based educational program planners had to develop educational opportunities focused on cultural competence, diversity, equity, and inclusion, and how to work in global teams, in order for employees to be successful in this new global workplace. The evolving nature of these topics means that these programs must also be updated frequently.
- The evolution of new careers, in areas from artificial intelligence to homeland security to social media influencing, has meant that all types of institutions of higher education, from community colleges to colleges and universities, have developed new degree and certificate programs.
- One of the fastest-growing sports in the United States is pickleball. As a result, community-based organizations such as YMCAs have started offering pickleball lessons, leagues, and tournaments in response to the growing number of people interested in learning to play the sport.

DOI: 10.4324/9781003259602-6

None of the education presented in the examples above would be possible without educational program planners. Before any educational program can be offered, it has to be developed, and that development is the responsibility of the program planner. The job of program planner involves creating new educational programs, but it also involves revising existing programs and making decisions on whether to keep or shelve programs that have run their course and are no longer relevant, even with revisions.

There are a variety of job titles for those who develop educational programs for adults. Program planning is a term that is used extensively in academia, and it is used in the workplace and in other venues, but terms such as instructional designer, program developer, or curriculum designer or developer are used as well (see Chapters 11 and 18). In other instances, program planning duties are combined with other job duties for those who work in the education of adult learners. The job titles "trainer" or "educator," for example, are often used for people who facilitate training programs, and frequently included in the job description for these types of positions are job duties that focus on developing the programs they will facilitate. The field of human resource development includes employees who develop and implement workplace training programs for employees. The duties of a human resource development specialist can include educational program planning. Because of the variety of titles and descriptions used in hiring program planners, people interested in careers in program planning should cast a wide net when looking for positions and should not only look for job titles that include the term "program planner." This does make searching for job postings for program planning positions challenging. Throughout Part II of this book, readers will find information regarding numerous spheres of adult education that require significant program planning skills and competencies. Focusing on the individual elements of a job description, rather than on job title, may yield more results in a job search.

The Program Planning Process

Just as there are a variety of titles used to describe program planners, there are several methods and models used by program planners. The first thing to remember is that despite the methods recommended and the models developed, program planning is a typically organized process, but is not necessarily linear. Even in the best of circumstances, it is an activity that involves crooked paths, full of twists and turns and starts and stops. Sometimes the end result of a program plan looks quite different from what was envisioned at the start of the process, and sometimes planning is done for programs that are never ultimately completed. It is important to keep all of this in mind when reviewing the models for program planning discussed below that this is the way program planning typically works.

One of the reasons program planning is a messy endeavor is because it does not happen in a vacuum. It typically involves a variety of people with an assortment of interests and priorities. The contextual environment includes "the surroundings, circumstances, environment, background or settings" (SAGE Flex for Public Speaking, n.d., p. 1) in which planners operate. Consider some contextual reasons why program planning is a "haphazard process" (Freeman & Wilmes, 2009, p. 224). First, program planning often involves multiple stakeholders, each with their own priorities and perspectives. The involvement of multiple stakeholders can make a program stronger, but it is rare that every stakeholder is on the same page with regard to what should be taught and how it should be taught. Second, delving into potential content for a training program can be a task akin to peeling back the layers of an onion. We may think we have a clear understanding of content only to learn that there is more to it than we expected. Plans we envision as being straightforward can become very complex; however, planners may not learn of these complexities until the planning process is well underway. Third, consider the speed of change in our world today. The continuous change in the environment in which program planners work can mean that things that may have been accurate at the start of the planning process are inaccurate or incorrect by the time the process is completed. Changes can be related to the content program planners are working on, but they can also be related to changes in organizational structure and the priorities of those in managerial and leadership positions.

All this is to say that when considering these models for program planning, an understanding of the environment in which the planner works is important. As mentioned above, multiple stakeholders can greatly influence the final program and its effectiveness. For instance, when developing a program, it is important to have all the stakeholders at the table (Cervero & Wilson, 2006). It is equally imperative to understand the power dynamics of the stakeholders. Some may have more power than others, for instance, the funders of a program. In addition, a representative of the intended participants also needs to be there. We as the planners may need to ask those with less power for their ideas, and try and incorporate them into our instructional design, if we want to develop an effective program.

Models are helpful, though, in that they assist in organizing things in the disorganized world of program planning. They provide structure and guidance to planners, and they help planners to consider parts of the process that they may not have considered. In that respect, they can help to ensure educational programs provide the participants with what they need and are more robust than might have been the case if the model was not utilized.

Models for Program Planning

Probably the most well-known model for educational program planning is the ADDIE model. (see Figure 4.1) The ADDIE model was developed in the 1970s, but its development was rooted in instructional systems design concepts developed by the U.S. Army in the 1950s (Molenda, 2003). ADDIE is an acronym for the series of steps involved in the program planning process: Analyze, Design, Develop, Implement, Evaluate. Early iterations of the ADDIE model presented each of these five steps in linear order, indicating that one step had to be completed before moving to the next step (Allen, 2006). Later versions of the ADDIE model depict the first four steps in a circle, with the fifth step (evaluate) in the center, connected to all of the first four steps (Kurt, 2017). This change to the model was done to emphasize the

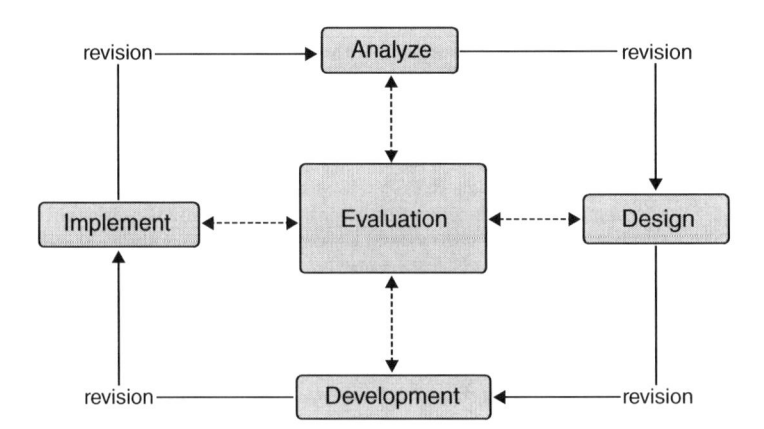

Figure 4.1 ADDIE model (updated)
Source: Kurt (2017)

importance of formative evaluation throughout the program development process and also to acknowledge the dynamic nature of program planning. In addition to being considered throughout, evaluation is the final step of this model. For additional discussion of the ADDIE model, see Chapter 10.

Since the development of the ADDIE model, others have developed models of program planning. Some are more detailed and some are simplified, but most start with the basic ADDIE structure. For example, Werner and DeSimone's (2012) human resource development process for program development consists of four steps:

1   Assessing needs
2   Designing programs
3   Implementing programs
4   Evaluating

Caffarella and Daffron's (2013) Interactive Model of Program Planning, consisting of 12 steps, provides much more detail than many other program planning models. Those steps are as follows:

1   Discerning the context
2   Building a solid base of support
3   Identifying program ideas
4   Sorting and prioritizing program ideas
5   Developing program objectives
6   Designing instructional plans
7   Devising transfer-of-learning plans
8   Formulating evaluation plans
9   Making recommendations and communicating results
10 Selecting formats, schedules, and staff needs
11 Preparing budgets and marketing plans
12 Coordinating facilities and on-site events

The authors also present their model in a circle to denote the fact that when the final step ends, the process starts again. While this model is more detailed, the authors point out that not all steps must be followed for every program developed and, even if all steps are followed, they may not be followed in the order presented in the text (Caffarella & Daffron, 2013).

Despite the fact that different models present different amounts of detail, at a basic level, all are structured fairly similarly. The beginning steps are typically related to analyses of learner needs and an understanding of the context in which the program is to be developed. These steps are followed by the development of content and the actual planning for the educational event. Here, the program planner takes a very broad topic and develops overall goals for the program, and from the goals creates specific learning objectives. Based on the overall goal and the specific objectives, content is then developed. After these steps are complete, a pilot of the program with actual learners is often implemented so the program planner can evaluate how it actually works in practice. Based on the results of the pilot, the planner may make revisions before the program is officially offered to learners. This is followed by evaluation and revision-related steps, whereby the planner gathers feedback from learners and uses it to improve the program. As denoted by the circular nature of some of the models presented above, the overall process of continuously improving the program based on learner input never ends, although working on revisions and updates based on learner input and other factors (which can be internal or external to the organization) is usually much more straightforward than the original program development process.

By now you may have a better understanding of why program planning is described as a messy process. Important to note, however, is that it can be an enjoyable process to work through, and it can result in great educational programs that help solve the problems and meet the needs of many adult learners. It can be very gratifying to develop a program that makes people's lives easier, helps them do their jobs more efficiently, or enables them to lead safer, healthier lives. In a lot of ways, program planners are both detectives and problem solvers. They see, or are presented with, problems to be solved by education, and they embark on the program planning journey to find answers and address those problems.

Competencies for Program Planners

The knowledge and skills involved in educational program planning cover a broad range of areas and often vary due to the specific context and support available. In larger settings, a program planner may serve more as a program manager delegating tasks and guiding team members throughout the process. Conversely, for adult educators in smaller organizations, program planning may be only one of many "hats" they wear. While many graduate programs in adult education offer courses in program planning, many practitioners gain expertise through hands-on experience with limited formal preparation.

Competencies for program planners can be grouped in a few distinct categories. First, an understanding of adult education practices and principles is necessary, as structure and learning experiences are built on this knowledge. Included in this category are competencies related to evaluation of programs through conducting needs assessments and using data to make informed decisions. Second, program planners should have exceptional project management skills. Third, because much of the work of program planners involves developing teams, working with diverse groups, and helping to build consensus regarding program content, people skills are necessary as well. Each of these three competency groups will be discussed in the following paragraphs.

Knowledge of Adult Education Theory

The content of educational programs varies widely, but all share the necessity of the program planner having a deep understanding of adult educational theory and curriculum development and design (see Chapters 1 and 2 for more information). Ideally, a program planner is familiar with educational psychology and various theories of adult learning. For example, theories of motivation and Knowles's tenets of andragogy (Knowles et al., 2020), along with Kolb's experiential learning (Kolb & Kolb, 2005) can guide new program development. Even though curriculum design may be managed by an instructional designer, an effective program planner will need to lead that process. Without a deep understanding of how to create an effective learning environment for adults, a program planner risks offering unengaging and ineffective learning experiences.

Evaluation Skills

Another crucial subset of skills in program planning is knowing how to design and implement data collection and analysis. These skills will be used in the crucial needs assessment phase and, when conducted successfully, will yield relevant information to guide decisions about program content, instructional methods, and scheduling, to name just a few. One common tool used to conduct needs assessments is the survey (Kirkpatrick & Kirkpatrick, 2016). Designing a survey is more than simply writing a series of questions for respondents to answer. The program planner must consider what information needs to be included. In addition, attention must be given to various aspects of the question format. For example, inexperienced survey designers may construct questions that require an advanced ability to read English for a survey to be used with English language learners, whereas an experienced planner will review the readability of all questions and possibly add graphics to accommodate all potential survey respondents. Another possible error is administering the survey without previously establishing a plan to make meaning of the data, which can result in biased or inaccurate findings. An understanding of data collection and analysis will also be used to guide program assessment and evaluation (see Chapter 5). Knowing how to develop valid and reliable assessment tools that align with program goals is the foundation of an effective learning program, enabling planners to examine program effectiveness, identify areas for improvement, and make data-driven decisions throughout the life of the program.

Project Management

Planning an educational program also requires strong project management skills. To be effective, a program planner must be adept at planning, organizing, and overseeing the development process while simultaneously following budgets and meeting timelines. In many cases, experienced and effective adult educators are asked to assume program planning responsibilities. Many of the planning skills used in classroom management easily transfer to the administrative tasks associated with program management. Adult educators are familiar with setting up collaborative teams, engaging in on-the-spot problem solving, and working with strict deadlines, all of which play a significant role in effective project management.

Collaboration Skills

The knowledge and skills mentioned so far are all invaluable to engage in effective program planning. However, as noted earlier, program planning does not happen in a vacuum. It is a process that usually involves many different people, each with different viewpoints, priorities, and perspectives. Being good at collaborating and communicating with diverse groups of people may be most important to a planner's success. This has been described as "the people-work" (Cervero & Wilson, 1994, p. 97) and the source of many challenges that arise throughout the planning process (Sandmann, 1993). Having good people skills helps program planners build productive relationships and strong networks of support. Planners work closely with stakeholders, administrators, and content experts as they gather input, share ideas, and build consensus. They need to build relationships across communities as they foster and nurture partnerships. To do this, they must be able to articulate their vision and opinions, listen actively and openly to feedback, and express sometimes complex educational concepts in a straightforward manner comprehensible to community members and stakeholders alike. An effective program planner exhibits strong emotional intelligence and is able to empathize and understand the perspectives of others throughout the program planning process.

Conclusion

It is our hope that we have provided you with an overview of the program planning process, along with the knowledge, skills, and attitudes necessary for effective program planners. Program planning can be complex work. Effective program planners are knowledgeable about all the steps involved and are able to be flexible as unexpected situations arise. Additionally, they are able to apply their knowledge to get things done skillfully and efficiently.

Because of the extensive list of competencies necessary for success in program planning, program planners can take a long time to fully master their skills. The necessary knowledge, skills, and attitudes cannot all be learned overnight. The best program planners are those who understand the importance of developing, and then continuously improving, their program planning abilities.

References

Allen, W. C. (2006). Overview and evolution of the ADDIE training system. *Advances in Developing Human Resources, 8*(4), 430–441. https://doi.org/10.1177/1523422306292942

Caffarella, R. S., & Daffron, S. R. (2013). *Planning programs for adult learners: A practical guide* (3rd ed.). Jossey-Bass.

Cervero, R. M., & Wilson, A. L. (1994). *Planning responsibly for adult education: A guide to negotiating power and interests* (1st ed.). Jossey-Bass.

Cervero, R. M., & Wilson, A. L. (2006). *Working the planning table: Negotiating democratically for adult, continuing, and workplace education.* Jossey-Bass.

Freeman, J. P., & Wilmes, D. M. (2009). Facilitating change through integrated strategic planning. *Planning and Changing, 40*(3–4), 224–241.

Kirkpatrick, J. D., & Kirkpatrick, W. K. (2016). *Kirkpatrick's four levels of training evaluation.* ATD Press.

Knowles, M. S., Holton (III), E. F., Swanson, R. A., & Robinson, P. A. (2020). *The adult learner: The definitive classic in adult education and human resource development.* (9th ed). Routledge.

Kolb, A. Y., & Kolb, D. A. (2005). Learning styles and learning spaces: Enhancing experiential learning in higher education. *Academy of Management Learning and Education, 4*(2), 193–212.

Kurt, S. (2017). ADDIE model: Instructional Design. *Educational Technology.* https://educationaltechnology.net/the-addie-model-instructional-design/

Molenda, M. (2003). In search of the elusive ADDIE model. *Performance Improvement, 42*(5), 34–36. https://doi.org/10.1002/pfi.4930420508.

SAGE Flex for Public Speaking. (n.d.). *Understanding the impact of context.* https://edge.sagepub.com/sites/default/files/elements_section_03_module02_0.pdf.

Sandmann, L. R. (1993). Why programs aren't implemented as planned. *Journal of Extension, 31*(4), 18–21.

Werner, J. M., & DeSimone, R. L. (2012). *Human resource development* (6th ed.). Cengage.

Chapter 5

Assessment, Evaluation, and Educational Research Skills

Lilian H. Hill

Introduction

My responsibilities as a professor at three universities have made me aware of the importance of assessment and evaluation, especially as change has occurred in adult education, and education in general, from a focus on facilitating learning processes in the 1980/90s to today's emphasis on student learning outcomes, assessment, evaluation, and accountability. I completed program evaluation courses during my master's and doctoral degrees in adult education, but little emphasis was placed on assessment. When I started university teaching, I emulated my professors' assessment practices but was not fully cognizant of the purposes, principles, and methods of assessment. Nevertheless, emphasis on assessment and evaluation increased with each successive academic role I held. I learned many assessment and evaluation skills as a professor, especially when I served on institution-wide assessment committees at two universities, created and analyzed data for inclusion in program accreditation reports, and served as a department chair needing to defend the value of my adult education program using data about program performance indicators (Hill & Isaac-Savage, 2022). As a result of these experiences, I published an edited book titled *Assessment, Evaluation, and Accountability in Adult Education* in 2020 and wrote a chapter on assessment and evaluation published in the *Handbook of Adult and Continuing Education* (2021).

As Hill (2020) notes, assessment can be defined as "measurement of individual student learning that may be used for screening, diagnosis, providing feedback, monitoring progress, and designing educational interventions" (p. 5). Evaluation involves the "application of learning assessments to make judgments for program improvement and providing information to stakeholders including regional and accreditation bodies, and accountability systems" (p. 5). While accountability is not a focus in this chapter, it relates to providing "evidence that education was conducted appropriately, progress was made, and resources, particularly tax monies, were used efficiently" (p. 6). Adult education programs need to be astute in their use of program funding and documenting program effectiveness.

You may not have chosen to become an adult educator to learn about assessment and evaluation. Nevertheless, they are both important skills related to effectively facilitating student learning; program creation and management; and administrative roles in adult education, especially now when education is often considered a commodity responsible for providing skilled employees to the workforce. Increased public, governmental, and accreditation agency scrutiny have all imposed requirements for documenting program and organizational success.

Difference between Assessment and Evaluation

Assessment and evaluation are often confused with one another, but each has different purposes and perspectives (Table 5.1). Assessment is formative in nature and its goal is to promote

DOI: 10.4324/9781003259602-7

Table 5.1 Distinguishing between assessment and evaluation

	Assessment	*Evaluation*
Definition	Information for improvement	Measuring value
Purposes	Gathering information used by educators and learners to improve learning	Making judgments about student learning outcomes based on predetermined standards
Focus	Attentive to adult learning theories and knowledge of learners' needs	Accountable to administrative, professional, and accreditation bodies
Criteria	Mutually set by instructor and learners	Determined by the evaluator
Process	Iterative	Summative
Goals	Continued learning, progression, and completion of learning processes	Determines whether goals have been met

Note: Adapted from Hill (2020)

continuous improvement in student learning. Assessment results provide information to instructors so they can adjust their instructional practices to improve student learning. For the same reason, results are provided to students so they can adjust their learning strategies. In contrast, evaluation tends to be summative and involves making judgments about the effectiveness of programs in achieving stated goals and objectives. When applicable, evaluation reports are shared with administrators and submitted to accreditation agencies. Assessment processes are usually conducted each time a course or program is offered, while evaluation is conducted periodically (e.g., every 3 to 5 years) or sometimes only once.

To illustrate the difference between assessment and evaluation, the following case study is presented. The case includes a Request for Proposals (RFP) and the information is divided into sections that address the purpose, goals, scope of services, and required competencies required of someone submitting a bid. Additional elements include information about time and place of submission, evaluation criteria, and the budget proposal that an assessment specialist or program evaluator would submit in response to the RFP.

Case Study

You have recently assumed responsibility as Chief Executive Officer (CEO) of a national non-profit organization experiencing financial trouble. An infusion of cash is needed for the organization to recover; however, before they will consider your application, funding agencies require demonstration of the value of the organization's educational programs. Before they invest, they want to know whether the programs meet their stated goals and objectives, comply with accreditation standards, and that clients are benefiting in tangible terms. You recognize the critical nature of assessment and evaluation, but also know that you are fully occupied in alleviating the fears of employees, determining the system's readiness for upcoming accreditation visits, and managing day-to-day operations. Despite financial limitations, you realize you need to hire an assessment specialist and a program evaluator. Therefore, you draw up an RFP for each role that includes detailed descriptions of the required competencies each professional should have (Table 5.2). For each role, some of the requested information will be the same and some will differ.

Considerations for Proposal Submission

Now imagine that you are preparing to submit a bid for one of these roles and consider the steps you would follow to write an effective bid. RFPs are a mechanism for providing detailed

Table 5.2 Request for proposals

Assessment Specialist RFP	*Program Evaluation RFP*
Purpose: Assessment Specialist to review, create, and implement detailed assessment of student learning outcomes of adult education programs offered by a non-profit agency focused on services for adult learners returning to learning. It is critical that information be provided about student learning outcomes (SLOs) to learners and program instructors so that each group can adjust their learning and teaching strategies to meet the program goals. Program goals must be compatible with meeting the requirements of Education for Mature Students™* accreditation (EME).	Purpose: Program Evaluator to use assessment data and other pertinent information to create a detailed evaluation of adult education programs offered by a non-profit agency focused on services for adults returning to learning. The evaluation will focus on (a) program implementation; (b) evidence of effectiveness; and (c) relationship between implementation and effectiveness. Results of this program evaluation will be used for program accreditation purposes and must be compatible with Education for Mature Students™* accreditation requirements (EME).

Required Competencies for Assessment and Program Evaluation
Knowledge of
- adults' learning needs
- effective instructional methods designed for adults
- Diversity, Equity, and Inclusion (DEI) to ensure that equal opportunities are available for instructors and students

Assessment Specialist *Knowledge of*	*Program Evaluator* *Knowledge of*
- purposes of effective assessment of learning outcomes - relationship among curriculum goals, student learning outcomes, assessment of adult learning, and program accreditation, with particular focus on EME accreditation standards - assessment software for record-keeping and report generation	- purposes of effective evaluation of adult education programs, especially process and end-of-program evaluations compatible with EME accreditation - current trends regarding employment for adults, criteria employers use when hiring, and soft skills desired by employers, e.g., communication, teamwork, leadership, growth mindset - educational research, especially related to adult students
Skills for	*Skills for*
- communicating well with internal and external stakeholders, including program managers, instructors, learners, and potential employers in the community of varied ages, races, social classes, and education levels - revising learning and course assessments - educating diverse program managers, instructors, support staff, and learners about creating assessments, using assessment information to facilitate improved learning and effective record-keeping - incorporating knowledge of DEI for effective instruction - making recommendations for program improvement	- conducting program evaluation research: qualitative, quantitative, and mixed method - analyzing program evaluation data, preparing reports, and providing information to the organization's administration, program managers, instructors, learners, and community - evaluating the incorporation of knowledge of DEI to determine whether effective instruction occurred - communicating with diverse internal and external stakeholders, including program managers, instructors, learners, potential employers, and local/regional/federal governing bodies in the community of varied ages, races, social classes, and education levels

Ability to	*Ability to*
• view assessment and evaluation holistically and provide recommendations for using assessment processes to enhance student learning • provide professional development for program managers, instructors, and learners	• clarify program objectives and ascertain whether there is clear agreement on these • identify and collect needed information to conduct effective program evaluation • conduct an environmental scan to determine key factors in program's internal and external context that may influence its success • identify program strengths and weaknesses, whether program is meeting its goals, and whether program was responsible for outcomes • make recommendations for program improvement

Time and Place of Proposal Submission

Proposals must be submitted electronically by June 30, 2023, at https://nationalnonprofit.org

Required Elements of Proposal

- Cover page stating name, proposer's company name, and full contact information including email and phone number
- Indicate availability for remote and in-person meetings in Central Standard Time
- Detailed documentation of proposer's credentials and experience with learning assessment, especially related to adult education programs
- Detailed proposal stating goals, processes, products, and timeline related to the RFP
- Detailed budget
- Complete resumé or CV of proposer(s) documenting experience with learning assessment or program evaluation
- Samples of reports of previous assessment or program evaluation experience
- At least three recommendations from previous learning assessment contracts or program evaluation contracts

Assessment Specialist Evaluation Criteria	**Program Evaluator Evaluation Criteria**
Successful bids will meet the following criteria: • The assessment processes will meet relevant curriculum standards of EME accreditation • The assessment processes must produce evidence of usability and efficacy with a full range of learners from basic to advanced • The assessment processes must promote rich learning experiences that build critical knowledge and skills fostering career readiness • Assessment processes should include technology and online resources calculated to enhance adult learning and facilitate effective record-keeping • Professional development and training must be furnished to the organization's program managers and instructors so that they can use the assessment processes in a manner that meets the diverse needs of the learners they teach.	Successful bids will meet the following criteria: • Program evaluation goals, processes, results, and reports will be consistent with EME accreditation requirements • Program evaluation will determine whether the program is meeting the expressed goals of internal and external stakeholders: organizational administration, program managers, instructors, learners, potential employers, and community members. It is possible that more than one report will be needed to reach each of these groups • Professional development and training must be furnished to the organization's administration, program managers, instructors, and learners so that they can use the program evaluation results in a manner that meets the diverse needs of the learners they teach.

Detailed Budget Proposal

Estimate of all costs and payments

Questions

Contact the CEO at CEO@nationalnon-profit or 888–555-xxxx. For questions to receive a response, they must be received no later than 10 days prior to the submission deadline.

information about projects, and your response is equivalent to a job interview where your knowledge and competencies are examined. The behavioral interview process provides useful guidance. In that format, you are asked questions like, "Tell me about a time when you were successful in following guidelines and meeting deadlines." You need to demonstrate your competencies by describing past successful work experiences.

In preparing to submit a bid there are several important steps to follow. These steps are detailed to help you secure a successful contract to perform the assessment or evaluation work described in the RFP.

Step 1: Study the RFP and Make Detailed Notes

RFPs provide detailed information, so it is wise to study the requirements to be sure you have sufficient interest to submit a bid. Check whether you are being asked to provide affirmative action or any other certification and declare any conflicts of interest. Do not ignore schedules, clauses, or attachments in the RFP. RFPs are designed to provide you with sufficient information to submit a successful proposal.

Step 2: Identify Areas That Are Unclear and Record Questions You Have

RFPs may be hundreds of pages long so having questions is natural. There is usually a defined time period to submit written questions; often it is no later than 10 days prior to the advertised date for receipt of bids.

Step 3: Assess Your Knowledge and Skills in Preparation for Writing a Bid

First, assess your skills to be sure you have the required competencies. If you are new to assessment and evaluation, you can use the RFP as a guide to competencies you want to develop. This RFP highlights the need for potential bidders to be knowledgeable about learning needs and suitable instructional methods for adult learners. People completing graduate degrees in adult education would have strong competencies related to this requirement. Be honest in your self-assessment; however, do not underestimate or underplay your abilities.

Assessment Specialist. If you are writing a bid for the assessment specialist role, the RFP clearly indicates required competencies, including knowledge of assessment principles and processes, ability to create and assess the value of assessment instruments, experience with promoting DEI, ability to communicate with internal and external stakeholders, and knowledge of software for collecting assessment data. Assessment goals, principles, and processes can be learned from texts that are a useful source of assessment methods and instruments, and that present the pros and cons of each method (Banta & Palomba, 2015; Kuh et al., 2015). However, few of them are directly pertinent to adult education so it may be necessary to look for sources specific to the field (Daffron & Caffarella, 2019; Hill, 2020).

Assessment must be purposeful and closely aligned with the learning objectives and goals articulated during the program's design. During the program design stage, program goals and related assessments should be planned together. Assessment results should be continuously used to inform adjustments to the program. A simplified program planning model has five steps: (a) assessing need for a program, (b) program objectives and specific goals based on established need, (c) assessment plans as part of planning objectives and goals, (d) program plan and assessment plans implemented on a concurrent basis, and (e) information gained from the assessments is used to refine the program and its implementation. Many cycles of this basic plan may be used over the lifetime of a program; however, the process can be more complex than the five steps (see Daffron & Caffarella, 2019). Many decisions require negotiations with varied stakeholders who bring different values and goals to the discussion (Cervero & Wilson, 2009). Planning for assessment is a step that is often missed, yet assessments created in a haphazard manner or at the last minute may be irrelevant to program goals and contribute little value to informing instructors and learners about adjustments they need to make to better facilitate student learning. See Chapter 4 for detailed discussion of program planning.

While books and articles provide valuable information about program evaluation, some of the skills delineated in the RFP can only be learned through experience. Promoting DEI requires knowledge of implicit bias, microaggressions, structural and systemic racism, cultural differences, social justice, and organizational development (Burrell et al., 2020). Beyond knowledge that you can gain by reading, effective DEI requires sensitivity, openness to different perspectives, tolerance of ambiguity, and cultural humility. Communicating with stakeholders requires well-developed social skills, including the ability to convey complicated information, demonstrate respect for diverse perspectives, and discern the meaning behind what people are saying. Collaboration skills can only be learned by working on projects with other people over time. Knowledge of software applications that can be supportive of assessment is also best gained through experience.

Program Evaluator. Like the assessment specialist position, a program evaluator responding to this RFP must have knowledge of adult learning, adult education instructional methods, and program evaluation. The person would need to be knowledgeable of the interrelationship among program objectives and goals, assessment, and program evaluation; cognizant about accreditation requirements; familiar with assessment documentation software; sensitive to DEI; have the social skills to communicate with multiple internal and external stakeholders; and be able to make recommendations for improvement.

As a program evaluator, your tasks are to identify program strengths and weaknesses, determine a program's effectiveness in meeting stated objectives and goals, and to make recommendations for program improvement. If an organization is working to meet accreditation requirements, you will need to familiarize yourself with the details of the goals of the organization, documentation required to meet the goals, reporting timelines, report formatting, and the review process. Many of these skills can be learned by reading a few of the available program evaluation texts, emphasizing sources specific to adult education (Cervero & Wilson, 2009; Daffron & Caffarella, 2019; Hill, 2021).

Martin and Roessger (2020) recommend that you begin by examining program inputs (instructors' knowledge, facilities, technology), components (teaching, course design, assessment), activities (learner participation in program), outputs (adult learning, course completion), and its short-term, medium-term, and long-term outcomes. An effective way to begin is to review the program's assessment results, sufficiency of its record-keeping, and discover whether program adjustments were made based on assessment results. You can use a logic model to visually display the program components to better understand the structure of the program (Figure 5.1).

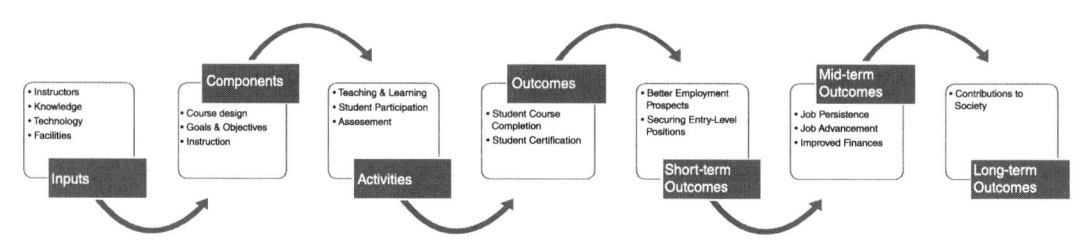

Figure 5.1 Logic model for case study

To fully determine the program's effectiveness, you need to be cognizant of the program objectives and goals, program delivery, and program outcomes. While these may be stated in the material provided to you, it is important to know that many programs have both stated and unstated goals. There may be differences in perspectives among program managers, instructors, learners, and organizational stakeholders. Therefore, you must ensure you can speak to the relevant people to identify varied perspectives and detect conflicting or hidden agendas. It is essential to detect whether any information is being withheld to make the program look good.

Qualitative, quantitative, and mixed-methods research methods can be used in program evaluation; therefore, you will need skills in all three domains. These are all skills you may have learned in your research courses in an adult education graduate program. Qualitative data can be created by conducting interviews, focus groups, observations, and document analysis. Qualitative research can help you determine which program components contribute to adult learning and whether other explanations are plausible. Quantitative analysis is used to verify which factors in the logic model are causally related to learner outcomes such as persistence and completion rates, grades, learner course evaluations, and other evidence. The specific statistical methods you choose to use would be based on the data you have access to or can create. Mixed methods combine the best aspects of qualitative and quantitative designs and can provide more complete information. In all cases, the evaluator must be conscious of threats to reliability and validity.

Finally, the last step would be to write reports and make formal presentations of your program evaluation results. You would provide information about how things currently stand with the program, the strengths, and weaknesses of the program, and make recommendations for improvement and future opportunities. By this time, you will have learned what information is sensitive and where disagreements exist so that you can present your results in a tactful and respectful manner.

Responding to the RFP

There are skills not as clearly stated in the RFP, such as budgeting skills. You need to carefully estimate your costs to conduct the project and calculate how much you need to charge for your work so you can make a profit. Budgeting is one of the most challenging skills for independent contractors and entrepreneurs to learn, and mistakes can be costly. For example, a company once wrote that the charge for each deliverable was 40 cents, but the actual cost should have been $4.00. The decimal error in the accepted bid meant that the company had to deliver the product even though they lost considerable money. Even when multiple people are involved in proofreading, this kind of mistake is easy to make and can put you out of business.

Excellent writing skills are needed to prepare an effective bid. You also need to be able to make formal presentations to sell your proposal and use negotiation skills to finalize the contract. Social skills are important to communicate your ideas to program managers, instructors, learners, and various external and internal stakeholders. Analytical skills are necessary to make sense of copious and varied data, whether you are using qualitative, quantitative, or mixed-methods research.

Step 4: Look for Pitfalls

Not all RFPs are worth your time to pursue. Before you submit a bid or accept a contract, it is helpful to beware of potential pitfalls that can occur. The following list provides only some of the problems you may encounter as an independent contractor.

- *RFPs may not include vital information.* The RFP may be designed to conceal organizational problems. Walking into this situation may be dangerous.

- *The RFP is vague, broad in scope, and lacks detail.* If the RFP does not clearly describe the need, it may mean that the organization's leaders are unclear about what they want. It is difficult to provide detailed and professional responses in this situation.
- *The turnaround time to submit a bid is so tight that it is unfeasible to respond with a well-written, professional bid.* You can wear yourself out quickly by chasing unrealistic RFPs.
- *There is no information about who to contact for questions, the period for clarification questions is noticeably short, or responses to clarification questions are vague or non-existent.* The people writing the RFP may be inexperienced or the RFP may be aimed at someone they know.
- *The RFP is seeking solutions for an urgent or high-risk situation.* You are submitting a bid to provide assessment or evaluation work and not to wave an imaginary magic wand.
- *Detailed information is sought that asks you to explain the methods you would use to tackle an organizational problem.* The organization could be fishing for information so that they can tackle the project themselves, without paying for your services.
- *RFPs are sometimes written for people with experience with the company.* There is no need to waste your time responding to an RFP tailored to favored vendors who have inside knowledge of the company.

Step 5: Mistakes to Avoid

Writing an effective bid for an RFP requires a significant investment of time. Avoiding the following mistakes can help you be more successful in securing contracts. If you have ever submitted an assignment or taught a university class, these items will not surprise you.

- *Not asking questions prior to submitting your bid.* Organizations that publish RFPs expect questions. Failing to ask questions, or making faulty assumptions, can result in rejection because your bid does not meet the organization's needs.
- *Not following the terms and conditions of the RFP.* Bidders are expected to carefully examine the terms and conditions and follow them closely. Attempting to negotiate changes in terms and conditions after the contract is signed is unlikely to be successful.
- *Lack of clarity in the bid.* CEOs are busy people who will not read lengthy information, especially when a brief statement is required. Details can be included in an appendix, if needed.
- *Ignoring instructions for document formatting and providing required information.* Evaluators of RFP bids will scan for information quickly, especially if many bids are received. If the information they are looking for cannot be found in the expected places, they are likely to move on to the next bid.
- *Not answering questions or saying information will be provided once the contract is signed.* If you do not provide the required information or sample documentation, the evaluator is likely to assume you do not have the relevant competencies.
- *Not addressing the selection criteria.* Make sure that your response meets each of the stated criteria.
- *Submitting the proposal late.* Submitting bids late is unprofessional and gives the impression that you are unable to handle a complex project. Most organizations will automatically eliminate late responses.

Practice and Theory

This chapter used the example of an RFP to investigate assessment and evaluation in adult education and illustrate the steps for writing a successful bid. It refers you to assessment and evaluation texts specific to adult education and describes the practices you would follow in working with an organization as an independent contractor. If you are involved in assessment, evaluation, and accreditation within your organization, many of the steps and cautions will be the same. You will have the advantage of insider knowledge and connections with other people who are involved in the same tasks. Disadvantages are that you can take familiar things for granted or hesitate to pursue controversial issues to protect your position.

Future of Adult Education in Assessment and Evaluation

The demand for stringent learning assessment and program evaluation is not going away anytime soon. Federal and regional funding agencies, grant funding agencies, regional accreditation of higher education, and state management of educational programs are all becoming more insistent that program decision-making is based on evidence derived from assessment and evaluation processes. When you are working to meet these requirements, it is easy to lose sight of the values and philosophies of adult education. Therefore, it is incumbent on adult educators to invest in developing the requisite competencies and motivation, as well as focusing on adult education's goals and objectives in order to conduct credible assessment and evaluation that meet stakeholders' criteria *and* preserve the integrity of adult education. There will be opportunities for adult educators to work within organizations and to serve as consultants.

Conclusion: The Three Takeaways

1. The need for learning assessment and program evaluation has become increasingly important and urgent. Therefore, adult educators need to develop the requisite competencies so they can conduct assessment and evaluation in ways congruent with program goals and adult education philosophies. To protect adult education programs, adult educators can invest in their own professional development to further develop their assessment and evaluation competencies.
2. While assessment and program evaluation require technical skills, what is most important is the focus on adult learners. Adult education graduate programs must emphasize the importance of learning assessment and evaluation skills consistent with adults' learning needs. While graduate students may not consider assessment and evaluation competencies as attractive as learning about social justice; technology skills; DEI; and adult learning theories, these competencies are crucial parts of effective adult education practice.
3. Ensuring that adult education graduate programs remain both viable and available to learners is a form of social justice. As higher education institutions respond to budget pressures, they are reducing the number of academic programs they offer, which restricts learner choices. Adult education programs are often vulnerable to elimination, attrition, or being subsumed into larger programs. Many analysts have commented that market economy logic has been incorporated into the academy with its expectations that education's sole purpose is employment preparation and requires time-consuming quantification (Gill, 2016). These are trends that contribute to obscuring the distinctive approaches of adult education (Milana, 2017). Adult education focuses on meeting the learning needs of diverse learners and social justice. While adult education is not the only discipline that upholds the need for social justice, we are possibly the only field that focuses on the roles of adult learning and social justice as inseparable.

References

Banta, T. W., & Palomba, C. A. (2015). *Assessment essentials: Planning, implementing, and improving assessment in higher education*. Jossey-Bass.

Burrell, S. L., Donovan, S. K., & Williams, T. P. (2020) *Teaching through challenges for equity, diversity, and inclusion*. Rowman & Littlefield.

Cervero, R. M., & Wilson, A. L. (2009). *Working the planning table: Negotiating democratically for adult, continuing, and workplace education*. Jossey-Bass.

Daffron, S., & Caffarella, R. S. (2019). *Planning programs for adults: A practical guide* (4th ed.). Jossey-Bass.

Gill, R. (2016). Breaking the silence: The hidden injuries of neo-liberal academia. *Feministische Studien, 1* (16), 39–55.

Hill, L. H. (Ed.). (2020). *Assessment, evaluation, and accountability in adult education*. Stylus.

Hill, L. H. (2021). Assessment and evaluation in adult and continuing education. In T. S. Rocco, M. C. Smith, R. C. Mizzi, L. R. Merriweather, & J. D. Hawley (Eds.), *The handbook of adult and continuing education* (2020 ed., pp. 140–149). Stylus.

Hill, L. H., & Isaac-Savage, E. P. (2022). Doors slam shut: Adult education program closures. *New Directions for Adult & Continuing Education, 2022,* 67–79. https://doi.org/10.1002/ace.20453

Kuh, G. E., Ikenberry, S. O., Jankowski, N. A., Cain, T. R., Ewell, P., Hutchings, P., & Kinzie, J. (2015). *Using evidence of student learning to improve higher education*. Jossey-Bass.

Martin, L. G., & Roessger, K. (2020). Program evaluation in adult education. In L. H. Hill (Ed.), *Assessment, evaluation, and accountability in adult education* (pp. 39–54). Stylus.

Milana, M. (2017). *Global networks, local actions: Rethinking adult education policy in the 21st century*. Routledge.

Chapter 6

Technology Skills

Michael D. Porterfield

Learning Process and Technology

In March 2020, as the COVID-19 pandemic started to take its toll on nations, families, and individuals, colleges and organizations in every field found that within days they had to switch from in-person instruction to online to preserve lives, as well as to keep the teaching and learning process going. Academics debated what to call this type of instruction, but they settled on "emergency remote teaching" (Hodges et al., 2020, para. 5). In this same blog, the writers also made the distinction that emergency remote teaching is not the same as quality online education which is carefully designed; in emergency situations, such as the pandemic, there is no time to be intentional, thoughtful, purposeful, and careful (para. 7).

To make this shift to emergency remote teaching, professionals at all levels realized that technology was the key to keep effective and necessary learning going. Early adopters of technology might have been aware of the various online tools, such as Zoom, but the pandemic forced everyone to adopt the latest education technology. Not only was technology reimagined, but also course design and distant facilitation of learning. Organizations asked: How does a course designer or facilitator move face-to-face instruction to online quickly? How does a seasoned face-to-face instructor, who relies on paper handouts and learning assessments, reimagine these analog lessons and assessments to an online format? The pandemic created many obstacles that could have derailed education, but because of hard work and reimagination by instructional designers, technologists, administrators, and instructors, this potential instructional obstacle was diverted to implement a rapid leap to remote instruction.

The pandemic of 2020 was the time when all areas of adult education rapidly moved to using technology. Martin and Xie (2022) emphatically stated: "Learning technologies and digital platforms are no longer an afterthought; they are critical for teaching and learning" (para. 1). How do we use technology to ensure learning technology is implemented with an intentional, thoughtful, purposeful, and careful design?

Freire (2004) foreshadowed the challenges to adult education as technology becomes more prevalent in life, especially in education:

> the education we need … cannot be an education that "trains" in place of educating. It cannot be one that "deposits" content into the "empty" heads of learners, but rather one that challenges us to think right. It is, therefore, the education that puts to educators the task of teaching learners how to think critically, while teaching them content …. For this reason, the technical-scientific education we urgently need is much more than mere training in the use of technological procedures. In truth, today's adult education, as well as education in general, must not forego the exercise of critically thinking about technique itself. (pp. 83 & 85)

DOI: 10.4324/9781003259602-8

Furthermore, Diamond (2008) noted that if technology is added to education without giving any thought to how it might impact instruction, there are only minimal benefits to learning. "Technology is best when considered more broadly, when you totally rethink how to teach a course rather than just taking what you have always done and simply do the same thing, but with technology" (Diamond, 2008, p. 220). Again, we need to focus on the process, but at the same time we need to know how the technology impacts course building, training, or other quality learning experiences.

Course Design Leading to Transformation

Freire (2004) and Diamond (2008) stressed the need to focus on course design and technology as complementing one another to create robust adult education. This next section will explore the elements of robust online learning.

Bloom's Taxonomy and Critical Thinking

At the root of every instructional event is a set of objectives; each objective usually starts with a verb. This is where a taxonomy of action verbs is handy, especially if there is a standard such as Bloom's Revised Taxonomy (Anderson et al., 2001).

> The revised framework was intended to broaden the typical set of learning outcomes that promote "retention" and "transfer." There exist several other taxonomies too (Biggs & Collis 1982; Fink, 2013; Gagné, 1985; Gagné & Briggs, 1974; Marzano & Kendall, 2001). All taxonomies are attempts to give a structure to the processes involved in learning based on the observations of learning behaviours and the limited understanding of how the brain functions. Nevertheless, most academics focus on Anderson–Bloom Taxonomy, also referred to as Revised Bloom's Taxonomy (Anderson et al., 2001).
>
> (Rao, 2020, p. 9)

As Rao (2020) stated, there are other taxonomies, but the Revised Bloom's Taxonomy (RBT) is the one used most often across many areas of adult education. It provides a list of various verbs associated with distinct levels of learning. The levels go from the starter level, *Remembering*, which deals with recall or the action of filling out a worksheet. At the highest level is *Creating* where learners produce a final product, for example, a multimedia presentation. At this level, the learner must integrate the other levels to create their final product. This process can lead to critical thinking. It introduces the importance of assessment or demonstrating mastery of the learning objective. Often technology is necessary in the construction of the assessment used to demonstrate mastery of the learning objective.

SAMR Levels of Technology Integration

SAMR is the acronym for a model developed for technology integration; it stands for Substitution, Augmentation, Modification, and Redefinition (Puentedura, 2006). With the rushed leap to remote work and learning during the pandemic, individuals were trained to use certain technologies to ensure collaboration for the work and learning environment. Training included: how to collaborate synchronously and/or asynchronously using a centralized hub which included video conferencing, messaging, and online document storage, viewing, and collaboration. Organizations did what was needed to ensure their teams or learning communities were able to engage with others while working or learning from home using various technologies. The goal behind the training on various technologies was to ensure effective communication. Palloff and Pratt (2007) made the connection between communication and community building: "Many of our attempts to communicate are, at the core, attempts at community building—a search for the community that connects us" (p. 35).

This need for connection using technology was brought into the spotlight during the pandemic, but this need for community building will never go away. It is important to continue to learn how to integrate these new technologies to enhance and transform communities so that they thrive. To help a community thrive, especially for adult learning programs and events, this takes time as the technology integration that connects us requires us to be intentional, thoughtful, purposeful, and careful in designing quality learning experiences. If technology is integrated properly into the learning or program design, this could lead participants to deeper or higher levels of thinking instead of rote recalling. Proper technology integration takes reflection, skill, and planning, but also a proficiency in the technology. Some users are novices, others are experts, while most users are somewhere in between. To help educators become more proficient in technology integration, this is where the SAMR model becomes formative.

Puentedura, (2006) developed the SAMR model. This model helps "teachers to 'move up' from lower to higher levels of teaching with technology, which according to Puentedura, leads to higher (i.e., enhanced) levels of teaching and learning" (Hamilton et al., 2016, p. 434). The SAMR model is divided into two tiers: enhancement at the lowest level with transformation at the highest level. Each tier has two levels:

- Transformation Tier (highest level)

    a   Redefinition—technology is used to create a task never imagined before.
    b   Modification—technology is used in a way that the task is significantly redesigned.

- Enhancement Tier (lowest level)

    a   Augmentation—technology is used as a direct substitute or task completed with some improvement.
    b   Substitution—technology is used in a way that it is a substitute or task completed with no improvement.

To help illustrate the enhancement and transformation levels of the SAMR model, an example might be helpful.

Enhancement Level. At this level, learners read a chapter from an e-book or online training manual instead of reading a physical book. This equates to the RBT level of Remembering. At the same time, the instructor or facilitator can create an auto-grading electronic quiz to test if the learners were able to recall important facts found in the learning module. Under RBT, the level of learning is classified as Understanding.

Transformative Level. In the workplace, specialized training modules with comprehension assessments are created to ensure security for employees and online company data, protection against harassment in the workplace, and fiscal procedures so that all employees have access to the same procedural information. This would be comparable to RBT's level of Evaluating. Or during a team video conference, after a short instruction by the team leader for new users in collaborating online, each team member synchronously types into a single online document to brainstorm their ideas and outline tasks for an upcoming presentation to present to a new client. In this instance the equivalent RBT level would be Creating.

In these examples, the facilitators or leaders had certain objectives or tasks that need to be achieved, and technology aided in this accomplishment. As more advanced uses of technology were integrated to demonstrate proficiency in the objectives, tasks were augmented or completed in a new way. As the technology integration level went up, so did the RBT. Finally, the more advanced application of technology skills, in conjunction with higher-level skills from Bloom's Taxonomy, "lead to deeper learning and transfer of knowledge and skills to a greater variety of tasks and contexts" (Adams, 2015, para. 11).

The Perfect Match: RBT and SAMR Model

When RBT and the SAMR Model are used together, they can make course and training design more robust. However, it does take particular skills to align the appropriate Bloom's action verb with the appropriate technology.

As noted in the previous section, the enhancement tier in the SAMR model contains Substitution and Augmentation levels. When enhancement is aligned with RBT, it is associated with Remember, Understand, and Apply—the three lower levels of RBT. The transformation tier in the SAMR model contains Modification, while Redefinition is aligned with Analyze, Evaluate, and Create—the three higher levels of RBT. Puentedura (2014) also noted:

> In turn, within each grouping a similar ordering occurs – e.g., Remember-type tasks are primarily associated with S(substitution)-level uses of the technology, Understand-type tasks are associated with either S(substitution)- or A(augmentation)-level uses of the technology, and so on. (para. 3)

This alignment between RBT and SAMR can also be very fluid. Not all advanced technologies need to be associated with the higher levels of RBT and vice versa. For example, creating a narrated PowerPoint presentation can help learners remember various facts. In this instance, learners compile a glossary and then turn this list into an online set of flashcards to help study for the next test. Again, Bloom's higher-order thinking skills do not always need to be transformative, but rather can be an enhancement.

Partner in Practice

The previous section outlined how technology impacts instruction with the "coupling" of RBT and the SAMR model of technology integration. As noted previously, Freire (2004) called upon adult educators today, as well as educators in general, not to "forego the exercise of critically thinking about technique itself" (p. 85). In other words, to design critical thinking activities using technology, one must be familiar with the various educational technologies and how to skillfully use them to achieve the desired outcomes and maximize learning. This section will focus on listing certain educational technologies and how to use them to enhance or even transform lessons or collaborations. Furthermore, as a partner in practice, the following information or practices are a starting point; there is always more to learn.

Learning Community

As noted earlier, any attempt at communication is an attempt to build community (Palloff & Pratt, 2007). Certainly, technology and the skills in using technology can assist in attempting to build community that connects us. As adult educators, we work with diverse populations in different programs and organizations, but what remains constant is the process in planning and achieving our goals and objectives set forth by these institutions; technology is a companion to assist with connecting and communicating and, if integrated appropriately, can be substantive or transformative in the process.

For a great example of this, see the qualitative study by Dirkx and Dang (2009) situated in workforce development. There are common elements both in process and technology integration that could apply to multiple areas of adult education, especially in the use of technology to communicate for community building. This next section will focus on a variety of these common communication technologies found in many areas of adult education as you develop your own toolbox.

Collaborating Using Microsoft Office 365/Google Workspace for Education or NonProfits

These are a suite of tools that contain online collaboration tools including email, calendar, video conferencing, online document storage, and the ability to create and share documents with others such as word processing, slide decks, surveys, spreadsheets, project management, and more. Collaborating with colleagues and learners or partners online is important. For instance, since the pandemic, many nonprofits and organizations have chosen to continue working from home to save money on office space. These online options offer a plethora of services for users to collaborate with their constituents. For example, these online tools make it easy for groups to create, maintain, and access all the documents necessary for a project or a slide deck for a group presentation to a potential client. Content creators can create training for employees or constituents using Google Classroom or OneNote Class Notebook to engage with one another, the facilitator, and a subject matter expert. When these tools are integrated properly in either a substantial or transformative way, they can help build community, as well as building robust learning modules. Therefore, "community is built upon what activities people do together instead of being based on geographical location" (Wellman, as cited in Rovai, 2002, p. 199).

An advantage to these online collaboration tools is that they can be used on a wide variety of devices, for example, laptops running various operating systems, tablets, or mobile phones. These tools rely on the internet for collaboration but can also be used offline as well. One time, a team of researchers tried collaborating on an article and they had difficulty because one did not have Word installed on the Mac. The rest of them were using Windows. The Mac user struggled trying to edit the document using Microsoft Word Online because it did not look familiar and, instead of learning how to utilize the software, the author just gave up and let another colleague edit the article. Reflecting on this example, if this one person knew the various available options, then much grief could have been potentially avoided. Furthermore, the manufacturers make these tools look and feel the same on purpose and even with similar options and features in the same place. This makes it easy to transition from one product to another.

Online Document Collaboration. In the past, learners would email their writing to their professor, facilitator, or editor. The person would then make edits or comments using features in Word, update the document title to reflect which version it was, and then email this updated document back to the learner. In the end, there might be multiple versions of an edited document, making it hard to keep track of all of them. Microsoft Word Online or Google Docs make it quite easy for multiple users to write, share, and edit a document by storing it in OneDrive or Google Drive. These tools even include different citation styles and reviewing tools in the online versions.

Video Conferencing. This has become a central feature of online collaboration tools, especially because there is only so much one can do by phone or through text-based communication. Video conferencing is an important way that individuals can engage in synchronous classes and connect with colleagues, doctors, and even distant loved ones. It is a vital tool to help maintain and sustain the learning community. Here are a few ways video conferencing could be used:

- Enhancement

  a Schedule appointments with clients or constituents to collaborate.
  b If the video conferencing service is integrated into a suite of tools, the convener can create an invitation, post it in an email, or share the link directly from the video conferencing tool.
  c Security is always a concern. Whenever the meeting link is created, it is recommended to enable the waiting room passcode, and only allow authenticated users to join; this ensures meeting organizers can see who is waiting to join and only the invited guests can participate.
  d For smaller meetings, sharing the screen might be necessary for all participants; this feature needs to be enabled.
  e Video conferencing services offer distinct levels of encryption. If the conversation during the meeting is a privileged conversation, please consult with your administrator because this will need a higher level of encryption to ensure privacy regulations.

- Transformative

  a If the convener is conducting a large meeting lasting for some time, here are some suggestions to engage the participants in an active manner:

     - Build in breaks.
     - Use the polling feature to gauge the participants' understanding of the material being presented.
     - Invite participants to enter questions into the Q&A tool. Ask a colleague to monitor these questions in order to answer them or to bring them to the attention of the presenter.
     - At the beginning of the presentation, ask participants to type into the chat an introduction so that they can meet each other.
     - Create a collaborative document as a back channel in which participants can take notes or use as a takeaway after the presentation.
     - Use breakout rooms to discuss various topics; this is another way for the participants to engage and communicate with others. Ask the group to appoint a facilitator to make sure everyone has a chance to share; a timekeeper to ensure the group does not run out of time; and a summarizer who will recap the conversation reporting back to the larger group.

  b If the sessions are for training, then these can be recorded and posted to an online training site for others to review, especially if the meeting is going over material for an upcoming test or online credentialing exam.

Using Video in a Training Program. Videos can be an important part of the learning experience. According to Kaltura (2019), a leading educational video vendor, "82% see learners' expectations for how much video should be part of their learning experience is increasing. [Also] 98% of respondents see video as having a part to play in personalized learning experiences" (p. 4). Video creation and viewing has become an integral part of the learning and training experience. These are a few ways of using video in an adult education experience:

- Enhancement

    a   LinkedIn Learning is one venue where adult educators/learners can access video tutorials on learning software, technology, business, and more, but usually one must pay for a subscription.
    b   Sometimes an organization or school might subscribe to various video/class resources.
    c   Check out your public library to see if LinkedIn Learning is available at your local branch. Your local branch might even have more eCourses you can access for free to enhance your professional or personal life.
    d   YouTube, Khan Academy, and TED Talks are other sources for learning through videos.

- Transformation

    a   TED has a resource called TEDEd in which a facilitator can create lessons by selecting multiple TEDEd animations, TED Talks, or even YouTube videos, and then add interactive questions, discussions, and more.
    b   After sharing these specially curated lessons to learners online, they can assess if they are comprehending the information or see what lingering questions they might have after viewing the videos.
    c   Facilitators can also create special collections of videos to share with online participants as well. Then these TEDEd lessons or collections can be embedded into a webpage or learning tool, for example, Google Classroom or OneNote Class Notebook, available in the collaboration suite.
    d   Recording videos are another of the available tools in an online collaboration suite of tools. Only a device with a video camera and microphone is needed. An example would be to have participants create brief introduction videos, so that they can get to know one another.
    e   If a participant is using the installed version of PowerPoint on a computer, they can create a slide deck, then add audio narration or screen recording to each slide. Once these elements are created in the slides, the whole presentation can be exported as a movie. Then this exported movie can be uploaded to an online site for viewers to watch.

Quizzes/Checking for Comprehension Survey. These are another common tool available to facilitators in collaboration suites. Some examples are as follows:

- Enhancement

    a   A multiple-choice, auto-grading quiz is given at the end of the module to see if learners mastered the content. This is a summative assessment.

- Transformation

    a   Frequent short multiple-choice quizzes are helpful to learners reviewing the material. This is a formative assessment.
    b   A quiz allows learners the opportunity to retake it twice, but after the first attempt if the learner does not attain a certain score, a module appears based on release conditions set by the learner's score containing extra study aids. After reviewing these study aids, the learner can retake the quiz.

Making Content Accessible. One of the first lessons I heard in my first adult education class was that adult education is about helping others to break down barriers that bar adults from learning. One of these barriers is accessibility. There are some simple things that can help, especially for those who use audio screen readers to access content.

- Use descriptive links. Normally, individuals will copy and paste links that are a mile long. If an individual using a screen reader came across this long link in the online text, the screen reader would start to read each letter of this long link. Using a descriptive link is better. To create a descriptive link:
    a   Simply type out a concise description of the underlying link.
    b   Copy the web link.
    c   Highlight the descriptive text.
    d   Go to Insert Link and paste the web address.
    e   This will help the user to access the linked content faster and not have the long link read aloud one letter at a time.
- Use built-in accessibility checkers to ensure that content is accessible to all users. This is an easy tool to access in Microsoft Office menus.
- Use Alt Text for images. When a screen reader comes upon the image, the alt text is what is voiced to describe this image and if it is marked descriptive, left blank, or contains the file name, this is not helpful. Simply write content as though the image is being explained out loud to another person.
- If a video or audio presentation is created for training, include a detailed outline or complete text of what is spoken.

Technology Skills: Other Areas of Adult Education Practice

The authors throughout Part II of this book note the increasing importance of technology in their adult education practice. If your role in the adult education sphere is in assessment and evaluation (see Chapter 5), you will need to be proficient in using spreadsheet software as well as quantitative and qualitative analysis software. Those who are involved with program planning (see Chapter 4) may need to use social media to publicize their programs and customer relationship management (CRM) software. For those readers with a passion for technology, specific positions within a given sphere of adult education may be of special interest, and examples of opportunities appear throughout this book. For example, Rowland (see Chapter 15) describes health information personnel as individuals who are responsible for organizing and maintaining the accuracy of data and other information using technology and data analysis.

Professional Development Example. A seasoned trainer attended a 9-week series to convert a face-to-face course to online. On the last day of the series, through listening to the presenters and completing this workshop incorporating best practices on how to include appropriate technologies engaging learners, the facilitator realized this also improved their face-to-face training. This individual engaged in reflection about the learning process and how training was delivered. They considered how to integrate appropriate technologies to improve teaching and learning. In summary, this instructor accomplished Freire's exhortation to critically think about the technique itself. How will you do this? For more on corporate training, see Chapter 11.

> **Technology Self-Assessment for Adult Educators**
>
> - What technology do you currently use and know how to use? You might surprise yourself and realize you already know a lot about using the appropriate technologies to do your job.
> - What goals or objectives are important for the audience of learners to accomplish or master?
> - Who are the learners and are these goals appropriate for them?
> - Start small. What one current learning activity do I want to enhance with technology?
> - Which technology can help make this enhancement possible?
> - Who is available to guide me if I know a specific technology will enhance the activity but do not know how to use it?
>
> Then practice, practice, and practice again. Do not be afraid to make mistakes. Mistakes can be the best teacher. When you feel comfortable with the technology, test it, and then implement it. Finally, evaluate how it went. Did the participants improve and meet the objectives of the lesson?

Success Strategies for Using Technology

- Bricolage. This is a French term from "bricoler," which means "to tinker." Try new techniques or tools to see how they work. Start thinking how you might apply them to your current practice to improve it. Communication with colleagues may help improve practice.
- Go to available workshops or professional development opportunities. Free or low-cost can be a great place to start. Also check out "boot camps" that are designed to get users up and running quickly.
- Look to your peers. Form a community of practice to discuss ways to improve instruction integrating technology.
- Work with an instructional designer, if you have access to one. The designer will listen to you, as the content expert, and help you determine your instructional goals and assist you in creating an appropriate learning experience.
- Look to your professional organizations to see if they offer any professional development opportunities.

Conclusion

This chapter offers examples and a method to integrate appropriate technologies with your instructional goals and objectives. The examples are provided to enhance and/or transform your own practice in educating adult learners when using technology. The path ahead is unknown, but it will be filled with many adventures. However, an apt metaphor might be the road not taken, as described by Robert Frost (2002) in his famous poem. Technology is here to stay and as adult educators we need to learn to use it in ways that are based on critical thinking about how it can be used to help learners to also think as critically as possible about the technology that is available.

References

Adams, N. E. (2015). Bloom's taxonomy of cognitive learning objectives. *Journal of the Medical Library Association: JMLA, 103*(3), 152–153. https://doi.org/10.3163/1536-5050.103.3.010

Anderson, L. W., Krathwol, D. R., Airasian, P. W., Cruikshank, K. A., Mayer, R. E., Pintrich, P. R., Raths, J., & Wittrock, M. C. (Eds.) (2001). *A taxonomy for learning, teaching, and assessing: A revision of Bloom's taxonomy of educational objectives.* Longman.

Biggs, J. B., & Collis, K. F. (1982). *Evaluating the quality of learning: The SOLO taxonomy (structure of the observed learning outcome)*. Academic Press. http://library.mpib-berlin.mpg.de/toc/z2007_963.pdf

Diamond, R. M. (2008). *Designing and assessing courses and curricula: A practical guide* (3rd ed.). Jossey-Bass.

Dirkx, J. M., & Dang, N. L. T. (2009). From laborer to learner: The experiences of former factory workers in a developmental education program. *Proceedings of the 50th Annual Adult Education Research Conference*, 107–112. https://digitalcommons.nl.edu/ace_aerc/1

Fink, L. D. (2013). *Creating significant learning experiences: An integrated approach to designing college courses* (revised and updated edition). Jossey-Bass.

Freire, P. (2004) *Pedagogy of indignation*. Routledge.

Frost, R. (2002). *The road not taken: A selection of Robert Frost's poems*. Henry Holt and Company.

Gagné, R. M. (1985). *The conditions of learning and theory of instruction* (4th ed). Holt, Rinehart & Winston.

Gagné, R. M., & Briggs, L. J. (1974). *Principles of instructional design*. Holt, Rinehart & Winston.

Hamilton, E. R., Rosenberg, J. M., & Akcaoglu, M. (2016) The substitution augmentation modification redefinition (SAMR) model: A critical review and suggestions for its use. *TechTrends, 60*(5), 433–441. https://doi.org/10.1007/s11528-016-0091-y

Hodges, C., Moore, S., Lockee, B., Trust, T., & Bond, A. (2020, March 27). The difference between emergency remote teaching and online learning. *EDUCAUSE Review*. https://er.educause.edu/articles/2020/3/the-difference-between-emergency-remote-teaching-and-online-learning

Kaltura. (2019). *State of video in education 2019*. Kaltura, Inc. https://corp.kaltura.com/resources/the-state-of-video-in-education-2019/

Martin, F., & Xie, K. (2022, September 27) Digital transformation in higher education: 7 areas for enhancing digital learning. *EDUCAUSE Review*. https://er.educause.edu/articles/2022/9/digital-transformation-in-higher-education-7-areas-for-enhancing-digital-learning

Marzano, R. J., & Kendall, J. S. (2001). *The new taxonomy of educational objectives*. Corwin Press.

Palloff, R., & Pratt, K. (2007). *Building online learning communities* (2nd ed.). Jossey-Bass.

Puentedura, R. R. (2006, November 26). *Transformation, technology, and education in the state of Maine*. Ruben R. Puentedura Weblog. http://hippasus.com/blog/archives/18

Puentedura, R. R. (2014, September 24). *SAMR and Bloom's taxonomy: Assembling the puzzle*. CommonSense. www.commonsense.org/education/articles/samr-and-blooms-taxonomy-assembling-the-puzzle

Rao, N. J. (2020). Outcome-based education: An outline. *Higher Education for the Future, 7*(1), 5–21. https://doi.org/10.1177/2347631119886418

Rovai, A. (2002). Development of an instrument to measure classroom community. *Internet and Higher Education, 5*, 197–211.

Part II

Practitioners' Voices

Chapter 7

Adult Basic Education/English as a Second Language/Family Literacy

Stephanie W. Collins

Introduction: My Journey to Adult Education

I am the first in my immediate family to graduate from high school and college. After earning a BSBA in Management and Organizational Behavior, I took a year off to decide on a graduate program. I was deciding whether to pursue an MBA or a teacher certification. One summer afternoon, I ventured into the education department at the University of Missouri–St. Louis (UMSL) to explore options and met with the late Dr. Mary F. Cooper. She introduced me to adult education (AE), which I considered a new phenomenon. Imagine hearing for the first time terms like lifelong learning, andragogy, self-directed learning, and learning contracts. It was because of Dr. Cooper's enthusiastic overview of the program that I began to envision a career focused on collaborative learning and program development, understanding learning styles, and where I could align my degree studies with my career goals. I began to see myself as an adult learner and a future adult educator, and I wanted to discover more.

To my surprise, being introduced to AE reignited my passion for education. Lifelong learning and how AE educates adults who take different pathways to formal education quickly captured my attention. Learning the functionality of AE programs within educational institutions was the most enlightening discovery. For example, it is possible to find AE programs offered through public school districts, community colleges, or universities. Among these are adult basic education (ABE), adult community or continuing education (ACE), adult education and literacy (AEL), adult literacy education (ALE), and adult secondary education (ASE). This chapter will focus on careers within this sphere of AE.

I was intrigued by theories of adult learning, andragogy, transformational learning, and self-directed learning. Consequently, the focus of my career changed from business to education. I had landed in an educational space that put in perspective the academic journey that, up to this point, I had been traveling for 22 years. Currently, I am pursuing a doctoral degree from UMSL in Adult Education, Workforce Development, Distance Learning, and Technology. I chose this program to help further my understanding of workforce readiness and technology, core academic competencies, personal and social capabilities, occupational competencies, career knowledge, and transitional skills. Ultimately, I believe this program will guide me in analyzing my doctoral research topics from a practitioner's point of view. I am researching AE and technology integration in the wake of COVID-19 while using my teaching background in General Education Degree (GED), now referred to as High School Equivalency (HiSET), preparation and English as a Second Language (ESL) or English to Speakers of Other Languages (ESOL) classes as a frame of reference. I remain confident that the AE graduate program at UMSL will continue to reshape and expand my educational and professional development with the possibility of serving and teaching a population of learners with whom I can identify.

DOI: 10.4324/9781003259602-10

As I reflect on the past and look to my future journey, I look forward to continuing collaboration and partnership-based work. There are many benefits to collaboration in education, whether in the classroom or between educational institutions and businesses. According to new research (Business-Adult Education Partnerships Toolkit, n.d.), through collaborative partnerships, adult educators and business leaders can create talent pipelines of workers ready to meet the needs of local in-demand industries and provide contextualized education for adult learners' career success.

Literacy Programs

Equally important are school and community partnerships that support family literacy programs. For example, Breiseth (2021) reported that when building a support network for English language learners (ELLs), community organizations play a valuable role and offer resources that schools may not have at their disposal to work with ELLs and their families. Research by Stefanski et al. (2016) reveals that partnerships between schools and neighborhood communities support student learning, improve schools, and strengthen families and neighborhoods. These partnerships expand the traditional educational mission of the school to include health and social services for children and their families and to involve the broader community.

The term lifelong learning is widely used in various adult education programs (ABE, ACE, AE, AEL) when referring to formal and informal learning opportunities. Both learning opportunities can be a bridge to the workforce, especially where the requirement is for workers to have some post-secondary education or training but less than a 4-year degree. See Chapter 23 on workforce development for an in-depth discussion.

Professional Qualifications

Throughout my career, I have always considered myself a teacher, regardless of the roles I have played or the jobs I held. When I received an opportunity to adjunct as an AEL and GED instructor at a community college, which required me to teach math, science, writing, reading, social studies, and critical thinking to adults, I began to identify as an adult educator. At the time, I was working in the corporate sector as a training specialist with a bachelor's degree in business. To qualify for the teaching assignment at the community college, I had to complete a two-part training program, the Precertification Workshop (PCW) and the Beginner Teacher's Assistance Program (BTAP). These workshops were the first step in becoming a certified adult education and literacy (AEL) educator in Missouri. (Each state has its own requirements.) The BTAP focused on providing an understanding of AE and the importance of the educator's role. It included discussions and activities related to data management, managed intake, AEL assessments, College and Career Readiness Standards, and the HiSET (*College and Career Readiness Standards for Adult Education*, n.d.). The PCW introduced the Test of Adult Basic Education (TABE) and provided strategies for understanding assessment results and using them to develop targeted instruction. It offered an overview of classroom management techniques and instructional strategies for multi-level classrooms where learners have different abilities, backgrounds, and interests.

The credentials I obtained for teaching literacy courses led me to an ESL instructor position at a university. This opportunity came after I had earned a master's degree in adult and secondary education. While I could have obtained the ESL teaching position without this credential, having a master's degree solidified my qualifications to teach in various adult learning environments, including ESL. In this position, I learned that ESL is just one way to refer to the field. To be more inclusive and because I was teaching English to learners who spoke more than two languages, I had to consider the terms Teaching English to Speakers of Other Languages (TESOL) or ESOL. I prepared and delivered competency-based ESL instruction to prepare learners to complete the 2-year English language study certificate program and pass the Test of English as a Foreign Language (TOEFL). I also developed basic and intermediate lesson plans for grammar, writing, composition, reading comprehension, vocabulary, oral communication, workforce entry skills, and technology.

> **TEFL – TESL – TESOL**
>
> Other English language teacher training courses and the qualifications that prepare instructors for different teaching environments are worth noting. Montrose (2015) details the differences between TEFL, TESL, and TESOL and what makes each teaching certification unique and valuable. In short, TEFL is for teaching English in non-native English-speaking countries to speakers of foreign languages. TESL is for teaching English in native English-speaking countries to speakers of foreign languages, whereas TESOL focuses on English in non-native and native English-speaking countries to speakers of foreign languages.

Facilitating Adult Learners' Life Transitions

Teaching GED and ESL require different strategies, but the goal is to help learners pass a competency test, consisting of either a high school equivalency or English language comprehension. My intention was to provide learners with academic knowledge and skills in the subject matter that would prepare them for post-secondary education, the workforce, or personal enrichment. Additionally, I aimed to help learners develop skills to become problem solvers, creative and critical thinkers, and lifelong learners. To accomplish this, I had to be adaptable, creative, sensitive to cultural differences, and present information in a real-life context to facilitate learners' grasp of the complexities of the language. I acted as a mentor, advisor, and liaison to learners and families who were just getting established in an unfamiliar environment.

Assessments

Understanding the purpose of assessments is key to the onset and continuum of any educational pursuit between educator and learner. If you do not know where learners are educationally when they arrive at your class, chances are you will not be able to help them to navigate to their destination successfully. Also, assessments help learners identify their strengths and weaknesses, allowing them to understand their learning process better. The worst scenario in a teaching and learning exchange is for a learner to physically reach the end of a course only to discover they mentally dropped out on the first day. Assessments can help educators implement practical and corrective instruction and help learners sustain progressive learning habits and development. See Chapter 5 for a complete discussion of assessment and evaluation skills.

Barriers for Adult Learners

Many adult learners face barriers such as financial obstacles, self-doubt, neuroplasticity, contradictory past knowledge, and reading. Reading skill deficits affect performance on every part of the GED test battery because they are written tests. Learners with reading problems must address them before they can hope to meet their goals. In my formative years in school, teachers often said that reading is fundamental. I fully understood the phrase's meaning when I became an ABE instructor. One of the most basic life skills is reading, and is perhaps the skill adult learners struggle with the most. Specific to reading and adult learning, Pickard (2016) expounds on the 2014 report by the Workforce Innovation and Opportunity Act (WIOA) regulator of ABE/ASE program operations. The report emphasized some of the ramifications for low-scoring adult readers. First, a classroom focus on workforce preparation and post-secondary education potentially limits reading and writing development opportunities. Second, WIOA performance measures may discourage programs from enrolling low-scoring adult readers by setting outcomes largely unattainable by those with significant reading difficulty. And third, these service shortcomings fall disproportionately on African American adult learners, who are over-represented among participants who test at or below the Low Intermediate Basic level. For adults with substantial reading difficulty, a focus on testing to the exclusion of other experiences with reading and writing is likely to have a negative limiting effect on their literacy development.

AE practitioners can help this population of learners by determining the reading comprehension strategies most important to adults' success on adult literacy outcome measures and aligning them with previously researched interventions (Hock & Mellard, 2005). The authors contend that when using a competency-based standardized test, adult learners need to be concurrently taught test-taking skills to reduce the test-related task demands and produce a better index of a learner's reading comprehension skills.

Job Opportunities in ABE/ESL/Family Literacy

There are numerous job opportunities for adult educators. An entry-level job would be instructing adults in preparatory and remedial classes such as high school equivalency, literacy, or ESL. As you reach higher levels of education, you may advance to a professorship or even take an administrative position. More than my literacy instructor credentials, having a master's degree prepared me for my current position as an AE program coordinator. I am responsible for developing career and trade programs, training, and supervising instructors, and advising learners. In addition to setting high expectations, demanding quality performance, and respecting the diversity of adult learners, learner interests have always been a priority. My AE graduate coursework promoted good communication skills, cultural sensitivity, patience, and resourcefulness and is a good foundation for aspiring AE practitioners in several settings.

Competencies Essential to Adult Education

There are a number of skills and competencies necessary to be an effective adult educator. According to *Adult Education Teacher Competencies* (n.d.), competencies identify the core knowledge and skills expected of any ABE/ESL/literacy educator. As reported in *How to Become an Adult Education Teacher* (All Education Schools, 2022), being an ABE educator takes a special sort of person. The following are some of the qualities and skills that make for the best adult educators. Communication skills are essential to help adult learners achieve their goals. You must be able to explain their progress and where they need to focus in terms they can understand. Cultural sensitivity is also essential, especially if you plan on teaching ELL. (See Chapter 14 for more information.) Resourcefulness is a must, as you need to be able to respond to all types of situations. Patience is the most crucial trait, as you deal with some learners who grasp the material quickly while others need more guidance and individual help.

Professional organizations also play an essential role in providing knowledge and skills necessary for the industry. One main reason for joining a professional organization is to network with fellow adult educators. This type of interaction can lead to discovering new resources and funding opportunities, learning new skills, and creating opportunities for collaboration. With the encouragement of my professors, mentors, and peers, I took advantage of numerous professional memberships and attended several education conferences, seminars, and webinars. I am a member of various organizations: American Association for Adult and Continuing Education (AAACE) (www.aaace.org), Coalition on Adult Basic Education (COABE) (https://coabe.org), Learning Resource Network (LERN) (https://lern.org), and Missouri Association for Adult Continuing and Community Education (MAACCE) (https://maacce.org). In MAACCE, I served as Community Education Liaison, Conference Planner, Treasurer, and President.

I have over 19 years of experience as an adult educator and literacy trainer. That experience includes the private, nonprofit, and community college sectors, along with curriculum development, program planning, teaching, and administration. I earned the State of Missouri Adult Education Vocational Supervisor Certification and am currently working as an Adult and Community Education (ACE) coordinator. I work to establish partnerships with businesses and industries to enhance program offerings. My expertise lies in managing a self-sustaining AE program. I oversee the development and implementation of programs that prepare adult learners to earn credentials to advance in post-secondary education or the workforce or to learn for personal enrichment.

It is important to note that some AE programs are autonomous and do not include literacy instruction. They operate within a public school framework and function as a community education program. As such, many community education programs are fee based and self-sustaining. They do not offer college courses or receive state funding. This type of program contrasts with a state-funded community college or university framework with continuing education programs, enabling them to provide an array of literacy programs at no charge to learners. For more information on community-based education, see Chapter 9.

Adult Education Learning Theories, Assumptions, and Implications

Adult learning theories provide insight into how adults learn and can help instructors be more effective in their practice and responsive to the needs of the learners they serve (TEAL Center Fact Sheet No. 11: Adult Learning Theories [TEAL Center], n.d.). While there are many adult learning theories, andragogy and self-directed learning are known to have staying power. These two theories are important components of our present-day understanding of adult learning. I will discuss andragogy, in particular, here. You will find a thorough discussion on self-directed learning in Chapter 2.

Malcolm S. Knowles, the Father of Andragogy in the United States, was one of the world's leading scholar-practitioners of adult learning. He was a member of a generation that experienced the fullest range of character-building phases the United States has known: a massive influx of immigrants, several wars, an economic depression, waves of technological advances, the civil rights movement, the dominance of the knowledge worker, and an optimism about the human spirit (Knowles et al., 2014).

Knowles (1980, as cited in TEAL Center, n.d.) explains that while attempting to document differences between the ways adults and children learn, he popularized the concept of andragogy ("the art and science of helping adults learn"), contrasting it with pedagogy ("the art and science of teaching children"). The article further states that Knowles posited a set of assumptions for the adult learner and implications for practice for adult educators.

> **Assumptions for Adult Learners**
>
> The adult learner:
>
> - Moves from dependency to increasing self-directedness as he/she matures and can direct his/her own learning.
> - Draws on his/her accumulated reservoir of life experiences to aid learning.
> - Is ready to learn when he/she assumes new social or life roles.
> - Is problem-centered and wants to apply new learning immediately.
> - Is motivated to learn by internal, rather than external, factors.
>
> *Implications for Practice*
>
> Adult educators:
>
> - Set a cooperative climate for learning in the classroom.
> - Assess the learner's specific needs and interests.
> - Develop learning objectives based on the learner's needs, interests, and skill levels.
> - Design sequential activities to achieve the objectives.
> - Work collaboratively with the learner to select methods, materials, and resources for instruction.
> - Evaluate the quality of the learning experience and make adjustments, as needed, while assessing needs for further learning.
>
> (TEAL Center, n.d.)

I agree with Kurt (2020) that adult learners retain information best when it is relevant and useful. Therefore, it is imperative for educators to explain the reason for learning a specific skill. As they possess a mature mindset, adults are often better at creating solutions to real-life issues as opposed to simply memorizing information. Problem-solving, immediate application, and performance-based tasks are all pillars of effective instruction.

Also worth mentioning is that andragogical principles must be sufficiently applied for adult learners (regardless of the English proficiency level: beginning, intermediate, etc.) to create and maintain experiences that are inviting, engaging, motivating, and personally rewarding (Finn, 2011). Finn further states that because of the variety of delivery contexts, "one of the more significant trends in adult ESL program development has been the efforts made by program planners, materials developers, and teachers to pay close attention to the needs of the learner and the social nature of learning" (p. 35).

As an experienced AE practitioner, I believe it is essential for adult educators to know adult learning theories and how they relate to the various learning styles and the unique ways adults respond to learning. I agree with Gouthro (2019) that the commitment to ensure that AE is a practice informed by theory enables educators to understand the complexity of the teaching and learning process. Additionally, it is important for ABE/ESL/family literacy educators to explore how power shapes personal and social learning contexts and fosters the development of a more critically literate and engaged citizenry.

Future of ABE: Technology Integration

Technology integration tops the list when reflecting on the future of ABE/ESL/family literacy and its unique infrastructure. It is like looking at an unfinished 1,000-piece puzzle! Where do you start, and what are the connectors? Using various technologies, educators can facilitate the achievement of learner and program objectives and outcomes (Boeren et al., 2020). Therefore, it is essential to understand the advantages of using technology for teaching and learning in ABE classrooms.

As stated by Basarmak and Hamutoglu (2020), the concepts of technology and integration are now widely used together because the presence of technology is advancing at an unbelievable pace in educational environments. As a result, instructional design is ever evolving, and a significant percentage of educators are responsible for designing their curriculum for online learning without losing sight of the learning experience (see also Chapter 2). The COVID-19 pandemic enabled online education to rapidly become a vital part of teaching and learning. According to Vargo et al. (2021), various types of human behavior shifted from offline to online, accelerating the diffusion of emerging digital technologies. As a result, educators had to adapt to the pace of online teaching and put greater effort into preparing for online courses by innovating and designing lessons while patiently turning adults from passive recipients to engaged learners.

Online classrooms and technology-based instruction offer significant opportunities for ABE/AEL instructors, learners, and institutions. They provide flexibility in the learning schedule, accommodate different learning styles, and allow for greater use of learning management systems that support blended learning. As previously mentioned, AE programs and course providers include school districts, community colleges, career centers, and community-based nonprofits. As such, and considering there may be similarities, no two entities operate exactly the same. A program's funding source can determine how much support it will receive for technology integration and professional development. However, the question remains: How can the infrastructure of AE programs support instructors and technology integration?

Even though integrating technology into the AE classroom is an important topic, it has yet to overcome perceived barriers and concerns about digital competency and educational infrastructure support. These concerns present a need for learners to acquire basic computer skills before educators can integrate technology into the curriculum. It also highlights the critical skills required for success in higher education, technical training programs, and the workforce. Many will agree with Rogers (2000) that the lack of adequate technology integration in the curriculum might be more related to institutional norms rather than teaching methods. Educators' perception of professional development for technology integration support solidifies this statement. The objective and outcome of professional development should be to improve student learning.

For professional development for adult educators to succeed, they must feel empowered to conduct the work of technology integration without institutional support. Having a sense of empowerment will aid educators in persisting against obstacles that may tempt them to switch back to traditional methods of teaching, which do not incorporate technology at all or integrate technology at a surface level (Kent & Giles, 2017). Additionally, opportunities for technological enhancements have emerged, and informal, self-directed learning has increased as the need for digital technologies increases. However, not all adult learners can utilize the technology to facilitate learning, due to unreliable or no internet access or lack of digital literacy skills required to participate in self-directed learning in a virtual environment. With these extrinsic, first-order barriers, educators face additional challenges in acquiring new skills and managing the teaching and learning process.

In some cases, the loss of informal learning caused by the pandemic will significantly impact disadvantaged and low-skilled workers who cannot complete their educational projects and need retraining. Consequently, this impact may take much work to reverse. This setback could lead to fewer opportunities in higher education, lower participation in the labor market, and lower future earnings. Nonetheless, the future for AE programs and educators remains bright. As reported by the American University School of Education (2019), the Bureau of Labor Statistics (BLS) projects an 8% growth rate for all AE educators between 2016 and 2026. Government funding for AE programs can directly impact the demand for ABE educators. The report also states that according to the National Center for Education Statistics, over two million students drop out of high school each year, and the US ranks 16th in literacy out of 24 countries. These statistics clearly show a need to invest in expanding AE programs nationwide.

Tips for Becoming a Successful Adult Educator in ABE/ESL/Family Literacy

Education is foundational and encompasses a myriad of challenges and possibilities. It is impossible to provide a finite list of knowledge, skills, and abilities required to be a successful adult educator. These are three tips that I have found particularly beneficial.

Complete a Degree Program

I suggest completing a master's-level training program to adopt a working knowledge of adult learning and how to design programs specifically targeted to an audience of adult learners. This level of training can also teach you the various learning objectives, skills, and knowledge required to be an adult basic educator and what career paths are available. A master's degree in AE emphasizing literacy will teach you how to design literacy programs for learners of all ages with diverse abilities. Learning the best practices of literacy education and planning literacy instruction are critical components for an adult educator practicing literacy. Research from GraduateGuide Team (2019) suggests that a master's in adult and continuing education enables you to teach adults beyond high school. Locations for teaching adults include institutions of higher learning, such as community colleges, universities, and technical and trade schools. It also opens the doors to career opportunities within community organizations, human resources development teams, academic admissions, and research groups. The research further contends that depending on your expertise, you can pursue more specialized teaching roles, including adult literacy and GED diploma, vocational instructor, remedial education teacher, TESOL or ESL educator, and community college professor.

Activate Prior Knowledge

Educating a diverse student body has shaped my teaching style and methods. The distinctions between learners were complex and they differed in demographic characteristics, with varying ethnic and racial backgrounds. Some learners, local and international, came from underrepresented communities. There were also differences in academic development, with some students having learning disabilities. As an educator, you can influence your learners' understanding of the material you share and the learning opportunities you present based on their background knowledge. One tip I found helpful in achieving this was focusing on the learners' prior knowledge and experiences. McPherson (2022) shares that this can help ELLs in particular because the knowledge they bring from diverse educational backgrounds can become an asset in the classroom. For example, if you ask learners to write an essay, it is helpful to know their understanding of and experience with essays in their previous learning. However, it is important to note that not all prior experience aids learning. Adult learners may have to unlearn conclusions from earlier experiences before accepting new ideas (Gibson, n.d.).

Storytelling

One sure way for educators to discover what the learner knows is through storytelling. Through storytelling, competencies are acquired in a context and may be more easily interiorized and linked to prior learning and experiences of learners. Stories and storytelling may be made part of adult learning activities for a variety of purposes (*Storytelling to Improve Adult Education*, n.d.). Having taught literacy in all content areas (math, language arts, social studies, science, reading, listening, speaking, and writing), I used this strategy to negotiate the complex dynamics that can arise in a classroom setting. The dynamics ranged from mediating in-class arguments and debates about the subject matter to noticing who remained silent during these discussions. What I found useful, especially with helping learners write an argumentative essay, was to engage in interactive learning activities. As I would tell stories, and as learners would tell or build their own stories, I corrected their spoken grammar for better articulation and grammatical structure for better writing and more precise communication.

Conclusion

In this chapter, it is impossible to convey the full richness of my experience as an adult basic educator. I could not have foreseen from that summer day when I first discovered AE that it would be my life's work. I am grateful for the guidance of mentors and peers and the opportunities to advance professionally throughout my career.

My journey to AE and thoughts on professional qualifications, competencies, theories, and tips for the future are all shared in this bird's eye view. In the context of literacy programs, AE includes GED, HiSET, ESL, and ESOL, among others. Literacy is the gateway to education and learning and gives families access to critical information and communication skills. By committing your life to the field of literacy and language, you will be helping facilitate those benefits for many people.

References

Adult Education Teacher Competencies. (n.d.). LINCS, U.S. Department of Education. https://lincs.ed.gov/state-resources/federal-initiatives/teacher-effectiveness/competencies

American University School of Education. (2019, August 27). *Bridging the skills gap: Becoming an adult education teacher*. https://soeonline.american.edu/blog/adult-education-teacher/

Basarmak, U., & Hamutoglu, N. B. (2020). Developing and validating a comprehensive scale to measure perceived barriers to technology integration. *International Journal of Technology in Education and Science*, 4(1), 53–71.

Boeren, E., Roumell, E. A., & Roessger, K. M. (2020). COVID-19 and the future of adult education: An editorial. *Adult Education Quarterly*, 70(3), 201–204. https://doi.org/10.1177/0741713620925029

Breiseth, L. (2021, November 22). *Working with community organizations to Support ELL students*. Colorín Colorado. www.colorincolorado.org/article/working-community-organizations-support-ell-students

Business-Adult Education Partnerships Toolkit. (n.d.). LINCS, U.S. Department of Education. https://lincs.ed.gov/state-resources/federal-initiatives/business-adult-education-toolkit

College and Career Readiness Standards for Adult Education. (n.d.). LINCS, U.S. Department of Education. https://lincs.ed.gov/professional-development/resource-collections/profile-521

Finn, D. (2011). Principles of adult learning: An ESL context. *Journal of Adult Education*, 40(1), 34–39.

Gibson, C. (n.d.). *Tips for being an effective instructor for adults*. Rent Smart. https://fyi.extension.wisc.edu/rentsmart/for-instructors/tips-for-being-an-effective-instructor-for-adults/

Gouthro, P. A. (2019). Taking time to learn: The importance of theory for adult education. *Adult Education Quarterly*, 69(1), 60–76.

GraduateGuide Team. (2019, April 3). *What can you do with a master's in adult education?* Graduate-Guide.com. https://graduateguide.com/what-can-you-do-with-a-masters-in-adult-education-2/

Hock, M., & Mellard, D. (2005). Reading comprehension strategies for adult literacy outcomes. *Journal of Adolescent & Adult Literacy, 49*(3), 192–200.

All Education Schools. (2022, September 27). *How to become an adult education teacher.* www.alleducationschools.com/teaching-careers/adult-education-teacher/

Kent, A. M., & Giles, R. M. (2017). Preservice teachers' technology self-efficacy. *SRATE Journal, 26*(1), 9–20.

Knowles, M. S., HoltonIII, E. F., & Swanson, R. A. (2014). *The adult learner: The definitive classic in adult education and human resource development.* Routledge.

Kurt, S. (2020, July 11). *Andragogy theory – Malcolm Knowles.* Educational Technology. https://educationaltechnology.net/andragogy-theory-malcolm-knowles/

Montrose. (2015). *TEFL, TESL, TESOL – What's the difference?* GoAbroad.com. www.goabroad.com/articles/tefl-courses/tefl-tesl-tesol-whats-the-difference

McPherson, G. (2022, January 24). *Delivering content to support adult learners – Supporting post-secondary English language learners.* Pressbooks. https://ecampusontario.pressbooks.pub/supportingenglishlanguagelearners/chapter/delivering-content-to-support-adult-learners/

Pickard, A. (2016). WIOA: Implications for low-scoring adult learners. *COABE Journal, 5*(2), 50–55.

Rogers, D. L. (2000). A paradigm shift: Technology integration for higher education in the new millennium. *AACE Review (formerly AACE Journal), 1*(13), 19–33.

Stefanski, A., Valli, L., & Jacobson, R. (2016). Beyond involvement and engagement: The role of the family in school-community partnerships. *School Community Journal, 26*(2), 135–160.

Storytelling to Improve Adult Education. (n.d.). EPALE – European Commission. https://epale.ec.europa.eu/en/resource-centre/content/storytelling-improve-adult-education

TEAL Center Fact Sheet No. 11: Adult Learning Theories. (n.d.). LINCS, U.S. Department of Education. https://lincs.ed.gov/state-resources/federal-initiatives/teal/guide/adultlearning

Vargo, D., Zhu, L., Benwell, B., & Yan, Z. (2021). Digital technology use during COVID19 pandemic: A rapid review. *Human Behavior & Emerging Technology, 3*, 13–24. https://doi.org/10.1002/hbe2.242

Chapter 8

Adult Environmental Education

Wendy Griswold

Overview of Adult Environmental Education

This section defines adult environmental education (AEE), acknowledges its theoretical roots and philosophical approaches, and provides a brief history. AEE is a process of supporting marginalized people and communities in addressing the myriad environmental injustices they increasingly face (Clover, 2003; Haugen, 2006). Although generally used as a definition of sustainability education, Meadows et al.'s (1992) conception of learning that helps people "to be far-seeing enough, flexible enough, and wise enough to contribute to the regenerative capacity of the physical and social systems upon which they depend" (p. 209) strongly resonates both with my AEE experiences and other adult environmental educators' conceptions. For example, Clover (2003) synthesized the common key characteristics of AEE to include:

- making explicit links between the environment, society, economics, politics, and culture.
- utilizing an engaged and participatory learning process not limited to individual behavior change and information transmission.
- focusing on root causes and critical questioning of market/consumer-driven capitalism and globalization; and
- learning that is community oriented and contextually shaped.

Sumner (2003) defines AEE as "a hybrid outgrowth of the environmental movement and adult education, combining an ecological orientation with a learning paradigm to provide a vigorous educational approach to environmental concerns" (p. 41). From these definitions, we can see glimpses of AEE's original theoretical roots.

AEE draws on adult learning theory in addition to feminist, popular education, and nonformal education to inform both theory and practice (Haugen, 2006). The connection between these is that they center the voices and meaning-making of marginalized people and communities. In addition, Walter (2009, 2021) provides a typology of AEE philosophical approaches, connecting them to liberal, progressive, behaviorist, humanistic, and radical thought and action. These theoretical and philosophical underpinnings are visible in the following historical overview.

Historical Overview

Haugen (2010) provides an historical overview of AEE, beginning with its emergence in the 1970s through the 2000s. In the 1970s, the field emphasized individual behavior change to address environmental problems. In the late 1980s, sustainable development moved into the foreground with a focus on improving the quality of life in developing countries. In the 1990s,

DOI: 10.4324/9781003259602-11

the focus on sustainable development continued with a shift toward a global context and questioning humanity's relationship with the earth. Involving the general public as active participants in making change began to be emphasized. This was also the decade that UNESCO, the United Nations Educational, Scientific and Cultural Organization (focused on international cooperation in education, arts, sciences, and culture) first recognized AEE as a distinct body of knowledge. In the 2000s, AEE was defined "not as top-down, monological learning, but rather as a dialogical, community-based approach to finding answers for environmental problems" (Haugen, 2010, para. 31) with transformation, experiential learning, and social movements as key theoretical and practice-based approaches. Adult environmental educators acknowledged that environmental problems are the result of intersecting social/ political, economic, and cultural behaviors and values, with public activism the necessary antidote. The 2010s, according to Walter (2021), saw an evolution from the 2000s with the emergence of critical place-based education (Greenwood, 2014), land-based education (Tuck et al., 2014), and ecojustice adult education (Dentith & Griswold, 2017).

My Career Path

Like many adult educators, I practiced adult education for years before I "discovered" the field. This discovery allowed me to enhance my intuitive practice with research-based theories and practices and to enhance my career skills. I began my adult education career as an administrative program associate for an environmental research studies center at a tribal college. This led to a program manager position (ultimately an education coordinator post-doctorate) at a Research 1 university where I worked directly with communities addressing hazardous waste sites impacting environmental and human health. I also developed and administered international exchange programs for Indigenous scholars in the United States and Russia focused on shared environmental concerns. These experiences were interwoven with earning a doctorate in adult education, allowing me to utilize my formal learning in my work and reflect upon my work experience while learning about adult education.

My professional career in AEE began at Haskell Indian Nations University (Haskell). Being interested in environmental issues, I applied for an administrative assistant job at the Haskell Environmental Research Studies Center (HERS). The job was assisting a program manager from Kansas State University (K-State) in running the NAOMI (Native American and Other Minority Institutions) program. Its purpose was to provide faculty and learners from tribal and other minority institutions with opportunities to participate in research on hazardous substances, which impact many marginalized communities. We developed educational programming on tribal environmental issues and coordinated research fellowships for faculty and learners from NAOMIs at research institutions where the U.S. Environmental Protection Agency (EPA) was funding hazardous substance research.

I worked with the NAOMI program for about 5 years, with a promotion to project manager after 6 months. We obtained additional AEE grants, and I became more involved in non-HERS work for K-State. This is where I began collaborating directly with communities. This involved CAGs (Citizen Action Groups), which were groups of local people living in communities impacted by Superfund sites on the National Priorities List (NPL) (U.S. EPA., n.d.). Superfund sites are the places in the U.S. with the worst levels of hazardous substance contamination. Our goal was to help residents understand the science and technology related to contamination and its cleanup, so they could weigh in on the EPA's remediation plans. We provided technical assistance and education to equip CAG members to interface with the EPA, state regulators, and consultants; understand and make meaning of highly technical and scientific reports and presentations; and make decisions and recommendations about cleanup processes impacting their community.

In the mid- to late 1990s, addressing brownfields became a federal priority, leading to the Technical Assistance to Brownfields (TAB) Program (U.S. EPA., 2022). Brownfields are sites such as former dry cleaners, gas stations, etc., where concerns about potential environmental contamination prevent their re-use. Brownfields programs work to address the blight affecting many communities. TAB was similar to CAGs. We helped build community capacity to engage on a more equal footing with the other players in the redevelopment process (e.g., regulators, property owners, real estate developers). During this time, I began to recognize the larger work we were doing. We were helping people engage in the democratic process at a very local level. Community engagement and involvement was sought to help local governments make redevelopment decisions serving community needs identified by community members impacted by brownfield sites. We were helping people access their power and agency as Americans to shape their communities. This work also provided my first opportunity to dive deeply into participatory processes.

In parallel with TAB, I began working in the Altai Republic, Russian Federation. This opportunity came through HERS, where I met a biologist with experience in the U.S./Russian scientific exchanges following the USSR's collapse. We wrote a successful grant to the U.S. Agency for International Development, which administers civilian foreign aid and development assistance. This launched a 10-year collaboration with Gorno Altaisk State University, involving exchanges for university faculty and learners in Kansas and Altai. During one of these trips, I decided to pursue my doctorate, which led me to the academic field of adult education.

From the first meeting of my first course, adult education felt like home to me. We sat in a circle. Learners' experiences were primary, respected, and integrated into the learning process. Pursuing that degree infused my work with more energy. My work became more interesting to me because more of it became visible. I began to recognize the experiences of community members as learning. I learned theories that explained what I was doing and experiencing in the field. The work touched people's lives in significant and meaningful ways. It was work worth doing. It made a difference. All of us could grow and learn together. Even when it did not reach its tangible goals, it was still worthwhile. It still made us all stronger, wiser, better.

My adult education degree helped me in many ways. It provided me with budding research skills, leading to my involvement in different research projects at K-State. This culminated in my serving as the lead principal investigator of Shared Air/Shared Action, a community-based participatory action research project focused on building community environmental organization capacity to monitor local air quality using low-cost sensors. I submitted the project proposal as an educational coordinator at K-State and began the project as an assistant professor at the University of Memphis.

Valued Skills in Varied Contexts

To identify highly valued adult education skills and adult learning theories and practices applicable to AEE, I sought the insight of three colleagues. Skills identified were program evaluation (Chapter 5) and planning (Chapter 4), creating effective learning environments, intercultural competence (Chapter 14), knowledge of adult development theories, designing learner-centered approaches, popular education strategies, and relationship building. These skills are discussed in detail below. In Chapter 1 of this volume, their connections to the Standards for Graduate Programs in Adult Education are discussed (Commission of Professors of Adult Education [CPAE], 2014).

"A Perfect Synergy": Technical Assistance to Brownfields

According to Blase Leven, K-State TAB Programs Director, and a geologist, having an adult educator on a technical assistance team was useful in two significant ways. First, it brought credibility to our outreach and education efforts. Increasingly, funders are expecting increased accountability and effectiveness. K-State TAB developed an evaluation program to document knowledge and perspective changes participants experienced (Daffron & Caffarella, 2021). While the technical assistance team embodied many kinds of expertise (e.g., engineering, environmental science, economic development, planning, etc.) to provide a variety of non-formal learning activities (Ross-Gordon et al., 2017), I was the only social scientist. I also had knowledge of Institutional Review Board (IRB) procedures, ensuring that research with human subjects was conducted in alignment with IRB and institutional procedures.

> No one else had a background or training in education or social science research, so a formally trained adult educator filled a skills gap. Specifically, Blase (personal communication, February 11, 2022) shared that, "the use of actual legitimate and credible procedures ... based on your adult education background and degree ... helped us be super organized [in a] very straightforward manner."

Second, I incorporated adult learning theory and practice into technical assistance programming. Drawing on the assumptions and process elements of andragogy (Knowles, 1985), I incorporated learners' experiences, readiness to learn, and their problem-centered orientation to create learning environments and activities tailored to adult learners. Our day-long workshops evolved from successive talking heads and PowerPoint presentations to interactive, learner-focused events. Blase (personal communication, February 11, 2022) recalled:

> grant writing workshops ... where we would do small group work to review proposals with some breaks [so] people could reflect on what they've done or heard and share what they're thinking ... in a group ... [It was] a nice interpersonal format ... where the ... attendees ... participated in co-learning and interacting.

The goal of these changes was to create more effective learning environments, which I learned in my adult education coursework. Blase (personal communication, February 11, 2022) described the impact of these changes as "help[ing] us slow down and ... do things more deliberately, allow[ing] time for it to sink in and ... be internalized with the attendees and even help them do that by interacting with each other and with the group [in] different ways." Blase and I have worked together for over 25 years, so he can offer his perspective both before and after my adult education degree. When asked how my degree changed me, he shared that he noticed an increased sense of purpose in my work. He also gained an appreciation for the relevance of adult education to our work.

> It's super relevant to what we do. And it became more and more relevant ... because of the way our center's mission migrated from a research audience to a multistakeholder [audience that] includes non-technical adults ... It was ... a perfect synergy.
> (personal communication, February 11, 2022)

Altering Educational Trajectories: International Exchanges

Having an adult educator as a collaborator in international AEE was also valuable. In this work, I partnered with Cynthia Annett, a biology professor. Cynthia acknowledged that I helped her to understand how to work with adult learners. "I never really thought about the difference between pedagogy and learning in an adult context, which is kind of strange, because I'm a university professor and I teach adults" (personal communication, March 21, 2022). Although this was an exchange program for learners and faculty focused on community water quality, Cynthia had a larger vision for the work, which aligned with my learning about intercultural competence and transformative learning (King et al., 2021).

> I wanted it to be something that would help [develop] worldviews, to give people this larger experience. But I never had a concept of that being within an educational framework ... What you helped me to do was to think about how the experiences were shaping the learning goals of the students, because I think we could see that essentially every student in the program had their educational trajectories at least somewhat altered.
> (C. Annett, personal communication, March 21, 2022)

Specifically, Cynthia (personal communication, March 21, 2022) credits my developing knowledge of adult education with:

> convinc[ing] us that everybody was bringing something to [the experience]. You taught me that the adult brain ... has opinions and life experiences, and you're not just pouring things in the ear ... That was very helpful in terms of getting us to lighten up, and to trust that something was going to happen.

Again, I was drawing on my growing understanding of andragogy as well as a variety of adult development theories (King & Kitchner, 1994; Mezirow, 1991).

Aside from student learning experiences, Cynthia found an adult educator useful in program planning. Developing a respectful partnership, which included elevating our Russian colleagues to full partners, was essential to the success of the program (Cervero & Wilson, 1994). Key to our partnership was building trust with Russians not far removed from their Soviet history and infrastructures.

> Interculturally navigating a trusting environment has got to be one of the most difficult things ... Even though you had the unenviable task ... of figuring out how things would be administered, which didn't always fit within the Russian system, you were able to engender enough trust that the Russian bureaucrats [were] able to trust that ... we were doing it in a way that was going to lead to good outcomes for everybody ... That level of trust, sometimes it's very, very difficult to create ... [In] the post-Soviet environment in Siberia, especially after the incredibly difficult 1990s, trust didn't come easily.
> (C. Annett, personal communication, March 21, 2022)

Like Blase, Cynthia knew me before and after my adult education degree. Her take on how it benefited me was similar to Blase's. She said:

> [it gave] you confidence in the things that you were doing ... In your case, your PhD validated things that are very deeply internal to you [and] your lived experience. You had many, many years as a professional [before]. It's kind of like you developed a theory in your mind, and then it was validated, and you then have the words to describe it.
> (C. Annett, personal communication, March 21, 2022)

"Folks Aren't Falling for the Same Old, Same Old": Community Air Monitoring

When engaging with communities learning about local air quality monitoring, being an adult educator skilled in applying popular education principles (Horton, 1998) is essential to successful outcomes. These principles are equitable relationships between facilitators and participants, addressing group/community identified needs, participant involvement in program design, and valuing community wisdom. When discussing our Shared Air/Shared Action work, Kim Wasserman, Executive Director of Little Village Environmental Justice Organization (LVEJO), communicated that our mutual alignment around educational values and processes was a key factor in our lasting relationship. "One of the most important things that folks don't get is it's not just a question ... project needs. It's a question of alignment on values and principles and accountability that make-or-break relationships" (K. Wasserman, personal communication, February 11, 2022).

Learning to create relationships was an outcome of the intersection of my professional experiences and adult education coursework. I was able to enter the space already in alignment with community partners. This ability to form a respectful partnership allowed for learning and project outcomes different from partners' past experiences. Kim (personal communication, February 11, 2022) shared that "we have so many folks who come to us just for the transactional purposes of a relationship. And I feel like our relationship is not based on that. Our relationship is based on transformation." Further, we created a learner-centered environment that valued the experiences and knowledge everyone brought (Vella, 2002). One of my goals was to create a space where holders of community and technical/scientific knowledge would both be valued and see their contributions as necessary and meaningful (Corburn, 2005). According to Kim (personal communication, February 11, 2022), initially the community partners:

> were very self-doubtful about our capacity ... in ... air monitoring ... And it's so funny because we do popular education, we talk about leadership development. But even as organizers every now and then we need to be reminded that we are the experts of our neighborhoods, that we do know what we're doing, that this ... is not new to us. It was incredibly empowering ... to be part of that project and see [we] could do this work, that ... [we] are the experts.

In addition to creating a learner-centered environment, I focused on relationships between project partners/learners (Vella, 2002), which provided community partners with a model for future relationships with external partners. Kim shared that this focus had beneficial outcomes.

> I fundamentally believe the process we went through is ... why folks not only have been able to talk about air quality but are interested in the continuation of air quality projects ... They're looking for that in anybody who approaches them ... Folks aren't just falling for the same old, same old. Folks are looking for key words and key things that they know ... they require to have a successful relationship. That would have never happened without [Shared Air/Shared Action].
>
> (K. Wasserman, personal communication, February 11, 2022)

Every learning experience has outcomes and for Shared Air/Shared Action community partners, key outcomes included their ability to engage with government and businesses concerning local air quality threats. Kim shared the following about LVEJO's ability to respond to a botched smokestack implosion in April 2020 (Peña, 2020):

[Shared Air/Shared Action] accelerated the conversation on air quality in Chicago. That project fundamentally empowered us to be able to speak to air quality issues in a way that we hadn't before and allowed us to really push the envelope. We would have never ... been as strong on the scientific portion of the Hilco implosion had it not been for this project.

(K. Wasserman, personal communication, February 11, 2022)

While equipping and empowering a community organization to defend itself against outside interests and threats is a goal of AEE (Clover, 2003), Kim reminds us that the processes used are also very important considerations.

> It's not just about having people participate; it's how we approach them in participating. It's how they feel in participating that will make or break the outcomes ... More importantly, make or break their experience in working with us. And that ultimately ... is equally as important, if not more important than the outcomes of the project.
> (K. Wasserman, personal communication, February 11, 2022)

Future Directions

My view of AEE's future is that it will continue its evolution into supporting marginalized people and communities in efforts to address all forms of injustice, not solely environmental. When I began my professional career in the 1990s, I identified as an adult environmental educator and that truly was the work I was doing, helping communities address environmental issues devoid of any critique or consciousness of the how and why these issues emerged. As the concept of sustainable development emerged, my focus shifted to adult sustainability education. This represented not only a shift in vocabulary, but a shift in who and what I was serving. I, like other adult environmental educators (Haugen, 2010; Walter, 2021), began paying attention to how our social/political, economic, and natural systems intersect to create and perpetuate the oppression, marginalization, and destruction of humans and the world upon which we depend.

A shift in the field is happening with respect to terminology and practice. Education for Sustainability (EfS) is replacing AEE. In practical terms, this shift allows us to undertake teaching and learning that makes explicit connections between the environment, society, and economics, with an expanded focus on equity and inclusion, of which EfS is in great need (Leach et al., 2018). This allows for equal concern and acknowledgement of the intersections of environmental, social/political, and economic inequity that are increasingly having disastrous impacts on humanity and the planet. This is crucial work to take on and adult educators are well equipped to serve society in this manner.

We need to emphasize the learning possibilities presented by everyday life. Not limited by the mundane, the everyday reaches from our families through our communities and nations into world society (Kalekin-Fishman, 2013). We need to connect the global concerns of social/political, economic, and environmental inequity and their implications for everyday life, making explicit how they play out in our individual lives and the lives of our communities. To become a sustainable planet, we need the human population to learn about sustainability throughout their lives and in all aspects of their lives (UNESCO, 2015). We also must communicate and demonstrate that change is possible, and that we have reasons to be hopeful. (Griswold, 2017, 2022).

The current and future role of adult educators working in this realm relate directly to our skills at creating learning environments and respectful relationships with and among learners.

We can be very useful in facilitating equitable interactions and activities that bring diverse groups of learners/stakeholders together to define mutual problems and devise solutions to our current and future problems. *This is the only way to ensure that emerging solutions are solutions for all of us, not just some of us.* We need to help community organizations and area experts (e.g., scientists, engineers, architects, economists), agricultural producers and regulators, and climate justice groups and the Big Greens (e.g., Environmental Defense Fund, Natural Resources Defense Council, Sierra Club) work equitably and productively, rather than continue historically extractive partnerships. We do this by relying on participatory strategies from popular (Horton, 1998) and dialog education (Vella, 2002). What my experience and AEE's history show is a decreasing emphasis on transmitting knowledge about the environment and an increase in engaging adults in learning how to advocate for changes impacting their own lives, their families, their communities, and the entire world.

Resources

Below are resources to learn more about AAE/EfS. They include organizations and suggested reading.

Organizations and Agencies

These organizations are locations to search for jobs, connect with others working in AEE/EfS, and learn more about current education efforts focused on the environment, justice, and inclusion:

- The mission of the North American Association for Environmental Education (https://naaee.org/) is accelerating environmental literacy and civic engagement to create a more sustainable future. They host an annual conference. Search for state-level environmental education associations to target specific states.
- The Climate Justice Alliance (https://climatejusticealliance.org/) is a nationwide network of organizations working toward a just transition from the extractive economy harming people and ecosystems. They have a newsletter and job and involvement opportunities.
- The Movement Generation Justice and Ecology Project (https://movementgeneration.org) inspires and engages in transformative action towards the liberation and restoration of land, labor, and culture. They provide curriculum tools and a critical framework for just recovery.
- The U.S. Climate Action Network (www.usclimatenetwork.org) facilitates trust and alignments among members to justly and equitably fight climate change. They also provide grant funding to support grassroots organizing efforts.

Aside from organizations, many federal and state agencies provide AEE programming, conferences, and grant programs. Agencies to target include the U.S. Environmental Protection Agency (www.epa.gov), NASA (www.nasa.gov), the National Park Service (www.nps.gov), and the U.S. Department of Agriculture (www.usda.gov). To search for federal level jobs, visit www.usajobs.gov. At the state level, target departments of environmental quality and health, state, and local extension offices, and university research centers.

Suggested Readings

The Long Haul by Myles Horton (1998) and *Learning to Listen, Learning to Teach: The Power of Dialogue in Educating Adults* by Jane Vella (2002) are recommended texts for learning

AEE/EfS. While these are not specific to environmental education, they are specific to the processes and techniques that educators working in AAE/EfS need to use. Following Horton and Vella's practical and sage advice has served me well.

> **Pro-Tips**
>
> 1. You do not need to be an expert on environmental issues. The expertise an adult educator brings is adult learning theory and practice. Your role is to infuse our field's knowledge and processes into the content knowledge your collaborators bring.
> 2. You need to be flexible and patient. When working with community organizations, build trust and alignment by letting them take the lead. When working with environmental or other content experts, your ideas may encounter resistance. Taking things slowly with all partners and meeting them where they are is key to moving forward together.
> 3. Volunteering is an effective way to learn more and develop your skills. It allows you to learn about an organization and for them to learn about you. Networking can lead to future job opportunities.

References

Cervero, R. M., & Wilson, A. L. (1994). *Planning responsibly for adult education: A guide to negotiating power and interests.* Jossey-Bass.

Clover, D. E. (2003). Environmental adult education: Critique and creativity in a globalizing world. *New Directions for Adult and Continuing Education, 99*, 89–95. https://doi.org/10.1002/ace.113

Commission of Professors of Adult Education (CPAE). (2014). *Standards for graduate programs in adult education.* American Association for Adult and Continuing Education. www.aaace.org/page/CPAEStandards

Corburn, J. (2005). *Street science: Community knowledge and environmental health justice.* The MIT Press.

Daffron, S. R., & Caffarella, R. S. (2021). *Planning programs for adult learners* (4th ed.). Jossey-Bass.

Dentith, A. M., & Griswold, W. (2017). Editors' notes. *New Directions for Adult and Continuing Education, 153*, 5–6. https://doi.org/10.1002/ace.20216

Greenwood, D. A. (2014). Culture, environment, and education in the Anthropocene. In M. P. Mueller, D. J. Tippins, & A. J. Stewart (Eds.), *Assessing schools for Generation R (responsibility)* (pp. 279–292). Springer.

Griswold, W. (2017). Sustainability, ecojustice, and adult education. *New Directions for Adult and Continuing Education, 153*, 7–15. https://doi.org/10.1002/ace.20217

Griswold, W. (2022). 'We can't wait anymore': Young professionals engaging in education for sustainability. *Adult Education Quarterly, 72*(2), 197–215. https://doi.org/10.1177/07417136211044153

Haugen, C. S. (2006). Environmental adult educator training: Suggestions for effective practice. *Convergence, 39*(4), 94–106.

Haugen, C. S. (2010). Adult learners and the environment in the last century: An historical analysis of environmental adult education literature. *Electronic Green Journal, 29*. https://escholarship.org/uc/item/8kw8q39h

Horton, M. (1998). *The long haul: An autobiography.* Teachers College Press.

Kalekin-Fishman, D. (2013). Sociology of everyday life. *Current Sociology Review, 61*(5–6), 714–732. https://doi.org/10.1177/0011392113482112

King, K. M., Dixon, K. V., González-Carriedo, R., & Dixon-Krauss, L. (2021). Transformation and cross-cultural adaptation of teacher candidates in an international teaching program. *Journal of Transformative Education, 20*(2), 138–158. https://doi.org/10.1177/15413446211028564

King, P. M., & Kitchner, K. S. (1994). *Developing reflective judgment.* Jossey-Bass.

Knowles, M. S. (1985). *Andragogy in action: Applying modern principles of adult learning.* Jossey-Bass.

Leach, M., Reyers, B., Bai, X., Brondizio, E. S., Cook, C., Diaz, S., Espindola, G., Scobie, M., Stafford-Smith, M., & Subramanian, S. (2018). Equity and sustainability in the Anthropocene: A social–ecological systems perspective on their intertwined futures. *Global Sustainability*, *1*(e13), 1–13. https://doi.org/10.1017/sus.2018.12

Meadows, D. H., Meadows, D. L., & Randers, J. (1992). *Beyond the limits: Global collapse or a sustainable future*. Earthscan.

Mezirow, J. (1991). *Transformative dimensions of adult learning*. Jossey-Bass.

Peña, M. (2020, April 11). *Dust cloud envelopes Little Village after smokestack demolition: 'My lungs started hurting'*. Block Club Chicago. https://blockclubchicago.org/2020/04/11/dust-cloud-falls-onto-little-village-from-smokestack-demolition-that-was-carried-out-despite-coronavirus-pandemic/

Ross-Gordon, J. M., Rose, A. D., & Kasworm, C. E. (2017). *Foundations of adult and continuing education*. Jossey-Bass.

Sumner, J. (2003). Environmental adult education and community sustainability. *New Directions for Adult and Continuing Education*, *99*, 39–45. https://doi.org/10.1002/ace.108

Tuck, E., McKenzie, M., & McCoy, K. (2014). Land education: Indigenous, post-colonial, and decolonizing perspectives on place and environmental education research. *Environmental Education Research*, *20*(1), 1–24. https://doi.org/10.1080/13504622.2013.877708

UNESCO (2015). *Rethinking education: Towards a global common good?* UNESCO Publishing. https://unevoc.unesco.org/e-forum/RethinkingEducation.pdf

U.S. EPA. (n.d.). *Superfund*. www.epa.gov/superfund

U.S. EPA. (2022, March 23). *Brownfields technical assistance, training and research*. www.epa.gov/brownfields/brownfields-technical-assistance-training-and-research

Vella, J. (2002). *Learning to listen, learning to teach: The power of dialogue in educating adults* (rev. ed.). Jossey-Bass.

Walter, P. (2009). Philosophies of adult environmental education. *Adult Education Quarterly*, *60*(1), 3–25. https://doi.org/10.1177/0741713609336109

Walter, P. (2021). Adult environmental education. In T. S. Rocco, M. C. Smith, R. C. Mizzi, L. R. Merriweather, & J. D. Hawley (Eds.), *The handbook of adult and continuing education* (pp. 314–321). Stylus.

Chapter 9

Community-Based Adult Education

Hleziphi Naomie Nyanungo

Practicing Community Education

Like most adult educators, I did not know that adult education was an academic field, and I certainly did not dream of being an adult educator when I grew up. However, I was familiar with the practice but did not know that it had a name. This is a familiar story for adult educators, and perhaps even more so for community educators. I was researching graduate programs in community development a few years after graduating from college when I stumbled across adult education as an academic field. Things fell into place for me when I came across community education as a component of progressive approaches to community development while reading about the philosophy of Julius Nyerere, the former president of Tanzania. Nyerere was affectionately known as "*Mwalimu*" (teacher in Swahili) because of his dedication to lifelong learning (Mhina & Abdi, 2009). The idea of using education to help communities enhance their capacity to address issues in their locality and transform their circumstances resonated with me. That informed my decision to apply to graduate programs in adult education instead of community development.

As a new graduate student in my adult education program, my professors asked why I wanted to focus on community education instead of something like workforce education or human resource development. The question made sense because the two degrees I had at that point were in business-related fields and so, on the surface, appeared better aligned to workforce education. My answer then (and now) is that I want to work with people and organizations engaged in efforts to transform place-based communities. Guided by a commitment to meaningful social change, I chose to focus on community education because of the promise and potential it presents to disrupt oppressive social structures in our world. I graduated with an adult education degree with a community education concentration many years ago and have been able to build a career that has featured community education in various contexts.

This chapter explores what a career in community education may look like. I start the chapter by sharing a little about how my own career has developed and my orientation to community education. This will be followed by a discussion of the competencies that I have found to be core to the practice of community education. In the concluding section of the chapter, I offer suggestions for seeking and/or creating job opportunities to practice community education.

A Career Featuring Community Education

My academic training as an adult educator with a community education focus has opened doors for me in different settings. What follows is a brief tour of my career to give you a sense of the variety of ways that my community education specialization is featured. My first job after

DOI: 10.4324/9781003259602-12

completing graduate school was a faculty position where I primarily taught courses to graduate students working in education and nonprofit settings. I was able to draw on my background in community education to design courses that helped students make connections between course content and real-world applications. For example, I developed and taught a course on youth development. My students and I connected with the community-based organizations engaged in youth development in that locality and developed mutually beneficial relationships where the class would do projects that supported the organizations in meeting their goals, while the class benefited from contextualized, on-the-ground experiences. In my faculty role, I also had the opportunity to plan, organize, and coordinate professional development opportunities to enhance skills of community-based practitioners. Furthermore, because of my interest and background in community education, I was invited to lead an initiative to establish a university-wide structure for facilitating community-based learning at that institution. I even had the opportunity to participate in collaborative community-based research projects with colleagues from other disciplines.

For a period of time, I worked outside academia in the public service sector. Working in the office of adult education, a city agency, I contributed to coordinating education services for adult learners and supporting practitioners and organizations providing adult education in a large metropolitan city. The office ran programs to build the capacity of individuals and organizations to deliver quality and coordinated educational activities for adults who faced barriers of literacy, language, and digital.

The next phase of my career was returning to higher education where I currently work in an academic administrative role as a faculty/educational developer in a teaching and learning center. When I was going through the application process for this job, I was asked the question: What unique contribution do you think you would bring to this job? My answer to this question was community education. Note, the job description said nothing about community education, but I highlighted it because I saw the potential value it presented for the position. Looking back at that application process, I think that my training and background in adult education qualified me for the job, but it was my interest and experience in community education (among other things) that gave me an edge as a candidate. I am now in a position where I draw on my community education knowledge and experience to promote and support faculty members who are interested and involved in community-based learning to make meaningful and mutually beneficial relationships with community partners. I also draw on my skills and knowledge of community education to cultivate and support faculty learning communities.

This brief tour of my career path demonstrates the versatility of community education. Essentially, wherever I go, whatever my role, I take community education with me. The perspective that I get from community education has been an asset in the development of my career as an educator. I see myself more as an adult educator with a specialization in community education, rather than a community educator. For me, this is an important distinction in that community education does not define my role but refers to my specific skill set, professional interests, and orientation to my work.

Community Education in Practice?

It is hard to provide a clear and concise definition of community education because the term is used in many ways. Some use the term as a reference to the site where educational activity is taking place (education *in* community) (Connolly, 2010). It could be used to refer to the intended participants or audience of an educational activity (education *for* community) (Mello & Braga, 2018). Community education may also refer to planning and/or delivery of programs (education *of/with* community) (Archibald, 2018; Brookfield, 1983). Complicating things further are the many related terms used in adult education literature, which include community action, emancipatory education, popular education, and so forth. For the purposes of this chapter, my definition and orientation to community education is based on critical pedagogy. In a keynote address delivered at an adult education association annual meeting, Phyllis Cunningham (1993) defined critical pedagogy as "the educational action which develops the ability of a group to critically reflect on their environment and to develop strategies to bring about democratic social change in that environment" (p. 8). Drawing on this definition, community education as used in this chapter refers to educational action which develops the ability of a group to critically reflect on their *community* (however defined) and to develop strategies to bring about democratic social change in that *community*. The practice of community education involves supporting individuals, groups, and organizations to critically reflect on existing circumstances, guiding them to articulate future aspirations to work toward, and identifying, planning, and delivering educational activities to facilitate the desired change.

The excerpt below from an address delivered by Michael Newman (1993) is an illustrative encapsulation of the practice of community education as organizing educational activities to build the capacity of individuals, groups, and organizations.

> When, a long time ago, I worked as a community education worker in inner London, people constantly asked me: "But what do you teach?" I would reply that I did not actually teach but that I organised educational activities for people in the local community. "What kind of activities?" they would ask. "Things like a series of meetings on welfare rights or an arts and crafts workshop for mothers and babies," I would reply. "Oh, you teach art," they would say. Back home in Australia I worked as a trainer in the trade union movement – labour educator, you call them here – and designed programs on recruiting, organising workplaces, running meetings, speaking effectively, campaigning, and negotiating. I remember one person looking in horror at me and saying: "You don't actually teach them to do that, do you?" And when I fetched up in a university educating adult educators and people asked me what I did, I would reply: "I am a university lecturer." "Oh," they would say, "and what do you teach?" "I teach adult education." "No, I meant, what is your subject?" "I educate adult educators." "Yes, but you must have a subject like history, or maths, or science, or English literature?" "I teach people about the processes of learning and organising learning." "Yes, of course you do," they would say, "but what do you teach?"

As implied in this excerpt, the ability to organize educational activities is the defining element of community education practice.

> Planning, designing, and facilitating educational activities to build capacity is at the core of community education practice.

In the next section of the chapter, I unpack these competencies in more detail.

Core Competencies for Practicing Community Education

As I discuss the competencies and skills that are core to the practice of community education, I will be sharing some ways in which I have developed and/or strengthened these competencies for myself. In sharing my journey of career development, I am not suggesting that this is THE path that everyone should take. I urge anyone interested in making a career that involves community education to find their own path or, even better, create a unique path for themselves. My hope is that my experiences will inspire you to figure out that path for yourself.

After identifying and analyzing a long list of skills and competencies that are essential to the practice of community education, three categories or skill sets have emerged. They are (a) skills for facilitating productive dialogue; (b) skills for designing, planning, and delivering educational programs; and (c) project management skills.

Facilitating Productive Dialogue

Dialogue starts with listening as this is the foundation of facilitating respectful dialogue. An example of this is a program that I was involved in when I worked in the Office of Adult Education. The office convened regular meetings to which community partners were invited to attend. I was responsible for planning and organizing these meetings. After a couple of poorly attended meetings shortly after I took on this role, I decided to visit each of our community partners. My initial thought was just to go and introduce myself to our partners so they would know who was inviting them to the meeting and figure out why they were not coming to the meetings. It turned out that in addition to the introductions, an even more important purpose for these visits was for me to listen. Listening to the partners allowed me to learn about them and their programs and it went a long way to building trust between us. I visited all the partners before I convened the next meeting. When the next meeting was scheduled, it had an agenda that was informed by the concerns and interest of partners that I had learned from listening to them. The meetings ultimately became a space for dialogue around common interests and concerns among partners. Based on this dialogue, my team and I were then able to develop resources and programs to build capacity based on the expressed and demonstrated needs of the community partners.

My sense is that adult educators are generally skilled facilitators of dialogue (see Chapter 3) and take it for granted. We do not highlight it enough as a core skill in our work. For the practice of community education, this is an essential aspect of the work in any context.

> Productive dialogue can only take place in a context where there is mutual respect and trust. The ability to build and sustain relationships is therefore critical to community education.

People are reluctant to work with someone they do not know and trust. My approach to facilitation is greatly influenced by participatory and learner-centered approaches to teaching that I was introduced to in my graduate work.

Designing, Planning, and Delivering Programs

I do not think it is a stretch to say that most practices of adult education involve program planning. Program planning involves assessing learning needs, identifying resources, planning programming, and evaluating programs (Daffron & Caffarella, 2021). For additional information on program planning, see Chapter 4. What makes this a core competence for practicing community education? I refer you to Michael Newman's (1993) description of his work a few sections ago. Each of the jobs he described involved designing, planning, coordinating, and delivering programs *with* participants. I have found adult learning theories and strategies to be helpful when thinking about the purpose of the educational activity and figuring out learning strategies for meeting the goals of the educational activity. Research skills that include data collection, analysis, and synthesis of information to share with specific audiences come in handy here too.

Initiatives that employ community education practices typically involve multiple players (individuals, groups, and organizations) who may have differing and sometimes conflicting viewpoints about what is happening in a given situation and what needs to happen to resolve issues and concerns in that situation. Practicing community education requires one to be attuned to power dynamics when designing and planning programs (Cervero & Wilson, 2006). An example that comes to mind here is of initiatives to enhance the capacity of individuals and groups to practice equitable or anti-racist teaching practices. Think of the varied opinions and agendas involved in that work in any given context. Who is supporting this work? Who is against it? What are the interests and agendas being negotiated in decisions about if and how to plan and deliver such programs? Who benefits from it and how? I am sure that adult educators who may be working in initiatives to promote and support diversity, equity, inclusion, and justice (DEIJ) are familiar with the tensions and dynamics in this work. In this regard, I have found theories of community organizing (Brager et al., 1987; Horton & Freire, 1990), community capacity building (Chaskin, 2001), and asset-based community development (Kretzmann & McKnight, 1996; Mathie & Cunningham, 2003) to be especially instructive to analyzing and negotiating contextual dynamics related to power, interests, and resources.

Project Management

In my practice of community education, I have come to appreciate project management as an important skill set for any initiative where the goal is to bring about change. While building the capacity of individuals and groups, we may find ourselves in situations where we are shepherding multiple projects to fruition. Managing projects includes skills such as formulating and communicating strategies, monitoring and evaluating progress, sourcing and allocating resources, communicating with multiple stakeholders, and providing strategic leadership.

Finally, there is one additional category that does not quite fit in the three above. This is a category that has to do with one's attitude towards community education practice.

> Working in community education requires patience and humility.

Change does not happen according to plans (no matter how good the plans are) and many of the variables that contribute to desired change are beyond the control of the community educator. What keeps me going is maintaining a sense of curiosity about the world and staying optimistic and hopeful for what is possible. To this end, I have found connections with friends and colleagues who share similar values and interests to be indispensable. Now that we have discussed core competencies for this work, we move on to the next section of the chapter: finding opportunities to practice community education.

Finding Opportunities

As I was writing this chapter, I decided to take a quick look at what jobs popped up when I used "community education" as the search tag on *www.Indeed.com*, a job search site. The jobs that I saw listed made mention of "community engagement" or "community outreach" but not "community education," especially as discussed in this chapter. I am not surprised by this. I have learned through my experiences that sometimes employers do not even know they need a community education expert until we show up and explain it to them. For instance, I was once offered a job for a position overseeing an apprenticeship program. The description of the position made no mention of community education as a required or desired competence. However, in my application and interviews I explained how the practice of community education could help the organization successfully meet their goals while also contributing to increasing equity in this arena. It was clear to me that the people who drafted the job specification did not think about community education, and that is understandable because there are not many people who know and understand the practice of community education. This is important to keep in mind when searching for work opportunities to practice community education. The responsibility of educating potential employers of the value that the practice of community education can bring to them is often on our shoulders. I try to find ways to convey to a prospective employer that "you may not be looking for a community educator, but a community educator is what you need for this position."

So how do you find these opportunities? If my experience is anything to go by, you need to be creative and strategic when seeking opportunities where you can practice community education. Here are a few questions you could ask when evaluating a potential job opportunity:

- *Is this a position that involves supporting teaching and learning?* Look closely at the description of the job and see if it mentions ways in which the person in this position would be involved in planning and supporting educational activities. Based on the context, you might not see the words "teacher" or "student" in the description. Terms like "professional development" or "workforce development" may be used when referencing initiatives that involve teaching and learning.
- *How does this position contribute to meaningful social change?* If, like me, you are interested in work opportunities where it is important for you to feel like you are contributing to a greater cause, this is an important question for you to consider. Does the job description reference social change or transformation? Do the programs described align with your approach to social change? Do not limit yourself to opportunities in organizations that share your philosophy but look for opportunities that can co-exist or support your philosophy. Working in contexts where there is an extreme contradiction in values can be draining psychologically, emotionally, physically, and spiritually.
- *How does/could the practice of community education bring value to this position and the vision and purpose of this organization?* This one is a key question because job descriptions often do not explicitly state this. For example, the job description of a Director of Equity and Inclusion at a medical school may not include references to community education. However, that is a job that will benefit from community education practice.

In general, any initiatives that seek to promote equal access to resources, equity, and social justice could benefit from the practice of community education. Examples of such initiatives include efforts to increase technology access and skills, address health disparities, promote equity and inclusion in education, promote gender justice, and environmental sustainability. When seeking opportunities, one needs to think about where community education can bring value to the mission and goals of the work. Being able to articulate the value that community education brings to a potential employer gives practitioners a unique advantage.

Thinking creatively, you will be able to find opportunities to practice community education in any given industry. See Table 9.1.

Table 9.1 Opportunities in community education

Industry	Potential Opportunities
Higher Education	Continuing education, community-based learning and research, teaching and learning, community engagement and external affairs, DEIJ initiatives (for additional information, see Chapter 14)
Health Sciences and Services	Health education/health promotion initiatives, DEIJ initiatives, community health services offices (for additional information, see Chapters 14 and 15)
Nonprofit/Public Service	Community engagement and relations, professional development, collective impact-based initiatives, DEIJ initiatives, workforce development, education coordination (for additional information, see Chapters 14, 17, and 23)
Corporate	Corporate social responsibility, social impact, sustainability, citizenship, public relations (for additional information, see Chapters 8 and 11)

What You Need to Know to be Successful as a Community Educator

- *Focus on the goals of the job, and not the job title:* You do not need the title of "community educator" to be a community educator. If the work you are doing involves building the capacity of residents and/or organizations to promote social change in their context, you are doing community education. If someone did a research study of people practicing community education, my guess is they would find that most of these people neither have the title of "community educator" nor do they think of their work as community education. Community education is an orientation to the work and can be practiced from whatever position you occupy.
- *Invest time and resources in building and maintaining relationships:* Success in achieving goals and implementing strategies depend on the relationships that you have with others. Hint: that means attending lots of meetings. I had a conversation with a colleague a while ago about how we were both finding it difficult to get our work done because of the many meetings we had to plan, attend, and facilitate. As I reflected on this conversation a couple of days later, I realized that I was wrong. The meetings are not getting in the way of my work; the meetings are my work. I am talking here about both formal and informal meetings where we are engaging in discussions that move our initiatives forward. It is because of those meetings that I can organize meetings and events that people will participate in because they feel connected to the work and see value in it. That is only possible through the work of establishing and nurturing relationships of mutual respect and trust with individuals and groups.
- *Be willing to learn:* If you are comfortable going into contexts that are unfamiliar to you, and you are willing to learn, you will do well practicing community education. The set of skills that community educators bring can be applied in any context or field of practice. For me, this has been one of the greatest rewards of practicing community education. I value the opportunity to learn and grow with every initiative in which I am engaged. With their skills, community educators can guide processes and to do that effectively, they need to learn about specific content and context. It is a humbling feature of this work because it requires you to show up in places where people may question what you may have to contribute with your limited expertise in their specific field of knowledge or context.

If you are considering a career that involves community education, the resources below may be helpful:

- Collective Impact Forum: https://collectiveimpactforum.org: Features a regularly updated blog and resources on topics relevant to community education.
- The Association for Community Organization and Social Action: https://acosa.clubexpress.com: A professional membership organization for learners and practitioners.
- *Journal of Community Practice* (published by Routledge): Peer-reviewed interdisciplinary journal with manuscripts on issues and topics relevant to community action.

Conclusion

One of my goals for this chapter has been to highlight the versatility of community education as a practice. If you are someone who has been interested in community education and wondered what this might look like in practice, I hope that this chapter gave you some ideas for how you might operate in different contexts. Wrapping up this chapter, I have been reflecting on what I would do differently if I was starting my career over again. I would have worked on articulating the value of community education to audiences outside of adult education much sooner.

> Final piece of advice to anyone interested in developing a career that involves community education: know the value of this practice and be able to articulate it to others.

References

Archibald, T. (2018). Community organizing in/as adult education. *Adult Education Research Conference*. https://newprairiepress.org/aerc/2018/papers/16

Brager, G., Specht, H., & Torczyner, J. L. (1987). *Community organizing* (2nd ed.). Columbia University Press.

Brookfield, S. (1983). Community adult education: A conceptual analysis. *Adult Education, 33*(3), 154–160. https://doi.org/10.1177/074171368303300303

Cervero, R. M., & Wilson, A. L. (2006). *Working the planning table: Negotiating democratically for adult, continuing, and workplace education*. Jossey-Bass.

Chaskin, R. J. (2001). Building community capacity: A definitional framework and case studies from a comprehensive community initiative. *Urban Affairs Review, 36*(3), 291–323. https://doi.org/10.1177/10780870122184876

Connolly, B. (2010). Community education: Perspectives from the margins. In K. Rubenson (Ed.), *Adult learning and education* (pp. 133–139). Academic Press.

Cunningham, P. (1993). Let's get real: A critical look at the practice of adult education. *Journal of Adult Education, 22*(1), 3–15.

Daffron, S. R., & Caffarella, R. S. (2021). *Planning programs for adult learners: A practical guide* (4th ed.). Jossey-Bass.

Horton, M., & Freire, P. (1990). *We make the road by walking: Conversations on education and social change*. Temple University Press.

Kretzmann, J., & McKnight, J. P. (1996). Assets-based community development. *National Civic Review, 85*(4), 23–29. https://doi.org/10.1002/ncr.4100850405

Mathie, A., & Cunningham, G. (2003). From clients to citizens: Asset-based community development as a strategy for community-driven development. *Development in Practice, 13*(5), 474–486. https://doi.org/10.1080/0961452032000125857

Mello, R. R., & Braga, F. M. (2018). School as learning communities: An effective alternative for adult education and literacy in Brazil. *Frontiers in Education, 3*, 114. https://doi.org/10.3389/feduc.2018.00114

Mhina, C., & Abdi, A. A. (2009). Mwalimu's mission: Julius Nyerere as (adult) educator and philosopher of community development. In A. A. Abdi & D. Kapoor (Eds.), *Global perspectives on adult education* (pp. 53–69). Palgrave Macmillan US. https://doi.org/10.1057/9780230617971_4

Newman, M. (1993). Throwing out the balance with the bathwater. *The encyclopedia of pedagogy and informal education.* https://infed.org/mobi/adult-education-throwing-out-the-balance-with-the-bathwater

Chapter 10

Consulting

Cathryn A. Hennes

If you are interested in a degree in adult education but are not looking to work for a single company full time, there are many opportunities as an education consultant. This chapter focuses primarily on technology education consulting. However, there are contract projects with client companies dealing with everything from soft-skills training to software/technology training. There are various job titles including Instructional Designer, eLearning Developer, Technical Writer, or Business Analyst. With each position, the job title may not completely reflect the project. The description may not even provide the complete requirements. If you are hired on the project, always understand and know that *flexibility* is the most important competency you must have. *Communication* is next. If you cannot communicate verbally and in writing, being a consultant is not a good fit. *Knowing your subject area* is another important competency. Get hired and get moving! Own your contract journey.

My Career Path

My career started in 1994 working with Ernst & Young. I was hired as a desktop publisher/word processor to support the instructional designers and graphic designers developing training within the department. I transitioned from this administrative support role to a programmer analyst position. As I worked closer with the instructional designers/organizational change management specialists, there was an opportunity to gain experience about how to develop training and train adult learners within the company. During the transformation of my position and responsibilities, I had an opportunity to develop a technology training day for new management consultants at all levels (new college graduates, experienced hires, and new partners). I worked on a team to design this training that covered all three levels but was also customized for the needs of each new hire type.

Seven years later, I was laid off. Over the years after my first layoff, I returned repeatedly to administrative roles and worked my way up the training ladder in new industries. I was hired for a nursing education program specifically for my technology knowledge where I developed training documentation for faculty, including one-on-one training, along with my daily administrative duties. Despite my skills and experiences in technology and training, the market demanded a more advanced degree. I started by adding to my Associate degree credentials and obtained a BA in English along with a Professional Writing Certificate. At the time of my college studies, I reasoned that since I had been developing training and technical documentation for my employers, I would earn my BA in English and continue into a technical writing profession.

At this point, I needed to return to work and repay my student loans. I found a position with a major professional tools manufacturer headquartered in my hometown. What luck! I was hired in the company on a part-time basis as a marketing assistant. Again, I returned to my administrative roots for the second, and last, time. As a marketing assistant, I was hired to learn their manufacturing software so that the marketing professionals could focus on developing new products to sell. After learning the software, I had an opportunity to use my degree by writing and editing operators' manuals for the products they were developing and selling.

Then, as I learned the software, individuals within their Product Engineering department started developing training on the same software and enlisted my help in developing the curriculum paths. The woman designing the training left the company, opening her position where I was then hired full time into the Product Engineering department. Half my new position was managing the data for all the products this company developed and sold. The other half was creating fully the curriculum paths for all employees using the software and training them.

My training career was launched! During my years in the manufacturing company, I returned to college and earned my Master of Education degree in Adult Learning & Development and then obtained a second master's in Educational Technology. My second master's program was focused on the K-12 arena, but before and during my program, I worked with my advisor and the professors to gear all my assignments toward the adult education environment. Each course started with a discussion with the professor/instructor. I explained my goal for the course and received approval for the exercises and projects. When the course required my activities to focus on K-12 activities, I developed exercises from my daughter's perspective. One project allowed me to build exercises my daughter could use for working with my bank's mobile phone application and managing a budget. This taught me the skills for the most important competency as a consultant: flexibility and communication.

While using the skills learned within the degree, I created a lifecycle approach to using my learning in my daily job and then using my daily job in my learning. After my first MEd graduation, internal political issues caused me to be laid off from the manufacturing company. This is where my career got interesting.

Since 2015, I have been engaged in consulting work. I have been hired by companies who are implementing new software or upgrading existing software. I learn how the organization uses the existing software or learn how the company expects to use the new software. Consulting positions vary by company. I have been hired as a technical writer and developed technical business process documentation that also doubled as baseline training documentation. I have been hired as a business analyst for training documentation. Currently I work in a niche, which in short covers senior instructional designer/eLearning developer/learning experience architect with a banking industry client. The job title does not typically dictate what the consultant will be hired to do. Therefore, I might be searching for an instructional designer position but find that some organizations wanting the same skills might use the title of technical writer. The description of duties is the most important aspect. Some organizations are only willing to pay specific amounts which are determined by the role name. Hence an organization may list an instructional designer position with the same requisite requirements as a technical writer position because they are interested in paying less to the consultant for their contract.

The Process of Obtaining the Contract

There are multiple career opportunities as an education consultant. You have an opportunity to work with small companies and large corporations. As a consultant, you might be hired as a part-time employee and receive a W-2; or you might be hired as an independent contractor and receive a 1099 at the end of the year. Another route would be to set up an LLC (limited liability company) and receive a 1099. All these options are viable ones for getting paid for your contracting work. This is an area where a good tax accountant would be able to give you some advice.

Searching and Applying for the Contract

Here you need to know how to read the postings, work with recruiters, and understand how to communicate with the potential client to earn the contract project. Within my specific niche of technology training with adults, it was important to note that companies post positions with various job titles. You may see a position for a technical writer, but within the job description, the posting's requirements include developing and teaching technical training. At the same time, if you are interested in an instructional designer posting, the position's description may require the need for technical writing. They tend to go together.

Working with the Recruiters

Once you have applied for the position, or the recruiter has contacted you, the recruiter will typically require a first-line interview with their company. Knowing how to communicate with recruiters is particularly important. Listen to their questions and confirm you understood the question prior to answering. With the global market of today, it is important to understand individuals when English may not be their primary language. When this happens, the recruiter and I have found communication easier through emails. Not only is strong verbal communication important, but also strong written communication.

Interviewing with the Potential Client

You have gotten the first and potentially only interview with the client. The recruiter converted your resume into one representing the recruiting company and forwarded it to the client. There are many different types of interviews that the client might conduct from one-on-one in person, a team with you in person, one-on-one or a team on a video interview (i.e., Skype, Microsoft Teams), to even just phone calls. The client is gauging how you answer their questions. They are also interested in knowing your level of knowledge of the company and the potential project they will award to you. What questions do you have? Always make sure you have questions about the company and the project. Specific types of questions might include who the learning audience is and what final learning deliverables (simulations, user guides, job aids, quick reference guides, etc.) are expected.

Working on the Project

Once you start the project, meet with your manager and team if applicable. For example, with my bank client, I was required to be in the office for only one day, and I have been working remotely ever since. Since *communication* is a theme for many different teams and employees, know who you are communicating with and how to communicate with them. For my bank client, I am working with many executive-level individuals. At the same time, there were different programming teams along with the associated organizational change management (OCM) team, and lines of business (LOB) and subject matter experts (SME). With all groups working together, the end-user (or the employee/learner) may not understand the impact the training will have on their jobs. Knowing who, how, and what to communicate with all the various groups is determined by the subject matter.

With this bank client, as an example, I focused on understanding the software because the client has hired me to develop training on software. The organization was implementing Salesforce and shutting down older systems. This meant rolling out technology enhancements monthly or bi-monthly. I needed to understand how every employee would see and use the software as each department will see and use the software differently. By using the software as each department uses it, I can more accurately design the best training for each employee. According to their website, "Salesforce unites your marketing, sales, commerce, service, and IT teams from anywhere with Customer 360 – one integrated CRM [customer relationship management] platform that powers our entire suite of connected apps." (Salesforce, n.d., para. 2). Most importantly, in order to do any project, I needed to know how to use the software required to develop and program all the training. I work with software applications like Adobe Captivate, Adobe Photoshop, TechSmith SnagIt, Microsoft 365, and Microsoft Teams. I have also needed to know specialized software like Assima. The client should always be willing to train the consultant for any required specialized software.

Important Terminology

- ADDIE is the acronym for the instructional design process or program planning process (Analyze, Design, Develop, Implement, Evaluate). This is the standard process for developing training for adults in the corporate world. You will often find most job postings require you to know how to use the ADDIE model (Allen, 2006).
- Agile is a project management software that breaks down projects into smaller releases for the client. "Agile is the ability to create and respond to change" (Agile Alliance, 2022, para. 1). Agile is just one of several products currently on the market. A project example is that they might start implementing software in one department and then roll it out to other departments. The overall project's timeline may be multiple years long, but each smaller learning project is within a shorter timeframe, allowing for enhancements and revisions as newer tasks are completed.
- SDLC is Software Development Life Cycle. This process is used in software projects to customize a packaged software such as Salesforce, based on a defined budget and timeline (Booch, 2018). This cycle is used by IT programmers who are designing, developing, and testing customization to software like this to align with their company's needs (Kneuper, 2017).

As my clients implemented new or upgraded software for their employees, I have engaged with all three processes at once.

Practice and Theory

There are various theories of how adults learn. They are addressed in more detail throughout this book (see Chapter 2). Here I will talk about two theories that are valuable in the realm of consulting and corporate training (see Chapter 11).

ADDIE Model and Program Planning

The military developed the ADDIE model for use as a systematic training development tool. Over time, improvements were made to this model to build in evaluation and feedback loops throughout the process and it developed into a training "problem-solving, decision-making model" (Allen, 2006, p. 439).

Allen (2006) explains the elements of this model. The first phase of this model is to **analyze** the immediate work-system requirements. Here the consultant or instructional designer would review the performance requirements of employees and compare these to the knowledge, skills, and abilities (KSAs) of current employees. Through this analysis, the training needs are established.

From there, the next step is the **design** phase. In this stage, instructional objectives and a detailed plan of instruction are created. The designer would select specific instructional methods, including reviewing any current related instructional materials, media, and strategies to teach the material to the participants.

The next phase is **development**. During this phase of the project, all related learning materials would be created, including videos, slide decks, quizzes to test knowledge learned, etc. This is also the stage where the confirmation of the match between each instruction module and the learning objectives would occur. At this point, pilot training would transpire with those in the field with revisions based on the feedback loop.

After revision, **implementation** of the training would follow to the entire training audience. The final step is **evaluation**. Evaluation (see Chapter 5) should be a continuous process from development to implementation. At each point, evaluation would provide the consultant with relevant information to ensure that the training model meets the organizational needs.

Self-Directed Learning

Employees are expected to be self-directed in their learning. While organizations may have mandatory training, additional learning is usually left to individuals to pursue on their own. In addition, as a consultant, there are many situations where you need to learn a system or procedures within the organization that you are working with, and your own ability to be a self-directed learner is essential.

In the literature, self-directed learning (SDL) has been characterized as a personal attribute, as well as a process (Merriam & Bierema, 2014). As a consultant, your focus is usually on SDL as a process. Knowles (1975) defines the SDL process as the point "in which individuals take the initiative, with or without the help of others, in diagnosing their learning needs, formulating learning goals, identifying human and material resources for learning, choosing and implementing appropriate learning strategies, and evaluating those learning outcomes" (p. 18). As an education consultant you might be asked to design learning modules that teach soft skills, as well as technical or knowledge-based skills to enable the client organization to provide many SDL activities for their employees at all levels.

Competencies

As a consultant, your strengths are your ability to manage multiple projects and be flexible. This section discusses aspects of time management and flexibility which will serve you well.

Time Management

As development teams and learning projects are built, being able to manage time for all the various learning deliverables can create many challenges. As an individual consultant, time management is primarily producing quality work per deadlines. However, as you take on more complex consulting work, this may include managing other contractors if the client's needs require that you move from being a one-person developer to managing a development team. Currently, I work with 19 different programming teams who are building a 100%-customized Salesforce. The client has over 55,000 employees. Training releases are happening monthly for the current year and will return to bi-monthly in the next year.

Flexibility

As mentioned above, the most valuable skill needed in consulting is flexibility. Flexibility is the skill of shifting and adjusting to meet the changing needs of your client and to make sure that you are keeping the communication channels open and functioning smoothly. This means actively listening and responding based on what is said. This does not mean always saying yes or no to assigned tasks, but understanding how to communicate with the client, as well as making sure everyone is aligned with requests and tasks, etc. An important part of flexibility is the ability to be agile. If you are agile, you are able to "think on your feet," anticipate potential changes, and quickly and easily change direction. As a consultant, you realize that change can and will occur as you move through your project(s) with the client. You will be working in a fast-paced environment.

The following job description is an example regarding a potential new contract for an instructional design project for the banking industry. It illustrates the various competencies that might be required. Depending on the consulting assignment that you are seeking, there may be differences.

- Work with multiple levels of employees.
- Design training curricula and materials.
- Design eLearning, using Adobe Captivate 2019 (or the latest software).
- Develop storyboards using Microsoft PowerPoint and establish learning templates.
- Load training deliverables to an established learning management system (LMS) or content site.
- Revise existing eLearning materials.
- Financial services experience preferred (this would change based on the industry that would be your primary consulting niche).
- Bachelor's degree in Instructional Design, Instructional Technology preferred.
- Specified technology: Adobe Captivate 2019, Articulate Storyline 360, Rise, 360 (preferred), Photoshop, Audition, and Microsoft 365.
- Understand ADDIE.
- Critical thinker along with excellent written/oral communications and listening skills.
- Ability to work in a fast-paced environment.

Notice that the description asks for knowledge of ADDIE, the instructional design process discussed above. However, throughout my 7 years as a consultant/contractor, not once have I been asked directly if I know ADDIE. Through the interview process, recruiters and/or hiring managers will know how much of the process you know by asking questions that indirectly will tell them if you know ADDIE and use it in practice. They review your resume and will ask you about prior projects you have completed. How did you complete the work? What process did you use? What happened when you had issues? Once you have the contract project won and are on the working on the project, your project team may not even ask those questions either. You won the project; that means you know the adult learning or instructional design theories. They assume because acronyms like ADDIE are on your resume, and your projects highlight your work, that you understand and use the required model(s).

Future of Adult Education in Your Career Area

Within adult education consulting, the future is bright. ALL companies hire new employees. The type of organization and employee skill sets will determine the amount of training that company provides. Corporations and large companies will provide more training to employees than smaller companies. Whether it is hardware or software, technology will continue to evolve. I am specifically working within the software side of the IT part of the organization.

This is also where my "elevator pitch" information helps potential clients understand what I do. There will always be a need for contractors/consultants to understand the software the organization wants to implement, as well as other training and development opportunities. In addition, organizations need to train employees on soft skills, on-boarding (new hires), basic job skills, and even leadership skills. Organizations often need consultants who understand the process of developing robust training for employees.

All companies use technology/software to run their businesses and the future is moving to online, just-in-time training. As a consultant, I have an opportunity to help craft the final training documentation from job aids, quick reference guides, or learning maps to e-learning simulation training. Therefore, it is important to understand all software being used by the client from LMS and/or content management systems to store training documents and software titles like Salesforce, Teamcenter, SyteLine, and Blackboard that are currently used in organizations.

My current banking client has multiple legacy software systems. A legacy software system simply means the software is older and needs to be replaced. Depending on the company, this process may be quick, but for other companies, like my banking client, it could have a multi-year completion timeframe. Most clients want their training to coincide with the rollout of new processes and software, so that the training launches alongside the rollout. Most firms use various forms of job aids, learning maps, and eLearning simulation training all stored on a single site, such as Microsoft SharePoint site.

Many companies are leveraging new software to solve a business issue with their processes. For instance, when a division or company breaks off from the parent or larger company, the new company may need to develop their own software or processes for the company as a whole and for various departments, such as accounting or training. There is usually a deadline when the new company needs to have its own systems in place and can no longer use the software and processes of the parent company. This can also occur when a company is acquiring a new company. An example would be when Microsoft acquired LinkedIn. Depending on the size of the organization, the break-off company may hire an outside consulting team to develop a full training curriculum and train its employees over a certain period. This may entail multiple projects that use various configurations of project team members and/or outside consultants.

Elevator Pitch

A great elevator pitch is essential (see the Conclusion chapter for a brief description of elevator pitches) in order to convey what you can do for a potential client. My elevator pitch helps potential clients understand my focus and expertise. "Companies hire me to learn new or upgraded software solutions and implementations by writing and developing the technical documentation and training programs, and then training their employees. I HELP companies to HELP their employees have better work lives."

Employees spend one-third of their lives on the job. Employees must know how to do their jobs and to use the software to optimize their output and productivity. Having training that is easy to understand is fundamental to having better work lives.

Success Tips

First and foremost, be honest. When you are discussing potential contracts with a recruiter and/or a hiring manager, if they ask you about a skill that you do not have, tell them you do not have that skill. Over my contracting career, most of my projects have been presented to me about software implementations that I have never used. A version of the following statement usually follows: "Well, if you've worked with (insert software that you do know here), then you can work with (insert their software name here)."

Finding Clients

LinkedIn, networking, and resumes are all important avenues for finding clients. LinkedIn is a business networking social media site. You can learn about specific companies that have your interests and network with recruiters and various others who can help you with your career. For those in the education realm, do not limit who you have connected to your network. Over the course of my career, I have collaborated with individuals in the following areas: military, healthcare, manufacturing, banking, government/public sector, and higher education. I am also connected professionally to transitioning service members (anyone from the military, active duty, veterans, military/veteran spouses), individuals from high school and college, former teachers, and professors.

Once I had an individual respond to my networking request with, "Why should I connect with you?" because I was not in their field. My response was,

> Why not? My career deals with working in as many different industries as I can. No. I cannot hire you, but through networking, someone who is connected to me may be looking for a new employee who could be you. So why not?

They accepted my connection request. Be willing to network with anyone and everyone!

Your LinkedIn Profile and Resume. You must have a resume if you wish to apply for contracts with recruiting firms and companies. Having a LinkedIn profile allows you to network with others and allows you to showcase your career. The following is the link to my LinkedIn profile: www.linkedin.com/in/cathrynhennes/.

Both my profile and resume are the same and are formatted similarly, allowing potential clients and recruiters the opportunity to see my entire career without having to download my resume, and then open it to read about my career. Over my consulting career, all projects have been presented to me. I never looked for the positions and applied to them. They have all come from LinkedIn with a recruiter searching for me. However, treat this advice as the exception to the rule and be as proactive as possible. You might have the same experience but leave nothing to chance.

Develop a Website. If you are working to have your own business, make sure you also have a website. My website displays my writing artifacts from my client projects. When you do that, make sure you never use company/client information within the documents. Always redact your documents to be generic. I say this because, as a consultant, you will sign contracts stating the final deliverables you build and write for the client are their property. They are not yours! That can create a difficult situation if new clients are asking to review artifacts you have written in the past. Keep your website current. You can find my website at the following address: www.go2learning.biz/home/

Be DIFFERENT! Be YOU!

References

Agile Alliance. (2022, March 21). What is Agile software development?www.agilealliance.org/agile101/
Allen, W. C. (2006). Overview and evolution of the ADDIE training system. *Advances in Developing Human Resources, 8*(4), 430–441. https://doi.org/10.1177/1523422306292942
Booch, G. (2018). The history of software engineering. *IEEE Software, 35*(5), 108–114.

Kneuper, R. (2017). Sixty years of software development life cycle models. *IEEE Annals of the History of Computing*, *39*(3), 41–54. https://doi.org/10.1353/ahc.2017.0022

Knowles, M. S. (1975). *Self-directed learning: A guide for learners and teachers*. Association Free Press.

Merriam, S. B., & Bierema, L. L. (2014). *Adult learning: Linking theory to practice*. Jossey-Bass.

Salesforce (n.d.). What is Salesforce? www.salesforce.com/products/what-is-salesforce/

Chapter 11

Corporate Training, Global Learning, and Talent Management

Murray Winland and Catherine H. Monaghan

Introduction

Adult education career opportunities are available in companies, corporations, and organizations across North America and around the world. Within these institutions, adult education career opportunities occur within departments with a variety of names such as Training; Training and Development; Learning and Development; Human Resource Development (HRD); Staff Development; Talent Management, and more.

Regardless of the department name, organizational learning is both the functional area and the framework for helping company, corporation, and organization employees develop their knowledge, skills, and abilities (KSAs). With solid KSAs, employees and their competencies are valuable resources who improve their organization's overall effectiveness. Acquiring competencies also helps employees to move forward in their careers and engage in work that fulfills their passions and can make a difference in the world.

This chapter reviews Murray's career journey, positions within the fields of corporate training, global learning, and talent management. In addition, competencies or KSAs are discussed along with success tips to choose and build a successful career in this area of adult education.

Murray's 30-Year Career

Like countless professionals in the adult education space, I fell into the career by total chance. I was selected to join a company's training department not for my adult education skills (I had none), but for my subject matter expertise. Specifically, I worked as a claims representative for a major insurance company, handling commercial vehicle claims that included tractor-trailers, buses, limousine services, and other business-owned vehicles. My company was expanding this part of their business and found themselves in a hiring frenzy to bring on board new claims representatives. Because I could string words and sentences together and knew things that other people joining the company would need to learn, the training department brought me on as a stand-up trainer or face-to-face trainer.

I quickly figured out that training was the right career choice for me. I also knew that I wanted to become much more knowledgeable and skilled in all facets of the craft. I pursued a master's degree in Adult Learning and Development at night while working full time. And I joined various professional organizations which we will discuss later.

Throughout my career, I attended numerous conferences, workshops, and seminars. I presented at multiple conferences myself and had the opportunity to give back to my profession and those hoping to be in it by speaking and teaching adult education classes at a few colleges and universities.

DOI: 10.4324/9781003259602-14

Over my career I worked at several different companies but always in the adult education space. I worked for two different Fortune 500 insurance companies, a company recognized as a global leader in energy and environmental technologies and services for the power and industrial markets, a multinational health care services company, a multinational e-commerce corporation, and a pioneering virtual customer management company.

Across these companies I progressed through a variety of adult education roles. These roles were exciting and rewarding. I would like to share some of those paths with you, as well as a few thoughts on ways you could explore your own adult education career aspirations.

Career Paths in Corporate Training and Global Learning

The career paths available to those who want to work in corporate training, global learning, and talent management are varied and occur on many rungs of the career ladder. This chapter will discuss the roles of trainer, instructional systems designer, measurement and evaluation, and leadership.

Trainer/Training Specialist

Adult education career paths in companies, corporations, and organizations are as varied as the institutions themselves. Murray began his adult education career as a stand-up (face-to-face) trainer. While formal classroom stand-up training opportunities have decreased over the years, the predicted death of stand-up training has not come to fruition. There has been a dramatic shift to "distance learning" or "online learning" that still has, as one of its model pieces, the need for live trainers. An example might be a TED Talk, or a workshop delivered on-site for an organization. Therefore, while the modality may have shifted toward the use of technology to deliver training experiences, live trainers are still needed and in demand.

Before my retirement (Murray), the last company I worked for delivered outsourced customer service support to some exceptionally large brand name companies. We did this by partnering with small, independent customer service businesses and individual customer service providers who needed training on the brand company's products, processes, procedures, and customer support expectations. The entire learning delivery experience happened via technology. This included the always-important instructor-led component. The instructors that we used were also independent business owners.

If you have a desire to deliver training as an instructor, there are still abundant opportunities to do so. Critical to success in this role are three things. First, strong facilitation skills are imperative. (See Chapter 3 for developing skills as a facilitator.) Secure the necessary training to be able to deliver live training in a way that resonates with the adult learner. These skills are important in both a brick-and-mortar classroom and an online classroom. Second, you will need subject matter expertise in the topic being taught. And third, in today's training environment, you will need to learn technology delivery platforms and the skills necessary to be effective while delivering through them. There are both similar and different skills that will be required as compared to a classic classroom (See Chapter 2 for practical teaching skills.)

Instructional Systems Design

Instructional Systems Design (ISD) provides a well-defined career path for adult educators in companies, corporations, and organizations. Instructional designers build training experiences. Some job titles might be Instructional Designer, Content Designer, or Education Technology/Media Producer. If you have an interest in this space, consider securing a graduate-level degree (both master's and/or doctorate) in the adult education or ISD discipline, through an adult education graduate program, as this will enhance your opportunities in the field. The ever-changing needs and preferences of the adult learner, coupled with learning technologies, has necessitated the need for strong expertise in the design and creation of instructional approaches and materials.

Instructional Design Models

You will need to be well-versed in the various ISD models to be effective as an instructional designer. The most traditional is the ADDIE model, of which there are several variations (see Chapters 4 and 10 for a further discussion of this model). But at the heart of the model are five phases: Analysis, Design, Development, Implementation, and Evaluation (Allen, 2006). These phases provide the necessary building blocks for creating effective training and performance support tools.

Another ISD model to be familiar with is the Agile Learning Design (ALD) model. Today's organizations, finding themselves in the ever-increasingly highly competitive global marketplace, are looking for their employees to quickly add value and "time-to-proficiency" has become an important human resource strategy. ALD refers to any of the ISD approaches to training content development that focus on speed, flexibility, and collaboration (Groves, et al., 2012).

The ALD model moves beyond the ADDIE model while using the elements of ADDIE. The important difference is that ALD uses the steps in the ADDIE model both simultaneously and in a non-linear fashion. Per Groves et al. (2012), the ALD model emphasizes:

- "Usable deliverables over comprehensive documentation" and "collaboration over negotiation" of the perfect module (p. 50)
- "Responding to change over adhering to a plan" (p. 51)

Initially, the instructional design effort meant that slides and speaker notes were created, based on input of subject matter experts, and then used in classic classroom surroundings by an instructor. Today's adult learners demand a variety of learning modalities such as instructor-led, self-paced, on-demand, and mobile approaches. Technology plays a critical role in the instructional design methods and eLearning deliverables necessary in today's organizational environments. Short, varied, and to-the-point learning events are key in today's organizations and to employees. Staying current in both the latest and future trends in the ISD space is important. The field has changed to a significant extent and that change was accelerated by the pandemic of 2020. That pace of change will continue and so there is a need for those in the corporate learning space to be lifelong learners to stay ahead of the curve.

Measurement and Evaluation

It is of paramount importance that any training organization measures, evaluates, and improves its training efforts. Measurement and Evaluation (M&E) career paths are plentiful for today's practitioners. Long gone are the days when organizational leaders considered training a necessary evil and relied on faith that the training experience was helping employees. Now executive leaders demand that training dollars are wisely spent—that there is a return-on-investment (ROI)—and skilled employees come out of learning experiences and add increased value to the company.

A working knowledge of, and the ability to practically apply, a training measurement model will be necessary if you would like to pursue this adult education specialty (see Chapter 5 for a more detailed explanation). People working in the M&E space normally bring an advanced degree in measurement and evaluation, statistics, qualitative/quantitative measurement, research, test theory, evaluation instrument design, or a related field. A PhD or EdD in adult education with a focus on research methods and evaluation would be invaluable.

Evaluation Models

At a minimum, be familiar with the classic Kirkpatrick (Kirkpatrick & Kirkpatrick, 2016) training evaluation model and the more contemporary and holistic Phillips model (Phillips & Phillips, 2008). Both models are in alignment on the first four levels of evaluation. The Phillips model adds an important fifth level that is critical in today's global learning and corporate training space. Let's briefly examine each of the five levels.

The first level of evaluation focuses on how well the learner reacted to the learning experience. Lovingly referred to as "smile sheets," historically this was the only type of training evaluation conducted. But this level of evaluation still provides valuable information that can be fed back to the instructional design staff and stand-up trainers, as appropriate. The next four levels of measurement and the evaluative outcomes derived from them are much more important to the adult education department and the parent organization. Level two answers the question, "Did the employee learn what they needed to learn?" Level three helps us understand if the employee is applying what they learned on the job. Was there a causal link between training and employee performance? And if not, why not? With level four measurement, we learn if the employee's application of the newly learned knowledge and skills results in improved business results, whatever they may be. Finally, at level five, we can determine if the monetary value of those improved business results exceeded the cost of the training program: the ROI.

As an adult educator, being able to talk about "business results" and ROI in a work environment will be of importance to your career. This is especially true for those of you with aspirations to work in adult education leadership positions.

Leadership

Depending on the size of the adult education group or training department, and the overall size of the parent company, various leadership roles and opportunities are always available. Murray worked in training organizations as small as three people but also had the opportunity to lead large, global adult education teams of over 100. In larger teams there are normally more leadership layers. Supervisory, managerial, and executive-level opportunities are common. Some leadership job titles might be Learning and Development Manager, Director of Leadership Development, VP of Learning and Organizational Development or Director of Talent Management.

In adult education training and development, the adult educator entering into a leadership role normally has expertise in one or more areas. As an example, leadership opportunities in the instructional design space are quite common. The leader in this area began first as an expert instructional designer. When the size of their team gets large enough because of an increased workload, leadership becomes important to ensure that multiple project deadlines are met and the quality of the design deliverables are achieved. In larger training teams you will also find leadership opportunities in the instructor-led space and the measurement and evaluation area, as well as within training administrative functions.

Senior and executive leadership opportunities, while less frequent, are also available. Large training teams are commonly led by someone at the executive level. This is especially true when the training organization and its people are spread across multiple geographic locations or even globally. In fact, many forward-thinking organizations have a C-suite learning executive commonly called a Chief Learning Officer, Director of Organizational Development, or Director of Talent Management.

Regardless of the level or levels of leadership within a training environment, leaders, of course, must bring management and leadership skills to the table (Monaghan, 2010). There are many leadership models (Northouse, 2021), but there are certain leadership characteristics that are important if one is to be successful in guiding a team of adult education professionals. Those characteristics start with integrity. But influencing, delegation, and communication skills are also fundamental. The ability to demonstrate respect, gratitude, and empathy toward your team members will go a long way in helping you be a great leader. Being strongly self-aware and taking action to personally improve is also crucial. In addition, a leader needs the necessary courage to make tough decisions, have tough conversations, and, especially at the senior leadership levels, have intentional interactions with other company executives as required to be effective and successful.

Practice and Theory

Regardless of the chosen path in adult education, it is important that all in the space have a clear understanding and working knowledge of the theory of adult education. You will be well served to research Malcolm Knowles (1995, 2020), considered by many to be the father of adult education, and his theory of Andragogy, synonymous with adult learning. He pointed out the significant differences between how adults learn as compared to children. While there are other thought leaders in the adult learning area, Knowles's assumptions and principles are still widely used in today's training organizations. This is especially true in the design and creation of learning experiences for adults.

The importance of obtaining the foundational knowledge necessary for working successfully in organizational learning cannot be overstated. Perhaps not surprisingly, there are certain truths when it comes to educating adults that are timeless. Yes, the mechanisms now available for delivering learning experiences—primarily technology-driven—have drastically changed. But how adults want to learn is still well explained with adult learning theory that goes back decades. Knowing these truths will be your foundational starting point for your entire career in training and development.

Because human performance can be influenced by complex factors that go beyond a person's own KSAs and, therefore, cannot always be simply solved with training, it is important to also have knowledge in Human Performance Technology (HPT). Also called Human Performance Improvement (HPI), this field of study acknowledges that a variety of methodologies should be understood and employed when trying to improve employee performance (Brinkerhoff et al., 2019; Etsey & Young, 2022; Rothwell et al., 2018). Specifically, HPT/HPI incorporates different disciplines to get a more holistic performance improvement outcome at the societal, organizational, process, and individual performer levels. Methodologies such as total quality management (Souza et al., 2022), lean Six Sigma (Bakke & Claudio, 2023), organizational development (Cheung-Judge & Holbeche, 2021), process improvement (Page, 2016), knowledge management (Li et al., 2022), performance support systems (Etsey & Young, 2022), and training combine to deliver the best performance solution. It would be beneficial for more practitioners in adult education to learn and incorporate these methodologies in their work.

In this global and diverse world, it is paramount that educators in this arena develop their cultural competencies. As outlined by Bohonos (2019) and Monaghan and Isaac-Savage (2023), these skills are necessary in terms of training, employee development, and leadership. These authors present frameworks for implementing diversity practices at all levels of the organization.

Career Opportunities

Adult education and training opportunities continue to be in abundance. Internal company postings, online job boards, professional organizations, college and university placement offices, professional recruiting firms that specialize in training positions, and word-of-mouth all provide venues to discover available jobs. The professional organizations listed have job postings and descriptions, as well as in-person chapters and conferences for networking opportunities.

When you get that interview, prepare for it. Research the company and have a working understanding of what they are all about. Be prepared to talk about the company and how you will add value to the company employees in the training space. Learn all you can about your interviewers. Listen closely to the questions. Speak to the things that are important to them. Training team members will want to know that you know something about adult education. Be prepared to talk in adult learning terms. Executive leaders will want to know how hiring you will impact their business and the bottom line. Talk about "business results" and ROI.

Of course, interviews are a two-way street. Get a sense of how the company and its executives view the importance of employee training. Run – do not walk – away from any organization where it is obvious that adult education and training are not considered essential to the company's current and long-term success.

An experience Murray remembers to this day is this: I was interviewing for a director-level learning leadership position at a Fortune 500 insurance company. The person they would hire would lead an adult education team responsible for the training of all information technology employees within the organization. My interviewer, who later was to be my boss, and I were halfway through our interview when I just put it out there by saying, "Mary. Let me be frank. I don't know a thing about information technology. It seems like a stretch that I'm being considered for this area's training leadership role." Her response is one that you will want to look for as you pursue your own adult education career. Mary said, "I have 2,600 information technology professionals. I need a training leader." I worked with and reported to Mary for 7 years, my longest tenure at any position in my career. Look for a boss like Mary.

Professional Organizations and Journals

- Association for Talent Development (ATD) (www.td.org/). This organization provides resources for members involved in developing the knowledge and skills of employees. They offer webinars, conferences, and certifications in areas such as human performance improvement, evaluation, coaching, and consulting (see Chapter 10). They also have a magazine and a job bank, as well as chapters around the world. You can also obtain a certification as an Associate Professional in Talent Development (APTD) (www.td.org/certification/aptd/introduction) and become a Certified Professional in Talent Development (CPTD) (www.td.org/certification/cptd/introduction).
- International Society for Performance Improvement (ISPI) (https://ispi.org). This organization also provides resources, webinars, journals, and certifications in facilitation and one in development of training, as well as a job bank.
- Society for Human Resource Management (SHRM) (www.shrm.org/). SHRM is focused on the human resources (HR) area of business. This often includes the training and talent development areas. They offer a plethora of resources, including templates, as well as a job site. They offer two certifications: SHRM Certified Professional (SHRM-CP) (www.shrm.org/certification/decide/Pages/shrm-cp.aspx) and SHRM Senior Certified Professional (SHRM-SCP) (www.shrm.org/certification/decide/Pages/shrm-cp.aspx).

- *TechTrends: Linking Research & Practice to Improve Learning.* Articles on all aspects of innovative technology in education and training in schools, colleges, and private industry for members of the Association for Educational Communications and Technology.
- *Chief Learning Officer.* Journal for executives in the learning and development spaces within organizations. Also includes annual conferences and other resources.

Future of Adult Education in Corporate Training, Global Learning, and Talent Management

We began writing this chapter in the midst of COVID-19. Prior to the pandemic, learning technology platforms had gained a foothold in North America. As it became necessary in mid-2020 – almost overnight – to continue business and education with stay-at-home employees and students, adult learning professionals scrambled to reposition many of their programs to online courses using learning technology. Many were ill-equipped to do so, and the adult learner suffered.

Technology will continue to play a major and expanding role in adult education, in companies, corporations, and organizations. Increasingly, adult education practitioners recognize the capabilities of learning technology. Organizations are embracing learning technology for both its effectiveness and cost benefits that increase the bottom line. Therefore, as discussed above in the ALD model, there will be more pressure on adult education practitioners to deliver meaningful training experiences in shorter timeframes and at less expense.

And yet we will not have to sacrifice best practices if we keep Malcolm Knowles and his theory of adult learning at the forefront of our adult education efforts (Knowles et al., 2020). The assumptions and principles are still as applicable today as they were 50 years ago and learning technology delivery mechanisms allow for good theoretical application.

Graduate-level programs in adult education will be well served to ensure that courses on learning delivery technology platforms and technology to build eLearning courses are included in the curriculum. Additionally, courses on training measurement and evaluation and supporting tools should take a more prominent place in the syllabus lineup.

Practicing adult education professionals should supplement their adult education knowledge with additional training in learning technology and add these types of skills to their toolkits. You can explore graduate programs, or the professional organizations already discussed, if you find that you need to increase this particular skill set.

Success Tips

I (Murray) have learned a lot over the years – much from classrooms and most from experience and the good people who were around me. But if I had to pick three things that I had always provided as advice to others wanting to do what I did, it would be the following.

First, be open to coming into the adult education profession through whatever door opens for you. You may recall that I, by chance, fell into it. Of course, you may know that you want to be in adult education but, if you need to, take other opportunities along the way to get there. A quick story may help illustrate this point better. I was helping an adult education graduate student prepare a résumé that would hopefully help them secure interviews in the training space. As I reviewed this person's first résumé draft, I pointed out that nothing in it suggested that they had any training background. "But I was just the shift supervisor at McDonalds" was the individual's response. I asked, "But did you not oversee both the formal and on-the-job training of new employees, among other things? Wouldn't it be good to document this training experience in a résumé written to get you an interview in the training field?"

Second, stay current in the field of adult education, as well as the professional skills necessary to enable long-term success. The amount of change that I experienced in my 30-year career was astounding. This pace of change will not slow down. Better yet, stay ahead of the game. Join professional organizations. Attend seminars and conferences. Seek partnerships with other practitioners whose work you admire. Be a mentor/find a mentor. Be a lifelong learner.

Third, pick the right organizations and the right bosses—especially the latter. If they, too, are an adult education professional that can be a plus. But even if they are not an adult educator, you will want to be sure that they want and trust you to implement your expertise in the organization. Your career in adult education will be much richer and fuller if you are serving the right organization and believe in their purpose.

In this branch of adult education, there are many exciting opportunities. Remember to remain agile about current trends in knowledge management, especially about the multigenerational needs of employees. Continue to develop your business acumen. This includes knowing the organizational vision, market strategy, and financials. Steep yourself in knowledge about the industry. Expect that visions, strategies, and markets will change and understand how that will impact the training needs of the organization. Build an excellent internal management network, so that you can be an effective voice at the table (Cervero & Wilson, 2006). This will enable you to be a leader in creating value and innovation, allowing you to be involved from initial concept through the strategy to the implementation through gaining executive support.

All the best in pursuing your adult education career in corporate training, global learning, and talent management. Your calling is an honorable one and we are thrilled that you are in the community.

References

Allen, W. C. (2006). Overview and evolution of the ADDIE training system. *Advances in Developing Human Resources*, 8(4), 430–441. https://doi.org/10.1177/1523422306292942

Bakke, M., & Claudio, D. (2023). Efficiency realization and capacity increase: Implementing lean six sigma in a growing startup. *Small Enterprise Research*, 30(2), 239–254. https://doi.org/10.1080/13215906.2023.2200746

Bohonos, J. W. (2019). Including critical whiteness studies in the critical human resource development family: A proposed theoretical framework. *Adult Education Quarterly*, 69(4), 315–337.

Brinkerhoff, R. O., Apking, A. M., & Boon, E. W. (2019). *Improving performance through learning: A practical guide for designing high performance learning journeys*. Promote International AB.

Cervero, R. M., & Wilson, A. L. (2006). *Working the planning table: Negotiating democratically for adult, continuing, and workplace education*. Jossey-Bass.

Cheung-Judge, M., & Holbeche, L. (2021). *Organizational development: A practitioner's guide to OD and HR* (3rd ed.). Kogan.

Etsey, J., & Young, R. (2022). Human performance improvement (HPI) is a modern approach to organisational performance. *Appita Magazine*, 2, 40–43. https://search.informit.org/doi/10.3316/informit.587883208603786

Groves, A., Rickelman, C., Cassarino, C., & Hall, M. J. (2012). Are you ready for Agile learning design? *T+D*, 66(3), 46–51.

Kirkpatrick, J. D., & Kirkpatrick, W. K. (2016). *Kirkpatrick's four levels of training evaluation*. ATD Press.

Knowles, M. S. (1995). *Designs for adult learning*. American Society for Training and Development (ASTD).

Knowles, M. S., Holton (III), E. F., Swanson, R. A., & Robinson, P. A. (2020). *The adult learner: The definitive classic in adult education and human resource development* (9th ed.). Routledge.

Li, Y., Shao, Y., Wang, M., Fang, Y., Gong, Y., & Li, C. (2022). From inclusive climate to organizational innovation: Examining internal and external enablers for knowledge management capacity. *The Journal of Applied Psychology*, 107(12), 2285–2305. https://doi.org/10.1037/apl0001014

Monaghan, C. H. (2010). Management and leadership. In A. Rose, C. Kasworm, & J. Ross-Gordon (Eds.), *Handbook of adult and continuing education* (pp. 177–186). Sage.

Monaghan, C. H., & Isaac-Savage, E. P. (2023). Community, intersectionality, and social justice in critical human resource development. In J. C. Collins & J. L. Callahan (Eds.), *The Palgrave handbook of critical human resource development* (pp. 307–323). Palgrave.

Northouse, P. G. (2021). *Leadership: Theory and practice* (9th ed.). Sage.

Page, S. (2016). *The power of business process improvement: 10 simple steps to increase effectiveness, efficiency, and adaptability* (2nd ed.). American Management Association.

Phillips, P. P., & Phillips, J. J. (2008). *Beyond learning objectives: Develop measurable objectives that link to the bottom line*. ASTD Press.

Rothwell, W. J., Hohne, C. K., & King, S. B. (2018). *Human performance improvement: Building practitioner performance* (3rd ed.). Routledge.

Souza, F. F. D., Corsi, A., Pagani, R. N., Balbinotti, G., & Kovaleski, J. L. (2022). Total quality management 4.0: Adapting quality management to Industry 4.0. *The TQM Journal, 34*(4), 749–769.

Chapter 12

Correctional Education

Rosary-Joyce Kennedy

> Restored citizens, returning citizens, justice-involved and immured, as well as other non-offensive, non-derogatory terminology, are often used to refer to the incarcerated, parolees, or offender populations to promote and support a more humane view and interaction with these individuals. The terms justice-involved and immured will be used interchangeably throughout this chapter.

Introduction

Since 1970, the incarceration rate in the United States has increased fourfold (Vera Institute of Justice, 2019) with a population that currently exceeds seven million individuals (Thoulin, 2021). As the general populace has burgeoned, the demographics of incarcerated individuals have also evolved. There is also a growing number of justice-involved learners who have a history of learning difficulties and/or disabilities. Thus, as the incarceration rate has increased, and the population has changed, the call to meet specific service needs for the immured has also proportionately changed, particularly for individuals who want to avoid recidivism and who aspire to rehabilitate. Many individuals who face release from institutions endure barriers to successful societal and familial reintegration such as acquiring safe, affordable housing, obtaining gainful employment, improving low levels of literacy, attaining high school equivalency credentials, and matriculating into post-secondary education. Participating in educational programming often involves both education and correctional staff managing many responsibilities and personal issues for future learners.

Education is prioritized and reprioritized by policy makers and program creators presenting education as both a currency to advance economically and a channel through which individuals may network for a better life. These encounters with adult education professionals who act as liaisons for success enable a transactional process where resources and opportunities are exchanged. Though navigating the terrain of maintaining basic survival often takes precedence over the urgency of obtaining educational and occupational credentials, there are professionals with instrumental roles who are impactful advocates and leaders who facilitate optimistic processes. This chapter will outline and describe roles, responsibilities, competencies, and various experiences of these correctional education practitioners within the context of adult basic education (ABE) and literacy. For more information on ABE, see Chapter 7.

Students' Barriers to Participation

Adult education programs in the United States provide services for several million learners, with a myriad of educational and occupational goals and objectives (Patterson & Mellard,

DOI: 10.4324/9781003259602-15

2007). Learners serviced by ABE and literacy programs face many obstacles and challenges to participation. Three primary categories of barriers to learner engagement are personal, institutional, and lack of professional experience. Within the general realm of ABE there are many personal barriers that adult literacy education students encounter that make it difficult for them to initiate or continue participation in adult education programs. The factors span a continuum that includes but is not limited to geographic location of residence juxtaposed with locale of class site, transportation, educational duties versus family obligations, work/school/family schedule conflict, lack of personal financial resources, or "general fear of returning to school" (Ritt, 2008, p. 12). This is often further complicated by negative past experiences with school, lack of employment experience, and/or inconsistencies in employment tenure. Students' occupational background is also an indicator of one's prior educational preparation and thus the scope of professional experiences. Institutional barriers, though frequently designated outside of the student's control, often pose as "limits that reduce access to adult students and may result in diminished interest or delay in degree completion" (Ritt, 2008, p. 14).

Learners who have experienced incarceration or who will face incarceration endure additional barriers to participation in education, whether personal, psychological, or situational. For justice-involved learners who require and/or have a desire to participate in adult basic literacy and education, secondary education, or post-secondary education, their hindrances to involvement are often complex. Incarceration poses a type of trauma that exacerbates pre-existing social, emotional, and cognitive problems. Many justice-involved learners have experienced a history of trauma which makes apparent various problems that they express in both the criminal justice system as well as the correctional education classroom. As these issues and experiences persist, educational programming continues to be developed, evolves, and provides avenues in which the immured may engage positive stimuli to improve their lives, requiring staff to facilitate and manage.

Program needs for the justice-involved are created and structured to address the academic, credential, or degree deficiencies that individuals may require for ABE and literacy, post-secondary education, and career training. If learners do not need specific services and programming, enrollment is impacted and may decline. Conversely, if there is a significant need for specific educational services, enrollment may then increase. As a result, for some government or nonprofit agencies, or educational institutions, contingent on class size, there may be delays enrolling aspiring students. Thus, for some potential students, skill acquisition, skill enhancement, and credential attainment are also delayed. As this time-chasm increases, a potential learner's momentum may slowly dissolve as "the success of offenders' education is dependent upon them actively participating in and completing education programs" (Desir & Whitehead, 2010, p. 12).

Correctional Education's Impact on Recidivism

There is an abundance of research that supports the theory that education reduces recidivism (Hall, 2015; Magee, 2021). Empirical evidence shows that education reduces the rate of recidivism by approximately 42% (Magee, 2021). Growing awareness of these facts and factors has informed criminal justice and correctional education reform as many programs restructure the focus on using education to rehabilitate the immured. Further research by Lee (2022) that endorses a more holistic process to engage the justice-involved suggests that a combination of "Andragogy, Counseling, and Therapy" (p. 1) be employed to involve a more "integrative approach" (p. 4). This particular methodology could facilitate a more lucrative process by which the formerly justice-involved may properly re-enter into society and their respective communities. Recidivism reduction is the desired outcome. Correctional education programs specifically often attract educators with a pedagogical background in a specific subject area as well as in the ABE field.

Correctional Education Programs and Settings

There are various settings in which correctional education is facilitated. Institutions or agencies in which correctional educators may work include detention centers, state prisons, community correctional organizations, and other social service agencies. There are also classes provided in non-profit organizations that often ally in partnership with educational or correctional institutions so that services such as transitional housing and occupational training may be facilitated. These carceral institutions and social service agencies engage dynamic activities with wraparound services provided in collaboration with educational and employment agencies. Consistency and frequency of learner participation in educational and occupational training opportunities may be unpredictable, however. For many programs, learner enrollment and completion outcomes are inconsistent. This is often complicated by the transient nature of the restored citizens' personal and legal responsibilities which impact their academic progress and overall goals. Furthermore, their enrollment is sometimes contingent upon the structure of the program, the program organization, course offerings relevant to students' needs, and related staffing responsible for executing program objectives.

Safety is an essential principle in correctional institutions. This may be defined as both maintaining one's physical safety as well as protecting various tools and instructional instruments from misuse and/or theft. Teaching, establishing, and reiterating this principle in training prepares the educator for continual awareness and proactive action. Safety training is facilitated by the institution but is not standardized throughout the United States. The level of content specificity and delivery method, whether small group classroom instruction or computer based, also varies. The safety of both employee and facility residents is discussed in training to protect the individual, whether employee or resident, from physical and/or emotional vulnerability during predatory instances of physical attack or psychological manipulation. One must also secure material property such as educational and personal belongings from theft, damage, or misuse. Last, all staff learn how to work cooperatively to deploy departmental policy, accurately report infractions, and identify examples of policy violation. Despite these issues, barriers, and fluidity of participation, educational and occupational training avenues for the justice-involved exist, persist, and are supported by dedicated staff.

Careers in Correctional Education

There are a myriad of job possibilities in correctional education. Thus, there are various professional roles in which one may engage and different routes in which an individual may participate to provide education to individuals experiencing incarceration. These professions range from and involve, but are not limited to, correctional education teachers, standardized test facilitators and proctors, correctional education administrators, post-secondary and continuing education instructors, correctional officers, and correctional librarians. What is also observable are instances where there is interdepartmental movement of these respective educators who either are promoted vertically or move laterally to assume an employment position in a different area of the correctional setting. One of the foremost jobs that is significantly impactful for professionals pursuing opportunities to support restored citizenship is the correctional education teacher.

Correctional Education Teachers

Working in the correctional education space is challenging and dynamic, often imbued with unpredictable events, expectations, and interactions. Correctional educators, thus, are individuals charged with many unique tasks and responsibilities. Likewise, correctional education teachers as correctional educators are individuals who service a diverse population of learners. They often manage and/or are involved with various aspects of educational programming which require creativity and flexibility. These processes foster a correctional education teacher's ability to respond to both the environment in which they work and the diverse needs of students.

Messemer (2006) studied various factors and situations that influenced correctional education teachers' instructional decision-making processes. Five types reported were: defense procedures (safety and security), attributes of classroom characteristics, relationship between correctional education colleagues, the justice-involved facility residents, and correctional education administrators. Though often an important member of the correctional education team, correctional officers did not have a statistically significant influence on educators' decision making.

Thus, individuals who bring educational opportunities to the immured provide resources that empower the justice-involved to work towards restored citizenship, which has a varied meaning to the individual, as well as the legal system. Though the restoration of voting rights depends on the individual's offense and/or the state in which they offend or re-enter, many restored citizens seek to successfully obtain gainful employment, further their education, and reunite with families. The immured or justice-involved students have an array of cognitive abilities, academic skills, personalities, social norms, socio-economic upbringings, and experiences that have posed prior or current barriers to educational participation, attainment, and advancement. Yet, the sustainability of professional success also hinges on the ideal that this profession is a calling or vocation.

> I first recognized this call or vocation when my journey started as an adult basic literacy education educator teaching single teen parents for an adult literacy program governed by a public city school system in the Midwest. During my travels on this occupational journey, my love for teaching was planted, germinated, and eventually blossomed. I continued working in ABE and literacy. Eventually, I gained experience as a high school equivalency test teacher working for a women's prison in the Southwest region of the United States. I encountered many justice-involved individuals with diverse backgrounds, educational experiences, and offenses. At each graduation ceremony, I was inspired as I witnessed the impact that education had on students. They spoke of the change in themselves and their goals for their lives. The trajectory of my career also changed as I shifted my educational and career plans to continue my tenure as a correctional educator.

This notion elevates one's expectations with the possibility of emotional rewards and the idea that positive influences and contributions are being invested in the lives of vulnerable individuals who are in the process of rehabilitating. For students as participants in these respective educational programs, success is not only academic, but also transformational, as evidenced by the positive, professional relationships with teachers and other correctional educators.

Correctional education teachers devise lesson plans by which formal daily instruction is delivered to the student. They provide formal education in preparation for test taking and skill application that builds towards higher levels of knowledge. Sometimes creative expressions of a lesson are stifled or diluted by institutional restrictions, where materials are not permitted on the premises or in the classroom due to content that triggers emotional responses, brings up negative past experiences, or is deemed inappropriate. Curriculum selection and implementation is often controlled by the institutional administration and is contingent on the structure of programs, funding resources, and the various programs' relationships with other entities or institutions, whether departments of education and/or post-secondary schools.

Competencies

Valuable competencies or skills that support an educator's success include flexibility, positivity, creativity, and diligent policy adherence. For example, flexibility and organization work in tandem as a teacher may create a lesson plan and organize materials, only to encounter students who were expected to attend, but do not arrive to class for many reasons. Students' attendance is often impacted by many factors which include but are not limited to: incarcerated units placed on restricted movement ("lockdown"), individual residents assigned to restricted movement ("lockdown"), illnesses experienced by students and/or staff, students who refuse to participate in educational programming, or students who cannot be escorted to class due to correctional officer staff shortages.

Correctional education teachers also serve as models for behavioral expectations that future restored citizens will need to demonstrate and employ in other formal and nonformal settings such as workplaces, homes, and communities. Occupational preparation skills such as resume writing, interview protocols, establishing good habits/choices, and workplace etiquette are also reflected in lesson plans and lesson delivery. Additional principles taught include punctuality, respectful dialogue, conflict resolution, problem solving, budgeting, and other topics that often help to contextualize curriculum and instructional topics. Those respective qualities are often regarded as soft skills and employability skills that have been formalized in programs currently acknowledged as *Transitions* or *Transitional Education*. Some transition programs are foundation courses that are prerequisites to college classes, occupational certificate programs, or skill trade programs. Skills taught in this area are modeled by the instructor who provides pro-social skills and demonstrates how a positive mindset may benefit engagement in the workplace and other environments as well.

In addition to providing services to their respective learners, correctional education teachers also fulfill the administrative duties, tasks, and requirements as defined by their programs. This frequently involves attending staff meetings; participating in continuing education or providing professional development with or to their colleagues; conducting research; attending or presenting at local, state, and national conferences; completing program forms and documents for compliance purposes; and complying with the execution of departmental policies and orders. Executing departmental orders is an essential demonstration of following compliance because departmental orders are the laws by which operations proceed and are managed.

Many educators who enter correctional education come with experience working in elementary and secondary education. Some also have prior experience working in ABE and literacy. Educational preparation for the position of a correctional education educator requires a minimum of a bachelor's degree, a teaching licensure endorsed by their respective states, and a preferred post-baccalaureate degree. Opportunities for promotion laterally or vertically include excelling into the role of an administrator, supervisor, or director, or that of other team members such as special education teacher, test facilitator, administrator, correctional officer, or correctional librarian if properly credentialed.

Exceptional Student Service Teachers

"Compared to the general population, the prison population represents a remarkably high percentage of adults with learning disabilities" (Koo, 2016, p. 240). Unfortunately, endeavors to address the needs of the justice involved with learning disabilities in correctional education programs have been inadequate and restricted (Bell, 2016). Therefore, instructors and educational support for these learners are needed to address their academic abilities and requirements. Thus, correctional education educators who have specialized credentials and duties are essential to service learners with learning challenges or difficulties.

In some states, they are recognized and categorized as Exceptional Student Services or ESS teachers. In other states they are recognized as special education teachers. Their purpose is to work with individual students to support and engage instruction that meets their educational challenges and unique learning mechanisms and cognitive abilities. Educators who encounter these learners must be properly trained to support robust opportunities to educate and rehabilitate these students as well.

Correctional education teachers who work in Exceptional Sstudent Services maintain portfolios of their students, attend Individual Education Plan or IEP meetings, and complete state and program mandates associated with the Individuals with Disabilities Education Act or IDEA law. These instructors have earned an accredited teaching credential and additional licensure to work with students with varying abilities. This additional credential is often earned post-baccalaureate or alongside a graduate degree.

This realm of correctional education is an area that can benefit from program growth and expansion. Many of these immured learners have either received services in the past or self-disclose their experience as having a "learning disability." Some learners have exceeded the age limit and no longer meet the age criteria for services. Typically, special education services are provided to justice-involved students who are 18 years of age and younger, leaving the remaining population subject to the support of their general education teachers. Contingent on the teacher, and/or the respective institution and program, students may or may not receive the adequate services required to make progress and achieve academic goals.

Test Facilitators/Test Proctors

Standardized tests are often utilized in correctional education programs as tools to measure student progress and to demonstrate program accountability. They are also mediums from which data is produced. The U.S. Department of Education (2022) defined standardized tests as "scientifically normed and machine-graded instruments administered to students and adults under controlled conditions to assess capabilities, including knowledge, cognitive skills and abilities, and aptitude" (p. 1). There are specific types of standardized tests that require facilitation in correctional facilities. Some tests facilitated are the *Test of Adult Basic Education*, *GED*®, and *HiSet*.© The *Test of Adult Basic Education* is one such skill assessment by which students' academic growth can be identified and reported as program data. The *Test of Adult Basic Education* provides K-12 grade level equivalent and scale scores to show students' academic educational functioning level, which is meant to drive both assessment of adult learners for teaching and learning transactions and curriculum delivery. The *GED*® and *HiSet*© are tests that produce post-secondary education credentials upon passage. According to the website of the Prison Policy Initiative (2018), "of the 33% of all formerly incarcerated people (age 25+) who hold GEDs as their highest degrees, the vast majority (73%) received them in prison. In total, we find that almost 27% of formerly incarcerated people attained a GED while incarcerated" (p. 1)

Standardized test facilitators or test proctors are essential staff members in correctional education programs and classrooms. These professionals adhere to the protocols of test proctoring, maintain physical and psychological safety of test participants, and prevent or report cheating. Test facilitators also function as data managers who capture, report, and monitor student data. In addition to being organized and detail oriented, test proctors/facilitators execute data management and analysis for future classroom application and program compliance. Their basic educational requirements include an undergraduate degree, but some individuals may possess a graduate degree dependent on previous careers or other occupational backgrounds. To administer these tests these individuals must also be licensed by the respective publisher for the test they will oversee and facilitate. The costs for licensure and training are paid by the correctional institution.

Correctional Education Administrators

Correctional education administrators are also essential personnel that facilitate program operations, educators' professional tenure, and immured students' academic successes. Their titles may be described or categorized as supervisors, principals, or directors. Minimum educational requirements include undergraduate and graduate degrees, teaching licensure as defined by respective states, and a principal's and/or superintendent's licensure. As leaders for both educators and learners, administrators function as liaisons who connect teaching staff with correctional operations to ensure compliance with program and department order directives, and state funding mandates. Administrators supervise curriculum development, departmental budgets, curriculum deployment and implementation, instructional delivery, and professional development. Correctional education administrators engage in communicating the needs of their department by networking with institutional operations, meeting compliance mandates of other state educational agencies, and facilitating memorandums of understanding with contractors employed by post-secondary institutions and non-profit agencies. This requires administrators also to be business savvy as acquiring, maintaining, allocating, and supervising funding to be monitored is critical to overall program operations. Another duty involves conflict resolution. Administrators periodically mediate problems or issues between staff and/or learners and resolve issues and/or complaints that may arise and come to their attention. There are instances in which administrators create, mandate, and disseminate policies for their respective educational departments. Administrators may be responsible for collaborating with other institutions to provide post-secondary education to the incarcerated for successful completion inside the facility. They also work with other staff and personnel to support additional educational and occupational opportunities for students before being released from the institution. Yet, irrespective of these various obligations, one of their most significant responsibilities involves ensuring the safety of staff and learners.

Correctional Officers

Correctional officers are also an educative element in the life of the immured or justice-involved learner. Their educational backgrounds vary with basic requirements including an undergraduate degree, completion of correctional officer training, and previous experience as a correctional officer. Correctional officers may advance to higher ranks in the profession. There are opportunities for officers to engage in re-entry efforts for the justice-involved when they are promoted to the third or fourth levels on their jobs. Then, they may work collaboratively with correctional education teachers to promote the students' successes by providing resources to support a successful transition towards restored citizenship. Many officers have had former careers as military members of the United States Armed Forces or local police departments. Some correctional officers who transition from working solely as officers will make a lateral career move, switching to the role of correctional education teachers, administrators, or librarians. This potentially involves additional education and training of a bachelor's degree and teaching licensure to successfully acquire a position in the education field.

Correctional Librarians

Improving literacy and a love of reading support the immured student with increasing their cognition, improving their academic abilities, and building the stamina for their journey towards restored citizenship. Essential to the correctional education program for this purpose are correctional educational librarians. They are responsible for managing libraries that are housed in various units in the correctional institution. Many are former correctional education teachers, certified librarians from the community, or correctional officers who have retired from correctional supervision, now working in a different role in the field. In addition, professionals who have worked in public libraries are recruited to bring their creativity and experiences to the correctional setting. Correctional librarians manage book lending, facilitate book delivery to individuals in high security levels of custody, and institute reading programs. Many correctional education programs are challenged by the lack of literary resources because they are dependent on donations from the community. Donations must also be screened for security purposes, yet this is one of the most common ways that materials are replenished for correctional libraries.

Continuing Education and Professional Development

Continuing education and lifelong learning are two hallmarks of successful adult education. They are components to formal education (Merriam & Brockett, 2007) that enable adult learners to engage in the process of lifelong learning. Post-secondary institutions are often the conduit by which these transactions occur. In addition, the professional development systems for ABE literacy instructors are governed by their respective programs and states. Though, historically, training, and professional development for adult literacy educators has not been succinct but "sporadic" (Eggleston, 1991), professional expectations for the field have become more rigorous recently within the past 5 to 10 years.

Professional development aids in shaping the educators' experiences so that andragogical knowledge and practices, for example, can be deployed to support the academic advancement of the immured adult learner. Avenues for professional development for aspiring correctional educators vary contingent on their occupational and educational backgrounds. Professional development often complements and supplements the foundational education and experiential knowledge of aspiring correctional educators to support the needs of the justice-involved learners they educate during their tenure in correctional education.

Opportunities in Correctional Education

Many professionals are not initially aware of the adult education opportunities in corrections post-graduation from baccalaureate- or graduate-level education programs. These opportunities are often communicated by current employees to their family, friends, or acquaintances. Many of these occupations can be found via online sites specific to job seekers such as www.indeed.com, www.higheredjobs.com, or on the website of the respective federal, state, or local agency or institution. Applicants may also network via www.linkedin.com. Additional opportunities exist to work and network through organizations such as the Correctional Educators Association (https://ceanational.org), Coalition on Adult Basic Education (https://coabe.org), American Association for Adult and Continuing Education, www.aaace.org), and Association of Career and Technical Education, (www.acteonline.org), which have contributed to the expansion and advancement of the ABE and literacy and correctional education fields. These organizations provide resources for curriculum and instruction, therefore enabling one to network, grow, and develop professionally. Annual conferences are hosted in cities across the United States and internationally where educators and administrators share best practices in teaching and learning. Keynote speakers deliver inspirational and motivational talks that remind practitioners about their purpose, mission, and values in the field. Vendors from educational publishing companies also market or advertise their materials. During these conventions, educators from across the country and world convene to educate, be educated, and accumulate resources to take to their respective programs and students to augment services provided by their program. This further supports learner progress and goal attainment. These educators also grow personally and professionally by immersing in breakout sessions to expand their knowledge and add to their resource bank to benefit their learners.

Recommended Reads

Flores, J., Barahona-Lopez, K., Hawes, J., & Syed, N. (2020). High points of learning behind bars: Characteristics of positive correctional education experiences for incarcerated girls. *International Journal of Educational Development, 77*. https://doi.org/10.1016/j.ijedudev.2020.102210

Flynn, N., & Higdon, R. (2022). Prison education: Beyond review and evaluation. *Prison Journal, 102*(2), 196–216. https://doi.org/10.1177/00328855221079276

Galeshi, R., & Bolin, R. M. (2022). The influence of correctional education, skill proficiency, and lifelong learning on social outcomes of incarcerated individuals: Results from PIAAC. *Social Science Journal, 59*(3), 424–438. https://doi.org/10.1016/j.soscij.2019.09.007

Hall, R. S., & Killacky, J. (2008). Correctional education from the perspective of the prisoner student. *Journal of Correctional Education, 59*(4), 301–320.

Future of Correctional Adult Education Careers

The future of careers in correctional adult education will certainly progress as professionals and programs develop and as people involved in justice movements advocate for restored citizenship for the advancement of individuals' social, civil, educational, and human rights. These issues and concerns are pertinent considering the current societal demands for restorative justice and policies that promote reducing recidivism and mass incarceration. As previously mentioned, traits such as professionalism, patience, flexibility, creativity, organization, and humanitarianism are helpful qualities if individuals are seeking to engage in the field of correctional education. Having a formidable work ethic is a positive asset, yet, if one is contemplating an extensive tenure in this career, it is advisable that they invest in robust self-care as it is easy to get burned out, particularly for educators who are empathetic in nature (Mielke, 2019).

The future of adult education careers in correctional education will also welcome educators who address the cognitive and behavioral deficiencies of adult learners with varying abilities. As the needs for those justice-involved learners grow, more specialized staff will be required. Likewise, as the occupational landscape changes, correctional institutions will need to forge and strengthen partnerships with post-secondary education institutions and agencies to prepare future employees for the workforce. Professionals will also be required to be technologically savvy for curriculum and instructional delivery. Technology plays an essential role in curriculum selection and instructional delivery as current "archaic approach(es)" in dire need of "reform" (Zitko, 2021, p. 3) dissolve. Yet, there are many institutions that have already incorporated technological devices despite restrictions that mandate cyber security. Tablets, stand-alone computers in classes and libraries, educational televisions, and other devices are useful to engage students in augmenting and enhancing their academic experience. The role of the correctional education professional, whether teacher, administrator, test proctor, or librarian, will continue to develop as the field grows and evolves, hopefully with the intent of supporting individuals who will contribute to a more humane society.

References

Bell, C. (2016). Special needs under siege: From classrooms to incarceration. *Sociology Compass, 10*(8), 698–705. https://doi.org/10.1111/soc4.12392

Desir, E., & Whitehead, C. L. (2010). Motivational strategies for correctional practitioners. In M. S. Plathotnik, S. M. Nielsen, & D. M. Pane (Eds.), *Proceedings of the Ninth Annual College of Education & GSN Research Conference* (pp. 12–17). Florida International University. http://coeweb.fiu.edu/research_conference/

Eggleston, C. R. (1991). Correctional education professional development. *Journal of Correctional Education, 42*(1), 16–22.

Hall, L. L. (2015). Correctional education and recidivism: Toward a tool for reduction. *Journal of Correctional Education, 66*(2), 4–29.

Koo, A. (2016). Correctional education can make a greater impact on recidivism by supporting adult inmates with learning disabilities. *Journal of Criminal Law & Criminology, 105*(1), 233–269.

Lee, H. T. (2022, April 10–13) *Correctional education: An integration of andragogy, counseling, & therapy* [Conference presentation]. COABE 2022 Conference, Seattle, WA, United States. https://coabe.org/wp-content/uploads/2020/12/Correctional-Education.pdf

Magee, G. (2021) Education reduces recidivism. *Technium Social Science Journal, 16*, 175–182.

Merriam, S. B, & Brockett, R. G. (2007). *The profession and practice of adult education*. Jossey-Bass.

Messemer, J. E. (2006). *Influences on teacher decision-making in correctional education classrooms* [Doctoral dissertation], University of Georgia.

Mielke, C. (2019). *The burnout cure: Learning to love teaching again*. ASCD. https://ascd.org.

Patterson, M. B., & Mellard, D. (2007). *Program characteristics that predict improved learner outcomes*. National Institute of Child Health & Human Development, National Institute for Literacy, the U.S. Department of Vocational and Adult Education.

Prison Policy Initiative. (2018). *Getting back on course*. prisonpolicy.org/reports/education.html

Ritt, E. (2008). Redefining tradition: Adult learners and higher education. *Adult Learning, 19*(1–2), 12–16.

Thoulin, C. (2021). The impact of state and federal policies on community college correctional education programs. *New Directions for Community Colleges, 196*, 69–79. https://doi.org/10.1002/cc.20484

U.S. Department of Education. (2022). *Structure of the U.S. education system: Standardized tests*. International Affairs Office, U.S. Department of Education. www.ed.gov/international/usnei/edlite-index.html

Vera Institute of Justice. (2019) *Incarceration in local jails and state prisons*. www.vera.org/publications/state-incarceration-trends

Zitko, P. (2021). Redesigning correctional education to meet 21st century learning modalities. *Academia Letters*, Article 691. https://doi.org/10.20935/AL691

Chapter 13

Cultural Institutions and Museum Education

Claire Aldenhuysen

Museums and other related cultural institutions (for the purposes of this chapter, I will use "museums" as an umbrella term) are often nonprofit organizations where staff members are expected to wear many hats. This is advantageous for emerging professionals in adult education who come from various backgrounds with countless skills that can be applied in many unrelated contexts. A career in the arts allows for those who are creative to flex their unique skill set in a way that is both personally fulfilling and advantageous to their home organization.

My Career Journey

My journey in this field began in college, when I was hired to work part time at a museum summer day camp, developing six weeks of educational programming for children in a number of different disciplines. It was a lightbulb moment for me, as I had not realized that museum education was a thing, let alone a potential career. I had always been an artsy kid who spent my childhood being driven to piano lessons, taking dance classes, or drawing little comics. I was never particularly good at any of these things, but I enjoyed them, nonetheless. Teaching in a formal classroom did not appeal to me but leading a group of 10-year-olds in a craft project to make a lizard keychain out of plastic beads was more my speed. I wanted to pursue a career in education without the baggage of tests and quizzes, to teach others how to learn something new for the sake of learning it, just for fun!

Unfortunately, my introduction to nonformal learning (in the museum world it is frequently referred to as informal learning) occurred just around the time of the Great Recession, which meant my life took an unfortunate series of twists and turns. This resulted in a few years of juggling several part-time jobs slinging lattes and hawking band t-shirts, a rather accidental year abroad, and an eventful summer at a Hollywood wax museum before I was able to get back on track and enroll in the Museology graduate program at the University of Washington in Seattle.

Specializing in museum education and administration taught me a lot about what I wanted to do professionally and how I could put my degree to good use. Immediately after graduating, I went to work at a small rural museum until COVID-19 hit. I lost my job and, having done some soul-searching, decided to go back to school to spruce up my resume and make myself more appealing to potential employers in the museum and nonprofit field. Fortunately for me, Ball State University (the "Harvard of Muncie," as some say) had an online master's degree program in Adult and Community Education that could be doubled up with Executive Development for Public Service. I saw this as the perfect opportunity to apply what I had learned both academically and professionally and develop myself as a leader in my field and, hopefully, get back on track (once again).

DOI: 10.4324/9781003259602-16

Museum Education as Adult Education

Adult education and museums have a long history together. References to museums in the adult education canon can be found as early as 1928, in the American Association for Adult Education handbook. Museum education is both similar and different from adult education. Adult educators have much to offer museum studies and vice versa. Grenier (2009) points out that:

> ... the work of adult educators and museums are often two sides of the same coin. To understand this two-sided coin, it is first important to consider the similarities. Both recognize the importance of lifelong learning in society and seek ways to reach learners across their life spans. Both integrate empirical research and practitioner experience in the development of new and existing theories. Finally, both recognize the role of context, content, and experience on the learner and seek out ways to facilitate learning. (p. 3)

Grenier also points out differences including vocabulary and research/studies. Adult education often has a strong focus on community engagement and development with continuing education for adults, such as literacy programs, GED preparation, professional development and training, and other forms of workforce preparatory education.

Regardless of their seemingly divergent paths, there are considerable similarities between the two fields, first and foremost is the focus on lifelong learning. Many people misunderstand the role of museums in their learning journeys, due to the fact that their experiences with museums are usually limited to field trips in elementary school. Museums are often seen by adults as boring, dusty spaces to spend a rainy day. Unless someone intentionally visits a museum as an adult, many "grown-ups" rarely return to these informal learning spaces outside of chaperoning their own children on a field trip. That is where adult educational programming comes in. One thing adults enjoy, and what often draws them to return to the museum as opposed to other forms of entertainment, is the promise of exclusive or "secret" knowledge. This makes behind-the-scenes tours immensely popular, and small wine-and-cheese tours of galleries after hours tend to be a big hit among the adult crowd. Therefore, many museums and science centers will have adult programming that is focused on speaker series, film screenings, and service projects, such as river cleanups. Individuals have limited free time; they have to spend it wisely and ensure that it has meaning and value. Spending a Saturday afternoon at the museum learning about an Impressionist painter can be a valuable, educational experience. It gives the attendees something to talk about and perhaps brag about when they return to the office on Monday morning.

While I was in graduate school, I was constantly applying for jobs that my new degree would help me qualify for. After six months of effort, I managed to land the role of Director of Education for a small, local nonprofit arts education organization, where I managed nearly two dozen part-time teaching artists, created educational programming for children and adults, and, yes, developed summer camps.

The skills I developed have served me well. The same can be said about what I learned in customer service during the years following the Great Recession. Those who have gotten lucky and "fallen into" ideal careers without having to go through years of self-doubt, borderline poverty, and toxic workplaces do not realize the value of the resourcefulness built out of necessity and survival. I can create a budget for art programs because I spent years tracking every penny that went in or out of my meager bank account. I know how to deescalate a situation with an unhappy client because I have been screamed at by customers whose coffees did not turn out right. One learns a lot working customer service and those lessons are not quickly forgotten, no matter how nice the office is now or how long it has been since you have been on the other side of the counter.

Adult Education: Applicable at all Organizational Levels

There are many roles within museums, cultural institutions, and arts organizations, from the unpaid intern to the CEO. At museums and other informal learning institutions, such as science centers, arts education, and libraries, you might see the following positions:

Senior Level

- CEO/Executive Director
- Museum Director
- Chief Executive Officer

Mid-Level

- Director of Education
- Director of Museum Learning
- Curator of Education
- Manager of Museum Education
- Manager of Adult Programs
- Director of Interpretation
- Deputy Director for Learning and Audience Engagement
- Head of Education
- Special Projects Coordinator

Entry Level

- Education Coordinator
- Adult & Community Education Coordinator
- Museum and Academic Programs Coordinator
- Educator
- Educational Program Manager
- Adult Program Manager
- Museum Educator
- Tour Guide
- Education Intern
- Research Associate

At the arts education organization where I worked, the organizational structure of the education department was structured (from top to bottom) beginning with myself as the Director of Education, followed by my direct report, the Education Coordinator, with whom I managed our art instructors and interns.

> **The Joy of Collaboration**
>
> There is never a dull moment when working in a museum or other cultural institution where the "customer" is a potential learner, and the "product" is knowledge. One thing I always enjoyed about working in museum education was the opportunity and ability to work together with other departments within the institution. Every aspect of the museum can benefit from input from the education department. Social media managers can glean "fun facts" (my favorite!) about the

collection or promote upcoming educational events. Administration can use the data and statistics from attendance to share with the board of directors to demonstrate the direction the institution should go in the coming fiscal year.

Some important questions that the administration might be asked about adult education programming are as follows: are the adult programs more popular than the children's programs? Do after-hours lecture series have greater response during certain times of the year? All of this information is beneficial. Even building maintenance and operations can benefit from coordinating with education staff – where is the best place for building signage? Are the restrooms easy for tour groups to find? Are the exhibits or activities ADA accessible? How can we make the space more friendly? – how about adding more seating throughout the building? Can the lighting and sounds be adjusted for sensory-friendly visits? Collaborating with other staff in these ways makes the organization a far more successful and welcoming space for all visitors.

Museum Education for Adults

One of the things that appealed to me about my adult education graduate program was the emphasis on lifelong learning and how to instill a love for the pursuit of knowledge in informal contexts. What I learned from the museum field prior to getting into adult education is that people do love to learn, so long as it is fun. As adult educators, it is our responsibility to create educational experiences that teach people something new without judgment, with joy, through memorable activities. In order to do this, the museum educator needs to intentionally plan programs. Chapter 4 in this volume does an excellent job of explaining the art of program planning, so there is no need for me to repeat it here – but it is certainly a huge part of this field of study and practice! I always used to joke that the best part of museum education was "tricking" people into learning something new – though in my experience, you very rarely need to "trick" adults who are intentionally seeking a learning opportunity. There is typically a spark of preexisting curiosity there that needs to be encouraged into a flame of lifelong learning. We are the bellows – we are there to cultivate that fire and keep it going, and keep individuals coming back for more, whether it is for painting lessons, a lecture series on chocolate, or a nature walk to seek out native birds.

In the 21st century, museums have shifted from a strategy of collection and display to one where educational programming is a driving force (Falk & Dierking, 2016, Weil, 2002). Lord and Lord (2009) suggest that there are "two qualities that characterize the successful management of public programs: visitor-responsiveness and creativity" (p. 87). That perspective continues to inform museum practice to this day (Corona, 2022).

This educational programming, especially in the adult education space, can take many forms: a guided tour with a lecture or an audio tour are two common formats. A tour directed in person provides adults with the opportunity to ask questions and engage more deeply with the subject matter (Grenier & Sheckley, 2008; Specht & Loreit, 2021).

Individuals who visit a museum do so at the intersection of three contexts (Falk & Dierking, 2016). The author classifies those as the personal, sociocultural, and physical. These contexts shape the adult visitors' experiences. As a museum educator, it is important to be cognizant of these aspects as you plan your educational offerings. "Visitors now cocreate and cocurate their journey with the museum, and that process is unending the way museums and exhibits are designed" (Walhimer, 2022, p. 3).

Important Competencies

Every single role in a cultural institution requires an individual to be (figuratively!) quick on their feet, knowledgeable about their organization, and willing to step in where needed. Museum education is most certainly the field of the generalists of the world, who may be coming into the organization with a completely different background than their colleagues. Every position is a little different and asks different things of the applicant, but the thread tying most, if not all, museum education roles together, is a responsibility to educate the public in some way. Museums are usually looking for someone who has expertise in at least one of the following: education, leadership, business, public relations, marketing, and even social media, as well as a background in the museum's primary focus (art or science, for instance).

Education departments in particular are often looking for expertise in program planning, developing curriculum, and leading educational activities. Although their primary aim is to be educational destinations, museums are still businesses and tourist destinations within their communities, which means they want someone who can be a spokesperson for the organization. In many ways, the representatives of the education department become the face of the museum in the public sphere, meaning they must cast their net wide to draw in all audiences. Outside of the primary duties of the position, job listings often mention that the ideal candidate is someone who is passionate, inspirational, collaborative, and visionary; someone who sparks interest, arouses curiosity, and engages others in learning; all this and more.

> **Success Tip: The Elevator Pitch**
>
> I always have an "elevator pitch" on hand about my organization when someone asks me what I do or where I work; it typically has the institution's name (of course!), what I do there, and what our upcoming programming looks like and how it might interest the other person. If your institution has any kind of discounted tickets or programs, it is great to carry around a day pass or two to give to interested folks with your business card stapled to them. I used to keep a handful of free admission tickets to the museum where I worked in my glove box in my car in case I ran into anyone who expressed more than a passing interest. You never know when you might help someone learn something new or discover a new passion!

Flexibility

It is important to be flexible when working in education in cultural institutions, because you might suddenly be asked to table a booth at a community event or run a summer camp because your instructors called out sick at the last minute. You should always have an activity or two on hand that can be done with limited or no supplies to entertain kids if you suddenly find yourself, for example, having to host a tour for a group of 80 second graders whose school forgot to schedule ahead of time and figured they could "just drop in for a field trip." It is good to prep these "just in case" projects and have them stashed away in your office or multipurpose room for these sorts of situations. You might be exhausted by the end of the afternoon, but everyone leaves happy and with a take-home craft in hand.

Improvisation

Now is your chance to flex those improv skills as a "professional edutainer!" There is also a considerable amount of stage presence required for this work, and you will learn quickly how to be "on" for your audience to both entertain and educate them... yes, you will be in the business of "edutainment"! But it is a ton of fun, and you will find that even the most introverted person will enjoy their moment in the spotlight as they lead a tour around the museum and share their knowledge. And if you are extroverted, you will thoroughly enjoy the opportunity to have a captive audience to (hopefully) laugh at your very cheesy jokes about airplanes, dinosaurs, or minerals. This tour totally *rocks*, amiright folks? I can hear your groans from here. *Good*. They replenish my electrolytes.

Creativity and Curiosity

In order to succeed in cultural institutions like museums or arts organizations, creativity and curiosity are an absolute must. These are places for people who read entire books on the history of salt (guilty) and spend the following week boring their family and friends with "fun facts" about salt; people who love to collect and learn about gemstones and minerals (or just like to pick up neat rocks they find while out on a walk); people who knit on the weekend; people who read for fun. These are the people who have dabbled in many creative endeavors throughout their lives and are prime candidates for this sort of work.

I would recommend as a precautionary tale to always have a hobby that is steadfastly and diametrically opposed to what you do every day for work – whether it is jogging, volunteering to care for exotic birds at the local shelter, or participating in a drum circle in the park – to keep yourself from burning out. Some of the best advice I got in graduate school was to not spend every weekend in a museum, because you will burn out on the very thing you were passionate about before you even get started. If you simply cannot help yourself, try visiting a museum or cultural institution that is quite different from the one where you work. Curator in an art museum? Try visiting a transportation museum to learn about trains and automobiles, or tag along with the local chapter of the Audubon Society on a birding hike. When you are in the business of learning, "treating" yourself to a new subject or topic is always a delight and can often remind you of why you got into this field in the first place. Plus, who knows? Maybe you will realize you *really like trains* or end up investing in some binoculars and downloading a bird identification app on your phone in order to identify the birds flitting around your backyard.

Like Being Indiana Jones (Sort Of)

Museum work can be wildly varied, especially when you work in education—sometimes, in many museums, the education department becomes the catch-all (especially in smaller institutions where staffing is limited) and you will wear many hats, which can be great for the multi-tasker. Hopefully, you can find a role where your primary focus is on education-related tasks, which, depending on your seniority or leadership level, can have differing degrees of audience engagement and community involvement.

Moving Up the Ladder

Entry-level museum educators will be the ones "in the field" so to speak, going to schools for museum-in-a-box programs, conducting tours aka being a docent, whereas middle management education staff would be in the office, developing programming for both permanent and rotating exhibitions, coordinating field trips, and creating outreach opportunities within the community. Depending on how introverted or extroverted you are, either one of these directions could be a great fit! I found that when I was newer to the field, I loved doing community events, but as I began to seek leadership roles, I wanted to focus more on the logistical and administrative side.

Similarly, in an arts education organization, the higher up your role within the organizational hierarchy, the less you will be interacting with the public on a daily basis. In a lot of ways, it is like being the principal of a school. As Director of Education, you will be dealing with things like analytics, databases, tracking revenue, purchasing art supplies, creating job postings, developing programming, coaching staff on classroom management, and curriculum development. This role is an excellent one for someone with a background in business, fundraising, teaching, or human resources. Having a background in art is not necessarily a requirement but having an understanding and appreciation of the arts and, more importantly, how artists themselves function in a work environment, can be invaluable. Collaborating with artists and creatives can often feel like herding cats, but it is ultimately an extremely affirming experience when you receive feedback from your learners about how much they loved their instructor and the class.

When I was in my previous role, my education coordinator and I sometimes described our positions as the principal and vice principal to people who asked what it was, exactly, we did. At my graduation from the University of Washington, our keynote speaker joked that this would be the final time we would be in a room full of people who actually knew what we did for a living. My experience with adult, community, and museum education as a field has turned out to be very similar; the only difference is that people tend to be a bit impressed when they hear what my degree is in, instead of misunderstanding and asking what instrument I play (museology sounds incredibly similar to musicology for the uninitiated—and for the record, I did grow up playing piano and clarinet but cannot profess much skill in either at this point in my life, certainly not enough to get a graduate degree!). Having a graduate degree in a discipline that is recognizable and easy to understand is very advantageous in the job hunt. I had considerably more call backs and invitations to interviews once I obtained my degree in adult education, because hiring managers actually knew what it was I studied. And while this may be exclusive to job hunting in a smaller community, I found that once I earned a degree from the local university, there was more interest in my applications from local organizations than ever before.

Finding That Coveted Museum Position

For museum professionals, the American Alliance of Museums (AAM) (www.aam-us.org) is a valuable resource for job postings, professional development, and networking, as well as for discounted tickets to the annual convention. Joining regional museum associations is equally, if not more, beneficial for the localized aspect of your network can pave the way for museum partnerships and programmatic crossover (statewide museum road trips, anyone?). There is also the Museum Education Roundtable (www.museumedu.org), the Visitor Studies Association (www.visitorstudies.org), and The Group for Education in Museums (www.gem.org.uk).

Finding a job in the museum field can be tough, but there are plenty of good websites to get your search started, including Indeed, LinkedIn, HigherEdJobs, and the American Alliance of Museums' job board. There are also job boards for regional and statewide positions; it all depends on where you want to live and what you want to do. If you are not tied down by obligations to one location, I would recommend casting as wide a net as possible and looking not only locally, but regionally, nationally, and internationally for positions in museums and adult education. There is opportunity everywhere for people in this field, especially with the degree of variety and experience that people bring into it. Begin your search by looking up any of the roles listed earlier in the chapter; it will give you a good idea of what is available in your preferred locality.

The Association for Arts Administration Educators (AAAE) (https://artsadministration.org) is a membership organization that functions similarly to AAM, but specifically for arts administration educators. A great deal of support can be found on the local level as well by getting involved in nonprofits with causes you care about and serving as a board member. You can also join professionals' groups either online or in person to network with others within and outside your field. This is helpful both in small towns and larger cities; regardless of population, you will frequently find yourself running in the same circles with the same people, especially if you are lucky enough to find a networking group that aligns with your interests. Leadership workshops for professional development are another excellent option to network and to get yourself immersed in your local community and understand its inner workings. I recently completed an 8-week workshop for emerging leaders and came out with over a dozen new friendships among fellow movers and shakers and a much stronger feeling of connection with my community. I realized how interconnected the nonprofit and for-profit organizations and businesses were and how they can help each other in countless ways. Networking is your friend here; the museum world is extremely small and knowing the right people can get you in the door when other tactics may fail.

Looking *Beyond* NYC, LA, and DC

Success can mean different things to different people. Working in this field can be incredibly fulfilling regardless of salary. There are plenty of museums and cultural organizations in smaller cities and towns throughout the United States where the cost of living is a fraction of what you will find in "the Big City," and quality of life is exponentially better too. So, living on a smaller salary is not always a deal breaker, especially if you love the work you do! I hope this advice will be a salve to those mid-career professionals who are already happily settled somewhere and would prefer not to move. It may take extra effort or time to find a suitable local role but it is worth it to not have to uproot yourself and your entire life if you do not have to! On the other hand, if you have the means and ability to move somewhere new (and your significant other/partner/family are on board), take a chance! You never know unless you take that leap!

Furthermore, many smaller organizations in smaller communities are more flexible and actually promote a work/life balance as well, which is priceless. It helps, too, to set boundaries sooner rather than later; the educational field is both gratifying and exhausting and you absolutely must protect yourself from burnout! The arts are incredibly diverse and can be a wonderful place for those of us who may not otherwise feel comfortable living our authentic selves. People who have suffered through toxic workplaces understand how valuable and affirming it is to work somewhere where you are not judged, harassed, or fired for your identity or ethnicity. To be surrounded by people who are not only accepting of you, but supportive, makes the work environment that much more positive.

To me, success in the museums and cultural organizations field means being doggedly persistent and continuing to improve yourself and move forward until you achieve your goals. Going back to graduate school and earning my double master's in Adult & Community Education and Executive Development for Public Service provided a competitive advantage and showed my dedication to the field in a way that my previous degree in Museology did not. Furthermore, it broadened my horizons both personally and professionally. I realized that I could apply my skills in the wider nonprofit sphere and do good for my community in more ways than one.

References

Corona, L. (2022). Digitization for the visibility of collections. *Collection and Curation*, *42*(3), 73–80. https://doi.org/10.1108/CC-06-2022-0024

Falk, J. H., & Dierking, L. D. (2016). *The museum experience revisited* (1st ed.). Routledge.

Grenier, R. S. (2009). The role of learning in the development of expertise in museum docents. *Adult Education Quarterly*, *59*(2), 142–157. https://doi.org/10.1177/0741713608327369

Grenier, R. S., & Sheckley, B. (2008). Out on the floor: Experiential learning and the implications for the preparation of docents. *Journal of Museum Education*, *33*(1), 79–93.

Lord, G. D., & Lord, B. (2009). *The manual of museum management*. AltaMira Press.

Specht, I., & Loreit, F. (2021). Empirical knowledge about person-led guided tours in museums: A scoping review. *Journal of Interpretation Research*, *26*(2), 96–130.

Walhimer, M. (2022). *Designing museum experiences*. Rowman & Littlefield.

Weil, S. E. (2002). *Making museums matter*. Smithsonian Books.

Chapter 14

Careers in Diversity, Equity, and Inclusion

Ian C. Barrett

My Experience

For 30 years, I have worked in human resource (HR) management and human resource development. My career happened by coincidence. After completing my MBA, I worked in pharmaceuticals sales. After trying that for a year, I moved into an operations analyst role with a security guard firm. The personnel specialist decided to leave the firm, and they asked me if I was interested in the role. I applied and was hired by the district manager. In the personnel specialist role, I led recruiting, benefits, HR compliance, payroll, and administration, and supervised two staff members. I also facilitated new employee orientation, which was my introduction to the practice of adult education. New employee orientation focused on four areas: organizational mission, vision, and values; federal and state laws and regulations; company policies and procedures; and employee benefits and payroll.

Years later, I moved on to work for a health insurance company and diversity was a priority in my role. I was a recruiter, and senior management was interested in hiring college graduates of color to join our professional staff. HR was tasked to lead this program. We identified underwriter and financial analyst roles for recruitment. We selected universities and contacted their career centers. We visited campuses and conducted interviews, invited finalists to our offices for additional interviews, and made job offers, many of which were accepted. We had several new college graduates of color join our organization as their first jobs post-graduation. The program was a success based on the established goal of hiring college graduates of color.

> At another employer, I developed an affirmative action plan. I had no formal training and learned through experience. I joined a large private research university in the late 1990s. The federal government had audited the organization's employment practices and identified areas of noncompliance. For the next year, my colleagues and I worked to capture demographic data on every applicant. While this data was voluntary on the applicants' part, we were required to ask for it. We analyzed job selection, promotion, and involuntary termination rates by race and gender. We identified deficient areas and implemented improvement actions. A subsequent audit found that we were complying with the federal standards.

Over the years, my roles have included experiences in the private, public, and nonprofit sectors. My positions have changed, from the entry-level role of personnel specialist to my current role as executive vice president and chief human resources officer. In summary, my diversity experience includes developing diversity vision statements and strategies, facilitating diversity councils, and leading diversity programs (e.g., recruiting, training and development,

DOI: 10.4324/9781003259602-17

mentoring and coaching, employee resources groups, climate assessment and external benchmarking, diversity events, and affirmative action), all with a goal of creating lasting change.

The Field of Organizational Diversity, Equity, and Inclusion

What is now known as workforce diversity, equity, and inclusion (DEI) began as affirmative action. To advance representation, affirmative action is the tool that federal contractors and subcontractors use to advance minorities, women, people with disabilities, and veterans in the workforce (United States Department of Labor, n.d.). Richard Nixon was the first president to sanction formal goals and timeframes to lower barriers to minority employment (Kotlowski, 1998).

Administered by the Office of Federal Contract Compliance Programs, affirmative action requires federal contractors to perform statistical data analysis to show that their hiring, promotion, and termination practices are fair to minorities and women. In addition, a plan of affirmative action outreach must be developed for minorities, women, people with disabilities, and veterans. Because of these federal requirements, the role of affirmative action manager was born.

The 1980s and 1990s saw a shift from affirmative action to a broader field of diversity management. Thomas in 1990 posited that we needed to move from affirmative action to affirming diversity and that the power of diversity is the mixture of both similarities and differences (Thomas & Woodruff, 1999). Today, many identities comprise diversity including

> race, color, national or ethnic origin, ancestry, age, religion, disability, sex or gender (including pregnancy, sexual harassment and other sexual misconduct including acts of sexual violence such as rape, sexual assault, stalking, sexual exploitation, sexual exploitation and coercion, relationship/intimate partner violence and domestic violence), gender identity and/or expression (including a transgender identity), sexual orientation, military or veteran status, genetic information, the intersection of these identities or any other characteristic protected under applicable federal, state or local law.
>
> (Tufts University, 2023, para. 1)

Roles and Responsibilities

Many roles exist in a DEI function. Industry, size, geographic footprint (i.e., local, regional, national, global), and maturity of the function all contribute to the team size and roles. Outlined here are some common roles.

Diversity Coordinator. This is a role that primarily provides administrative and operational support. Duties include performing customer service for leaders, employees, board members, vendors, and the public. The responsibilities encompass general office tasks (e.g., processing transactions, coordinating meetings, and managing files) and supporting the leader and staff on the diversity team. The diversity coordinator may lead diversity events and celebrations (e.g., Women's History Month) by working with the diversity team to identify overall goals, select speakers, create communication, plan refreshments, and manage logistics (see Chapter 4 for additional information about program planning). The incumbent may schedule organizational leaders to attend community and civic events. A diversity coordinator is an entry-level role, which can be found in any-size organization.

Diversity Program Manager. A professional role that has some autonomy, discretion, and decision making. The incumbent may lead diversity programs, such as affirmative action planning, diversity training, and employee resource groups. For diversity training, this role may use a curriculum design model such as ADDIE – assessment, design, development, implementation, and evaluation, which is one of a plethora of curriculum design models (see Chapter 10 for more details about this model). This professional may engage in problem solving through internal consulting engagements. For example, an organizational leader may ask for assistance to help with a problem. The diversity program manager would collaborate with the client to assess and diagnose, and then plan, implement, and evaluate an intervention (Chapter 5 provides more details about evaluations). The professional may align their work with other colleagues in recruiting and selection, training and development, and community relations.

Diversity Director. Leads a DEI function and people. This director may lead a diversity program for a small- to medium-size organization or a new program. The focus of the role is operational in nature, ensuring that programs are well run and well liked. The programs may include all those managed or coordinated by the diversity coordinator and diversity program manager. The director is responsible for leading the employees and managing the processes of recruiting, training, performance management, and career coaching for the team.

Chief Diversity Officer. Also known as the CDO, they are the strategic leader for a medium- to large-size organization or a more mature program. They function as a member of the organization's executive team, which works to identify the organization's vision, mission, strategies, priorities, and outcomes. As a senior leader, the CDO focuses on the organization's reputation with stakeholders, such as customers, employees, board members, and the community. DEI have an impact on stakeholders, and the CDO makes sure the diversity lens is brought to important decisions. The CDO takes the organization's plan to craft a diversity strategy with associated outcomes and assigned persons to tasks. This leader is the facilitator of the DEI plan and adapts it based on emerging external issues and internal focus areas.

The National Association of Diversity Officers in Higher Education (2020) website provides the 16 professional standards developed for CDOs in colleges and universities. They are:

1 Frame the work based on comprehensive definitions of diversity, equity, and inclusion.
2 Embed diversity, equity and inclusion in organizational mission, vision, and strategic plan.
3 Facilitate organizational change.
4 Work with leaders to revise policies, procedures and practices that create structural barriers to access and success.
5 Promote inclusive excellence in teaching, learning, and cocurricular programs.
6 Promote inclusive excellence in research, creativity, and scholarship.
7 Engage in evidence-based practice.
8 Collaborate to plan and develop diversity, equity, and inclusion infrastructure.
9 Optimize the balance between centralized and decentralized work.
10 Build organizational capacity for diversity, equity, and inclusion.
11 Conduct periodic climate assessment to identify strengths and gaps.
12 Take a lead role to address hate-bias incidents.
13 Partner with others to mentor diversity activities.
14 Commit to advance diversity throughout the organization.
15 Lead compliance with laws, regulations, and policies.
16 Display high levels of ethical practice.

Diversity Consultant. An outside subject matter expert who provides services to an organization. This professional may function in several ways. First, the diversity consultant can bring expertise from consulting widely across industries and deeply within organizations. They bring expertise that the organization needs. For example, as people from Afghanistan and Ukraine come to the United States because of political unrest and war, health systems and public schools may engage consultants with expertise in the Afghan and Ukrainian culture with a goal of providing culturally appropriate services. Another example is diversity assessment and strategy. Oftentimes, an organization wants to start a diversity journey. Its executives may believe that it is the right thing to do, and stakeholders (especially employees) are pushing it to act. The organization may bring in a diversity consultant to help it assess its current internal climate and external marketplace. Based on the assessment results, the consultant would work with senior leaders to develop a multi-year diversity strategy with some immediate next steps. A second way that a diversity consultant may be used is to function as an additional resource. If an organization wants to provide diversity training, it may buy the curriculum and services of a facilitator versus developing and facilitating its own program. Diversity consultants can facilitate focus groups and meetings, develop diversity scorecards, and co-author and co-deliver presentations to various stakeholders. Diversity consultants are ubiquitous and much of the business is based on relationships and word-of-mouth referrals. (Additional information on consulting can be found in Chapter 10.)

Competencies, Degrees, and Career Pathways

In the previous section, various roles and titles, along with day-to-day activities, have been discussed for careers in DEI for adult educators. Now, the topics of competencies, credentials, degrees, and pathways will be addressed.

Competencies

The diversity coordinator's role is like that of the administrative coordinator, administrative assistant, or executive assistant. The competencies necessary for this position include verbal communication and client service, written communication and document production, technology management, records management, event management, and project coordination (International Association of Administrative Professionals, n.d.).

The diversity program manager, diversity director, chief diversity officer, and diversity consultant roles, which are professional positions, have a core set of competencies that they share. Sometimes the proficiency-level requirements are different (e.g., more advanced for the director role compared to the program manager role). The director and CDO role have additional competencies. The U.S. Government Office of Personnel Management website (n.d.) publishes Proficiency Levels for Leadership Competencies in their *Policy, Data, Oversight Assessment & Selection* section. The overall competencies are leading change, leading people, results driven, business acumen, building coalitions, and fundamental competencies. What follows is an analysis using sub-competencies, which are components of the overall competencies.

For the professional roles, the key competencies are creativity and innovation, external awareness, conflict management, leveraging diversity, problem solving, technical credibility, partnering, political savvy, and influencing/negotiating. External awareness and technical credibility are extremely important. Stakeholders look to diversity professionals to know what is going on in the world (e.g., racial equity, #MeToo, and reproductive rights movements), along with the impact on internal and external priorities. Diversity professionals need to have technical credibility in topics such as white privilege, institutional racism, imposter syndrome, tokenism, and performative activism or slacktivism—defined as feel-good activism with little meaningful social or political impact (Kristofferson et al., 2013). Diversity professionals need to be knowledgeable to facilitate discussions and guide people to resources.

The diversity director role both leads the work and manages the people. While partnering, political savvy, and influencing/negotiation are important in the diversity program manager role, the proficiency level for the director is higher. The diversity director may be the highest diversity professional in the organization. They may be called on to be a thought partner with executive leaders and leaders in other functions. For example, an employer may have a no tobacco use policy for new hires. The intended goal could be to improve the health of the employee population and decrease health insurance costs. An unintended consequence could be excluding certain demographic groups from employment at higher rates because of the prevalence of tobacco use in those groups. To change a policy such as this one, the diversity director may need to build a partnership with HR and Finance to influence the decision-making of executives. Developing others, team building, human capital management (e.g., recruiting, training, performance management, and career coaching), and financial management are required competencies.

For the chief diversity officer, the additional competencies are strategic thinking and vision. The CDO begins with the organization's strategy and leads the development of a diversity strategic plan that is aligned to the organization's strategic plan. The CDO develops a diversity vision to guide the work of the diversity team and the actions of leaders at all levels and employees. The vision should be inclusive and detailed enough so that people can see how their role contributes.

The diversity consultant role requires a competency in business development. To remain viable, the consultant identifies new clients and manages current clients. Business development involves prospecting, client identification, needs assessment, solution generation, negotiation, implementation, evaluation, and after-sale servicing.

Degrees and Credentials

The diversity coordinator role generally requires a high school diploma and administrative experience and can be the entry point for a person with a bachelor's degree. The diversity program manager position requires a bachelor's degree and 3 years of related experience and can be the entry role for an individual with a master's degree. Individuals come into the field with business, education, psychology, and ethnic studies degrees, among others. The diversity director role often requires a master's degree. A doctorate degree is looked upon favorably for the chief diversity officer role. While educational attainment is not a requirement for the diversity consultant role, degrees add credibility and many consultants have earned degrees.

The curriculum of adult education programs – Standards for Graduate Programs in Adult Education (Commission of Professors of Adult Education, 2014) prepares graduates for roles as diversity professionals. Diversity training, program planning, and outcomes measurement are three standard responsibilities in DEI. First, diversity training is ubiquitous and occurs in many workplaces (Newkirk, 2019). Oftentimes, diversity training is focused on knowledge acquisition. Adult educators have the proficiency to incorporate adult learning theory into a diversity curriculum (see Chapter 2), make training more experiential, identify how to incorporate technology, and focus on skill development. Second, diversity professionals plan many types of programs (e.g., cultural events and award ceremonies). Program planning (see Chapter 4) is essential for developing and implementing diversity programs and adult educators are well skilled in producing programs. Third, much of the work in DEI involves evaluating outcomes (see Chapter 5). For existing programs (e.g., hiring, pay, promotions, and terminations), adult educators can analyze outcomes along racial, gender, and other diversity dimensions to identify and highlight bias (Newkirk, 2019). For new programs, adult educators are skilled at needs assessment, objective setting, implementation of evidence-based programming, and outcome measurement, with a goal of achieving planned outcomes.

Certifications

Many organizations offer diversity certifications as an opportunity for individuals to develop knowledge and skills in DEI. Certificates may not be included as job required qualifications but are included as preferred qualifications and looked upon favorably. Universities offer DEI certifications as continuing education and professional development programs.

Cornell University has a series of long-running and well-respected Diversity & Inclusion certificates including, for example, programs for HR professionals, women, and one specifically focused on change initiatives. https://ecornell.cornell.edu/certificates/diversity-inclusion/

Georgetown University offers a six-course Executive Certificate in Diversity, Equity & Inclusion, which prepares professionals to analyze, diagnose, and address DEI issues in organizations. https://scs.georgetown.edu/programs/396/certificate-in-diversity-equity-inclusion/

The University of Nevada, Las Vegas, College of Education, offers an 18-hour credit program: Graduate Certificate Chief Diversity Officer in Higher Education. www.unlv.edu/certificate/chief-diversity-officer-higher-education#catalog

The goal is to prepare professionals to be proficient in the National Association of Diversity Officers in Higher Education Standards of Practice.

Some of the top 10 schools on the 2023 Best Education Schools list offer DEI certificates (U.S. News, n.d.). For example:

Harvard University Graduate School of Education: Leading for Excellence and Equity: A Certificate in Advanced Education Leadership Module. www.gse.harvard.edu/ppe/program/leading-excellence-and-equity-cael

Teacher College Columbia University: Reimagining Education for a Racially Just Society. www.tc.columbia.edu/admission/reed/

University of Pennsylvania: Race, Diversity, and Equity in Higher Education. www.gse.upenn.edu/academics/center-professional-learning/race-diversity-equity-higher-education-certificate

Professional organizations and online educational platforms offer certification programs as well. For example:

American Hospital Association Institute for Diversity and Health Equity: Certificate in Diversity Management in Health Care, https://ifdhe.aha.org/certificate-diversity-management-health-care-cdm

American Management Association: Diversity, Equity, and Inclusion Certificate Program. www.amanet.org/diversity-and-inclusion-certificate-program/

Association for Talent Development: DEI in Talent Development Certification. www.td.org/education-courses/dei-in-talent-development-certificate

edX and Catalyst: Inclusive Leadership, www.edx.org/professional-certificate/catalystx-inclusive-leadership

edX and Catalyst: Race, Gender, and Workplace Equity, www.edx.org/professional-certificate/catalystx-race-gender-and-workplace-equity

Career Pathways

DEI roles are found in public, private, and nonprofit sectors. Cooper and Gerlach (2019) found that one in four of the 250 largest cities in the United States hired a chief diversity officer. People with interest and/or experience can find opportunities across industry, size, geographic footprint (i.e., local, regional, national, global), and maturity of the diversity function.

People come from a variety of work and educational backgrounds to DEI work. The common path is that a person works in human resource management and has diversity work as a part of their portfolio. It could be through recruiting for job openings, with a focus on inclusive pools of diverse applicants. It could be managing the firm's affirmative action program.

A second way that individuals enter the field is via education. Some professionals come with K-12 education experience. Some are college professors and instructors who transition to diversity work. Others may be engaged in other forms of adult education, such as adult basic education, human resource development, or corporate learning before they enter diversity work.

A third way that people come into the field is through community relations. Oftentimes the issues are similar (e.g., equity), the skill sets are similar (e.g., relationship building, influencing), but the audiences may be different (e.g., diversity may be internal focused versus community relations, externally focused). Some community relations professionals leverage their knowledge, skills, and competencies to transition into diversity.

Finally, another entrance into the field is to learn from experience. First, many work organizations have diversity councils and employee resource groups. Often, the diversity team leads this work. Leaders and employees serve and do this work as part of their regular jobs. Second, diversity may be built into a job. For example, a school principal may work with her team to disaggregate student achievement based on demographic factors (e.g., race, ethnicity, zip code, free/reduced-fee lunch status). The purpose would be to find any significant differences and address them with evidence-based interventions. The goal would be equity in student achievement across groups. Third, many boards of directors have diversity committees or diversity components in their human resources or governance committees. Through education and experience, these three groups of individuals develop diversity competence, and some people take these skills into full-time diversity roles.

> A few years ago, I worked at a university, and we employed a diversity program manager. The incumbent had left more than six months earlier, and we determined that we still had a need for this role. Responsibilities included leading the diversity council, employee resource groups and the affirmative action program. A diverse pool of people applied for this role, and they came from a variety of backgrounds. One person was a higher education diversity professional who focused on working with students. They had been a student at this university and was hired to join the staff upon graduation. Another person had 8 years' experience working at the university. Along the way, they volunteered with a group of colleagues to start an employee resource group. Not only did this individual produce professional development programs but also built relationships, showcased their talents, and developed new skills. In addition, this person created a community foundation to serve others. Another person had experiences in qualitative research, grant writing, fundraising, marketing, and volunteer management, all in the nonprofit sector. This candidate had more than 10 years volunteer leadership experience with an LGBTQ civil rights organization. Finally, a fourth person had been a student and graduate assistant at a large public research university where they earned both a bachelor's and master's degree. After graduation, this individual remained at the university as assistant director and then director of diversity for one of the colleges within the university. These candidates met the knowledge, skills, and experience requirements for the position, and we enthusiastically interviewed all of them.

Adult Education Practice and Theory

Groen and Kawalilak (2014) provide a review of the foundational theories of adult learning, which are andragogy, self-directed learning, experiential learning, and transformative learning. Each theory has its place in DEI. Andragogy is the art and science of learning in adults (Knowles, 1980). Adult life experiences serve as a foundation for learning. DEI professionals and learners in organizations also bring their life experiences to this work. Self-directed learning is systematic learning that occurs in adults and is independent from an instructor or classroom (Merriam & Bierema, 2014). This type of learning occurs with DEI professionals as they work to improve their practice, and with adult learners who seek to enhance their DEI competence. Experiential learning is key as it encourages "adult educators and learners to recognize, design, engage in and value learning beyond formal, classroom-based, cognitive activities" (Groen & Kawalilak 2014, p. 75). Finally, transformative learning should be the focus of diversity work. "Transformative learning is a process of changing perspectives and habits of mind, ultimately resulting in changes in behavior" (Owen, 2021, p. 125). To advance DEI, transformative learning can be a tool for both diversity professionals and learners as we seek to change. (More information can be found in Chapter 2.)

Current and Emerging Trends in the Field

The field of DEI continues to grow and develop. One trend is the growth in diversity jobs. Organizations in the for-profit, public, and nonprofit sectors, of assorted sizes and a variety of geographic footprints (i.e., local, regional, national, global), have added diversity roles (Cooper and Gerlach, 2019; Newkirk, 2019). A second trend is the simultaneous advancement of both social justice movements and political polarization. In the United States, government programs meant to level the playing field and make up for past discrimination (e.g., affirmative action) have come under greater scrutiny. Some organizations have chosen to remain silent, while others have chosen to respond both internally and externally. Third, stakeholders want organizations to take actions and achieve results. It is no longer okay to engage in performative activism, like a public relations statement condemning racial injustice. Stakeholders are holding organizations accountable for real change.

Professional Associations

Here are some professional associations for persons interested in DEI careers.

- American Association for Access, Equity and Diversity (AAAED): www.aaaed.org/aaaed/default.asp
- Association of Law Firms Diversity Professionals: https://alfdp.com
- National Association of Diversity Officers in Higher Education: www.nadohe.org

Job Listings

DEI roles may be found on general job boards. Association websites also list DEI career opportunities.

- Association for Talent Development: www.td.org
- College and University Professional Association for Human Resources: www.cupahr.org
- Society for Human Resource Management: www.shrm.org

Three Recommended Readings

Klagge, J. (1996). The leadership role of today's middle manager. *Journal of Leadership Studies, 3*(3), 11–19. https://doi.org/10.1177/107179199700300303

McDonald, D. M. (2016). *What is a diversity manager? Developing a study framework from an analysis of the literature.* [Unpublished manuscript]. https://doi.org/10.13140/RG.2.1.1411.6248

Williams, D., & Wade-Golden, K. C. (2013). *The chief diversity officer: Strategy, structure, and change management.* Stylus.

References

Commission of Professors of Adult Education. (2014). *Standards for graduate programs in adult education.* https://cdn.ymaws.com/www.aaace.org/resource/resmgr/Engage/Commissions/CPAE/cpae_2014_standards_update.pdf

Cooper, C. A., & Gerlach, J. D. (2019). Diversity management in action: Chief diversity officer adoption in America's cities. *State and Local Government Review, 51*(2), 113–121. https://doi.org/10.1177/0160323x19879735

Groen, J., & Kawalilak, C. (2014). *Pathways of adult learning: Professional and education narratives.* Canadian Scholars Press, Inc.

International Association of Administrative Professionals. (n.d.). *IAAP cap body of knowledge.* www.iaap-hq.org/page/CAPBOK

Knowles, M. S. (1980). *The modern practice of adult education: From pedagogy to andragogy* (2nd ed.). Cambridge Books.

Kotlowski, D. (1998). Richard Nixon and the origins of affirmative action. *Historian, 60*(3), 523–541.

Kristofferson, K., White, K., & Peloza, J. (2013). The nature of slacktivism: How the social observability of an initial act of token support affects subsequent prosocial action. *Journal of Consumer Research, 40*(6), 1149–1166. https://doi.org/10.1086/674137

Merriam, S. B., & Bierema, L. L. (2014). *Adult learning: Linking theory to practice.* Jossey-Bass.

National Association of Diversity Officers in Higher Education. (2020). *Standards of professional practice for chief diversity officers in higher education 2.0.* https://nadohe.memberclicks.net/standards-of-professional-practice-for-chief-diversity-officers

Newkirk, P. (2019, October 21). Diversity has become a booming business. So where are the results? *TIME Magazine, 194*(16–17), 38–39.

Owen, R. (2021). Using mindfulness to promote transformative learning in implicit racial bias training. *Adult Learning, 32*(3), 125–131. https://doi.org/10.1177/1045159520981165

Thomas, R. R. (1990). From affirmative action to affirming diversity. *Harvard Business Review, 68*(2), 107–117.

Thomas, R. R., & Woodruff, M. I. (1999). *Building a house for diversity: How a fable about a giraffe & an elephant offers new strategies for today's workforce.* AMACOM.

Tufts University. (2023). *Nondiscrimination statement.* Office of Equal Opportunity. https://oeo.tufts.edu/policies-procedures/non-discrimination/non-discrimination-statement/

United States Department of Labor. (n.d.). *Affirmative action.* www.dol.gov/general/topic/hiring/affirmativeact

U.S. News. (n.d.). *2023 best graduate schools.* www.usnews.com/best-graduate-schools

U.S. Office of Personnel Management. (n.d.). *Policy, data, oversight assessment and selection.* www.opm.gov/policy-data-oversight/assessment-and-selection/competencies

Chapter 15

Health Professions Education

Michael L. Rowland

Career Background

My career in the healthcare field started over 30 years ago. Although my path into the healthcare field and adult education has been rather circuitous, it has still been a truly rewarding career and I would not change anything about my journey. I began my employment career in higher education as an admissions/recruitment counselor working with prospective undergraduate students, their parents, and many returning adult students who were often displaced by their employers but seeking to develop new skills and interested in pursuing higher education. In my role, I represented the university at recruitment events, toured high schools in the area, met with guidance counselors to explain admissions criteria, and described undergraduate majors offered for undergraduate students and the benefits of enrolling at a large research university with many unique opportunities.

Three years later, an opportunity opened up for me to move into a similar recruitment-type position; however, it was with the dental school at the same institution. My duties consisted of conveying admissions criteria to potential applicants, undergraduate advisors, and parents. I read and evaluated applicants' admissions files, based on stated admissions criteria, such as grade point average, dental admissions test scores, student essays, and other variables, and selected top candidates for the admissions committee to interview. At the time, competition for admission to dental school was quite competitive. There were often 10–15 applicants for each available seat in the class. I also advised applicants who were not admitted on how they could become more competitive applicants. After a few years in this position, I was promoted to the position of Director of Admissions & Recruitment at the same dental school. With this promotion, I focused more on strategic recruitment efforts of students at surrounding colleges and universities interested in dental education. I conducted numerous recruitment presentations that required me to further develop my public speaking and communication skills. Also, the institution began to focus efforts on the recruitment of a more diverse pool of candidates so I met and counseled students from predominantly minority-serving institutions. I analyzed admissions data and maintained records to enhance the admissions/recruitment/interview process. During this time, I had a staff of two to three working with me in different positions.

> While working as the Director of Admissions for the dental school, a colleague introduced me to the field of adult education as she was pursuing her doctoral degree in the area. Within a few years, I began pursuing the same doctoral degree. I had a strong interest in working in continuing and professional education in the health professions. My interest in working with adult learners/faculty grew, and I became more interested in how to design effective learning programs utilizing my knowledge, background, and skills.

DOI: 10.4324/9781003259602-18

Along with my major in adult education/learning, my cognate area was in counseling. My training in counseling served me well as I was often called upon to manage highly delicate and sensitive issues with faculty and sometimes students. Understanding how to listen intentionally and appreciate the perspective of two opposing sides helped me provide impartial, yet sound, counseling and consultation to learners, faculty, and administrators. A key to my success in this position was networking with colleagues who held similar types of positions at other dental institutions. A national presence was also helpful for me to find collaborators to further pursue scholarly activities.

Upon completion of my doctorate in adult education, I eventually sought and achieved a full-time faculty position as Assistant Professor of Medical Education and Health Professions Education at a different university. I was hired specifically because of my background in adult education and experience in recruitment. This position was a joint appointment between the Office of Medical Education (80%) and the College of Education and Human Development at the same university (20%).

> While I did not have any experience in medical education, the primary focus of the position was seeking individuals with strong skills in educational research, curriculum design, program planning, and program management. The hiring committee sought to find someone with an adult education background to provide educational and faculty development activities to healthcare professionals, specifically to physicians, nurses, dentists, public health professionals, and others working in the healthcare environment.

In that role I ran the Certificate in Health Professions Education (CHPE) program. It was a collaborative program developed between the College of Education and Human Development (CEHD) and the School of Medicine. During the time I directed the program, it was a 12-credit hour program designed for healthcare professionals who took courses in four areas: (a) teaching and learning, (b) program planning and evaluation methods, (c) introduction to research methods, and (d) adult learning. I was also responsible for the recruitment of qualified applicants to participate in the program. My job was to advise students and maintain learner records, along with other duties. There were some learners involved in the program who were not healthcare professionals, i.e., who did not possess a healthcare degree, but had experience working in a healthcare environment. For example, there were adults enrolled who had a background in healthcare finance, health librarians, or those who worked in continuing education but sought additional education and training to be successful in their current jobs and eventually move up the career ladder.

After 5 years at this medical school, I accepted a new position as Associate Professor (tenured) and Associate Dean for Faculty & Professional Development at another medical school. I was recruited to design, create, develop, implement, and evaluate all faculty and professional development initiatives and resources to enhance and promote overall faculty excellence, including preparing healthcare faculty for the process of promotion and tenure. In this role, I provided faculty development activities not only for physicians but also to basic science faculty members (generally PhDs) as well. Faculty development plays an essential role in the academic vitality and ongoing personal and professional development of faculty in healthcare institutions. Steinert (2014) provides a great resource for anyone interested in faculty development in the health professions. Faculty development is important to enriching the knowledge, skills, and career advancement of faculty at all levels. A key competency of faculty development is bringing faculty scholars together to establish connections, collaborations, and form a learning community of scholars.

Another key aspect of my role as Associate Dean was to provide new faculty with a formal introduction to the institution, help them to further understand their role, and share expectations with them not only as clinicians and basic scientists, but also as academicians. The New Faculty Orientation (NFO) program focused on helping new faculty understand how they fit into the mission, vision, and strategic plans of the institution. As new faculty joined the school at different times, our NFO programs were presented two to three times each academic year to accommodate all new faculty and provide smaller, more intimate gatherings to help them become better acquainted with the institution. These NFO programs were offered in various lengths and formats, including online.

Due to extremely heavy demands on healthcare workers and the high rates of burnout and turnover among healthcare workers, I started an initiative focused on the health and wellness of our faculty. These types of programs have become a significant focus in healthcare institutions, with some institutions hiring a senior-level person to be exclusively responsible for the overall health and well-being of an organization (Dyrbye et al. 2020; Pipas et al., 2021; Ripp & Shanafelt, 2020). These positions are generally classified as Chief Wellness Officer or Health and Wellness Coordinators. They are sometimes held by a healthcare professional but can also be a non-healthcare professional with a background and understanding in organizational culture and training. Stanford University Medical School offers a Chief Wellness Officer training program for healthcare physicians and other more senior leaders in the organizations. For more information, visit https://wellmd.stanford.edu/knowledge-hub/courses-conferences/cwo-course.html

Key Competencies

An abundance of positions exists in the healthcare environment for those without a specific health professions degree. Those with a degree in adult education can be a tremendous asset to the healthcare enterprise. Yet, there are some key competencies and skills required and expected for those interested in careers in the field of healthcare.

Knowledge of Adult Learning

Awareness, knowledge, and understanding of adult learning, lifelong learning, learning styles and practices, and an understanding of the different orientations toward teaching and learning (see Chapter 2) is critical and program planning skills (see Chapter 4) are essential for those interested in working in health environments and with healthcare professionals. Non-healthcare workers with a knowledge of adult learning, andragogy, self-directed learning, and orientations to learning such as behaviorist, cognitivist, humanist, social learning, and constructivist in addition to having skills in the organization of teaching and learning activities (Merriam & Bierema, 2014), such as the flipped classroom approach (Talbert, 2017) or self-directed learning activities (Raidal & Volet, 2009), would do well in healthcare offices of training and development. A cursory knowledge of the five perspectives of teaching by Daniel Pratt is helpful to someone beginning a career in healthcare (Pratt & Associates, 1998).

Evidence-Based Research Skills

Comprehension of evidence-based research skills and statistics are beneficial for those who can analyze data and present findings to groups of health administrators and others in the organization. A good text for those interested in research would be Jacobson's (2020) text, *Introduction to Health Research Methods in Healthcare: A Practical Guide.*

Access to Key Resources

Proficiency and capacity to access key resources to assist the learning healthcare organization, patients, and/or community is essential to assist in a healthcare enterprise. Working within the learning functions of the healthcare organization requires the ability to interface with and understand on-going changes across the system, including patients and community resources.

Cultural Competencies

Ability to work well with diverse groups and colleagues. This is a particularly useful skill for patients and healthcare providers from diverse backgrounds who speak different languages and have different cultural norms (see recommended readings below on how culture and language play a significant role in healthcare).

Program Evaluation

Familiarity with program evaluation in order to systematically collect and analyze program data for further development and enhancement. Chapter 5 in this volume describes the skills needed for program assessment and evaluation.

Knowledge of Medical/Health Terminology

Understanding and knowledge of medical/health terminology, such as Health and Insurance Portability Accountability Act (HIPAA) rules and regulations. For more information on HIPAA see, www.cdc.gov/phlp/publications/topic/hipaa.html

Analyzing Effects on the Healthcare Environment

Analyzing influences on the organization or the healthcare environment, whether the influences are internal or external to the healthcare organization. Part of the analysis involves designing interventions, when needed.

Interpersonal Communication Skills

Strong interpersonal communication skills are essential to understanding and building trust with patients, healthcare providers, administrators, and others in the healthcare environment. As health information and new diseases become increasingly complex and require a certain level of health literacy, adult educators can design healthcare programs for those struggling to understand complicated health jargon. As Hill (2011) states, "Since learning is central to health, adult educators' insights regarding adult learning are critical in helping adults learn about their disease states and appropriate actions they can take" (p. 101). This is a unique time in the healthcare workforce. The healthcare enterprise is comprised of at least three different generations of learners: Baby Boomers, Generation X, and Millennials. In some instances, due to workforce shortages or issues of burnout among other faculty groups and the strain of working during a pandemic, members of the "silent generation" or those born between 1928 and 1945 remain in or have returned to the workforce.

Providing Effective Feedback

An essential skill needed in the healthcare environment, or any learning organization, is proficiency in knowing how to deliver effective feedback. One of the most researched topics in health professions education is how to deliver effective feedback to learners. (Bing-You et al., 2017; Jug et al., 2019; Rami & Krakov, 2012). Jack Ende is often credited with being the father of feedback in medical education. His article on providing feedback in the clinical environment (Ende, 1983) has created multiple methods and means of providing feedback in healthcare. Adult educators can assist healthcare professionals in their understanding of how to deliver effective feedback to learners and staff, whether in the clinical setting or in the classroom setting.

Networking

Networking with others in the healthcare organization and field is a necessity. You can learn essential skills and information from others about healthcare, the opportunities that are available, and which skills are needed for certain types of positions. Networking includes meeting and learning from those who are higher in the organization as well with those in key lower-level entry positions. Everyone can serve as a source of knowledge.

Healthcare Opportunities and Responsibilities

The healthcare industry has a plethora of opportunities for those who have a background in adult education and/or are interested in educating adults across the spectrum from continuing medical education (Cervero & Gaines, 2015) to patient and community education (Dietz et al., 2023). This section discusses a variety of those careers along with the competencies needed.

Community Health Workers and Organizers

Those working in this area provide education and support to individuals and communities about their particular health and wellness issues or concerns. Community health workers and organizers work in a variety of settings, such as community health centers, schools, libraries, and YMCAs. Individuals with degrees in health education, social work, or community health would be well suited for this type of role. (For more information about community education, see Chapter 9 in this volume.)

Cultural/Diversity Trainers and Experts

Individuals with knowledge of other cultures, languages, and customs who can assist healthcare workers and institutions in a variety of roles, such as language interpreters, by explaining and defining cultural norms of certain populations are needed in the healthcare field. Cultural trainers and experts can often work via telehealth when emergencies arise.

Health/Patient Advocates

Those with strong health literacy skills are needed to facilitate communication and learning between patients and others unfamiliar with medical terminology in an effort to promote patient understanding and decision-making. The healthcare environment sees patients from a wide range of backgrounds with varying healthcare knowledge, ranging from those with little to no knowledge of healthcare or health insurance, who do not understand the jargon and lexicon of healthcare, to those with professional degrees.

Health Information Personnel

Individuals working in this area are responsible for organizing and maintaining the accuracy of data and other information collected. Other key competencies include knowledge of medical terminology, coding, and classification systems and healthcare rules and regulations. This career would be suitable for anyone with a background in information technology or data analysis.

Health Coaches

Similar to a community health worker, a health coach typically works one-on-one with patients and/or their family members to help them adopt and learn healthy new habits, behaviors, and skills. This type of work can be done in a variety of settings.

Healthcare Administrators

Those with an adult education degree and a business background of public health can use their skills to provide overall leadership and problem-solving skills and work to educate and train employees and improve patient education and engagement. Key is an understanding of healthcare rules, regulations, policies, and practices, together with strong leadership skills.

Health Promotions Personnel

Someone who is interested in developing health programs and information can work in a variety of healthcare institutions, including hospitals, nursing homes, and wellness centers. The primary competency here is planning educational programs for clients.

Learning/Instructional Designer

This position is ideal for adult educators with a background and knowledge of adult learning and development, program design, and evaluation. With a degree in adult education, individuals can use their skills in developing a needs assessment, assisting in curriculum design, and crafting evaluation strategies to create effective training programs that meet the needs of healthcare professionals. For more information on instructional design, see Chapter 18.

Medical Writers

Medical writers are often required to disseminate information that requires writing in language that is easily understandable and effectively written for a wide array of audiences. They can work in healthcare communications departments and write newsletters and other information for non-healthcare and healthcare personnel.

Patient Care Coordinators

Coordinators come from a variety of backgrounds. They assist patients and families in the care and coordination of their healthcare. Requirements include strong communication skills and the ability to work under pressure. They should be caring and compassionate individuals who often must be able to lift patients or other heavy loads.

Future of Adult Education in Health Professions Education

The future of adult education in healthcare and the health professions is an ever-growing, developing, and accelerating enterprise and there are no signs of slowing down or this pattern changing anytime soon. Having the knowledge, skills, and understanding of education and learning situates adult educators in a unique position to thrive in health professions education. There is an urgent need in health professions education to address and explicitly focus on issues of diversity, health equity, social justice, and inclusive training practices at all levels. The health professions literature has noted the lack of diversity in most healthcare sectors and the lack of socio-cultural understanding of some healthcare providers and their patients (Brottman et al., 2020; Gwayi-Chore et al., 2021; Landry, 2021: McElfish et al., 2018; Neff et al., 2020; Sullivan, 2016). There is a concern that minoritized and underserved populations who lack racial concordance with their provider are less likely to follow treatment. Many patients prefer to have a provider who is of the same race/ethnic background and gender as they are, and research indicates that racial concordance can often lead to better health outcomes (LaVeist et al., 2000; Nazione et al., 2019; Takeshita et al., 2020). Adult educators can also assist healthcare professionals with not only creating the mechanics of online instruction but can also guide them in understanding how to create a sense of community and sense of engagement with online learners.

Key Resources and Information on Careers in Healthcare Professions

- American Association of Health Coaches. (2023). *Health coaching*. www.healthcoach.org/health-coaching
- American Association of Medical Colleges Career Connect. https://careerconnect.aamc.org
- American Dental Education Association. https://dentedjobs.adea.org
- American Health Information Management Association. (2022). *Health information technician*. www.ahima.org/careers/health-information-technican
- American Public Health Association. (2016). *Health communication specialist*. www.apha.org/policies-and-advocacy/public-health-careers/health-communication-specialist
- Bureau of Labor Statistics. (2023). *Occupational outlook handbook: Medical and health services managers*. www.bls.gov/ooh/management/medical-and-health-services-managers.htm
- Cleveland Clinic Health Professions Education. https://my.clevelandclinic.org/departments/health-sciences-education/careers/career-options
- National Commission for Health Education Credentialing. *Guide to health education careers*. www.nchec.org/guide-to-health-education-careers
- National Health Careers Association. (2023). *Medical secretary*. www.healthcareers.org/career/medical-scretary.
- National Patient Safety Foundation. (2016). *Patient educators*. www.npsf.org/patient-educators/

Recommended Readings on Influences of Language and Culture on Healthcare

Argueza, B. R., Saenz, S. R., & McBride, D. (2021). From diversity and inclusion to antiracism in medical training institutions. *Academic Medicine*, 96(6), 798–801. https://doi.org/10.1097/ACM.0000000000004017

Dreachslin, J. L., Gilbert, M. J., & Malone, B. (2013). *Diversity and cultural competency in healthcare: A systems approach*. Jossey-Bass.

Fadiman, A. (2012). *The spirit catches you and you fall down: A Hmong child, their American doctors, and the collision of two cultures.* Farrar, Straus and Giroux.

Galanti, G. A. (2015). *Caring for patients from different cultures: Case studies from American hospitals.* University of Pennsylvania Press.

Hsieh, E., & Kramer, E. M. (2021). *Rethinking culture in health communications: Social interactions as intercultural encounters.* John Wiley & Sons.

Kidder, T. (2003). *Mountains beyond mountains: The quest of Dr. Paul Farmer: A man who would cure the world.* Random House Publishing.

Pratt D. D., & Collins, J. B. (2000). *The Teaching Perspectives Inventory (TPI).* Proceedings of the Adult Education Research Conference. https://newprairiepress.org/aerc/2000/papers/68

Reiss, H., & Kraft-Todd, G. (2014). E. M. P. A. T. H. Y.: A tool to enhance nonverbal communication between clinicians and their patients. *Academic Medicine, 89*(8), 1108–1112. https://pubmed.ncbi.nlm.nih.gov/24826853/

Skloot, R. (2011). *The immortal life of Henrietta Lacks.* Crown Publishing.

Snyder, C. R, Frogner, B. K., & Skillman, S. M. (2018) Facilitating racial and ethnic diversity in the health workforce. *Journal of Allied Health, 47*(1), 58–65. https://pubmed.ncbi.nlm.nih.gov/29504021/

Conclusion

There is an explosive array of career opportunities for non-healthcare professionals in the healthcare industry. For those with some of the key competencies/skills needed for this field and with some additional training and development, opportunities in this field are abundant. Health professions learners are in a continuous mode of learning and training; adult educators as program planners who can understand the diverse needs of a group of learners and then design and assess learning activities are sorely needed to achieve effective learning. In each stage of health professions education, from the early years of training, during the growth and development as a health professional to the late stages of a career in health professions, working with adult learners is inevitable and adult educators can lead much of the teaching and learning in health professions. While the most difficult part of the COVID-19 pandemic may be behind us, it has also alerted and motivated many healthcare enterprises and educational institutions to continuously search for alternative methods of teaching and learning and providing patient care. Therefore, there are many emerging opportunities for those with a background in adult education.

References

Bierema, L. L. (2018). Adult learning in health professions education. *New Directions for Adult and Continuing Education, 157,* 27–40. https://onlinelibrary.wiley.com/doi/abs/10.1002/ace.20266

Bing-You, R., Hayes. V., Varaklis, K., Trowbridge, R., Kemp, H., & McKelvy, D. (2017). Feedback for learners in medical education: What is known? A scoping review. *Academic Medicine, 92*(9), 1346–1354. https://pubmed.ncbi.nlm.nih.gov/28177958/

Brottman, M., Char, D., Hattori, R., Heeb, R., & Taff, S. (2020). Toward cultural competency in health care: A scoping review of the diversity and inclusion education literature. *Academic Medicine, 9*(5), 803–813. https://pubmed.ncbi.nlm.nih.gov/31567169/

Cervero, R. M., & Gaines, J. K. (2015). The impact of CME on physician performance and patient health outcomes: An updated synthesis of systematic reviews. *Journal of Continuing Education in the Health Professions, 35*(2), 131–138. https://doi.org/10.1002/chp.21290

Cranton, P., & Kompf, M. (1989). Adult education and health professions training: A paradox? *The Journal of Educational Thought, 23*(1), 15–26. www.jstor.org/stable/23768634

Daley, B. J., & Cervero, R. M. (2018). Moving forward together. *New Directions for Adult and Continuing Education, 157,* 97–101. https://onlinelibrary.wiley.com/doi/10.1002/ace.20272

Dietz, C. J., Sherrill, W. W., Ankomah, S., Rennert, L., Parisi, M., & Stancil, M. (2023). Impact of a community-based diabetes self-management support program on adult self-care behaviors. *Health Education Research, 38*(1), 1–12. https://doi.org/10.1093/her/cyac034

Dyrbye, L. N., West, C. P., Leep-Hunderfund, A., Johnson, P., Cipriano, P., Peterson, C., Beatty, D., Major-Elechi, B., & Shanafelt, T. (2020). Relationship between burnout and professional behaviors and beliefs among US nurses. *Journal of Occupational and Environmental Medicine, 62*(11), 959–964. https://pubmed.ncbi.nlm.nih.gov/31734790/

Ende, J. (1983). Feedback in clinical medical education. *Journal of American Medical Association, 250*(6), 777–781. https://pubmed.ncbi.nlm.nih.gov/6876333/

Gwayi-Chore, M. C., Del Villar, E. L., Fraire, L. C., Waters, C., Andrasik, M. P., Pfeiffer, J., Slyker, J., Mello, S. P., Barnabas, R., Moise, E., & Heffron, R. (2021). "Being a person of color in this institution is exhausting": Defining and optimizing the learning climate to support diversity, equity, and inclusion at the University of Washington School of Public Health. *Front Public Health, 9,* 642477. https://doi.org/10.3389/fpubh.2021.64277

Halalau, A., Falatko, J., & Mi, M. (2016). Application of adult learning theory in teaching evidence-based medicine to residents. *Journal of Medical Education, 15*(4), 185–193. https://brieflands.com/articles/jme-105528.html

Hall, L. H., Johnson, J., Watt, I., Tsipa, A., & O'Connor, D. B. (2016) Healthcare staff wellbeing, burnout, and patient safety: A systematic review. *PLoS One, 11*(7), e0159015. https://pubmed.ncbi.nlm.nih.gov/27391946/

Hansman, C. (2018). Starting a health professions education graduate program. *New Directions for Adult and Continuing Education, 157,* 77–86. https://onlinelibrary.wiley.com/doi/10.1002/ace.20270

Hill, L. H. (2011). Health education as an arena for adult educators' engagement in social justice. *New Directions for Adult and Continuing Education, 130,* 99–104. https://onlinelibrary.wiley.com/doi/abs/10.1002/ace.414

Jacobson, K. H. (2020). *Introduction to health research methods in healthcare: A practical guide* (3rd ed.). Jones and Bartlett Learning.

Jug, R., Jiang, X. S., & Bean, S. M. (2019). Giving and receiving effective feedback: A review article and how-to-guide. *Archives of Pathology and Laboratory Medicine, 143*(2), 244–250. https://pubmed.ncbi.nlm.nih.gov/30102068/.

Landry, A. M. (2021). Integrating health equity content into health professions education. *AMA Journal of Ethics, 23*(3), E229–E234. https://pubmed.ncbi.nlm.nih.gov/33818374/

LaVeist, T. A., Nickerson, K. J., & Bowie, J. V. (2000). Attitudes about racism, medical mistrust, and satisfaction with care among African American and white cardiac patients. *Medical Care Research and Review, 57,* 146–161. https://pubmed.ncbi.nlm.nih.gov/11092161/

McElfish, P. A., Moore, R., Buron, B., Hudson, J., Long, C. R., Purvis, R. S., Schultz, T. K., Rowland, B., & Warmack, T. S. (2018). Integrating interprofessional education and cultural competency training to address health disparities. *Teaching and Learning in Medicine, 30*(2), 213–222. https://pubmed.ncbi.nlm.nih.gov/29190158/

Merriam, S. B. (1996). Updating our knowledge of adult learning. *Journal of Continuing Education in the Health Professions, 16*(3), 136–143. https://doi.org/10.1002/chp.4750160303

Merriam, S. B., & Bierema, L. L. (2014). *Adult learning: Linking theory to practice*. Jossey-Bass.

Michaelson, L. K., Parmelee, D. X., Levine, R. E., & McMahon, K. K. (Eds.). (2008). *Team-based learning for health professions education: A guide to using small groups for improving learning* (1st ed.). Stylus Publishing.

Nazione, S., Perrault, E. K., & Keating, D. M. (2019). Finding common ground: Can provider-patient race concordance and self-disclosure bolster patient trust, perceptions, and intentions? *Journal of Racial and Ethnic Health Disparities, 6*(5), 962–972. https://pubmed.ncbi.nlm.nih.gov/31119610/

Neff, J., Holmes, S. M., Knight, K. R., Strong, S., Thompson-Lastad, A., McGuinness, C., … Nelson, N. (2020). Structural competency: Curriculum for medical students, residents, and interprofessional teams on the structural factors that produce health disparities. *MedEdPORTAL, 16*: 10888. www.mededportal.org/doi/pdf/10.15766/mep_2374-8265.10888

Parmelee, D., Michaelsen, L. K., Cook, S., & Hudes P. D. (2012). Team-based learning: A practical guide: AMEE guide no 65. *Medical Teacher, 34*, e275–e287. https://pubmed.ncbi.nlm.nih.gov/22471941/

Pipas, C. F., Courand, J., Neumann, S. A., Furnari, M., Abaza, M. M., & Haramati, A. (2021). *The rise of wellness initiatives in health care: Using national survey data to support effective well-being champions and wellness programs.* Association of American Medical Colleges.

Pratt, D. D., & Associates. (1998). *Five perspectives on teaching in adult and higher education.* Krieger Publishing Company.

Raidal, S. L., & Volet, S. E. (2009). Preclinical students' predispositions toward social forms of instruction and self-directed learning: A challenge for the development of autonomous and collaborative learners. *Higher Education, 57*, 577–596.

Rami, S., & Krakov, S. K. (2012). Twelve tips for giving feedback effectively in the clinical environment. *Medical Teacher, 34*(10), 787–791. https://doi.org/10.3109/0142159X.2012.684916

Ripp, J., & Shanafelt, T. (2020). The health care chief wellness officer: What the role is and is not. *Academic Medicine, 95*(9), 1354–1358. https://pubmed.ncbi.nlm.nih.gov/32324635/

Steinert, Y. (Ed.). (2014). *Faculty development in the health professions: A focus on research and practice.* Springer.

Sullivan, L. W. (2016). Diversity and higher education for the health care professions. *Milbank Quarterly, 94*(3), 448–451. www.milbank.org/quarterly/articles/diversity-higher-education-health-care-professions/

Takeshita, J., Wang, S., Loren, A. W., Mitra, N., Shults, J., Shin, D. B., & Sawinski, D. L. (2020). Association of racial/ethnic and gender concordance between patients and physicians with patient experience ratings. *Journal of American Medical Association Network Open, 3*(11), e2024583. https://pubmed.ncbi.nlm.nih.gov/33165609/

Talbert, R. (2017). *Flipped learning: A guide for higher education faculty.* Stylus Publishing.

Chapter 16

Military Education

Royce Ann Collins and James B. Martin

Adult Education Career Paths in Military Education

Our personal paths to this area of adult education were quite divergent. As a career educator, one of us moved from General Education Degree (GED) and adult literacy instructor to working with adults in higher education. She began her career as an advisor and worked with thousands of adult learners at one institution, progressed in her career and expanded duties over curriculum, faculty, and assessment of learning. She went on to complete a doctorate in adult education and gained a full-time faculty position in adult education. Military-affiliated learners became a part of the student population she served. She was hired as an adult education faculty member who was primarily responsible for the programs at a local post. Her teaching and advising grew from working with a few military-affiliated learners to teaching graduate courses and advising cohorts of active-duty and retired military learners on post. Master's and doctoral programs in adult education were offered on post and she was the primary advisor for both. To help these learners achieve their education and career goals, she learned the Department of Defense (DoD) job classifications in order to guide learners to the correct courses in the curriculum that would meet the requirements. This created an opportunity to learn more about career paths affiliated with the military which used adult education principles and theories. The other author started his path to military adult education when he was given the opportunity to teach at the United States Military Academy while on active duty. This sparked an interest in higher education and when the opportunity came to teach at one of the Army's two graduate schools the doorway to adult education opened. A few years on the faculty there led to positions in adult education programs at civilian universities after military retirement and a journey that would encompass the remainder of his working life was on. A move back to the Army graduate school to positions as a faculty member, Associate Dean, and eventually Dean resulted in deep expertise and passion for the DoD's education programs, which by their very nature are all in the area of adult education, regardless of specific discipline needs.

Professional military education across DoD is fertile ground for graduates of adult education programs. Whether active military, veterans, or graduates of adult education programs with no military experience, there are positions which require adult education degrees or positions where the degree and competencies achieved in such a program are valuable. Most of the armed services, but particularly the Army, have learning concepts or strategies which are based on the theory and practice of adult education. Active-duty military officers and noncommissioned officers can utilize the competencies from an adult education degree while teaching in any of the professional military education schools in any service or as a faculty member in the various civilian education systems. In the federal sector, there are two U.S. Office of Personnel Management (OPM) (2018) civilian career fields dedicated to education: Career Programs 31 and 32. These programs include positions which advise adult learners, positions which focus on teaching, and positions which are administrative in nature.

DOI: 10.4324/9781003259602-19

Civilian Positions

Educational positions in the military or government world often appeal to individuals who enjoy working in structured environments. An excellent example of this is the pay system in the Federal service. The position level and pay systems are, for the most part, the same across the Federal government based on grade level and years of service. In most cases, these positions are in what is called the General Service (GS) and are most often referred to as GS positions. This title refers to the pay scale published by OPM which lays out the pay ranges for every one of the 15 GS pay grades. Because these pay grades identify different levels of education and/or experience, there is a very large difference in the pay ranges between the various grades. Each pay range has 10 steps which sequentially increase compensation. For example, in 2022, a GS1 has a basic pay range of $20,172 to $25,234. On the other end of the grade scale a GS15 has a basic pay range of $112,890 to $146,757 (OPM, 2022). Actual pay rates vary based on a locality where pay is adjusted for cost of living at specific locations. A major difference between working in civilian higher education and the military is that, based on your grade and years working, everyone will progress with pay raises regardless of the agency you work for, race, gender, or any other identifying characteristic (see Figure 16.1). While some employees can receive pay raises based on merit, all employees receive raises based on time in the position. Most new hires will begin at step 1 on their grade's pay scale. In each of the first three years, they will receive a one-step increase as a matter of policy. From year 4 to 9 they will receive a step increase every 2 years and from year 10 to 18 they will receive a step increase every 3 years (OPM, n. d.). If a person stays on schedule with no merit raises, they will still reach the maximum pay for their grade level in 18 years.

Education and training positions in the military are most often part of what is referred to as the 1700 occupational group. This group has a variety of different occupational series with a unique number code and different responsibilities and required competencies. Most involve adult education, but not all. The specific list of occupational series in this group that pertain to adult education careers includes:

1. 1701 – General Education and Training Series
2. 1702 – Education and Training Technician Series
3. 1712 – Training Instruction Series
4. 1740 – Education Services Series
5. 1750 – Instructional Systems Series

All of these have connections to the study and practice of adult education, such as adult learning and program planning, though they may require other specific skills and competencies to accompany that preparation. The initial series, 1701, is a very broad category that allows multiple positions that include a wide variety of academic disciplines. Other series have specific fields attached to them, such as vocational education, but all of them require or benefit from a common underpinning of adult education. A unique aspect of adult education is its application alongside other disciplines to improve the educational quality of that discipline. Again, using the vocational education series, an applicant may have the necessary background for such a position from their undergraduate preparation, but the addition of graduate-level preparation in adult education,

GS12																		
Full Years in Grade	1	2	3	4	5	6	7	8	9	10	11	12	13	14	15	16	17	18
Pay Step		2	3	4		5		6		7			8			9			10

Figure 16.1 Pay raises based on time in position
(OPM, n.d.)

specifically in the area of adult learning theories and program planning, greatly enhances their ability to plan and administer such courses. The organization of occupational series by OPM makes just such a marriage of undergraduate and graduate preparations a superior combination for any of the 1700 group of occupational series. Posting of these jobs may be found at the USAJobs.gov website by searching for any of the 1700 group series. All these series are used throughout the Federal government, so there are many such positions managed by OPM. Below is an explanation of each series common in the military along with its official description.

1701 – General Education and Training Series

> Typically includes position titles such as Instructor, English as a Foreign Language Instructor, Supervisor Instructor (Dean), Chief Academic Analyst, Education Specialist, Training and Curriculum Specialist, Instructional Development Specialist, and STEM Education Administrator.

This series covers education and training positions that primarily require full professional knowledge of a subject field not covered by another established series in either the Education Group, GS-1700, or any other occupational group. This includes instructors in college or equivalent-level programs, when the area of expertise is in a subject matter field not classifiable to an established series, and when no other series is more appropriate, e.g., instructors of English, instructors of foreign language (OPM, 1991).

As mentioned above, this series is the most general of the occupational group and has a broad variety of different position titles. Overall, the Federal government employs 14,026 individuals in the 1701 series; over 5,300 employed in the Army, Navy, Marines, and Air Force; 7,498 within the DoD outside of the services; and 166 within the Veterans Administration (Federal Government Jobs, n.d.).

1702 – Education and Training Technician Series

> Typically includes position titles such as Training Technician, Lead Training Technician, Supervisory Education Specialist, and Educational Technician.

This series includes positions that involve nonprofessional work of a technical, specialized, or support nature in the field of education and training when the work is properly classified in this group and is not covered by a more appropriate series. The work characteristically requires knowledge of program objectives, policies, procedures, or pertinent regulatory requirements affecting the particular education or training activity. Employees apply a practical understanding or specialized skills and knowledge of the particular education or training activities involved, but the work does not require full professional knowledge of education concepts, principles, techniques, and practices (OPM, 2018).

This series is the least technical of the 1700 occupational group, with some positions only requiring practical experience while others benefit greatly from a preparation in the field of adult education. The pool of positions for series 1702 is smaller than the 1701 and includes 7,632 throughout the Federal government. These are distributed across the government, but include 4,300 within the military services (Army, Navy, Marines, Air Force) and another 829 strictly within the DoD (Federal Government Jobs, n.d.).

1712 – Training Instruction Series

> Typically includes position titles such as Training Instructor, Training Specialist, Lead Training Specialist, Supervisory Training Specialist, Training Administrator, Training Branch Chief, and Accreditation Division Chief.

This series covers positions concerned with administration, supervision, training program development, evaluation, or instruction in a program of training when the dominant requirement of the work is a combination of practical knowledge of the methods and techniques of instruction and practical knowledge of the subject matter being taught. Positions in this series do not have either a paramount requirement of professional knowledge and training in the field of education, or mastery of a trade, craft, or laboring occupation (OPM, 2018).

This is a common position series for positions in the military's non-degree-granting institutions, though such positions can be found in the colleges and universities within the services. While the official position definition has a focus on the practical side of the training world, many positions in this series benefit greatly from a preparation in the field of adult education. Across the entire Federal government, 9,213 individuals are employed in the 1712 series. Of these, over 6,600 are employed in the services (Army, Navy, Marines, Air Force) and 559 within the DoD itself (Federal Government Jobs, n.d.).

1740 – Education Services Series

> Typically includes position titles such as Education Services Specialist and Supervisor Education Services Specialist.

This series includes professional positions where the duties are to administer, supervise, promote, conduct, or evaluate programs and activities designed to provide individualized career-related or self-development education plans. The work requires knowledge of education theories, principles, procedures, and practices of secondary, adult, or continuing education. Some positions require skill in counseling learners or enrollees to establish educational and occupational objectives (OPM, 2018).

Positions in this series require the application of professional knowledge of education to educational and vocational testing and counseling, and the application of the administrative policies and procedures of the education services program. Employees apply this knowledge in providing guidance and assistance to training program enrollees seeking to develop their full potential by pursuing job-related instruction or self-improvement courses. The work involves furnishing support to programs of general education for adults, including occupational specialty-related courses, basic academic courses, and other adult programs. Across the Federal government there are 995 such positions, with 790 individuals from the 1740 series employed in the services (Army, Navy, Marines, Air Force) (Federal Government Jobs, n.d.).

1750 – Instructional Systems Series

> Typically includes position titles such as Instructional Systems Specialist and Supervisor Instructional Systems Specialist.

The 1750 series is one of the few occupational series in OPM that have specific educational requirements to qualify for positions. These requirements are focused on the adult education field and guarantee a level of academic preparation for those applying for 1750 series positions. These requirements include 24 semester hours in fields such as learning theory, psychology of learning, and educational psychology; instructional design practices; educational evaluation; instructional product development; and computers in education and training. Across the Federal government there are 2,029 such positions, with 1,353 individuals from the 1750 series employed in the services (Army, Navy, Marines, Air Force) (Federal Government Jobs, n.d.).

This series includes professional positions where the duties are to administer, supervise, advise on, design, develop, or provide educational or training services in formal education or training programs. The work requires knowledge of learning theory and the principles, methods, practices, and techniques of one or more specialties of the instructional systems field. The work may require knowledge of one or more subjects or occupations in which educational or training instruction is provided (OPM, 2018).

Active-Duty Military Positions

While most of the previous information about adult education positions within the military have focused on civilian employees, there are a significant number of positions for uniformed educators also. Each service has its own unique system for assigning officers and enlisted personnel to education positions. The armed services represent the largest training programs in the USA and educate or train from GED preparation to complex scientific and technical education. Positions and opportunities within military education for adult educators require very similar competences and the application of similar theories as found in most universities around the nation. Many of the military learning institutions are degree granting, including both undergraduate and graduate degrees. In fact, the Army's senior noncommissioned officer school, the Sergeants Major Academy, grants an undergraduate degree in Leadership and Workforce Development (Sergeants Major Academy, 2021). This is the undergraduate foundation for adult education and the Army invests in it every year by sending active-duty soldiers to graduate schools in adult education to teach at the Academy. Faculty and staff members in these institutions require skills in assessment and evaluation, program planning, strategic planning, accreditation, faculty development, curriculum development, and educational leadership. All of the service staff colleges and war colleges are accredited to grant master's degrees and the Navy has an institution located in Monterey, CA, which grants terminal degrees in various fields (Naval Postgraduate School, n.d.). Along with the faculty at these institutions, academic support positions exist which could be filled by applicants with adult education backgrounds.

Practice and Theory

Adult education and the military have been intertwined for decades. Cyril Houle et al.'s (1947) book on the armed services and adult education demonstrated how adults were learning in military training. Ever since, the two entities have been linked. More recently, the Army Learning Concept, which has now evolved into an Army Learning Model, was developed from adult education theory (Department of the Army, 2011, 2017). Further, if the field of adult education is a "big tent tradition, welcoming all who seek to support the learning of adults as individuals as well as in groups organizations, and communities" (Ross-Gordon et al., 2017, p. 4), then the education and numerous activities of active-duty military and all the civilian offices that support the enterprise are wrapped in adult education. These careers cut across leadership, administration, teaching, and assessment. The careers with the military are far from just basic training companies. As Zacharakis and Van Der Werff (2012) discussed, education of the armed forces is more than behavioral in nature, but includes many learning theories and philosophies to develop the critical thinking skills necessary to embrace ambiguous problems. The DoD needs civilians to develop curriculum and to teach in the numerous armed forces schools.

Individuals interested in careers in the military need a comprehensive understanding of learning theories, including andragogy, self-directed learning, experiential learning, and transformational learning. As noted above, many of these careers deal with instruction and assessment of learning. Knowledge of adult development and cognitive development as well as instructional design are a part of the job requirements (e.g., GS1750) (see also Chapter 2). Whether in a formal classroom setting or an organizational department, these professions deal with preparing people for their current and future jobs and organizational policy and adaptation for the future.

Another important element of the field of adult education is program planning. Careers associated with the military focus on developing individuals, the organization, and society. The interactive model of program planning developed by Daffron and Caffarella (2021) parallels many of the models in military decision making. The flexibility of the model allows for incorporation into different settings as program planners work with a variety of components and tasks simultaneously. For further information about program planning, see Chapter 4.

There are many current military and civilian employees with degrees in adult education working in the civilian series listed above and serving currently in the armed forces. Their continued comments about how much they use the theories and practices learned in their degree programs on a daily basis is a testimonial to how well a background in adult education fits with military careers. There is a strong link between the theories and research in adult education from adult learning to planning programs to assessment of learning and the many careers associated with the military.

Future of Adult Education

Military education has been steeped in adult education theories and practice for many years, with the Army codifying it in the Army Learning Concept published in 2011 (Department of the Army, 2011, 2017). For over two decades the Program for the Accreditation of Joint Military Education (PAJE) has had requirements for size of classes, percentage of instruction which must be active learning, and outcomes-based education. These requirements, particularly the one concerning outcomes-based education, are codified by the DoD and in some cases by Federal statute (H.R. Rep. No. 117–88, 2022). Adult education is on a path to grow in its importance in the military across all services. The Army's faculty development program, a decentralized program at each institution, is a learning community with its central hub at the Army University located at Fort Leavenworth, KS. This program is based on principles and characteristics of adult education and prepares faculty members to teach and facilitate in Army classrooms throughout the United States. Many of the experts operating in this program are graduates of major adult education programs across the country. Over the past 20 years, adult education positions have grown year after year across the DoD and that growth will not abate any time soon.

With the emerging DoD requirements for outcomes-based education, several fields pertinent to the adult education world will grow in importance. Expertise in academic assessment and program review will become standard requirements for those seeking to find opportunities in military education, particularly in the Joint Professional Military Education (JPME) world (Collins et al., 2020). For further information on assessment, see Chapter 5. Each service has its own set of colleges, normally including a staff college for mid-career officers and a war college for more senior officers. These institutions are located throughout the United States and educate a prescribed service mix of officers. The Navy's staff and war colleges are located in Newport, Rhode Island; the Air Force's is in Montgomery, Alabama; the Marines Corps' in Quantico, Virginia; and the Army's are split between Leavenworth, Kansas, and Carlisle, Pennsylvania. Each of these degree-granting institutions have significant opportunities for adult educators and will have the need to strengthen their programs in assessment and program review. Additionally, all the services have other schools, which are not accredited for degrees but have the need for adult educators to create curriculum, provide instruction, and evaluate programs. The military is a data-driven organization, and it conducts regular reviews of curriculum and performance, thus driving a requirement for evaluation skills even in the non-degree-granting institutions. These skills will continue to be in great demand.

Three Keys to Success

The positions within the military education system that are steeped in adult education have very specific requirements that may seem overly structured to most in the adult education fields. When pursuing adult education positions with the military or Federal government, educators should do research on the specific requirements through the OPM website. For example, to successfully apply for a position as an Instructional Systems Specialist, also referred to as a series 1750, applicants must have 24 semester hours in four of the following five areas: learning theory, psychology of learning or educational psychology; instructional design practices; educational evaluation; instructional product development; or computers in education and training. A successful application for such a position should clearly show how the educator meets this specific requirement. These requirements, for all the education occupational series, are available on the OPM website. Job applications are completed on USAJobs.gov. This system is not intuitive and is steeped in military language and acronyms. Preference is given to veterans, so if you have prior service, make sure to note it accordingly. The words you use matter and using the exact phrases in the job requirements is important. Be extremely careful to note the requirements and fulfill them in their entirety.

As with any professional culture, working as a civilian educator requires an understanding of the cultural background and language specific to the military culture. Even if an educator has no military background, they can pick up these cultural cues if they pay specific attention to these unique cultures. We use the term cultures because each of the uniformed services has their own unique language and set of expectations. The Air Force and Navy are culturally more relaxed than the Army, and the Marine Corps is the least relaxed of the group. Which service you choose to work with could depend on how formal or relaxed you wish to be, or you could end up working for the Army as that is where the largest concentration of positions exists. In any case, taking the time to speak to coworkers and supervisors about expectations, learning the ranks of the specific service, and understanding the education and training programs of that specific service are all very useful bits of information. While the education world commonly uses acronyms, the armed services each have their specific set of acronyms which almost make up a different language. Early on in a new educator's career with one of the armed services, particularly if they have no military background, we recommend seeking a mentor on the critical acronyms to their work. Picking these up quickly will save time and allow you to sit through critical meetings and understand the verbal shorthand that is being used. Being an educator for the military is very similar to working in the civilian world as far as the use of theory and practice of adult education. Assessment of student learning concepts are no different; it is just applied to a different set of learning outcomes (Collins et al., 2020). Learning about the culture and history of the organization that an educator joins will make the work more interesting and rewarding.

The skills and experience which make you successful in one military service carry over to any other service or federal entities. The occupational series are the same across the DoD, along with other federal organizations that are associated with the OPM. Educators can flow between different organizations within the military or Federal government, as they have common classification systems and occupational requirements. There is far more flexibility within the system than most civilian academics and practitioners might imagine.

References

Collins, R. A., Welch, R., & Martin, J. (2020). Assessment and evaluation practices in army military education. In L. Hill (Ed.), *Assessment, evaluation, and accountability in adult education* (pp. 72–85). Stylus Publishing.

Daffron, S. R., & Caffarella, R. (2021). *Planning programs for adult learners: A practical guide.* (4th edition). Jossey-Bass.

Department of the Army. (2011). *The U.S. Army learning concept for 2015.* TRADOC Pamphlet 525–528-2. U.S. Army Training and Doctrine Command.

Department of the Army. (2017). *The U.S. Army learning concept for training and education 2020–2040.* TRADOC Pamphlet 525–528-2. U.S. Army Training and Doctrine Command.

Federal Government Jobs. (n.d.). *Education jobs – Instructors and teachers.* https://federaljobs.net/occupations/gs-1700_jobs/#General_Education_and_Training_Series,_GS-1701

Houle, C., Burr, E., Hamilton, T., & Yale, J. (1947). *The armed services and adult education.* American Council on Education.

H.R. Rep. No. 117–188. (2022). www.govinfo.gov/content/pkg/CRPT-117hrpt88/pdf/CRPT-117hrpt88.pdf

Naval Postgraduate School. (n.d.). *Programs and degrees.* https://nps.edu/web/guest/degree-programs

Ross-Gordon, J., Rose, A., & Kasworm, C. (2017). *Foundations of adult and continuing education.* Jossey-Bass.

The Sergeants Major Academy. (2021). *Bachelors of arts in leadership and workforce development.* www.ncoworldwide.army.mil/Portals/76/courses/smc/ref/20210607_BoA-LWD_trifold.pdf?ver=T9q5FHaWy-YovUAQnWtcmg%3d%3d

U.S. Office of Personnel Management (OPM). (1991, October). *Position classification flysheet for general education and training series, GS-1701.* www.opm.gov/policy-data-oversight/classification-qualifications/classifying-general-schedule-positions/standards/1700/gs1701.pdf

U.S. Office of Personnel Management (OPM). (2018, December). *Handbook of occupational groups and families.* www.opm.gov/policy-data-oversight/classification-qualifications/classifying-general-schedule-positions/occupationalhandbook.pdf

U.S. Office of Personnel Management (OPM). (2022). *Salary table 2022-GS.* www.opm.gov/policy-data-oversight/pay-leave/salaries-wages/salary-tables/pdf/2022/GS.pdf

U.S. Office of Personnel Management (OPM). (n.d.). *Policy, data, oversight: General schedule classification and pay.* www.opm.gov/policy-data-oversight/pay-leave/pay-systems/general-schedule/

Zacharakis, J., & Van Der Werff, J. (2012). The future of adult education in the military. *New Directions in Adult and Continuing Education, 2012*(136), 89–98. https://doi.org/10.1002/ace.20038

Chapter 17

The Nonprofit Sector

Paul G. Putman

There are many different nonprofit roles that are well suited for individuals with expertise in adult education theory and practice. Broadly, careers in the nonprofit sector include programs/services, administration (human resources, finance, information technology, data management, evaluation, etc.), fundraising/development, marketing/communications, and leadership roles. These careers may include work managing a board or advisory committee. With a background in adult education, you can thoughtfully plan how and when information is shared as well as how meetings are designed and facilitated. Your knowledge of leadership theory will be helpful as you will often be working with people in positions of leadership. This could include board members who are corporate or organizational leaders as well as other types of community leaders.

Nonprofit careers are a great match for candidates passionate about organizational missions/causes. There are many opportunities in the nonprofit sector for those with degrees in adult education. Entry points into jobs in the sector are plentiful and career pathways are myriad. This chapter begins with a brief overview of my experience and continues with a definition of the nonprofit sector and other terms before presenting six common roles and accompanying responsibilities. The section on adult education competitive advantage will help readers make connections between adult education and the sector. Program planning, leadership, and adult learning theories are just a few of the advantages that candidates with adult education degrees will bring to the table. Many resources for additional information are presented. The chapter concludes with some predictions for the future and advice for those interested in exploring a career in the nonprofit sector.

Author's Nonprofit Experience

Throughout my life I have been connected to the nonprofit sector as both a volunteer and employee. For me, the mission of an organization is a powerful motivator. My first paycheck came from a job shelving books at our local public library. I have been involved for several decades as a volunteer with arts-affiliated nonprofits in roles ranging from Manager of Theater Operations for the Cleveland International Film Festival to usher and house manager for several community theaters to a supernumerary (equivalent of an onstage "extra") with the Cleveland Opera. I have worked for five different universities (large nonprofits) in the areas of leadership and community service/service learning and as an adjunct professor. In the subsector of philanthropy, I have worked for United Way Services and the Cleveland Foundation, the world's first community foundation (see the box in this chapter). It is at that foundation (for more than 14 years) that I gained experience as both a program officer and fundraiser. I currently serve as the President and CEO of the Tree Research and Education Endowment (TREE) Fund, a national organization that funds scientific research related to tree care and urban forestry, supports student scholarship in this area, and presents educational programs. I have also served as a board member for local and national organizations.

DOI: 10.4324/9781003259602-20

The Nonprofit Sector

The nonprofit sector, sometimes referred to as the third sector (the first two sectors are public and private), is as complex as the field of adult education, with several dozen subsectors and types. As described in this chapter, the sector is presented in the historical context of the United States. The U.S. nonprofit sector employs 12.3 million people, about 10.2% of the total workforce (U.S. Bureau of Labor Statistics, 2018).

When thinking about nonprofit organizations, some key characteristics (Salamon, 1999) are that they are private (institutionally separate from government), non-profit distributing (they do not return profits to their founders/owners like the private sector), self-governing, voluntary, and of public benefit. U.S. tax laws contain nearly 30 different types of tax-exempt organizations. "While disagreements exist over how 'distinctive' nonprofit services are compared to those provided by businesses or government, nonprofits are well known for identifying and addressing unmet needs, for innovating and for delivering services of exceptionally high quality" (Salamon, 2015, p. 14). Nonprofits can range in size from small volunteer-led grassroots organizations with budgets under $100,000 to giant healthcare systems, major museums, and ivy league universities.

> **Philanthropy**, also sometimes referred to as the philanthropic sector, is a segment of the nonprofit sector. Philanthropy, translated from Greek as "love towards mankind," entails the process of people giving to others. **Foundations** are entities that provide support for the charitable activities provided by other organizations. Some foundations also maintain their own programs. Both private (created typically by a single corporation or donor/family) and public foundations can employ staff who work with the family, corporation, or donors to distribute money to other nonprofits via a grantmaking system. A **community foundation** is a public charity, a type of foundation that typically supports a specific geographic area. Individuals with backgrounds in adult education are well suited for programmatic/grantmaking, fundraising, convening, facilitating, and other roles at foundations.
>
> For more information see the following:
>
> - *Understanding Philanthropy: Its Meaning and Mission* by Payton and Moody (2008)
> - *The Almanac of American Philanthropy* by Karl Zinsmeister (2016)
> - The Council on Foundations (www.cof.org)
> - Candid (www.candid.org)

Roles and Responsibilities

This chapter explores nonprofit careers not explicated elsewhere in this book: program manager, fundraiser, foundation program officer, grant writer, scholarship officer, and volunteer administrator. In this section, six different types of positions that might be of special interest for candidates with degrees in adult education are described, followed by a list of frequently requested position competencies and helpful credentials.

Program Manager

Many professionals with degrees in adult education manage programs at nonprofits. In this context, a program can be defined as what the nonprofit does to implement its mission. The types of programs will vary widely depending upon the organization's mission, and while many have an educational focus, there are numerous other types of programs. A program manager at a nonprofit focusing on services for the unhoused might work to connect clients to services and stable housing. A program manager at a refugee resettlement agency may help newcomers learn processes and systems ranging from opening and managing a bank account to navigating school enrollment. At smaller organizations, managers may run the programs and work with adult learners or other nonprofit clients directly, and at larger organizations they may supervise a team of professionals in those roles. More detailed explanations of many sectors (adult basic education, etc.) appear throughout Part II of this book.

Fundraiser

Fundraisers in nonprofit organizations are responsible for securing funds to help the organization meet its mission. Tasks associated with these positions may include managing an annual fund appeal, facilitating donor solicitations, working to secure major gifts by meeting with donors one-on-one, securing planned gifts to be realized once current donors have died, and/or organizing large annual events like galas, golf outings, races, or concerts. Fundraisers may work with a team or primarily on their own. Depending upon the size of the organization, fundraisers may be generalists performing a wide variety of tasks and functions or may specialize and focus more intensely on a specific function.

Fundraisers primarily work with two populations: prospects and donors. Prospects are individuals who have not yet supported the organization but have the potential to do so. Donors are those who have already given. Donor stewardship involves working with each donor/donor family and tailoring communication and services to meet their needs and to help them meet their philanthropic goals, often through the engagement of donors in educational or experiential activities.

Grant Writer

Grant writers compose and curate proposals to funders to secure support for a nonprofit's programs, services, and general operations. The first thing a good grant writer will notice is that technically the role is grant *proposal* writer, not grant writer. That said, the common usage of grant writer persists. These jobs require a professional who is not only a superb writer, but a competent researcher and a critical thinker able to translate nonprofit programs into compelling proposals for funders. This is a nonprofit function that can often be done as a freelancer.

Program Officer

The other side of writing grant proposals entails reading and evaluating them. A grantmaker or program officer helps a foundation/funder meet its mission by connecting nonprofit applicants with funding to carry out the work. At some foundations, particularly community foundations, the focus is on being responsive to the needs of the community and working with a broad swath of nonprofits. At other foundations (community, family, and national), program officers may have an area of specialization and work with a select group of nonprofits within a specific sector (arts and culture, education, health, etc.).

These jobs typically involve a lot of reading and review of grant applications, reports, research, and supporting material. They also include meetings with nonprofit representatives, including program staff, executive directors, and board members. Officers write summaries and recommendations for foundation board members and correspondence to nonprofits and other funders. They may be engaged with additional writing in the form of reports, white papers, blog posts, articles, and more. Program officers hold great positional power and must be cognizant of that throughout their work. Working at a foundation requires a level of comfort in navigating power differentials.

> **Convening Community Stakeholders**
>
> One of the first grants I reviewed as a program officer at the community foundation stemmed from a proposal submitted by an organization that was working with Bhutanese refugees. The organization had seen a need for an education program working with mothers. Since I was unfamiliar with the lived experiences of refugees, I experienced a steep learning curve and worked with local refugee-serving organizations to hear more about the needs of refugees and the organizations serving them. This path of inquiry eventually led to the foundation providing funding not just for that program, but for an emerging Refugee Services Collaborative of about 12 nonprofits supporting this vulnerable population.
>
> My background in adult education provided me with insights into supporting the self-organizing collaborative in a way that helped sustain their collective work. For this group of service providers, they simply needed a neutral facilitator which the grant supported, and the time and space to work together to better serve people. I made it a point to not attend more than one meeting as I did not want my presence (representing a funder) to unduly impact their learning or collective work. In a single meeting I witnessed the group quickly organize agenda items ranging from the mundane ("We have a family that just arrived that needs winter clothing" – "Oh, we have extra clothing that was just donated – we should talk.") to the profound ("What are the biggest barriers facing refugees and us as supporters of refugees and how can we work to address them?").
>
> I have sadly witnessed other collaborative efforts fail due at least in part to well-intentioned funders overly engaged in the process. I believe that my familiarity with concepts such as self-directed learning (Knowles, 1975), program planning (Cervero & Wilson, 2005), and leadership served me (and in turn the community) quite well during my time as a program officer. See also the work of Myles Horton (2003) and Part I of this book for additional information on these theories and concepts.

Scholarship Officer

Institutions of secondary and higher education, as well as some independent nonprofits focusing on scholarships, have specific staff members responsible for coordinating the scholarship process from advertising available scholarships, coordinating the selection process, working with partners to administer the grants, facilitating donor appreciation, and conducting reporting. Many community foundations also have staff known as scholarship officers who do similar work, partnering with secondary and higher education institutions. Individuals with backgrounds in adult education will be well familiar with education and those seeking to attend institutions of higher education. Additionally, you may be working with donors passionate about education and can help them shape their visions of support for students.

> **Working with Scholarship Donors**
>
> The best part of this work is often the donors themselves, who are passionately committed to making a difference. One of my favorite donor stories entails an anonymous donor couple who,

after volunteering with a local kindergarten class, were inspired to create a "college promise" program. The kindergarteners and their families were selected to participate in a program designed to facilitate college readiness. Throughout their middle and high school years, the students participated in additional academic support and college visitation trips. A scholarship program staff person at a partner nonprofit served as program coordinator and mentor for the students. The donor couple pledged to cover any tuition costs not covered by Pell grants or scholarships. This was a substantial philanthropic investment on their part. It was also very important to them to remain anonymous, so they never met the students or their families.

With my background in adult education and my experience working at a university, I was able to support the donors' own learning journey by talking through their expectations and providing resources for their own exploration. In recent years, I was lucky enough to witness the students graduating high school and entering college. There have been enough twists and turns with their student journeys to fill a substantial case study white paper, but through it all my knowledge of adult education helped my own understanding and, in turn, I hope my insights provided reassurance to the donor family.

Volunteer Administrator

Volunteer administrators engage and coordinate volunteers for nonprofit programs or organizations. They assist and support nonprofits in meeting their mission. Volunteers can be committee or board members, individuals working directly with clients or program participants, or volunteers performing tasks or roles that might otherwise be fulfilled by staff members, but for free. Examples include coordinating individuals and groups sorting food at a food bank, tutoring students, or providing free legal advice at a clinic. These roles involve the recruitment, training, supervision, recognition, and retention of volunteers critical to helping the organization fulfill its mission.

Competencies and Credentials

The following list of competencies represents a sample of what might appear in position descriptions for nonprofit jobs. Entry-level positions may require a minimal level of skill while more senior-level positions will require a greater level of expertise.

- Passion for the mission of the organization
- Strong project management skills
- Exceptional communication skills – both oral and written
- Emotional intelligence and experience building relationships
- Ability to manage stakeholder expectations
- Program planning
- Ability to synthesize and translate complex concepts and frameworks into language that is clear for a wider audience
- Project accountability skills including contract management
- Ability to organize data and track logistics from inception to execution
- Maintain positive relationships with funders and other stakeholders
- Ability to handle confidential matters with utmost integrity
- Specific content knowledge or an area of expertise
- Experience training, coordinating, and inspiring a team of volunteers

Jobs and careers in the nonprofit sector are plentiful, and professionals often advance to positions of increasing responsibility, often fairly quickly, especially if you are flexible as to location and subsector. Much depends upon the exact role/position along with the type and size of the organization. You can be a big fish in a small pond or small fish in a big pond. If you are working at a smaller organization (big fish, small pond), you may need to know about many different types of tasks or position responsibilities. For example, if you work in fundraising at a smaller nonprofit you may need to have some knowledge about planned giving vehicles, basic tax law, how to run a campaign, and database management. In a larger office or organization, you may have colleagues with expertise in those areas so you might just need to know enough to communicate understanding. Nonprofit careers with smaller organizations can be great for professionals who aspire to move into C-suite roles quickly. They can also be appealing for those who value task diversity. Working in a smaller role at a larger organization (small fish, big pond) can allow you to gain expertise and knowledge by working with and learning from colleagues. Your position may focus on a very specific set of tasks that allows you to gain expertise.

Typical Requested Degrees and Credentials

Just like the corporate sector, this will vary widely by specific position. For most entry-level positions a bachelor's degree will suffice, and a master's degree is frequently listed as preferred (i.e., master's degree in nonprofit management *or a related area* such as adult education). Often, professionals in mid-level and upper-level roles will carry additional credentials beyond a formal degree. If it is a content-focused role, a doctoral degree is often desirable.

In addition to academic courses and programs, there are some additional certifications that may be useful once you have been in this field for a while and would like to advance in your career:

1 Certified Fund-Raising Executive (CFRE) – www.cfre.org
2 Chartered Advisor in Philanthropy® (CAP) – www.theamericancollege.edu/designations-degrees/CAP
3 Certified Grant Writer® (CGW) – www.agwa.us/CGWSeriesOnline
4 Grant Professional Certification (GPC) – www.grantcredential.org

Adult Education Competitive Advantage: Practice and Theory

While a degree in adult education is not often mentioned in position descriptions, the skill sets and desired competencies make this degree an extremely competitive "or a related area" option and degree holders should not hesitate to "throw their hat in the ring." Most of these roles include relationships with people. With a degree in adult education, you know how adults learn as well as what drives and motivates them. Having knowledge of program planning is a plus, as is understanding leadership theory and a firm grip on how to work well with those identified as leaders. For those with doctoral degrees, qualitative and quantitative research methodology coursework completed to support your dissertation and the ability to utilize existing literature helps you synthesize research and broad perspectives to communicate effectively with donors, funders, or organizational leaders. Implementing and reporting on program evaluations (necessary for effective programs and for most grants) will also be easier given your academic experience.

Program Planning Theory

In nonprofit careers, practitioners are often responsible for program planning, whether it be educational workshops, luncheons, or large fundraising events. Program managers can oversee individual programs/events, or the program could be a complex series of activities designed and implemented over a longer period of time—sometimes a year or longer. This typically entails managing a team of staff and volunteers. Your knowledge of program planning for adults will give you insights into how best to present information and create innovative and meaningful experiences that inspire volunteers, staff, and donors to support your organization and its mission. Most adult education programs discuss planning theory as important to planning educational programs. See Chapter 4 for more information on program planning.

Knowledge about the Field of Education

According to research conducted annually by the Indiana University Lilly Family School of Philanthropy and published in *Giving USA: The Annual Report on Philanthropy* (GivingUSA. org), education remains a top sector for charitable giving. If you work for a community foundation, or a nonprofit or foundation that focuses on education, having background knowledge in education theory and practice can set you apart from other applicants.

Foundations that work within the realm of education may specifically seek program officers with adult education degrees and experience. For example, a Spring 2020 posting for the Vice President of Mission and Programs for the Barbara Bush Foundation included the following qualifications:

- This position requires at least 7–10 years of experience, a master's or doctoral degree, and:
- Knowledge of adult learning theory and at least five years of experience managing adult education and/or training programs

(www.barbarabush.org/jobs/, accessed May 25, 2020)

Leadership Theory

Many board members and major donors have started their own companies or worked in executive (C-suite) roles. Many have also been involved in civic and community leadership roles such as serving on nonprofit boards or holding public office. Knowledge of leadership theory and working with leaders will provide insights into their mindsets. Professionals supervising staff or volunteers will also benefit from this knowledge. See Putman (2017) for more information on leadership competencies.

Adult Learning and Development Theory and the Donor Development Cycle

There are a variety of models or theories related to the identification of potential donors (prospects) and the process of individuals becoming more involved and giving more to the organization over time through a process called cultivation or stewardship (Sargeant, 2014). Visualized often as a ladder, or pyramid, fundraisers work to identify and secure gifts or donations. They strategize plans to encourage repeat giving, special gifts (often as part of a campaign for a specific project need), major gifts, and planned gifts. Over time, fundraising has moved from transactional paradigms to focusing on relationship building. Like adult learners, each donor is going to require an individual approach. For individuals with experience in adult education or adult learning and development, knowledge of the concepts of adult learning will be a boon to this work. (See Part I of this book for more information on adult learning theories.)

For More Information

The listings below provide greater detail about the various nonprofit roles and help give you a better sense of the range of salaries and benefits available. Note that salaries vary widely based upon subsector, size of organization, and location. What follows are a few professional associations to investigate as well as a few sites for nonprofit job listings. Use keywords connected to the type of job within the sector that intrigues you and note that often entry-level positions will use the word assistant or associate (i.e., development assistant). With nonprofit jobs, experience as a graduate assistant or other paraprofessional and sometimes even volunteer roles will often count towards the advertised years of professional experience.

Professional Associations

1. American Grant Writers' Association (AGWA): www.agwa.us
2. Association of Donor Relations Professionals (ADRP): www.adrp.net
3. Association of Fundraising Professionals (AFP): www.afpnet.org
4. Grant Professionals Association (GPA): http://grantprofessionals.org
5. Association of Leaders in Volunteer Engagement (AL!VE): https://volunteeralive.org

Job Listings

1. *The NonProfit Times* Nonprofit Career Match: https://careercenter.nptimes.com
2. Bridgespan Group Nonprofit Job Board: www.bridgespan.org/jobs
3. Grantmakers for Education: www.edfunders.org/job-announcements
4. *Chronicle of Philanthropy*: https://jobs.philanthropy.com
5. Council on Foundations: https://jobs.cof.org
6. *Philanthropy News Digest*: https://philanthropynewsdigest.org/jobs
7. Grants Professionals Association: https://grantprofessionals-jobs.careerwebsite.com

Four Trends Impacting the Future of Adult Education in the Nonprofit Sector

As we look to the future of the nonprofit sector, four trends seem particularly applicable for adult education practitioners. An increased level of engagement, technology, and diversity are balanced with shifting social expectations of the sector itself.

Greater Engagement and More Personalized Engagement

Program participants, donors, and volunteers are all looking for more personalized engagement, which will require thoughtful attention. National U.S. trends point to donors (younger donors in particular) who increasingly want to do more than just write a check or swipe a credit card, first becoming engaged in the mission of the organization, often as volunteers (Goldseker & Moody, 2020). An adult education background will equate to knowledge of HOW to engage meaningfully with these various constituencies. This skill set will become increasingly valuable.

Increasing Use of Technology

"Technology has become one of the wildcards of nonprofit evolution" (Salamon, 2015, p. 45). Whether it is facilitating communication, managing relationships, program delivery, or measuring results, these tools continue to become more sophisticated and robust, and a certain level of comfort with technology will be necessary for nonprofit jobs. One major trend is the increasing use of artificial intelligence (AI).

Integrated AI is the ability of a computer to perform tasks usually completed by human beings. This is not a "robots are coming for our jobs scenario," but rather the utilization of technology to gather and anticipate the needs and wants of people. For example, based upon where a person clicks within an organizational website, presenting content based upon their interests. This already occurs commonly on the internet, as anyone who has purchased an uncommon item as a gift for someone can attest as they are subsequently shown advertisements for related items. Another example is an automated chat function with a database of answers to the most-asked questions.

Diversity, Equity, and Inclusion (DEI)

Florenthal and Awad (2021) describe it nicely: "For some organizations, the diversity of the potential volunteer or donor population is increasing. For others, it is shifting. For most, diversity in those populations has been greater than the organization's capacity to engage fully that diversity" (p. 1). While DEI work can be its own adult education position (see Chapter 14), every role or position within the nonprofit sector will continue to be impacted as awareness of and support for various dimensions of human diversity expands. This will take time and attention if the sector hopes to approach this work meaningfully. It will be important to ensure that good intentions do not lead to negative impacts for staff, volunteers, or clients. See also the work of Villanueva (2021) and others.

Re-examination of the Value Proposition of the Sector

For those considering a long-term career in the nonprofit sector, the role of the sector in the United States in particular has a fascinating history, and a future that will certainly be interesting to say the least. Shifting societal expectations of the role of government, public understanding and support, and often-challenging funding models are just a few issues explored by Salamon (1999, 2015) and Ott and Dicke (2021), among others. The nonprofit sector is not going away any time soon, but at some point (U.S.) society is going to have to contend with the realities of the size and scope of some of the issues facing us and the capacity of the nonprofit sector to meet those challenges.

> **Advice for Nonprofit Careers**
>
> **Be passionate about the mission** of the organization and the work that it does. If you are managing programs or working directly with clients, you want to find an organization that speaks to your heart as well as your mind. If you are trying to build relationships with volunteers or donors and encourage them to give of their time, talent, or treasure to support your organization, it is extremely difficult to do so if you do not personally care about the mission. These careers can also be intensive, and during the busiest of days, grounding yourself in the mission will help keep you motivated.
>
> **Volunteer with or join a board of a nonprofit** whose mission you find personally compelling to explore the possibilities. If you are curious about fundraising, for example, volunteer to be a part of the development committee where you are exposed to asking others to support causes. Eventually, talk with staff about their roles and career paths to get deeper insight into the work to see if it is for you. For example, after learning more about proposal writing, you may want to give it a try but are unsure if you want to do it full time; then offer to be a pro-bono proposal writer for a small nonprofit.

> **Gain experience and expertise in a subject area** about which you are passionate. Present and publish. Foundations seeking program officers are often drawn to practitioners who bring the real-world experience of what the work entails "on the ground." This grounded experience pairs well with the work of foundations and philanthropy, which can often be working from a "30,000-foot perspective."

References

Bearman, J., Ramos, H. A., & Pond, A. N. S. (2010). Moving diversity up the agenda: Lessons and next steps from the diversity in philanthropy project. *The Foundation Review*, 2(2), 85–99.

Burlingame, D. F. (2016). *Achieving excellence in fundraising*. Wiley.

Cervero, R. M., & Wilson, A. L. (2005). *Working the planning table: Negotiating democratically for adult, continuing, and workplace education*. Jossey-Bass.

Fithian, S. C., Fithian, T., & Tolman, J. S. (2007). *The right side of the table: Where do you sit in the minds of the affluent?* FPA Press.

Florenthal, B., & Awad, M. (2021). A cross-cultural comparison of millennials' engagement with and donation to nonprofits: A hybrid U&G and TAM framework. *International Review on Public and Nonprofit Marketing*, 18(4), 629–657.

Goldseker, S., & Moody, M. (2020). *Generation impact: How next gen donors are revolutionizing giving*. John Wiley & Sons.

Grant, A. S. C., & Schiller, R. J. (2020). *Diversity, equity, and inclusion in advancement*. Council for Advancement and Support of Education.

Horton, M. (2003). *The Myles Horton reader: Education for social change*. University of Tennessee Press.

Knowles, M. S. (1975). *Self-directed learning*. Association Press.

Ott, J. S., & Dicke, L. (2021). *The nature of the nonprofit sector*. Routledge.

Payton, R. L., & Moody, M. P. (2008). *Understanding philanthropy: Its meaning and mission*. Indiana University Press.

Powell, W. W., & Bromley, P. (Eds.). (2020). *The nonprofit sector: A research handbook*. Stanford University Press.

Putman, P. G. (2017). Strategic leadership competency development. In *Encyclopedia of Strategic Leadership and Management* (pp. 1495–1520). IGI Global.

Salamon, L. M. (1999). *America's nonprofit sector: A primer*. Foundation Center.

Salamon, L. M. (2015). *The resilient sector revisited: The new challenge to nonprofit America*. Brookings Institution Press.

Sargeant, A. (2014). *Fundraising management: Analysis, planning and practice*. Routledge.

U.S. Bureau of Labor Statistics. (2018, August 31). Nonprofits account for 12.3 million jobs, 10.2 percent of private sector employment, in 2016. *The Economics Daily*. www.bls.gov/opub/ted/2018/nonprofits-account-for-12-3-million-jobs-10-2-percent-of-private-sector-employment-in-2016.htm

Villanueva, E. (2021). *Decolonizing wealth: Indigenous wisdom to heal divides and restore balance*. Berrett-Koehler Publishers.

Zinsmeister, K. (2016). *The almanac of American philanthropy*. The Philanthropy Roundtable.

Chapter 18

Online Learning and Instructional Design

Caryn Lanzo and Michael D. Porterfield

Virtually all organizations require training or educational activities, and many now offer these activities in an online format. Positions may be situated in higher education, training organizations, the technology sector, human resources, and other areas. A variety of positions exist in this space, but the role of "instructional designer" is most common. Other job titles include Instructional Technologist, Learning Designer, eLearning Developer, and Learning Management Systems (LMS) Administrator. Those with experience in the field may wish to progress to various positions including Coordinator, Manager, Director, or Assistant Dean. Some colleagues pursue doctoral studies which may prepare them for faculty, research, or higher education administrative positions that oversee entire units for online learning. Garrett et al. (2021) reports that the title of Chief Online Officer is the title that universities increasingly use as a designation for the online education executive in higher education. This demonstrates the importance of online learning within the organization and puts that position on the same level as Chief Financial Officer or Chief Executive Officer.

We believe that to be successful in this field, it is imperative that professionals have a solid foundation in instructional design. Courses in adult learning theory and instructional design, including objective/course alignment, plus how to create significant learning experiences, are an important piece of this foundation. Fink (2013) wrote of this experience:

> The central idea of this phrase – "significant learning" – is that teaching should result in something others can look at and say, "That learning experience resulted in something that is truly significant in terms of the students' lives" … significant learning is learning that makes a difference in how people live – and the kind of life they are capable of living. (p. 7)

Furthermore, professional development courses offered by organizations such as Quality Matters (QM) or the Online Learning Consortium provide an overview of best practices in developing quality online courses, as well as providing an opportunity to practice these principles.

Instructional designers have a wide range of responsibilities, which allows them to understand the entire development cycle of online course and program development. Since graduates of adult education understand how adults learn, they may find the field of instructional design particularly appealing. Professionals in this field often work with faculty or subject matter experts to develop courses and programs.

In 2022, we reviewed 35 positions in the instructional design/online learning field. Positions were posted on the Higher Education Jobs website, LinkedIn, or acquired through the Educause Instructional Design listserv. Chapter 11 on careers in corporate learning also provides additional information and websites for these types of positions in the corporate environment. Most positions were mid-entry level that assumed a combination of education, skills, and experience in instructional design. Positions primarily included those with the title of Instructional Designer. We also reviewed positions with titles such as LMS Administrator and

DOI: 10.4324/9781003259602-21

Instructional Technologist. In addition, similar positions such as Learning Designer, eLearning Developer and Learning and Experience Designer were included in the review. Key competencies emerged across the various position descriptions that are summarized below.

Key Job Responsibilities

Instructional Design

- Work with faculty/subject matter experts (SMEs) to develop online, remote, and hybrid courses that meet best practices and accessibility standards.
- Contribute to planning of online course production with SMEs and other project teams.
- Partner with SMEs to translate challenging business problems into engaging learning solutions.
- Research, design, and establish best practice models for the incorporation of online pedagogy, technology, instructional design principles, and learning standards in projects.
- Choose and apply appropriate instructional design principles, teaching strategies, and media formats to help develop written scripts/storyboards and transform them into clear, meaningful, engaging educational content for learners.
- Serve as a cross-functional team member on projects.

Content and Media Development

- Use a variety of technology and instructional design software to create and deliver learning content.
- Use fundamental digital design principles to develop, illustrate, and produce complex visual representations (such as learning objects, course enhancements, e-books, and video) through the mastery of key software programs and tools.
- Research and evaluate new educational technologies for improving student learning in online courses.

Quality Assurance

- Execute learning strategies in alignment with objectives that drive results.
- Review and edit curricular materials, including competency statements, learning objectives, and assessments, to construct effective course curricula.
- Assess effectiveness and evaluate completed learning modules after development.

Project Management

- Function as project manager for multiple course design projects.
- Oversee and implement course design and development projects.
- Utilize project management software to ensure courses and programs are designed in a timely manner with transparency to team members and leadership.
- Perform usability studies and create reports on project status within the project management framework established by the unit.

Teaching and Training

- Design, develop, and conduct instructional technology professional development activities to promote technology integration and enhance instruction and student learning.

- Develop documentation and manuals as required.
- Assist SMEs in implementing new technologies and approaches for online learning.

LMS Administration

- Provide implementation, management, and technical oversight of the LMS.
- Manage technical and functional integrations of related applications and software.
- Provide day-to-day operations of system integration, data synchronization, tool configuration, and implementation and updates for e-learning management systems.
- Perform system analysis and project management activities.
- Diagnose, troubleshoot, and resolve system issues.

Instructional Designers

> **What Do instructional designers Do?**
>
> - Work with SMEs to develop and design learning content.
> - Develop and deliver professional development on topics such as instructional design and specific technologies.
> - Develop media and interactive content that support achievement of learning outcomes.
> - Collaborate on cross-functional teams.
> - Participate in the planning of online courses and programs, and manage projects.
> - Assess quality of online courses to determine effectiveness as well as adherence to best practices and established benchmarks.
> - Resolve technical issues related to the LMS or other tools and technologies.

Most instructional designer positions require a bachelor's degree. Some instructional designer positions require a master's degree. In general, experience requirements range from a minimum of 1 to 5 years, depending on the position. Adult education graduates may compete with some applicants who have degrees in the field of instructional design. However, this is not necessarily a barrier for individuals who have previous experience in developing or delivering online education. Interestingly, no postings specified that a degree in instructional design was necessary, an acknowledgement that instructional designers may emerge from different fields of study. Instructional design, education, adult education, and instructional technology degrees were listed as examples of acceptable degrees, along with "or related field."

Areas of Experience Requirements

Employers want applicants to have experience in a variety of activities. They include:

- Designing instruction for adults
- Determining learning goals/outcomes
- Developing meaningful learning experiences
- Developing media and/or interactive content
- Designing assessment to improve instructional design
- Teaching online in an adult education setting

An instructional designer candidate would ideally have knowledge of instructional design methodologies and the ability to learn new instructional technologies. Two of these methodologies are knowledge of the ADDIE model (see Chapter 10) or the ALD model (see Chapter 11) of instructional design. Individuals with a background and/or degree in adult education are a good fit for the instructional design field due to their knowledge of adult learning theories, learning, and assessment, which is discussed in more detail later in this chapter. Salaries are typically posted in ranges, depending on qualifications and experience. The ranges were approximately $50,000 to $120,000.

Instructional Technologist

Instructional technologist positions reviewed were similar to instructional designer positions with regards to knowledge, skills, and experience (KSAs). These positions emphasize developing specific types of content rather than entire courses or programs and require strong technical skills in the areas of LMS usage, multimedia development tools, cameras, and recording hardware. Instructional technologists are generally part of an online learning team in an organization, but they may also support libraries or classrooms in colleges and universities, depending on the institution and the needs of the instructors. Salary ranges across positions reviewed were $48,000 to $78,000.

LMS Administrator

LMS administrators configure and maintain the LMS environment or software (as opposed to instructional designers, who use the LMS to present the content they create). This may include coordinating integrations with other systems to facilitate courses and enrollments, integrating with third party platforms such as lecture capture systems, synchronous meeting platforms, publisher platforms, and others. LMS administrators have the ability to customize the LMS with both branding and user experience preferences to best suit the needs of the organization's instructors and learners. LMS administrators provide support and troubleshooting for the LMS. They may also provide reports on teaching and learning activities in the LMS, such as learner achievement, predictive analysis, and standards achievement. Sometimes, LMS administrator positions are blended positions where roles are split between LMS administration, instructional design, or content/media development. Many of the LMS positions reviewed required a bachelor's degree. A few positions listed a master's degree as a preferred qualification. The LMS administrator desired skills were more aligned with the technical aspects of the learning environment. Salary ranges were $38,000 to $77,000.

Adult Learning Theory and Practice

There is a significant overlap of KSAs across these three diverse types of positions. In addition to the degree requirements and skills listed above, most positions require additional knowledge and skills including experience with MS Office applications, project management knowledge and experience, excellent communication skills, problem-solving abilities, and the ability to work independently and as a member of a team. Many positions request experience in teaching or learning in an online format, as well as experience instructing users in specific tasks such as using the LMS and related tools or designing an online course.

Social Constructivism

At the heart of these positions is adult learning, which helps make someone with an adult education degree a preferred candidate for these positions. There are several adult learning theories important for these roles. One theory is Vygotsky's (1978) social constructivism, which views knowledge as being constructed by learners through social interaction with one another. Furthermore, Smith and Ragan (2005) (as cited in Chuang, 2021) presume social constructivism in which "learning is collaborative with meaning negotiated from multiple perspectives" (p. 7). Again, learning happens when others interact with one another. According to Palloff and Pratt (2007), this takes "honesty, responsiveness, relevance, respect, openness, and empowerment" (p. 22), which are key in creating a learning community. Many current authors (Han et al., 2022; McGee & Tashakkori, 2021; van der Meer et al., 2021) continue to use McMillan and Chavis's (1986) foundational definition of community; they define a sense of community as "a feeling that members have of belonging, a feeling that members matter to one another and to the group, and a shared faith that members' needs will be met through their commitment to be together" (p. 9).

Infusing social constructivism or a sense of community becomes paramount and essential to learning, especially for online learning. Instructional designers need to consider this, plus realize "community is built upon what activities people do together instead of being based on geographical location" (Wellman, 1999, as cited in Rovai, 2002, p. 199). This can be difficult for those who define community based upon a geographical location. This is the reason meaningful and intentional interactions are imperative to learning.

Interaction Framework of Online Course Design

In 1993, Moore introduced a foundational interaction framework which determined an effective online course as having three meaningful interactions: learner-to-learner, learner-to-educator, and learner-to-content. Studying the underlying theory behind significant interactions has real-world ramifications upon teaching and learning, especially for adult learners. These significant interactions are defined and codified by the United States Department of Education (DoE) guidance in "regular and substantive interaction" language, which was first used in the Higher Education Act of 1965. This law provides the creation and access to financial aid, but in July 2021, the DoE gave further guidance on how "regular and substantive interaction" is defined in relation to distance education and innovation (Office of Postsecondary Education, 2021). To help ensure quality online courses and interactions, institutions and organizations developed rubrics. QM, a nonprofit, quality assurance organization that promotes quality course design for online courses, developed a rubric that course developers can use to measure course design. The State University of New York (SUNY), through SUNY Online, later partnered with the Online Learning Consortium to develop the Online Course Quality Review Rubric (OSCQR), which focuses on the instructional design and accessibility of an online course. According to the OSCQR website (Online Learning Consortium, n.d.), this rubric was influenced by Knowles's (1973) principles of adult learning and other influences including the Community of Inquiry model (Garrison et al., 2000), along with best practices. From a higher education standpoint, if a college or university does not meet these new requirements, this could threaten the institution's ability to access financial aid (Downs, 2021).

Personal Recommendations for Success

Both authors have worked in the field for many years and hold management positions that hire many of the positions described in this chapter. Also, both are adult education practitioners and want the reader to be successful in the field. With this in mind, each author offers their personal perspective to be successful. Remember that success can only be defined by you, the reader. Each has their own path to follow. In a history of Miguel de Cervantes, who is the author of *Don Quixote*, Brown (n.d.) wrote about success,

In every case, the remedy is to take action. Get clear about exactly what it is that you need to learn and exactly what you need to do to learn it. BEING CLEAR KILLS FEAR. Make it thy business to know thyself, which is the most difficult lesson in the world. (para. 14)

Caryn Lanzo

As a director who is responsible for hiring instructional designers, course and online material developers, and an LMS administrator, I have found that experience and skills are important, but it is not necessary to match experience and skills to our specific work environment. Regardless of who we hire, we know that we are going to need to train that person on our workflows and processes. If someone has the same type of experience in a different LMS or different type of software or tool, we are confident we can train that person in our specific software or tool. Knowledge on how adults learn, the ability to learn new technologies, and the capacity to work with and instruct others are equally important.

Adult education learners interested in this field might pursue an internship, student position, or graduate assistant position at the institution where they are studying, particularly if they do not have experience in online teaching and learning. Positions related to online learning and training might be found on college campuses in online learning offices; teaching and learning centers; information services and technologies; or human resources. Likewise, opportunities exist in the private and nonprofit sectors as well where organizations conduct training activities for continuing education, employee training, certifications, licensures, and more.

Experience as an instructor in an LMS and using related tools such as lecture capture, proctoring tools, and synchronous platforms such as Zoom are good skills to learn. Gaining knowledge about best practices for course design is also invaluable across all the different types of positions. Experience acquired using a specific LMS, as well as related tools, is typically transferable to different platforms. For example, if you have experience developing a module in Blackboard, that is useful when setting up a module in Canvas. Experience in multimedia development is also an area worth investing your time if you have access and the opportunity to do so.

While many employers prefer Adobe Captivate or Articulate Storyline software, I would recommend starting with Articulate Storyline. It is more user friendly than the Adobe platforms. Several instructional designer colleagues at my institution learned Articulate Storyline over the past few years. They had various experiences with other multimedia tools such as Adobe Captivate and audio/video production (from beginner to experienced). They used tutorials available through Articulate and other self-directed tutorials such as LinkedIn Learning (linkedin.com/learning) to help them learn to work with the program. Their experience with various learning technologies, knowledge of instructional design, and storyboarding skills were key factors that contributed to their success in using the software.

Michael Porterfield

For over 8 years, I have been an instructional designer/learning designer for both a public university and private one. My public university experience was mostly academic focused, while the private university was career focused. For me, the public university gave me the most experience and ability to grow professionally; also, the instructional designers were housed in a Center for Teaching and Learning within Academic Affairs, not Information Technology (IT).

In the Center for Teaching and Learning, our focus was on one-on-one consultations, faculty orientations, workshops, and quality online course design. We could focus, think, and collaborate with instructors to figure out what would help their participants learn, remember, and integrate the content in such a way that they would remember it 3 to 5 years after they took the class. If the instructional designers were housed within the IT department, there could be a different focus because they are more concerned with technical issues rather than teaching and learning. Even at the professional-focused university, it was about making the content interactive and presentable. These were my experiences; you might have a different one. In short, the working community is extremely important. Wherever you decide to work, you want to make certain you can grow professionally and individually while helping the learning community grow as well.

One of my mentors passed on this pearl of wisdom to me: technology should be at the service of the learning. Technology can always be learned, but the "learning about learning" and "reflecting on what you learned" are key to integration as a professional in online learning and development. As an adult education learner, you are keenly focused on learning and reflecting on your learning. This gives you an advantage when applying for a job in these areas. Again, technology can be learned; focus on quality course design, alignment, integration, and community. To me, these are key. Plus, do not be afraid to ask questions to learn more so that you can share this with others and help them grow professionally and as individuals. This was one of the main reasons why I received my terminal degree in teaching and learning with an emphasis in adult learning. In short, we are called to be educators. The piece of advice that has been most meaningful to me has been what Freire (1998) wrote: "Teachers who do not take their own education seriously, who do not study, who make little effort to keep abreast of events have no moral authority to coordinate the activities of the classroom" (p. 85).

Benefits of Professional Organizations

Joining organizations or forums related to instructional design can be beneficial both in terms of sharing knowledge and ideas, as well as networking. Teaching and learning communities (even those not specifically for online learning) can also be helpful to learn about different technologies and methodologies used by instructors and trainers. Exploring options with the online learning units, teaching and learning units, or libraries at your current organization or university is an effective way to get access to these different types of communities. Developing networks that allow for professional development, discussion, collaboration, and collegiality are important in any field, but especially so in positions in online teaching and learning, where technologies and practices are continually being updated and improved. There are additional resources in Chapters 10 and 11.

Professional Organizations

- American Association for Adult and Continuing Education/Commission on Distance Learning and Technology (AAACE/CDLT): www.aaace.org
- Educause: Instructional Design community group/listserv: https://connect.educause.edu/community-home?CommunityKey=3ff54e87-21c2-47a6-9791-19af491cdd80
- Educause: Instructional Technologies community group/listserv: https://connect.educause.edu/community-home?CommunityKey=0fc977l9-flfd-4a09-a3e6-f8ee2f412f71
- Educause: Teaching and Learning Initiative: www.educause.edu/eli
- Online Learning Consortium (OLC): onlinelearningconsortium.org
- Quality Matters (QM): www.qualitymatters.org
- United States Distance Learning Association (USDLA): https://usdla.org

The Future of Adult Education in Online Learning

The demand for instructional designers has increased over the past several years. Instructional designers work in higher education, private companies, and nonprofit organizations. Online courses and programs in higher education continue to grow. In April 2020, *Inside Higher Ed* published an article titled "Instructional Designers: The Hottest Job in Higher Education," where they describe instructional designers as "sherpas of online learning teams, experts in *how* to teach and design a course" (Decherney & Levander, 2020, para. 6). For private companies and nonprofit organizations, technological changes and advances in the workplace occur on a regular basis, making instructing employees on new and specific skills an essential practice. Guild Research predicted that the role of instructional designer would continue to expand due to these technological advances (Wagner, 2019). Additional growth in this area can be expected due to the rise in hybrid and remote working arrangements.

According to a Labor Insight Report from Burning Glass Technologies (as cited in St. Thomas University Online, 2019), in 2017, there were 7,000 postings for instructional designers in the United States. In 2018, there were 9,659 postings. A search of LinkedIn for "Instructional Designer" in 2022 yielded 7,346 results – on a single day. Opportunities in instructional design are likely to continue to increase.

The Changing Landscape of Online Education (CHLOE) project produces a yearly report that reviews the growth of online education in postsecondary education. This research project is part of the QM organization discussed above. Online education leaders are surveyed each year to contribute to the report. In the 2021 CHLOE 6 report (Garrett et al., 2021), changes to online education driven by the COVID-19 pandemic are highlighted. The report showed that most institutions increased investments in technologies during the pandemic. This investment was most pronounced in specific educational technology tools. Those showing the largest proportional increases in adoption included: video conferencing, video recording, accessibility tools, and virtual labs and simulations. Over 86% of respondents reported an increased or greater priority for online learning. A majority of institutions (57%) reported they were likely to reevaluate their strategic priorities and increase online course and program options.

The 2022 Educause Horizon Report – Teaching and Learning Edition (Pelletier et al., 2022) identified trends across five categories, including social and technological. Expert panelists weighed in on important trends likely to shape higher education in the near future. The 2022 report identified hybrid and online learning, skills-based learning, and remote work as important social developments. Learning analytics and big data, redefining instructional modalities, and cybersecurity topped the list of technological trends. These are important trends for instructional designers and others in positions related to online learning in higher education. See Chapter 11 for more information regarding corporate instructional designers.

Developing meaningful social interactions in learning spaces will be a significant focus as higher education navigates the transition from "emergency" remote learning to mainstreaming different types of hybrid modalities. The focus on artificial intelligence both for learning purposes as well as monitoring learner progress is a trend with much potential to improve the quality of learner–content interaction as well as improve learner success.

Recommended readings

- Darby, F., & Lang, J. M. (2019). *Small teaching online: Applying learning science in online classes.* Jossey-Bass.

- Fink, L. D. (2013). *Creating significant learning experiences: An integrated approach to designing college courses (Revised and updated edition).* Jossey-Bass.
- Morrison, G. R., Ross, S., Morrison, J. R., & Kalman, H. K. (2019). *Designing effective instruction.* Wiley.

In conclusion, a career in instructional design or related roles will prove to be a valuable opportunity for graduates of adult education programs. As the landscape for adult and higher education continues to change due to technological and other influences, instructional designers must always learn, adapt, and be flexible to create online learning environments that meet the needs of today's learners, regardless of the learning context.

References

Brown, L. (n.d.). *Miguel de Cervantes: History of Don Quixote.* www.spanish.academy/blog/history-of-don-quixote-author-cervantes-and-his-buried-remains

Chuang, S. (2021). The applications of constructivist learning theory and social learning theory on adult continuous development. *Performance Improvement, 60*(3), 6–14. https://doi.org/10.1002/pfi.21963

Decherney, P., & Levander, C. (2020, April 24). *The hottest job in higher education: Instructional designer.* Inside Higher Ed. www.insidehighered.com/digital-learning/blogs/education-time-corona/hottest-job-higher-education-instructional-designer

Downs, L. (2021, August 26). *Regular and substantive interaction refresh: Reviewing & sharing our best interpretation of current guidance and requirements.* Frontiers. https://wcet.wiche.edu/frontiers/2021/08/26/rsi-refresh-sharing-our-best-interpretation-guidance-requirements

Fink, L. D. (2013). *Creating significant learning experiences: An integrated approach to designing college courses.* Jossey-Bass.

Freire, P. (1998). *Pedagogy of freedom: Ethics, democracy, and civic courage.* Rowman & Littlefield Publishers.

Garrett, R., Simunich, B., Legon, R., & Fredericksen, E. E. (2021). *CHLOE 6: Online learning leaders adapt for a post-pandemic world.* Quality Matters. www.qualitymatters.org/qa-resources/resource-center/articles-resources/CHLOE-6-report-2021

Garrison, D. R., Anderson, T., & Archer, W. (2000). Critical inquiry in a text-based environment: Computer conferencing in higher education model. *The Internet and Higher Education, 2*(2–3), 87–105.

Han, J., Jiang, Y., Mentzer N., & Kelley, T. (2022). The role of sense of community and motivation in the collaborative learning: An examination of the first-year design course. *International Journal of Technology and Design Education, 32*, 1837–1852, https://doi.org/10.1007/s10798-021-09658-6

Knowles, M. (1973). *The adult learner: A neglected species.* Gulf Publishing Company.

McGee, J., & Tashakkori, R. (2021). STEM scholars' sense of community during the COVID-19 pandemic. *Journal of College Science Teaching, 51*(1), 49–57.

McMillan, D., & Chavis, D. (1986). Sense of community: A definition and theory. *Journal of Community Psychology, 14*(1), 6–23.

Moore, M. J. (1993). Three types of interaction. In K. Harry, M. John, & D. Keegan (Eds.), *Distance education theory* (pp. 19–24). Routledge.

Office of Postsecondary Education. (2021). *Distance education and innovation: Final regulations.* U.S. Department of Education. www2.ed.gov/policy/highered/reg/hearulemaking/2018/distanceandinnovationunofficialreg.pdf

Online Learning Consortium. (n.d.). *The OSCQR process.* https://oscqr.suny.edu/about/about-oscqr/the-oscqr-process

Palloff, R., & Pratt, K. (2007). *Building online learning communities* (2nd ed.). Jossey-Bass.

Pelletier, K., McCormack, M., Reeves, J., Robert, J., Arbino, N., Al-Freih, M., Dickson-Deane, C., Guevara, C., Koster, L., Sánchez-Mendiola, M., Skallerup Bessette, L., & Stine, J. (2022). *2022 EDUCAUSE horizon report: Teaching and learning edition.* https://library.educause.edu/resources/2022/4/2022-educause-horizon-report-teaching-and-learning-edition

Rovai, A. (2002). Development of an instrument to measure classroom community. *Internet and Higher Education*, 5, 197–211.

Smith, P. L., & Ragan, T. J. (2005). *Instructional design* (3rd ed.). John Wiley & Sons.

St. Thomas University Online. (2019, September 19). *Instructional design: A growing field.* https://online.stu.edu/articles/education/instructional-design-growing-field.aspx

van der Meer, G. H., Milota, M., de Jonge, R. R., & Jansen, R. S. (2021). Practical guidelines to build sense of community in online medical education. *Medical Education*, 55, 925–932. https://doi.org/10.1111/medu.14477

Vygotsky, L. S. (1978). *Mind in society: The development of higher psychological processes.* M. Cole, V. John-Steiner, S. Scribner, & E. Souberman (Eds.). Harvard University Press.

Wagner, E. (2019). *Learning engineering: A primer.* The eLearning Guild Research. www.learningguild.com/insights/238/learning-engineering-a-primer

Chapter 19

Policy Leadership in Adult Education Reform

Elizabeth A. Roumell, Alexis T. Cherewka and Aaron J. Reyna

Post 2020, the need for adult learning and a variety of key literacies is as critical as it has ever been in the United States, but the policies and programs supporting such programming are multifaceted and vary considerably from state to state. More leaders in the areas of adult and workforce education (AWE) public policy and adult and lifelong learning programming are needed to present these needs to the wider public and to key decision-makers locally, at the state level, and nationally. Ideally, leaders in the AWE policy area are able to effectively communicate with data; are highly capable at building coalitions and partnerships to promote adult learning infrastructure and opportunities; and are not afraid to engage private industry, businesses, or stakeholders of the public sector at the local, state, and federal levels. Adult education policy leaders must regularly work with a variety of partners to build robust service networks and local, regional, and state institutional capacity in support of increasing access to a wider variety of educational opportunities for working learners. AWE policy experts are deeply engaged in creating, enacting, and studying new visions for adult and workforce education, and must develop the knowledge, skills, abilities, and relationships needed to do so.

While we (the chapter authors) have all pursued advanced degrees in the field of adult education, which have proven effective in developing our own knowledge, skills, and abilities as related to AWE policy research and analysis, we have also accumulated relevant professional experience as practitioners in the field. Below, we briefly share our own background and introduction to the areas of research and policy analysis in the area of AWE.

Liz Roumell

I started my career teaching English as an instructor in Germany and later in the United States, as well as proctoring language and high school equivalency exams. I then moved into grant work, where I served as an external evaluator and technical support for various providers and grant-funded communities, and as a trainer for data collection and input, and data-driven decision-making. Later, I pursued my PhD in education with a focus on post-secondary and higher education, and later became a university faculty member teaching courses related to adult education. I began researching AWE policy development over time in order to mature my understanding of the architecture and processes behind AWE programming and learning opportunities for adults in the US and the European Union. These roles have actively contributed to the experience and knowledge I currently bring to my role as Executive Director of the Center for the Advancement of Literacy and Learning (TCALL) funded by the Texas Workforce Commission.

DOI: 10.4324/9781003259602-22

Alexis Cherewka

I began my career teaching English to speakers of other languages. After teaching in intensive English programs at the university level, I transitioned to working in an English for Speakers of Other Languages (ESOL) program at a community-based organization. It was during this time that I became more familiar with adult education policy through my work on grant assistance for the Workforce Investment Act (WIA) and the Workforce Innovation and Opportunity Act (WIOA). It was this experience that led me to consider the role of public policy in the classroom. Eventually I returned to school in an effort to better understand how policy affects instruction. As a doctoral candidate at Penn State University, I research the impact of the WIOA for adult foundational education. I have also worked as a consultant for the Migration Policy Institute's National Center on Immigrant Integration Policy, which gave me an opportunity to explore other adult educators' experiences under a WIOA program called Integrated English Literacy and Civics Education.

Aaron J. Reyna

My original rationale for pursuing a master's degree in adult education at Florida State University was to become a corporate trainer. However, due to the program's unique focus on social justice and my professional interest in policy and education, I decided to work in the public sector. My first full-time job was at a local nonprofit as a GED and college advisor in the San Antonio area. I became increasingly interested in workforce development and education, program development and evaluation, grant writing and management, and adult education policy and advocacy. Through these experiences I decided to pursue my doctorate in education policy and evaluation and became solely interested in studying policy and how to conduct and synthesize research.

Career Paths in Policy Leadership

Education policy is understood as a set of established principles, assumptions, and norms that govern education decision-making and practices. Such policy includes laws as well as processes and policies that educational organizations, local districts, states, and nations implement and follow to achieve educational goals (RAND, 2022). A specification of principles and actions related to educational issues which are followed, or should be followed, are designed to bring about desired goals in the public education sector.

> A career in education policy leadership consists of supporting educators, administrators, public stakeholders and leaders, education providers, and systems in addressing long-standing inequities in adult learners' educational experiences and outcomes. Policy leaders are also tasked with pursuing these aims within dynamic, rapidly evolving educational, social, and political contexts in which novel approaches to adult education and workforce development are being advanced alongside innovative models for creating improved access to learning opportunities across the lifespan.

Like many professional roles in the field, a career in AWE policy development, advocacy, and/or analysis often is not an intentional vocational choice, but rather a career development of happenstance. Work within the AWE policy area generally comes about through experience and time in the field and/or advocacy for AWE at various levels. People enter this work with a variety of backgrounds, professional experience, credentials, and personal career goals. Professionals in this area may have degrees and qualifications in various specialties in education, business or public administration, language teaching and acquisition, human resource (HR) development/management or career counseling, organizational psychology, instructional design, training and development, and continuing education. Often, they also bring specific expertise in a particular vocation or occupation (e.g. nursing, cyber security, technical fields, hospitality services). The types of institutions and organizations that AWE policy specialists work for also vary widely from federal and state agencies to local city governments, public and private educational providers, K-12 school districts, community college systems, and other institutions of higher education, to nonprofit organizations that support the development and advocacy for AWE policy change.

Historically, policy advocacy played an important role in the establishment of adult education programming in the US. In the 1960s, adult educators and their advocates were highly influential in the public and political arenas, which led to the eventual initiation of formal, public adult education programming under the 1966 Adult Education Act (AEA) at the federal and state levels. The AEA was a major turning point in the history of adult basic education in the US, marking the beginning of federal government funding for adult basic education (defined as pre-high school) and for English as a second language education. All 50 states receive federal monies to fund AWE programming across their regions and communities. The National Literacy Act (NLA) of 1991 was incorporated into the AEA. Until the Department of Labor's 1998 Workforce Investment Act (WIA), adult education programs were located within education legislation. The WIA repealed the AEA and the NLA. The WIA Title II, Adult Education and Family Literacy Act of 1998 (AEFLA), provided funding for adult basic education to:

- assist adults to become literate and obtain the knowledge and skills necessary for employment and self-sufficiency;
- assist adults who are parents to obtain the educational skills necessary to become full partners in the educational development of their children; and
- assist adults in the completion of a secondary school education.

In 2014, the WIA was replaced by the WIOA. The resulting federal block grants to states based on these iterations of federal legislation provide public AWE programming, serving as the foundation for the ongoing proliferation of a variety of adult learning opportunities across the country.

States may also have their own legislation and established public services in the AWE policy area, which can go beyond the basic federal funding or be coupled with other agencies or sources of funding. Some cities, such as Houston, Texas, have their own adult literacy blueprint and plan with a city office specifically dedicated to adult education provisions. Primary, secondary, and higher education systems often coordinate with AWE programs to establish clearer career pathways for adult learners that aim to assist them in earning the necessary credentials so they can obtain more stable work and family-sustaining incomes.

The Three Core Competency Areas

There are three primary areas of knowledge and experience that are important when it comes to working in the AWE policy arena: practitioner experience, policy processes and development, and research and analysis. These areas of experience should not be viewed as levels, nor as a particular order in which one must gain professional knowledge and experience. Often, people come to the field with a variety of previous professional experiences and may be gaining experience in more than one area of knowledge at a time. Even so, we will use these three areas to organize and present the relevant knowledge, skills, and abilities (KSAs) for AWE policy careers.

Practitioner Experience

Exceptional experiences that can meaningfully inform policy analysis:

- practical experience as an adult educator and/or as a program coordinator in the public sector;
- working with partner institutions and providers;
- obtaining and maintaining various types of funding sources (from foundations, government grants, donors, and sponsors); and
- managing stakeholders' expectations, performance measures, and outcomes.

AWE practitioners and professionals are often program directors and managers for AWE providers who coordinate across various services and institutions to help working adults gain access to the services they need for identifying, enrolling in, and continuing to pursue learning opportunities. Adult learning professionals (ALPs) (including adult educators, workforce specialists, adult education leaders, and others in supporting roles) must be able to identify key stakeholders in the areas of concern and continuously build networks across agencies, education providers, and relevant public service agencies. Practitioners also work to interface with relevant businesses and industries in partnership to inform, establish, and maintain access to various occupational training. They regularly work to collaborate and build partnerships and memorandums of understanding (MOUs) to develop robust referral systems and wraparound services for adult learners. An MOU is a formal document that describes and broadly outlines the elements of an agreement between participating parties, including the mutually agreed-upon expectations and responsibilities between each of the collaborating entities. AWE professionals must also be adept at identifying and pursuing a variety of funding opportunities to ensure the continuation of AWE programming. They are often tasked with managing public perceptions of the available services where necessary. Table 19.1 summarizes some of the KSAs practitioners can bring to the AWE public policy arena.

When it comes to advocating for public AWE services, policy advocates also need a working understanding of the actors and processes involved in the creation and implementation of germane policy initiatives at varying levels.

Table 19.1 Practitioner KSAs

Knowledge	Skills and Abilities
Familiarity with: • The field of education in general • Adult learning theories and teaching methods (see Chapter 2) • Learner assessment • Evaluation models and strategies (see Chapter 5) • Relevant data systems • Familiarity with several types of funding opportunities (see Chapter 17) • How to understand and use community and population-level statistics to inform strategic planning and decision-making	• Experience working in adult learning environments • Strong communication and coordination skills • Program development and planning (see Chapter 4) • Build budgets and budget justifications for projects/analyze proposed budgets • Conduct needs assessment/environmental scans • Perform program evaluations • Building partnerships with a variety of stakeholders • Cultural competence • Political savviness • Time management • Project management • Technology acuity

Policy Processes and Development

Policy is developed and implemented through a series of complex processes. Adult educators can better understand this process by participating in various professional organizations and becoming acquainted with the literature on adult education policy, both peer-reviewed scholarship and policy analysis.

Adult education appears in several areas of public policy (educational, labor and workforce, K-12 and higher education, and more), but the Adult Education and Family Literacy Act under the 2014 WIOA legislation represents primary federal legislation that directly addresses adult education policy. Under this policy, federal monies are handed to state education agencies such as the departments of education or labor, which in turn hold local competitions to award local grantees within their states. States build the requests for proposals, which are then comparatively reviewed to determine local grantees and educational priorities for their states and to elect how to spend money on professional development. State education agencies wield tremendous power in implementing adult education policy (Belzer, 2007). The federal office, the Department of Education Office of Career, Technical, and Adult Education (OCTAE), provides guidance and technical assistance for state agencies and local programs. At the same time, many other professional organizations and associations support policy implementation, raising awareness of new policy, providing policy analysis, and advocating for policy change. Table 19.2 highlights several of these organizations, what they contribute to the policy process, and their role in the adult education policy field. These organizations may also serve as resources for identifying up-to-date career opportunities in the field and offer access to the AWE professional community.

Within the area of AWE policy, it is especially important to develop an understanding for how various AWE delivery systems function, and that these vary considerably between states. For example, some states deliver programming primarily through their community college systems while others are coordinated within the K-12 public school systems. In other states, AWE may be partnered with higher education, with workforce development programming, or perhaps combinations thereof. A professional in this area also works to analyze the climate of leadership and the public's amenability to an idea when it comes to policy initiatives (i.e. is there buy-in and support, is there proper public knowledge and awareness, are there cultural norms or resistance one must be aware of?). There is also a vibrant nonprofit and faith-based sector that supports and provides AWE and community-based programming.

These noted system architectures for program delivery bring different and braided sources of funding and require collaborations with community, local, and regional actors, and potentially additional government agency partnerships. Cities like Houston, Texas, have also designed and implemented their own adult and family literacy blueprints to support their diverse communities and to address the high need for literacy support and AWE programming. Within these diverse contexts, policy advocates must be able to assess the infrastructure of a community, be aware of relevant programming and partnerships, and understand the core elements of building community capacity and capabilities. Understanding capacity building, policy implementation, and evaluation of such initiatives can also be extremely useful. Table 19.3 briefly summarizes some KSAs in the area of policy processes.

A professional who works in the area of AWE policy advocacy must be able to identify key stakeholders in the areas of concern and build networks across agencies, providers, funding opportunities, etc. They may also be present for and participate in the policy-making process, and actively work to build support and buy-in for various AWE policy perspectives. It is important to be able to frame key issues in a compelling way that resonates with key stakeholders and leaders. The AWE policy professional must also be able to provide concise,

Table 19.2 Field-related organizations

Organization	Policy Involvement?	Policy Area
American Association for Adult and Continuing Education (AAACE)	Policy research	Broad spectrum of topics related to adult learning
American Institutes for Research (AIR)	Policy research	Educational policy, program evaluation, and workforce development
Coalition for Adult Basic Education (COABE)	Policy advocacy	Adult foundational education
Migration Policy Institute (MPI)	Policy research	Immigrant integration and adult education
National Coalition for Literacy (NCL)	Policy advocacy	Adult foundational education
National Council for Workforce Education (NCWE)	Data, evaluation, policy recommendations	Career, technical, vocational, and workforce development programming, career pathways
National Skills Coalition (NSC)	Policy advocacy and research	Adult foundational education
ProLiteracy	Policy advocacy and research	Adult foundational education
World Education, Inc.	Policy research	Adult education, workforce development, and educational technology
Coalition for Adult and Higher Education (CAEL)	Engage with educators, employers, and community leaders to align learning and work so that adults achieve continuous, long-term career success	Foster a healthy workforce ecosystem partnering with a spectrum of entities supporting adult learners to create actionable career pathways
National Association of State Directors of Adult Education (NASDAE)	• Serve as a catalyst for public policy review and development related to adult education • Online resources to provide state policy and procedure models and options	• Coordinate, develop, and conduct programs of professional development for state adult education leadership • Disseminate information about the field of adult education • Network among members and with partner organizations
National Association of State Workforce Agencies (NASWA)	• Leading national advocate for workforce development policy and catalyst for system advances • Defining national policy on workforce and related issues	• Represent all 50 state workforce agencies and respected voices of these systems • Align work with national partners • Build an active network for state administrators • Provide workforce program and technology solutions
National Governors Association (NGA)	• Work with state policy leaders and other experts in fostering information sharing between states • Research, develop, and implement innovative solutions to public policy challenges	• Voice of the leaders of 55 states, territories, and commonwealths • Advocate for the bipartisan policy priorities of governors among federal agencies, Congress, and the White House
Barbara Bush Foundation for Family Literacy	Expand access to literacy services for adults nationwide	• Support to literacy programs in all 50 states and the District of Columbia • Coordinate efforts to improve access to literacy programming for all adults and families

Table 19.3 Policy process KSAs

Knowledge	Skills and Abilities
Familiarity with: • General knowledge about the field of education • How policy is made, and the processes involved in its implementation • Primary professional organizations and associations at the state, regional, or national level • How various AWE delivery systems vary from state to state • Leadership theory • Core elements of community capacity building (see Chapter 9) • The strengths and needs of adult learners who are targeted in policies	• Political savviness • Excellent report-writing skills and sharing targeted information with relevant audiences • Communicate and adjust message based on audience and purpose to non-subject-matter experts (SMEs) • Cultural competence • Explain the governance structures at the appropriate level (local, state, federal) • Research skills: mine, analyze, and interpret relevant data • Analyze public perception of the issues, programming, or initiatives • Build key partnerships and collaboration • Project management • Perform stakeholder analyses and environmental scans • Assess the infrastructure and capabilities necessary for proper implementation • Network actively and broadly with partners invested in AWE policy success • Technology acuity

compelling data and information to key stakeholders to promote information-rich decision-making processes. Understanding the complex background, context, and the relevant systems that support AWE public policies and programming may also require additional knowledge and support that researchers and analysts can contribute.

Policy Research and Analysis

It is also valuable to cultivate the ability to understand research and how it can be leveraged to help inform policy development and advocate for the field of adult education and adult learners. Similar to the other areas, a policy researcher/analyst also needs to be able to communicate and adjust a message based on audience and purpose, especially in communicating key information to non-SMEs in plain, accessible language. In this area, the policy researcher/analyst needs to be able to effectively communicate with researchers and experts as well as with educators, administrators, and the public at large. Researchers/analysts work to interpret and convey critical data to help promote an understanding of why AWE policy is important to the public. A summary of the KSAs for policy researchers and analysts are outlined in Table 19.4.

Research on key topics for the field, including numeracy, writing, digital literacy, and integrated education and training approaches, has not yet provided a clear picture for effective AWE policy and practice. The field lacks a strong portrayal of the very diverse range of learners, their motivations, supports and barriers for participation, and the outcomes of participation in AWE programming. There have also been limited studies on the return on investment (ROI) and social return on investment for AWE programming. In addition, clearly establishing how AWE programming contributes to the health of communities and society more broadly has been difficult to establish. Further, an understanding of topics that support the "infrastructure" for effective AWE programming, including what constitutes effective program formats and professional training of the workforce, is also still insufficient. The research that does exist tends

Table 19.4 Policy research and analysis KSAs

Knowledge	Skills and Abilities
Familiarity with: • Theoretical perspectives on adult education policy • Foundational knowledge of general public administration principles • The varieties and kinds of adult education and workforce development programming, and which ones fall under the purview of state or federal policy • A variety of research methods in order to be able to evaluate studies (see Chapter 5) • The relevance of policy analysis findings within the public context	• Strong communication and writing skills and ability to adjust message based on audience and purpose, especially with non-SMEs • Project management and implementation • Research skills: mine, analyze, and interpret relevant data • Analyze public perception of the issues, programming, or initiatives • Applied quantitative research skills and familiarity with statistics programs • Read and analyze public policy documents identifying the framing and rationale for policy development • Synthesize various sources of data on a policy subject/area • Interviewing, conducting focus groups, and other qualitative research skills • Cultural competence (see Chapter 14) • Technology acuity

to be fragmented and inconsistent, often leaving policy makers in the field dependent on research from other educational sectors, which is not AWE focused and does not provide well-defined knowledge related to adult learners who participate in AWE programming.

In light of the significant public investment made at the federal, state, and local levels, the field needs a more developed and robust knowledge base specific to adult learners and a well-trained workforce that knows how to, and is supported and incentivized to, use that knowledge base in support of AWE policy and programming. Such a research base and evidence-informed programming need to be specific enough to create a clear focus for action, but also broad and inclusive enough to respond to the diversity of learners, practitioners, and learning contexts that are characteristic of AWE programs. Therefore, more research, venues for research dissemination, and a highly functional, research-based professional development system are needed to establish such a knowledge base. In order to be most helpful, new research should be actionable, high leverage, written for a diverse audience of practitioners, and target key areas of need. The research should focus on increasing and improving adult learner participation, professional development, program and instructional quality and equity, as well as addressing an ever-changing adult education and literacy context. Research objectives in the field should work to:

- better understand the full range of learner sub-groups with regard to characteristics, needs, supports, barriers, and motivations to enroll in public AWE programming among both participants and non-participants in order to responsively (re)design programs and instruction to be as learner centered and learner responsive as possible;
- better understand and identify key strategies, modalities, resources, and supports that can enhance enrollment and intensity of participation for adults who could benefit from participating in AWE in order to increase the number and longevity of those who enroll and complete AWE programming.

Research is needed for a broad audience that includes practitioners, learners, policy makers, funders, community leaders, and community members. For practitioners and learners, it should inform programmatic and instructional decisions to improve learner outcomes. For policy makers it should help craft wise and effective policy that increases the potential for practitioners and learners to be successful. Funders, policy makers, community leaders, business and industry, and labor organizations also need research that convinces them of the importance of investing in AWE with money, time, and other valuable resources. Further, research and policy analysis should make a robust argument for funding AWE programming based on findings that demonstrate a wide range of positive short- and long-term outcomes of participation. The intended audiences for such research would be practitioners, researchers, funders, learners, and policy makers and leaders in the field.

Policy Leadership

Policy work in the field of AWE is a lot like playing a detective who is developing a "wall of potential suspects." As a highly *decentralized* field, policy work is heavily impacted by the fact that very few agreed-upon definitions exist; there is a plurality of organizations and agencies plus a multitude of entities and actors involved; and funding, in-kind support, and collaboration come from a variety of sources with varying requirements and regulations. It can be challenging to connect the plethora of dots into meaningful patterns, but it is also rewarding to collaborate with diverse groups of professionals who actively work to support adult learners and AWE programming.

Like all of the areas presented thus far, the specific KSAs required for a policy leadership role will vary by the community, the level and kind of leadership, and the particular kinds of programming that are being addressed. Despite the many variables, there are some core areas of knowledge that need to be built-out in the field. Facilitated by the Barbara Bush Foundation for Family Literacy, a 2020 national working group was specifically tasked with identifying needed areas of professional development (PD) and continuing education for ALPs as part of the *National Action Plan for Adult Literacy 2021*. The following competency areas were identified by a diverse group of ALPs across the country:

ALP PD Core Competency Areas (evidence-based training for all ALPs):

- Principles of adult learning (see Chapter 1)
- Principles of adult literacy/literacy in the 21st century (see Chapter 7)
- Principles and methods of second/additional language acquisition (see Chapter 7)
- Classroom management and the teaching/learning transaction (see Chapter 2)
- Integration of technology and digital literacy (see Chapter 6)
- Equity, diversity and inclusion, social justice, empowerment strategies (see Chapter 14)
- Learning modalities (face-to-face, blended, online, etc.) (see Chapter 6)
- Learning disabilities and teaching approaches for neuro-divergent learners
- Career Pathways, Integrated Education and Training (IET) practices, and other context-based teaching models
- Assessment and accountability (see Chapter 5)

PD Competency Areas for Administrators and Leadership (in addition to the content above):

- Program planning, design, and management (see Chapter 4)
- Grant writing, reviewing (see Chapter 17)
- Budgeting
- Program implementation (see Chapter 4)

- Supervise/evaluate instructional performance and practices (performance accountability) (see Chapter 5 on assessment and evaluation)
- Funding mechanisms (federal rules, fundraising, etc.)
- Legal, HR, employment rules
- Network with strategic partners
- Technology integration and digital inclusion strategies
- Leadership development
- Diversity, inclusion, and equity within organizations (see Chapter 14)

All competency areas are interdependent and dynamic. A multitude of diverse professionals and experts are needed in the AWE policy arena to advocate for and continue to build impactful and meaningful educational opportunities for working adults across the country. Professionals who understand this important public policy arena are in high demand.

> **Recommended Reading**
>
> Belzer, A. (2007). Implementing the Workforce Investment Act from in between: State Agency responses to federal accountability policy in adult basic education. *Educational Policy*, 21(4), 555–588. https://doi.org/10.1177/0895904806289263
>
> Pickard, A. (2021). Barriers to access in public adult literacy education. *Educational Policy*, 35(5), 721–747. https://doi.org/10.1177/0895904819843602
>
> Roumell, E. A., Todoran, C., & Salajan, F. (2020). A framework for capacity building in adult and workforce education programming. *Adult Literacy Education: The International Journal of Literacy, Language, and Numeracy*, 2(2), 16–32.
>
> Roumell, E. A., Salajan, F. D., & Todoran, C. (2019). An analysis and illustration of the U.S. adult and workforce education policy domain. *Adult Education Quarterly*, 69(4), 295–314. https://doi.org/10.1177/0741713619856097

Future of Adult Education in the Public Policy Arena

There is a clear and growing need for policy experts and professionals who have studied various models for educational programming at the local, state, and federal levels. Our adult working learners are ever in need of improved access to lifelong learning opportunities and support, which demands advocates and champions throughout the public sector. Policy research and analysis meets at the intersection of AWE practice and theory. The range of perspectives at different levels are necessary in working toward the kinds of policies that would best support adult and workforce education. The abundance and variety of expertise and skills contribute great value to the field, but there are also many areas of improvement that call for more intentional, evidence-informed, and targeted policy work.

Advanced graduate studies in the field of adult education provide foundational knowledge combining theoretical knowledge and methodological tools for applied research. Graduate programs also help ALPs develop strong analytical, communication, presentation, and writing skills. They also need to know how the educational systems and programming work in their region; who the key agencies and actors are related to AWE programming; have experience with grantsmanship, budgeting, and management; and in building partnerships to build healthy support networks and wraparound services for adult learners. Adult education graduate programs support targeted professional development and professional skills development that connects ALPs to people, data, content, resources, expertise, and learning experiences that can empower and inspire them to provide more effective learning opportunities for all adult learners.

Highly skilled ALPs who represent adult learners, educators, and programs need to be present on regional workforce development boards, in local and regional coalitions, and to be experts who are active across a variety of organizations. An important skill set that policy advocates can bring to the table are experts who can concisely and effectively convey information related to adult learning, including its social return on investment and economic impact, conveying data to communicate adult working learner and community needs, and to represent the interests of a variety of providers on various boards and governing committees.

References

Barbara Bush Foundation for Family Literacy. (2021). *National Action Plan for Adult Literacy 2021*. www.barbarabush.org/wp-content/uploads/2021/11/BBF-National-Action-Plan-for-Adult-Literacy-2021.pdf

Belzer, A. (2007). Implementing the Workforce Investment Act from in between: State agency responses to the federal accountability policy in adult basic education. *Educational Policy*, *21*(4), 555–558. https://doi.org/10.1177/0895904806289263

RAND. (2022). *Education policy*. www.rand.org/topics/education-policy.html

Chapter 20

Professional Development within the K-12 Setting

Christina Meecha

My Career in Professional Development

My career started in elementary education in 2003 as an intervention specialist. My role as an intervention specialist was as a teacher of students with disabilities. This position required me to engage with multiple grade levels, educating students with mild to moderate disabilities for success. This role is not just about teaching students but involves significant time working with the adults who are also part of the students' team. This team consists of assistants within the classrooms, special education aides, regular education teachers, administrators, outside consultants, school therapists, and parents. Staff who are hired through the district need specific training depending on their background, experience, and student needs (social/emotional, physical, and academic) in the building where they work. Along with creating a team that provides the students with what they need to be successful, it is also important to communicate with the families of the child and gain consistency for home-to-school collaboration. My first year was a whirlwind of constant collaboration to ensure students were getting everything they required for the best education possible. There were many challenges to work through. With so many stakeholders, I realized the importance of how I approached the adults with whom I worked. I knew that I needed more tools in my toolkit to manage working with so many team members.

After my first year of teaching as an intervention specialist, it was important to get started on a master's program that would be useful for my work within this role. When reflecting on everything within teaching, it became clear that only half of my job was educating young scholars with varying needs, and the other half was educating and training adults who were impacting students. Constant collaboration and training was necessary and it was important to do it effectively. To be effective, it needed to be done with an understanding of each adult's background. After doing my research, it was clear that a master's in adult learning and development would best serve me in my role as a professional development educator and expand my toolkit if I wanted to move into a different position outside of classroom education.

During my career, I have been part of various leadership teams within my school district. These committees where I served were not just building-wide but also district and statewide: Building Leadership Team representative for Intervention Specialists, Family Literacy Night Chair, Superintendent's Advisory Committee Representative, Building Advisory Committee, Diversity Committee, District Strategic Planning Committee Member, District Continuous Improvement Plan Committee, Summer Programming Principal, and Ohio Department of Education (ODE) Math Content Advisory Committee. All these committees were charged with decision making and how to best inform staff of goals and decisions made from these committees at all levels and positions to move our district forward.

DOI: 10.4324/9781003259602-23

As an educator, it was important to understand all levels of the K-12 grades even if that was not the level I was teaching at the time. I then needed to translate that knowledge and educate my peers about it.

> **Reading Organizational Culture**
>
> To take on roles where you are educating adults, you have to understand the bigger picture. In the *Jossey-Bass Reader on Educational Leadership* (Grogan, 2013), the author shares that "to be effective school leaders one must read and understand their school and community culture. Reading culture takes several forms: watching, sensing, listening, interpreting, using all of one's senses, and even employing intuition when necessary" (p. 198). For myself, it was learning about my district as a whole; not just my building that I work in, but all the schools. Then I worked on community committees to have a better understanding of both my school district and how other districts locally were working too. Lastly, I applied to be part of state committees through the ODE. All these specific experiences have helped me build the knowledge needed to assume training or coaching roles.

Within my district there are many leadership roles that allow me to use what I know about adult development and learning. I have been a mentor through the state of Ohio Resident Educator Program. This has been an extremely rewarding role because I assist first-year teachers as they work through their first 4 years of teaching. The state provides guidelines and trains mentors to assist their mentees. During this time of coaching, I have thought often of my adult education classes that discussed generational learning. Mentoring a millennial versus a Generation Xer means that your approaches will be different because of what typically drives that generation. Even though the generational approaches may be different it is important that you gain trust and treat the adults with respect. As Grogan (2013) states:

> Coaches assist people to move forward toward their goals through conversation and their way of being with people. They know when to push and when to back off based on the needs of the situation. They show genuine concern for both the task at hand and the welfare of those that have to accomplish that task. (p. 104)

Growing people professionally at the start of their first or new career is one way to utilize an adult education degree.

Another way that I was able to utilize the skills that I learned in my master's program was by chairing the Building Leadership team. Within this role, I led and collaborated with my peers, in my building, to problem-solve and create a positive culture. Some of the topics that emerged often dealt with new initiatives that came from the district's strategic improvement plan. Many of these initiatives dealt with rolling out training for teachers and staff. I was able to use my knowledge of program planning (see Chapter 4) to move the rollouts forward. One of the skill sets that I utilized was administering a needs assessment (see Chapter 5) for our aides in the building who were dealing with the most difficult students daily. Once we identified areas of need from them, we were able to create monthly classes that covered the crucial topics in a way that was comfortable and appropriate to enable learning. We also asked them about areas where they felt comfortable and if they would be willing to take part in teaching their peers. These trainings were a success and we saw the impact it made on the students and teachers, because people were more confident and competent in their roles in the building.

I have now moved into a promotion as a special education coordinator, which has brought many new responsibilities. There is a large number of people within the elementary system with many moving parts; therefore, constant communication with principals and staff is essential. This new role also means that questions come up about situations that may be new or more difficult than usual. Constant research is ongoing to be able to provide correct guidance to staff when situations occur. Since these questions often have a time-sensitive response, getting information in a timely manner is necessary. The biggest responsibility is balancing what is necessary to promote student safety and success while motivating and educating administration and staff to achieve this success.

Competencies

In my roles of training others through professional development in the K-12 education world, the philosophies and competencies I learned in my Master's of Adult Learning and Development Program have shaped how I approach every situation. The main competencies that have come to the forefront are the following:

- Connections: drawing out relevant experiences and knowledge to connect to theory
- Synthesizing: taking parts of the learning and creating a full picture for the learner
- Valuing: creating a relationship of respect and understanding what each person brings to situation
- Adapting: changing presentation styles for the adult learner depending on their needs so that they can be successful
- Collaborating: working alongside the learner and helping them to find the different resources they need

I consistently use these competencies to bring the best learning and outcomes for the adults with whom I collaborate. This helps decrease barriers and enhance learning for success.

When you are an educator in the K-12 arena, teaching students appears to be your biggest role. Most people seem to think that the only option to move into a job outside of the classroom teacher is to become an administrator. Many districts see the need for varied positions that are not necessarily administrative but are more coaching options. These districts are then allocating money within their budgets or using state grants/funding to create professional development opportunities for staff. Since many initiatives are state driven and vary depending on school districts within that state, it is important to look carefully for these types of positions through your local districts' websites and job posting sites. These opportunities are not just about the professional development (PD) days that are on the school calendar, but positions that are implemented to train and develop staff throughout the entire year. In the article "District- or school-based coaches? Research shows it makes a difference" Jacobson (2019) shares that:

> Diana Quintero of the Brown Center on Education Policy at the Brookings Institution believes that professional development programs like instructional coaching are more effective than the traditional PD workshop model because they are integrated in a teacher's day-to-day activities at the school and respond better to the active way teachers learn best. (para. 5)

Career Opportunities

In the following section I discuss the varied career opportunities for adult educators in this area. Within each career, I expand on the competencies, as well as talk about where they are situated within the K-12 setting.

Instructional Coaches

Many districts have implemented instructional coaches due to varied district needs.

> The role of an instructional coach can vary from place to place ... the definition is relatively similar across the board. Instructional coaches are educational leaders that train teachers and provide resources, feedback, modeling, and professional development to help schools meet instructional goals and school improvement goals.
>
> (Nelson-Danley, 2020)

These needs have opened more opportunities for educators to move into roles outside of the classroom without becoming administrators. The district areas' needs for improvement also provide opportunities for people who are specialists in areas such as data analysis, reading interventions, or other specialized areas.

Districts have shifted focus primarily to data and research-based strategies. Education now has more tools than ever to gather data for teachers to break down and utilize in their classrooms. These tools can be informative but require assistance and proper training on how to take that data and then understand the curriculum to best assist student needs. Wolpert-Gawron (2016) states that:

> Some teachers, instead of leaving, are finding new and professionally satisfying pathways within the education system, a move that's helping to redefine the teaching profession. As teachers put their extensive knowledge to use in these positions, they can become effective change agents for their schools and districts. (p. 56)

When I was interviewing educational leader and consultant Kathi Maxwell, she shared that:

> The instructional data can be used to show individual strengths and weaknesses to measure where students are at and where the next steps can be in their learning. This person has to have knowledge on state standards and how to take a student's data to identify where they are at in the learning continuum and then the next steps in the learning process.
>
> (Personal communication, April 18, 2022)

Within many districts the coaches meet with teachers as a team or individually. Teachers work with the coach to identify areas of need when looking at the data and teacher feedback. The coach then collaborates with the team or teacher on creating lessons that utilize research-based strategies the district has adopted as best practice. This may seem like a clear-cut process, but when you are dealing with varied personalities, new and veteran teachers, classrooms with an eclectic group of needs, and varied views on assessments and curriculum, it takes many adult learning and development competencies to be effective in this leadership role.

To be successful when performing the role as an instructional coach:

> district and school leaders need to put in place clear structures and expectations that allow them to have an impact on teacher practice. It is essential that this is made clear because "coaching" has become a dirty word because it has been used the wrong way — as an evaluative tool, as a way to "fix" teachers or with the idea that coaches are "resource gatherers".
>
> (Michelson, 2021)

When information is communicated correctly, it assists teachers in understanding that the coaches are collaborating with them to enhance student success, not to make them feel uncomfortable or professionally inadequate. Therefore, to be effective you need to understand the people on your team to best support them and in turn support student needs.

> Roles within coaching can vary depending on the needs of the organization:
>
> - Literacy/Reading Instructional Coach
> - Behavior Specialist
> - Family Liaison
> - Instructional Technology Coordinator
> - English as A Second Language Coordinator
> - Dyslexia Coordinator

Some districts have instructional coaches that focus solely on literacy within the district. These coaches, depending on the grade level, not only coach the teachers, but also help to implement reading strategies within the classroom. This same concept and model is used for math coaches as well.

Behavioral Specialist

Behavioral specialists are utilized to assist with the tougher behaviors that teachers deal with in the classroom. For example, we have seen an increase in students at the elementary level showing more signs of trauma from the COVID-19 pandemic. Students' increasing mental health issues are arising at a younger age and numerous school districts are implementing more supports to assist students and teachers. Most states mandate schools to create positive behavior instructional strategies; therefore, schools are creating positions to assist with mental health and other emotional support needs. These coaching positions are often created as a preventative measure. Working side by side with the teachers that you are coaching builds trust but also embeds modeling within the environment and gives the coach a better understanding of the needs of the students. There are many benefits for all stakeholders when coaching is done this way.

Family Liaisons

With more family involvement, districts are starting to create family liaison positions to bring the community and schools together. These liaison roles are dependent on the needs of communities and families within the district. For example, according to the Ohio Department of Education (2022a) for the Family and Community Partnership Liaison Program:

> School district staff, community partners, and other stakeholders can contact their Family and Community Partnership Liaison for resources and information regarding the following:
>
> - Connecting to high-quality family engagement supports;
> - Identifying opportunities to connect students and families with community partners and resources;
> - Locating direct service providers and community partners and agencies; and
> - Supporting local school district staff to serve highest need students and families.
>
> (Ohio Department of Education, 2022a, para. 6)

Instructional Technology Coordinator

The role of instructional technology coordinator is essential because there are various software programs utilized within a school district. Educational consultant Kathi Maxwell (personal communication, April 18, 2022) states that: "All districts by law have to use an Information Technology Center in which their data flows from various systems into the ODE student information system software. Other types of software are used for recruiting, attendance, time sheets, and onboarding for hiring." This shows that technology assistance is not just for the classroom teacher but also to run the business side of school districts. This is one side of IT, but these coordinators can also be utilized in the classroom.

In *A Day in the Life of an Instructional Technology Coach*, Engler (2021) shares that their role is ever-changing, and they have tried to schedule their day to meet these needs. Since an educator's time is precious, Engler shares their strategy for good adult learning:

> Every conversation I have is based on these three questions:
>
> - How are you?
> - What can I do for you?
> - What do you need?
>
> It's a great way to make connections and build relationships, and it often leads to meaningful discussions, planning activities together, scheduling meetings, or coaching opportunities.
>
> (Engler, 2021, para 3).

Engler shows that the competencies of valuing and collaborating about learners' needs are essential.

English as a Second Language Coordinator

Many children live in homes that speak more than one language. Those learning English are referred to as English Language Learners (ELL) (or alternatively as students with English as a second language, bilingual, or multilingual learners). The U.S. Department of Education states:

> English learners (ELs) are a growing part of the K–12 student population. Between the 2009–10 and 2014–15 school years, the percentage of ELL students increased in more than half of the states, with increases of over 40 percent in five states. Under the *Every Student Succeeds Act*, states must annually assess the English language proficiency of ELs, provide reasonable accommodations for them on state assessments, and develop new accountability systems that include long-term goals and measures of progress for EL.
>
> (U.S. Department of Education, 2017, para. 1)

Kathi Maxwell (personal communication, April 18, 2022) states that this is a "complex program to oversee. It is a self-reported, home language survey and not always accurate from families. They are often transient so there is a larger learning gap." Being able to understand the needs of ELL students depending on their home language is very important. A district's number of languages can vary. One local district has 14 different languages spoken by various students at home. The coordinator must assist the ELL teachers with finding time to give support and how to identify areas a student needs to work on to begin reading. Their primary focus is on vocabulary acquisition. Many school districts are writing grants for TESOL: Teachers of English to Speakers of Other Languages endorsements, so that more educators and coordinators can be prepared for these students in the classroom.

Dyslexia Coordinator

Certain states have legislation for reading and dyslexia specialists. As an example, a new Ohio law will require school systems to have specialists in screening for dyslexia. They will work with teachers to screen and provide guidance on interventions for dyslexia. The Ohio Department of Education (2022b) website states the following was required for school districts by January 2023:

- Establish a multidisciplinary team to administer screening and intervention measures and analyze the results of the measures. The team shall include trained and certified personnel and a stakeholder with expertise in the identification, intervention, and remediation of dyslexia.
- Starting in the 2023–2024 year, each local, city and exempted village school district, community school, and STEM school must establish a multi-sensory structured literacy certification process for teachers providing instruction to students in grades K-3.

(para. 1)

Gifted Coordinator

With gifted criteria changing often in education, many districts are hiring coordinators in this area. Gifted services must be provided to students depending on state indicators used. Since indicators for services determined by the state adjust and change year to year, it creates varied needs for administration, gifted specialists, and regular education teachers providing services. "Administrator license and/or state-required professional development that helps to meet the need of gifted students may be needed" (Kathi Maxwell, personal communication, April 18, 2022). A gifted coordinator often has to understand the revised codes within state guidelines for gifted services, train the teachers that offer services to these students, and maintain curriculum that is identified to provide deeper understanding of state standards (Ohio Department of Education, 2021, September).

Diversity and Social Emotional Needs Coach

Student diversity within districts has expanded over time. Districts are recognizing that student needs are ever-changing, and it is important for educators to remain current on these needs. As a result, districts are hiring diversity and social emotional needs coaches.

> District-wide diversity, equity and inclusion training has gained significant popularity in recent years as policymakers and administrators became more convinced by research that academic disparities between white students and students of color were partly caused by some educators' false beliefs of the intelligence levels and behaviors of students of color. Districts could start to systemically address those disparities once educators start to recognize racist or biased ideas and build systems to protect students from them.
>
> (Najarro, 2022, para. 4)

These roles vary depending on the district's needs, legislation passed in education, and societal needs within districts. Educators that fulfill these roles require varied skill sets dealing with people, legislation, and needs that arise. Districts look for people who have certain educational degrees or certifications specifically related to behavior, counseling, and social emotional licenses. Degrees or certificates in adult education are a plus in this arena.

Professional Organizations

It is important to stay abreast of the ever-changing world of education. As a professional, it is advantageous to become involved in professional organizations. Therefore, within a role that you are pursuing, it is necessary to find local, state, and national groups, publications germane to the field, and other professional opportunities. Below are some examples of state and national professional organizations:

Professional Organizations (Ohio Examples)

- Ohio Association of Elementary School Administrators
- Ohio Middle Level Association
- Buckeye Association of School Administrators
- Ohio Department of Education or any other state education department

Professional Organizations (National):

- ASCD: Association for Supervision and Curriculum Development (www.ascd.org)
- Council for Exceptional Children (https://exceptionalchildren.org)
- National Education Association (www.nea.org)
- TESOL International Association (www.tesol.org)
- American School Counselor Association (www.schoolcounselor.org)

Job and Career Boards

- EdWeek (www.topschooljobs.org/jobs/instructional-coach-pd)
- SchoolSpring (www.schoolspring.com)
- K-12 JobSpot (www.k12jobspot.com)

Future of Adult Education in K-12 Professional Development

The needs within K-12 education are constantly changing as new laws are put into place and more research is being established on best practices. Districts are creative in the ways that they respond to these changes and making sure that their staff continue to increase their knowledge in these areas. When districts are planning for professional development, it is important that it is not done to just check off a box, but to provide the meaningful development experiences that staff desire. Educators and staff are teaching much more than state standards; therefore, when planning it is essential that time is used wisely and content delivery is creative.

Schools are seeing many new needs arising due to the pandemic and other factors. Educators are tasked with filling gaps for students now that they are back into a more "normal" school day. Educators are also tasked with the social emotional fallout that happened for numerous students during the time of virtual learning. Educators are working to give students and parents experiences that build community within their districts. Because educators are being asked to do all of this, it is important that they are given the correct tools. When looking at the best professional development for districts, the challenge is not only presenting them with tools that are effective for students but also recognizing the human side of educators who have worked hard to maintain a calm normal in a time that was anything but normal. Many teachers have exited the profession; therefore, recognizing that self-care for staff is part of your developmental agenda is also essential. In the role of adult learning and development, it is important to keep these factors in mind.

> **Keys to Success**
>
> To be successful in one of these roles, learn to listen and observe the needs presenting themselves. It is important to provide information in a creative way that adult learners can understand. Do not forget that needing to learn something new as an adult can make people anxious, defensive, and worried. Be prepared to handle varied emotions in a professional, kind, and respectful manner. Remember that it is ok to not have every answer but to kindly let people know you will try to find out for them. Lastly, make yourself approachable so that people can come to ask for help.

Learning for adults is constant in the world of K-12 education. When you can have a role in which impacting adult learning will in turn influence the way students are educated, the rewards are many. If you are ready for a challenge and a new way of educating within the K-12 educational world, know that there are many opportunities for growth in this field.

References

Engler, T. (2021, April 27). *A day in the life of an instructional technology coach.* https://blog.teachboost.com/a-day-in-the-life-of-an-instructional-technology-coach

Jacobson, L. (2019, October 23). *District- or school-based coaches? Research shows it makes a difference.* www.k12dive.com/news/district-or-school-based-coaches-research-shows-it-makes-a-difference/564916/

Grogan, M. (Ed.). (2013). *The Jossey-Bass reader on educational leadership* (3rd ed.). John Wiley & Sons.

Michelson, J. (2021, October 27). *5 tips for setting up and sustaining coaching in your district.* https://k-12leadership.org/5-tips-for-setting-up-and-sustaining-coaching-in-your-district/

Najarro, L. (2022, March 24) K-12 diversity, equity, and inclusion trainings: Are they divisive or effective? *Education Week.* www.edweek.org/leadership/k-12-diversity-equity-and-inclusion-trainings-are-they-divisive-or-effective/2022/03

Nelson-Danley, K. (2020, February 5). *Educating implementing instructional leadership PD through coaching.* Educators Blog. www.graduateprogram.org/2020/02/implementing-instructional-leadership-pd-through-coaching/

Ohio Department of Education. (2021, September 14). *Rules, regulations and policies for gifted education.* https://education.ohio.gov/Topics/Other-Resources/Gifted-Education/Rules-Regulations-and-Policies-for-Gifted-Education

Ohio Department of Education. (2022a, January 14). *Family and community partnership liaison program.* https://education.ohio.gov/Topics/Student-Supports/Family-and-Community-Engagement/Family-and-Community-Partnership-Liaison-Program

Ohio Department of Education. (2022b, April 21). *Dyslexia supports.* https://education.ohio.gov/Topics/Learning-in-Ohio/Literacy/Dyslexia

U.S. Department of Education. (2017). Data story. Introduction. *Our nation's English learners.* Retrieved August 23, 2023. www2.ed.gov/datastory/el-characteristics/index.html

Wolpert-Gawron, H. (2016). The many roles of an instructional coach. *Educational Leadership, 73*(9), 56–60.

Chapter 21

Professional Organizations

Shawna L. Strickland

Professional Organizations

When I was recruited by a national nonprofit association for an executive-level education position, I was a faculty member and program director at a large Midwestern university. I had earned my doctoral degree a couple of years prior in education leadership and policy study and, before that, my master's degree in adult and higher education. Though I loved academia, and working with students was a fulfilling experience, the prospect of developing education that could impact the careers of over 150,000 professionals around the world was tempting. However, I was still concerned about how that environment would be different from the academic setting in which I had worked for a little over a decade. I was confident in my skills within academia; how was I going to meaningfully contribute to this organization and the membership? Were my skills going to translate well to the educational needs of the membership served by that organization?

Thankfully, this organization was not new to me. I had been a member since I earned my first undergraduate professional degree and had volunteered in a variety of capacities for years. I knew the mission and vision of the organization, I knew the staff, I knew the volunteers, and I knew the audience. Within about a month of starting the new position, it was clear that the skills I had gained during my graduate education were vital to my success in this role. Again, the position was focused on education, so that created a logical alignment. There were other aspects of the role, though, that were not as obvious to me in the beginning. In some respects, I was surprised at how well the skills I gained through that journey in adult education prepared me for the job and meeting the needs of the membership as well as my colleagues within the organization. This chapter will explore careers in professional organizations.

Overview of Professional Organizations

Professional organizations, also called professional associations or professional societies, serve a specific job field or industry, the individuals engaged in that field or industry, or the public interest in that field or industry. These organizations vary in size and scope, with some organizations relying completely on volunteer efforts and others with thousands of employees and multi-billion-dollar budgets. The way the professional organizations serve their constituents also vary, including membership, certifications, regulations, and advocacy.

Most professional organizations are nonprofit. This does not mean the organization is not interested in generating revenue or profits; rather, the nonprofit organization is not permitted to distribute those generated profits to its directors and officers (Renz & Associates, 2016). For more information on nonprofit organizations, see Chapter 17. Professional organizations are frequently categorized by their IRS tax status, of which 501(c)(3) and 501(c)(6) are the most common.

DOI: 10.4324/9781003259602-24

Professional organizations, regardless of tax status, engage in education at some level. That education may be targeted at the public, the membership, or other stakeholders. Regardless, there are many positions within the professional organization that would benefit from a candidate with a background in adult education.

Key Roles of Association Professionals

Within the professional organization structure, there are many different roles that would benefit from a candidate with a background in adult education. The education positions are the most logical positions that align with a background in adult education, as these positions focus on learning styles, continuing education, education technology, professional development, education accreditation practices, and certifications. Depending on the size of the organization, there may be one or two positions that are responsible for the entirety of the organization's educational efforts or there may be several smaller divisions within the education department with focused educational goals. Other positions range from executive leadership to coordinators of membership or other volunteer-facing positions. Detailing the nuances of these positions in context with the organization can be a helpful step in identifying a fit for persons with a background in adult education.

Learning Leaders

While each professional organization is structured uniquely, all will have a leadership position for education. This may be at the manager or director level, or it may be at the executive level. The level of this position will be dependent upon the positioning of education within the organization and the extent to which the educational activities contribute to the strategic plan.

If the leadership position responsible for the organization's education is at the executive level, it may be titled Vice President, Associate Executive Director, or Chief Learning Officer. At this level, they would direct the strategic and operational aspects of education: management of the learning management system (LMS), integration of the LMS within the association management system (AMS), educational content library, certification and/or credentialing programs, and assessment of professional needs. They would also contribute to the strategic direction of the organization as a whole, collaborating with other department leaders to meet the mission and vision.

The organization may employ an education director in addition to or in the place of an executive-level leader. This position manages the development and administration of content for the target audiences. If the organization offers professional training or certificate programs or specialized workshops or courses, this position may be responsible for coordinating, implementing, managing, and evaluating those programs. This director may also contribute to the strategic direction but is more department-level focused.

The education manager is responsible for administering programs that have been developed and implemented by the organization. They may have a role in designing the programs with subject matter experts, registering participants, and/or coordinating the accreditation of the content by various continuing education accreditation agencies. This role is likely to interact closely with volunteers and members of the organization.

In all of these positions, skills in developing behavioral objectives (see Chapter 2), developing educational content and curricula, creating in-person or e-Learning content, developing evaluation measures, and analyzing evaluation data are important. The more senior the position, the more skill is required in needs assessment for products and audiences, evaluation of learning outcomes (see Chapter 5), alignment of educational products, and evaluation of technology as well as leadership development, conflict resolution, team building, strategic planning, and environmental scanning.

Certification Leaders

Some professional organizations provide certifications and/or credentials. These activities provide an avenue for learners to demonstrate mastery of content or competencies needed in the profession. The activities can range from a certificate verifying completion of an educational course to successfully earning a credential based on industry-accepted standards. In these organizations, the staff responsible for these activities can range from a director or manager level to a specialist level. The more senior position is responsible for developing and administering the administrative aspects of the programs while the specialist level is responsible for the technical activities, such as product research and testing, coordinating the development of product standards, certification of products, field testing, technical manuals, and other technical aspects (ASAE Research Foundation, 2020). Competencies necessary for these positions include standards development, needs assessments, objective development, test creation, and continual evaluation of the industry and changing landscape.

Executives

The most senior position employed within the professional organization is the chief staff executive, usually titled Executive Director or Chief Executive Officer. This position is responsible for the strategic operation of the organization and management of all staff employed by the organization. They envision change and innovation and work closely with the board to develop the strategic plan and direction to achieve the mission and vision of the organization (ASAE Research Foundation, 2020; Renz & Associates, 2016).

In many organizations, an executive staff is established to strategically lead key business units, such as education, marketing, and information technology. The number of these positions and the scope of the role depend on the size and nature of the organization. The teams established for each executive staff role, sometimes titled Vice President, or Associate Executive Director, are typically aligned based on similarity in business units and experience of the executive staff. Skills necessary to function effectively in both of these roles include the ability to assess the environment – both internal and external – to identify drivers that will impact the function and contribution of the professional association, plan for the future amid risks and threats, strategically implement programs and products, and evaluate the impact of the organization as a whole and its products and programs effectively.

Practice and Theory

Many professional organizations provide professional development and training programs. In addition, about one-third provide accreditation or certification programs. On average, these programs account for a significant portion of the organization's revenue, after membership dues, meetings, and events (ASAE Research Foundation, 2018). This presents a significant opportunity for this major revenue-generating department to reap the benefits of the knowledge and skills of a professional with a background in adult education.

Understanding the adult learner and how they are motivated to pursue education and professional development is a vital competency in associations. Whether the goal is developing engaging, relevant, and accurate continuing education; planning and executing an in-person, virtual, or hybrid conference; or constructing a volunteer leadership development strategy, the association professional must be able to assess and diagnose the learner's needs and desired outcomes.

Professional Development versus Continuing Education

The terms *professional development* and *continuing education* are frequently used interchangeably. However, professional development focuses on enhancing one's current skill set for future growth. This may include pursuing a higher academic degree, earning credentials within the field, or engaging in specialty workshops to develop new skills. Continuing education is concentrated on maintaining current knowledge and industry practice, typically after the individual has earned a degree or credential in that field. Continuing education may take the form of a webinar or professional conference. Both of these activities are important within the field, and both may be supported by the professional organization.

Understanding Adult Learners

The very nature of professional organizations – serving a specific job field or industry, the individuals engaged in that field or industry, or the public interest in that field or industry – means that the organization's audience is composed of adult learners. Professional organizations, therefore, must understand the needs of adult learners and how they seek, consume, and apply educational activities in their professional lives. The learners will represent a wide variety of professionals in the field, meaning that their learning needs will differ based on several factors, including their career stage, experience level, and specialization in the field. Learners' needs will change over time as they progress through career stages, make changes to their career direction, and develop new skills and competencies based on the latest technology and science.

> **Adult Learners:** During the COVID-19 pandemic, healthcare providers (HCPs) were stressed by a variety of factors: lack of personal protective equipment, dwindling patient care supplies, surge of critically ill patients, lack of space, uncertain futures, and exposure to a highly contagious illness, to name a few. Though the organizations supporting HCPs had vast libraries of continuing education courses, those HCPs had little time to dedicate to learning. Many professional organizations dedicated a significant amount of resources to develop content that provided the most up-to-date, pandemic-specific, profession-specific virtual education to meet this new need level of the learners. One example was a short, just-in-time YouTube video demonstrating how to safely put on and remove personal protective equipment in airborne infection isolation in hospitals. To date, that video has been viewed over 15,000 times.

Andragogy. Within Knowles' theory of andragogy, the learner's life experiences are central to the learning process (Knowles, 1970; Knowles, 1975; Knowles et al. 2020). Andragogy was constructed on two concepts: learning theory and design theory (Henschke & Cooper, 2007). The design theory of Knowles' andragogy is based on processes of learning. It provides an opportunity for the educator to become a facilitator and assist the learner in acquiring the new knowledge or skill (Knowles, 1975; Knowles et al., 2020). These elements encourage the learner to take more responsibility and be more self-directed in their learning endeavors, facilitating professional development.

Self-Directedness. Self-direction in learning has two purposes: a method of learning and a goal of learning. The focus within a professional organization is on self-directedness as a goal of learning for the members and other stakeholders. Continuing education is a requirement in many professions. For example, with regards to medicine, the Institute of Medicine, now the National Academy of Medicine, stated that continuing education enables healthcare professionals to keep their knowledge and skills up to date, with the ultimate goal of improving performance and patient outcomes (Greiner & Knebel, 2003). Fostering self-directedness within the professional members of the association can improve their willingness to engage with the educational activities offered.

The level of self-directedness will vary from learner to learner. Past life and education experience influence the learner's willingness and ability to be self-directed. The subject matter can also impact readiness to learn; just because a learner is self-directed in one situation does not mean they will be self-directed in all situations. The educator developing content for the professional organization's stakeholders must understand the educational context and need for the activity.

Learning Expectations

The alignment of course objectives and outcomes are a vital component of developing educational content within a professional organization. Not only is this good education practice but accreditation agencies like the Accreditation Council for Continuing Medical Education (ACCME) require that all accredited courses clearly state the educational needs and competencies addressed within the educational activity and clearly communicate what the learner can expect to gain from participation. The educational professional within the organization should consider the audience, purpose, desired outcomes, and professional need to not only develop individual learning activities but also consider developing curricula and learning pathways that scaffold to enhance the professional development of the learner.

Competencies, Credentials, and Career Pathways

Careers in professional organizations that align with a background in adult education can be found for all career stages. For all career-level opportunities, effective communication skills, ability to function successfully within a team, conflict resolution, and relationship building are important attributes.

Entry-Level Skills and Competencies

Overall, there are certain skills needed for any association professional. However, the degree of skill tends to increase with the hierarchical level of the position.

Analytical and Critical Thinking. Analytical and critical thinking are skills that improve with practice, though a certain skill level is necessary upon entry into the field. Analytical thinking requires logical reasoning and problem-solving skills. It is the ability to identify and define problems and then extract pertinent information that can be used to arrive at a logical solution. Critical thinking also involves logical reasoning and problem-solving skills but also requires the ability to question assumptions associated with that problem (Brookfield, 1997). It is an objective analysis and evaluation of an issue in order to form a judgment, not only analyzing the issue but considering the way the issue is perceived. Overcoming implicit and explicit biases and being able to bracket oneself to explore the core issue presented is important to finding feasible solutions.

> **Critical Thinking:** My team was facing a significant data integration problem between the learning management system (LMS) and association management system (AMS). The information was not passing through as originally designed and the result was negatively impacting members who had purchased educational courses. During a meeting with the education team, the customer

> service team, and the information technology team, we completed a root cause analysis and identified the source of the issue. However, we were unable to reach a resolution. The conversation became strained, as each department had technical limitations on parameters around the data. At one point, the customer service manager asked, "Why must the information be formatted in this way?" The answer: because we've always done it that way. By verbalizing this statement and acknowledging that the barrier wasn't technical, we changed the way the team was considering the problem and potential solution. Once we removed our biases, we were able to formulate a solution that not only solved the problem but also streamlined the process.

Emotional Intelligence. Emotional intelligence was defined by Salovey and Mayer in 1990 as the ability of an individual to process emotions to guide thinking and behavior. Over the years, this concept has expanded to include many different traits and concepts. The 1997 Four-Branch Model of Emotional Intelligence provides a framework for both fundamental and higher order skill sets included in the spectrum of emotional abilities. The four branches consist of (a) managing emotions to attain specific goals; (b) understanding emotions, emotional language, and the signals conveyed by emotions; (c) using emotions to facilitate thinking; and (d) perceiving emotions accurately in oneself and others (Mayer & Salovey, 1997). As with many employment venues, persons employed by professional organizations are required to collaborate and interface with a variety of stakeholders, including internal colleagues, volunteers, partner organizations, elected officials, and funding partners. The ability to use, understand, and manage emotions is a valued skill, as is the ability to understand and manage these interpersonal relationships.

Digital Literacy. Digital literacy is defined as the ability to understand and use information from a variety of digital sources (Gilster, 1997). Within professional organizations, digital literacy includes the skills necessary to use the tools that manage members' data, content development and delivery, reporting metrics, marketing and communication strategies, and communication. For persons engaged in the educational endeavors of the professional organization, tools include not only commonly used suites of programs such as Microsoft 365 (including Word®, PowerPoint®, Excel®, Teams®, etc.) but also those platforms provided by third-party vendors: the LMS, AMS, virtual event platforms, and team-based project management tools. It is impossible for a candidate to be proficient in all types of these third-party platforms; however, an aptitude to learn new technology quickly and efficiently is an important skill.

Typically Requested Degrees and Credentials

Most leadership positions at the executive level within an association will require at least a master's degree. In the education division, preference may be given to applicants with a degree focused on education. Positions such as manager or coordinator may require a bachelor's degree. Most learning positions will require an understanding of that profession's credentialing requirements. If the candidate also has a background in the field served by the organization, those professional credentials may be required or preferred as well. Specialty credentials and certificates related to education are beneficial, as are credentials and certifications specific to association management. Typically, though, the credentials and certifications specific to association management are earned after employment and experience in the field.

The Certified Association Executive (CAE) credential reflects the breadth of knowledge gained by the association professional. Administered by the American Society for Association Executives (ASAE), this credential requires at least five years of experience as an association staff member (or one year as either the chief staff executive or other executive-level position), a bachelor's degree or higher, and at least 100 qualifying continuing education hours related to association management. The earned CAE credential must be renewed with continuing education hours every 3 years. If the goal is to become an executive-level employee of a professional organization, studying for and successfully earning the CAE credential can be a powerful tool. The content is diverse – including finances, human resource management, meeting planning, education planning, globalization of associations, and advocacy, to name a few. Earning the credential demonstrates a dedication to leadership within the association sector.

> **Credentials:** It was through my position as a respiratory therapy educator that I was recruited for the Associate Executive Director – Education position with the American Association for Respiratory Care. The profession-specific credentials that I had already earned were required in that position, as industry-specific knowledge was important to the organization for that position. The desired candidate needed knowledge of credentialing and continuing education requirements of the profession as well as subject matter expertise. In contrast, when I was recruited for the Associate Executive Director – Programs role at the American Epilepsy Society, the Certified Association Executive (CAE) credential was more attractive. This position, in addition to education, focuses also on clinical activities, research, and grant management. Specific knowledge in the field, in this case, epilepsy and its consequences, was not necessary to be successful.

Role-specific certificates and certifications are earned by association professionals as well. Again, these are typically earned after experience in that role has been established. Many of these certifications, like the relatively new Digital Events Specialist certification, are focused on very specific processes and outcomes.

A variety of microcredentials are earned by association professionals, though they are typically very focused on department-level skills. These short, competency-based credentials may represent skills in managing virtual events or compliance processes with specific accreditation agencies. More recent microcredentials include incorporating diversity, inclusion, and equity practices in associations, not only with staff-to-staff engagement but also with volunteer engagement and with business practices.

Adult Education Competitive Advantage

Diagnosing education and learning needs of the audience, writing behavioral objectives, constructing summative and formative evaluations, collaborating with subject matter experts, planning meeting logistics, delivering content, analyzing the evaluation results, and debriefing for future planning needs are all activities that reflect the professional role in associations. The critical thinking and evaluation skills needed by an association professional are developed during the adult education academic journey and are applied through assessing new technologies, such as the AMS and LMS, and through the evaluation of funding proposals and grant applications.

Professional Associations

Ask an association professional about the nature of professional organizations and they will likely respond that there is an association for everything – there are even associations for people who work for associations! The national American professional association for employees of associations and professional organizations is the ASAE. This organization provides career development, education, advocacy, networking, and resources for association professionals of all levels. Some US states and regions are home to smaller association professional societies that serve their state and regional professionals.

Salaries and Benefits

Many association professionals join professional organizations after employment in other industries, like healthcare and higher education. As such, salary expectations may not be accurately aligned. It is important that the applicant is as informed as possible about the salary expectations commensurate with the professional organization role so that they do not undervalue their potential contribution to the organization.

Salary ranges are dependent on the role and the size of the organization. The ASAE conducts and publishes a compensation and benefits study every two years that can be valuable when looking at a prospective job or during salary negotiations. Association organizations serving local areas, like Association Forum, which serves association professionals in Chicago, and state organizations also publish this information specific to their geographic service area.

Salary information can also be found by searching the job database provided by the US Bureau of Labor Statistics (www.bls.gov). Other sources may provide more robust information about annual salary, incentives, and job descriptions, though the information is obtained via paid subscription to the company's services. One example is the Economic Research Institute (www.erieri.com/salarysurveys/survey/nonprofits).

Another avenue to predict a realistic salary range is to review publicly available information about the professional organization. Organizations' filed 990 forms are publicly available on websites such as GuideStar (www.guidestar.org) and websites of the Secretary of State or Attorney General in the state where the organization is incorporated. While not every position within the organization may be included on the form submission, more senior positions, like Chief Learning Officer or Education Director, are likely to be included. These can provide a reference point for compensation expectations within the organization.

Education and Credentialing

Large professional organizations may include an executive-level education position. The most recent ASAE benchmarking data, published in 2020, reported a median base salary of $140,000 for this position, generically titled the Chief Education/Content Officer. In a smaller organization, the highest-ranking education position may be the Education/Content Director or the Certification Director. The median base salaries for these positions were reported as $98,336 and $100,712, respectively. Various other positions within the organization focused on education include education assistants, education coordinators, and education managers and the median base salary for these positions range between $49,706 and $67,030 (ASAE Research Foundation, 2020).

Executive Office

As previously identified, the top-paid position within the professional organization is the Chief Staff Executive. Based on the same ASAE 2020 benchmarking data, the median base salary for this position is $211,097. However, it is important to understand that this position is likely to have a compensation package that is more robust than other paid positions. Traditional benefits – health insurance, life and/or disability insurance, retirement, etc. – may be similar to other staff but the amount of annual bonuses and supplemental benefits may be significantly higher. Other executive positions range in base salary between $160,000 and $190,000, depending on the scope of the job descriptions (ASAE Research Foundation, 2020).

Job Listings

A commonly used source for finding employment in the association industry is the ASAE's job board, currently hosted on a third-party platform called CareerHQ. (https://careerhq.asaecenter.org/jobs). Within the platform, the candidate can browse posted positions by geographic location, industry, job category, education requirement, and career level. The advertisements typically include the required skills, competencies, and education background as well as a brief position description, information about the organization, and application instructions. Other search platforms include companies that are not industry specific, such as Indeed.com and Monster.com, and on social professional networks, like LinkedIn.

Some organizations continue to only advertise on the organization's website or within the profession that organization serves. Some organizations may use executive search services to recruit for higher-level positions, such as the Chief Staff Executive. Executive search companies work with the leadership of the professional organization to identify the preferred qualifications for the job and seek out candidates who meet those requirements.

The Future of Adult Education in Professional Organizations

A mainstay of professional organizations is the continuing and professional education provided to the membership. However, the changing environment and the way members view professional organizations impact how the organization can meet the members' needs. On-demand continuing education content is available from a wide variety of sources and the professional organization must position itself for success in a competitive environment. How members consume educational activities has changed dramatically since 2020; in-person professional conferences had to cease during the COVID-19 public health crisis and many organizations transitioned to virtual education platforms as a substitute. Providing around-the-clock access to on-demand content is very convenient and, having avoided in-person conferences for almost two years during the pandemic, may influence the way learners select educational activities in the future.

Automation and data analytics play a large part in the success of the association and this role will grow rapidly in the future. A 2018 study noted that 68% of professional organization members are interested in personalized content (Jordan et al., 2018). Automatically analyzing user data – for example, when learners access learning activities, the types of activities accessed, the relationship between self-identified data and the type of learning activity accessed – can provide an opportunity to develop individualized learning pathways.

Microcredentialing, discussed earlier in this chapter, is predicted to continue to grow. As the cost of higher education continues to rise, the opportunity to earn skill-specific digital badges and microcredentials becomes increasingly attractive. For a small price, if not free, the learner can gain skill in a targeted area, demonstrate competency for job promotion or career development, and promote their achievement. Organizations offer digital badges through a third-party vendor, like Credly or Accredible, for educational courses that can then be posted to social media sites like LinkedIn and Twitter for recognition. This, in turn, promotes the organization's educational offerings and may increase usage.

Keeping diversity, equity, and inclusion factors at the forefront is a vital component for success of the professional organization. Several aspects of diversity to consider, in addition to race and culture, include age, gender, sexual orientation, physical ability spectrum, and neurodiversity. Important for the development of educational products for the professional association is ensuring that content is accessible by all. Accommodations include ensuring content can be read by a screen reader for persons with low vision or blindness; transcripts or captions for persons with hearing impairment or deafness; and file types that can be accessed by persons with motor-skill impairment or immobility.

Conclusion

I have now been employed in the nonprofit association sector for about a decade. My experiences during that time have included two different association employers, association volunteer opportunities, and my own educational development to become an effective association professional. I have benefited from mentoring within the field, which led to preparing for and successfully challenging the CAE examination. My role, which started out with a singular focus on developing continuing education, has expanded over the years to include leading departments such as information technology, customer service, clinical activities, and research. The knowledge and skills I gained through my academic journey in adult education continue to benefit my performance in each of these roles.

References

ASAE Research Foundation. (2018). *Benchmarking in association management: Policies and procedures, volume 1.* American Society of Association Executives.

ASAE Research Foundation. (2020). *Association compensation & benefits study, 2020–2021 edition.* American Society of Association Executives.

Brookfield, S. D. (1997). Assessing critical thinking. *New Directions for Adult and Continuing Education, 75*, 17–29.

Gilster, P. (1997). *Digital literacy.* Wiley.

Greiner, A. C., & Knebel, E. (Eds.) (2003). *Health professions education: Bridge to quality.* Institute of Medicine (US) Committee on the Health Professions Education Summit. National Academies Press.

Henschke, J. A., & Cooper, M. K. (2007). *Additions toward a thorough understanding of the international foundations of andragogy in HRD & adult education* [Paper presentation]. Commission on International Adult Education Pre-Conference, American Association for Adult and Continuing Education Conference, Milwaukee, WI.

Jordan, T., Pawlak, T., Switzer, T., & VanDamme, S. (2018). *Digital evolution study: Insights on the past, present, and future of member expectations and association technology.* Community Brands.

Knowles, M. S. (1970). *The modern practice of adult education.* Association Press.

Knowles, M. S. (1975). *Self-directed learning: A guide for learners and teachers.* Association Press.

Knowles, M. S., Holton, E. F., Swanson, R. A., & Robinson, P. A. (2020). *The adult learner: The definitive classic in adult education and human resource development* (9th ed.). Routledge.

Mayer, J. D., & Salovey, P. (1997). What is emotional intelligence? In P. Salovey & D. Sluyter (Eds.), *Emotional development and emotional intelligence: Educational implications* (pp. 3–31). Basic Books.

Renz, D. O., & Associates. (2016). *The Jossey-Bass handbook of nonprofit leadership and management* (4th ed.). Jossey-Bass.

Salovey, P., & Mayer, J. D. (1990). Emotional intelligence. *Imagination, cognition and personality, 9*(3), 185–211.

Chapter 22

Religious Education

Trammell L. Bristol

Early in my career, I knew that my forte was teaching. As a public-school teacher, I relied heavily upon the traditional models of formal education. My role was that of the expert because the students started the school year as blank canvases. I transferred knowledge to them, and they rarely challenged me or the curriculum that I delivered. However, when I began to work with adult learners, I found that we brought our experiences to the classroom, and we learned from one another. I was intrigued with the collaboration that took place in the classroom and ultimately realized that I was better suited to work with adults. Therefore, I entered the doctoral adult education (AE) program at the Pennsylvania State University. This AE program encompassed learners from various vocations who desired to further their careers. The program strengthened my understanding of AE and provided me with the knowledge and skills that became the foundation for my practice as an adult educator.

In the program, I was fortunate to collaborate with professors who exposed me to different aspects of AE. My advisor was a proponent of social justice and spirituality, and I loved being a part of her classes. The graduate program also provided insights into how I could best collaborate with adult learners and focus on the factors that impact learning environments, such as the teaching methods and learning philosophies (Knowles et al., 2020; Merriam & Brockett, 2007). My ultimate career goal was to work in training and development with motivated adult learners to enhance their knowledge about the workplace.

However, along the way I found that my knowledge and skills could benefit my church. When I graduated, my pastor requested that I develop an educational program and serve as the Director of Christian Education (DCE). I stepped into this role because I view the church as a place that promotes growth and development in people, so that they can live more fulfilled lives. My pastor knew that I had the organizational skills to develop and maintain an educational program. My communication skills were key to allowing me to collaborate with the educators and learners who would be a part of the program. In addition, the graduate AE program provided the understanding I needed to execute program planning (see Chapter 4) so that I could develop meaningful learning opportunities for our church and community. Our vision was to go beyond the typical Sunday school or Bible study class. We did this by providing learning experiences that focused on daily life issues.

The Black church has been a trusted institution in the community (Brand, 2019; Hodges et al., 2016) and has encouraged the attainment of education (Brand, 2019). Growing up I can remember the importance of the church, especially within the social justice movement that Dr. Martin L. King, Jr. championed (Dorrien, 2023). Black churches have promoted the growth of their communities by facilitating learning opportunities like understanding voting and civil rights (Dorrien, 2023).

Therefore, I saw my working in the church as an opportunity to continue in the traditions of the Black church. To begin this endeavor, I asked learners about the types of learning

DOI: 10.4324/9781003259602-25

opportunities they would enjoy. We held focus groups and administered surveys with prospective learners to assess their needs. As a result of the feedback, we initially provided learning opportunities that enhanced the knowledge and skills of those who were or who desired to become clergy. For example, one program focused on preparing deacons or deaconesses to serve in the church and community, while another class worked with aspiring ministers to prepare them to serve.

As the DCE, I also developed learning opportunities to prepare adult learners to not only work in the church and community, but to also strengthen their understanding of Christianity. We provided instruction on a variety of topics, which included health, nutrition, finances, and growing in the faith. We also collaborated with the local community college and professionals to explore higher education and career paths. The success of the educational program was the result of the knowledge that I gained in the graduate degree program in AE. The program prepared me to create learning opportunities for diverse audiences and settings. During the COVID-19 pandemic, as the DCE, technology became a tool that I had to utilize to connect with adult learners. In fact, many houses of worship used technology during this time (Dias, 2021; Fadel, 2020; Gjelten, 2020). The role that technology has played in religious education (RE) will be discussed later in the chapter.

Community Organizations

AE occurs in various contexts and one setting that has been important to RE has been community organizations (. See Chapter 9 in this volume for more information about community organizations. The government has collaborated with community organizations since the 1990s (Clarke & Jennings, 2008) and today the Center for Faith-Based and Neighborhood Partnerships (CFBNP) continues this tradition, under the Department of Health and Human Services (HHS). The primary goal of HHS is to serve families and individuals who are in need. A CFBNP partnership that has flourished has been with Gracious Center for Learning and Enrichment Activities (GCLEA), a faith-based organization (FBO) in New Jersey. GCLEA provides AE classes on Islam and knowledge about life (such as cultivating father and son workshops and/or engaging with nature).

Isaac and Rowland (2002) argue that FBOs are important because they provide relevant AE. For example, the Salvation Army has an AE program in Idaho which offers classes that are pertinent to the community (the topics include grief counseling, knitting, and estate planning) (Salvation Army, n.d.). President Obama also collaborated with FBOs to create various initiatives within the My Brother's Keeper (MBK) program; one example, was the partnership between South Louisiana Community College and the Senior Pastors United Alliance (Hodges et al., 2016). They provided mentoring for first-generation college students to help them apply to college and become successful students (Hodges et al., 2016).

Formal and Informal Religious Education

Adult RE's main goal is to develop an understanding of a particular religion (Carr-Chellman et al., 2021; R'boul, 2021). This understanding is accomplished by exploring themes of the sacred texts within that religion. RE can be formal and take place in a variety of settings such as a university or community organization. Formal RE can be beneficial to those who desire to pursue it as a career choice or those who choose to gain the knowledge and skills that are the foundation for a particular religion.

Informal RE can include learning activities such as self-directed learning, incidental learning, and socialization (Isaac, 2014). Informal education can take place in various settings. For example, within the Baha'i faith, education is centered around peer leaders who facilitate study circles. They use a standard curriculum to explore the pillars of their faith and the educator facilitates instruction and encourages informal learning (Closson & Kaye, 2012).

Philosophical Approach

There are two AE frameworks that are integral to RE's practice. Both constructivism and lifelong learning provide a context for religious educators to use as their guiding framework. Constructivism has several guiding principles (Hein, 1991, as cited in Bristol & Isaac, 2009). First, learning is an active process and requires sensory input to construct meaning. Second, learning is a social activity associated with our connection to others. Third, learning requires reflection upon the material and does not occur instantly. Fourth, learners must be self-directed and motivated to learn. Finally, learning is contextual; learners relate the material to what they know or have previously learned. Additionally, the concept of lifelong learning is a part of AE. Hein further purports that lifelong learning, as a concept, was mainly used to address the need to build a skilled and knowledgeable workforce. These workers needed to be competitive and have access to the learning opportunities that could further their knowledge base. He proposes that religious institutions have become centers for nonformal learning. As a result, he found that older adults gained knowledge, spiritual guidance, and social capital when they participated in informal learning within religious institutions (Findsen, 2012). As older adults leave or prepare to leave the workforce, RE is one form of informal learning they pursue. Religious institutions also have other types of learning that may enhance the knowledge of these adults.

RE needs to value lifelong learning so that adults will continue to be a part of the learning environment. Hein (1991) (as cited in Bristol & Isaac, 2009) outlined the principles of constructivism and they should be utilized to create RE opportunities for adult learners. Research on adult learning has shown that there is significant support for the constructivism framework (Mayombe, 2020). Learning needs to be an active process in order to construct meaning. The material that will be used in any learning environment needs to help the learner make a connection to the material and create an opportunity for reflection on how the material relates to them. Learning opportunities must be self-directed and allow learners to use their previous experiences and learning to connect with the material.

Competencies, Credentials, and Career Pathways

There are several common careers for those who desire to pursue RE as an undergraduate major. According to the Bureau of Labor Statistics (2022), philosophy and religion majors generally worked in occupations that are in the field of education, or community and social service jobs. What these occupations have in common is that they interact with people and their goal is to support our society.

The website O*NET OnLine provides additional relevant information for those seeking to pursue a career in RE. The concluding chapter of this handbook will provide more details about this website for those seeking job opportunities in RE. Some of the skills that are needed include: (a) a knowledge of the basic principles of different religions; (b) principles of AE; (c) administration skills; and (d) communication and technology skills (O*NET OnLine, 2021). The addition of a master's or doctorate degree in AE can create a vital skill set needed to provide quality education for adults in a religious setting. The next part of the chapter will explore two career options that may entice those who are looking to enter the RE field.

Community Organizers in Faith-Based Organizations

One occupation that aligns with RE is that of a community organizer. FBOs or other nonprofits use this job title; their goal is to improve the plight of the less fortunate (Johnsen, 2014). The focus of a community organizer is to educate people on how to improve social problems that impact communities and then plan to problem solve for change. They also develop media to communicate their message and educational programs for volunteers and the community. (For more on community organizing and education, see Chapter 9.)

The approximate annual salary for community organizers is about $40,000 (Zippia, n.d.). A bachelor's degree may be required but a graduate degree in adult education is an advantage. In the AE field, there are adult educators who have a long history of being proponents for social justice. Brookfield (2016) states that he has seen adult educators in various settings and what remains constant is their commitment to activism and developing self-determination in people.

A community organizer advocates for those who are marginalized. The knowledge required for this role includes (a) basic principles of different religions; (b) psychology and counseling; (c) communication and technology; and (d) adult education principles. The most important characteristic of a community organizer is that they have a passion to improve the lives of those who are less fortunate. A person in this role educates others as a means to improve the community. They also must be comfortable interacting with the community because they are focused on external factors in the community. For example, the Muslim Women of Central Florida (Muslim Women's Organization, n.d.) is a community organization that seeks to empower Muslim women by providing them with support, resources, and dignity. They also educate women about issues that impact them such as voting rights and gender equality.

Another example of an organization that values community organizers is the Catholic Campaign for Human Development (CCHD). CCHD advocates for marginalized communities by bringing people together to address systemic injustices in areas such as housing and the courts. After the death of George Floyd, CCHD collaborated with a community in Maryland as they sought to eliminate legislation which allowed juveniles to be questioned without a parent's consent or attorney representation. This legislation unfairly impacted Black people. CCHD collaborated with the community organizers to provide resources and training so that they could gain support for this proposed legislation. "CCHD annually distributed about $10 million to its grantees in community organizing and economic development grants" (Grindon & Sadowski, 2021).

Director of Religious Education (DRE) or Religious Activities

Another career opportunity is that of a Director or Assistant Director of Religious Education or religious activities. The other possible titles within the career could include Adult Ministry Director, Young Adult Education Director, Assistant Religious Education Director, Senior Adult Education Director, or Women's Education Director. According to O*NET OnLine (2021), the role of the assistant director is to coordinate or design programs for a particular house of worship or community organization; this role may be used by any religion or faith. The mean annual salary for the DRE would be approximately $53,000 (O*NET OnLine, 2021); therefore, the assistant's salary would be less.

This position would be a great fit for someone with an AE degree. They could work for a church in a particular community or for a larger denomination or organization such as the United Methodist Church or the Union for Reform Judaism. The director or assistant director would be responsible for helping to manage the RE programs sponsored by the FBO. The breadth of their role is broad because they serve the interests of the DRE, learners, educators, and the FBO or educational organization, all at the same time. They would engage in various tasks, including creating and planning programs, updating curricula, developing program budgets, and communicating with learners and educators effectively. The goal is to lead a team of professionals and/or volunteers with diverse interests so that they can support a quality program. Therefore, they need to engage in evaluating (see Chapter 5) their program effectively so that it provides meaningful learning opportunities for all adults. Additionally, they must stay abreast of trends in the AE field and technology to make improvements when needed. The knowledge required for this role includes (a) basic principles of the religion with which you would like to affiliate; (b) psychology and counseling; (c) communication and technology; and (d) adult education principles.

Directors and assistant directors of RE promote learning or extra-curricular activities within their organization; they may instruct a class or develop educational opportunities. They may also have to fulfill other roles as needed, such as providing counseling, guidance, and leadership in reference to marital, health, financial, and religious problems. This job requires at least an undergraduate degree in RE. However, a graduate degree in AE would better prepare a candidate in understanding how to balance the competing priorities within their organization.

> **Professional Associations**
>
> The following professional associations have job postings and information about various career opportunities. This is not an exhaustive list; other faith traditions will have their own websites.
>
> - American Association for Christian Counselors: www.aacc.net
> - Christians Engaged in Faith Formation: https://cefumc.org
> - National Association of Directors of Christian Education: https://nadce.wildapricot.org
> - National Conference for Catechetical Leadership: www.ncclcatholic.org
> - National Presbyterian Church: https://nationalpres.org/connect/adults/
> - The Religious Education Association: https://religiouseducation.net
> - The United American Muslim Association: https://uama.us/en/who-we-are/about-us/

Technology in Religious Education

This next section discusses the use of technology within RE and the challenges that have resulted. According to Frye (2012), most of the world's religions have been utilizing distance education to reach more people. This is because not everyone is able to travel or attend services when and where they are held. Some consider the Bible as an early form of distance education (Asumanf, 2016).

The beauty of distance education is that it utilizes various formats to connect with people to deliver education. Therefore, the DRE must possess skills to use technology that will enhance learning opportunities. An adult educator would be integral in this role because they would possess the skills to train and develop instructors and learners on how to use the technology.

First, most religious organizations (large or small) have a website that allows people to view material about the organization such as the types of learning opportunities offered. For example, the IslamiCity website was founded in 1995 and its aim is to share Sunni Muslim resources. The website promotes education and shares the messages of the Qur'an such as peace and goodwill for the world (Frye, 2012). In the U.S., online and tele-programming have been utilized in Islamic spaces because of the lack of access to a place of worship in their community (Fadel, 2020). In fact, the website Black Iftar was an online learning resource during the pandemic that was developed to meet the needs of Black Muslims (Abderahman, 2021). In addition, other online platforms were established prior to the pandemic and continue to serve those who desire to know more about the Muslim religion (Fadel, 2020; Masruri et al., 2022).

While podcasts were created as a form of entertainment, they also provide knowledge to listeners. Podcasts have advanced informal learning in RE. Listeners value podcasts because they are able to control the content and context of the material they consume (Chan-Olmsted & Wang, 2020, as cited in Hackley, 2022). Therefore, the experience is individualized, and the listener selects the knowledge and its depth (Hackley, 2022).

This platform is valuable because it can connect learners who are new to a particular faith tradition. To illustrate, Bailey (2020), as a religious educator, developed a course for chaplains to understand how to collaborate with community organizers and activists as they toiled for social change. A podcast was created to deliver the curriculum. The benefit of the podcast was that it enabled her to reach a larger audience (including those who may not have been part of her target audience).

Using technology to access RE gives learners an opportunity to remain connected to their religious institution without the pre-pandemic challenges of transportation and/or scheduling constraints (Gjelten, 2020). For instance, Facebook developed an app for the Potter's House (a church in Dallas, Texas) that uploaded continuing education programming for its 30,000 members (Dias, 2021). Christian educators value the use of technology (Dunlow, (2021) (i.e., Zoom, Facebook, and YouTube) and the use of online learning has resulted in increased participation. For example, my pastor, Bishop Kenneth White, reported that he gained more adult learners utilizing technology (especially from different parts of the U.S.) (personal communication, March 2, 2022). Similarly, online learning has enhanced Islamic education in Indonesia (Maemonah et al., 2022). Online learning eliminated at least one of the barriers of in-person learning, in terms of classrooms that can only accommodate a limited number of learners. Online learning has the potential to reach more learners who may have no formal connection to a specific FBO or religion. Even as religious institutions have returned to in-person learning opportunities, online technology has continued to flourish (Dias, 2021; Dunlow, 2021).

While technology has enhanced the learning experiences of some, those who are without the technology (computers, internet access, etc.) or skills to navigate these platforms need to be accommodated. Adult educators must address how they will facilitate meaningful learning opportunities for all. A religious educator should explore how they can ensure that there will be a variety of learning opportunities. For example, one way that FBOs are connecting with those who do not have access to the internet is the use of conference call lines. In my church, we have senior citizens who lack the technology (i.e., internet access, smart phone, computer) or the skills to use the technology. Therefore, we use a conference line which allows multiple callers to hear the church services and/or participate in other learning opportunities. A religious educator needs to ensure that learners have the necessary technology prior to the start of classes. If they do not have the technology, or are not savvy with it, it is imperative that a plan is developed to meet the needs of the learner (such as setting up a conference line so that adult learners can participate).

Conclusion

AE influences many fields because learning is a lifelong process. As Hein (1991) (as cited in Bristol & Isaac, 2009) highlighted, learning is an active process, and it is imperative that AE facilitates a connection to the material so that learners can bridge that link to the material. Most often that connection relates to their lived experiences. Within RE, this enables them to connect to the curriculum and understand their life in context to their faith.

There are career opportunities in the RE field that would benefit from having a graduate of an AE program. Two specific opportunities that are closely aligned with AE are that of a community organizer and director/assistant director of religious education or activities. These careers can be found in the local community or at a national level within an FBO. What they have in common is a focus on enhancing the knowledge and skills of those who are part of their organization. Adult educators are positioned to contribute to the RE field because they have the knowledge and skills to enhance the learning environment of adults. The field of RE encompasses many diverse religions and an adult educator has the knowledge and skills to build a learning environment that supports all adult learners (Carr-Chellman et al., 2021; Closson & Kaye, 2012; Isaac, 2014).

When I began working in the field of education, I realized that I enjoyed the connection that I shared with adult learners. I felt energized by the conversations that we had about the curriculum and the connections that we shared about our life experiences. This same energy motivated me to become the DRE at my church. I enjoy creating a space for adult learners from diverse backgrounds and affirming that they belong and have a voice. Too often those who have been marginalized are left out of formal learning experiences; RE has the opportunity to transform this. This is my passion and the reason I encourage people to become religious educators.

References

Abderahman, S. (2021). *Peace*. Black Iftar. www.blackiftar.com

Asumanf, A. (2016). Fostering spiritual formation at a distance: Review of the current debates and a Biblically grounded proposal for maximizing its effectiveness as part of ministerial formation. *Conspectus, 22*, 1–38.

Bailey, J. (2020). Blooming beautifully: Emerging tools for religious education. *Religious Education, 115*(1), 34–45.

Brand, D. (2019). Barriers and facilitators of faith-based health programming within the African American church. *Journal of Cultural Diversity, 26*(1), 3–8.

Bristol, T., & Isaac, E. P. (2009). *Christian education and constructivism: Learning through the adult education Sunday school class*. Proceedings of the 50th Annual Adult Education Research Conference, Chicago, IL. https://digitalcommons.nl.edu/cgi/viewcontent.cgi?article=1000&context=ace_aerc#page=74

Brookfield, S. (2016). The future of social justice in adult education. *Dialogues in Social Justice, 1*(1), 27–30.

Bureau of Labor Statistics. (2022). *Occupational outlook handbook: Field of degree: Philosophy and religion*. www.bls.gov/ooh/field-of-degree/philosophy-and-religion/philosophy-and-religion-field-of-degree.htm

Carr-Chellman, D., Kroth, M., & Rogers-Shaw, C. (2021). Adult education for human flourishing: A religious and spiritual framework. In T. S. Rocco, M. C. Smith, R. C. Mizzi, L. R. Merriweather, & J. D. Hawley, (Eds.) *The handbook of adult and continuing education*, (2020 ed., pp. 297–304). Stylus.

Clarke, G., & Jennings, M. (2008). Introduction. In G. Clarke & M. Jennings (Eds.), *Development, civil society and faith-based organizations: Bridging the sacred and the secular* (pp. 1–16). Palgrave Macmillan.

Closson, R., & Kaye, S. (2012). Learning by doing: Preparation of Bahai nonformal tutors. *New Directions for Adult and Continuing Education, 133*, 45–57.

Dias, E. (2021). *Facebook's next target: The religious experience*. https://religionandpolitics.org/rap-sheet/facebooks-next-target-the-religious-experience/

Dorrien, G. (2023). King & his mentors: Rediscovering the black social gospel. *Commonweal*. www.commonwealmagazine.org/king-his-mentors

Dunlow, J. (2021). Digital discipleship: A study of how churches in New York used technology for adult discipleship during the COVID-19 pandemic. *Christian Education Journal, 18*(3), 458–472. https://doi.org/10.1177/07398913211046364

Fadel, L. (2020). *Ramadan, A month about community for many Muslims, goes virtual*. NPR. www.npr.org/2020/04/23/841894002/ramadan-a-month-about-community-for-many-muslims-goes-virtual

Findsen, B. (2012). Religious institutions as sites of learning for older adults. *New Directions for Adult and Continuing Education, 133,* 71–82.

Frye, S. (2012). Religious distance education goes online. *New Directions for Adult and Continuing Education, 133,* 13–22.

Gjelten, T. (2020). 'Things will never be the same.' How the pandemic has changed worship. NPR. www.npr.org/2020/05/20/858918339/things-will-never-be-the-same-how-the-pandemic-has-changed-worship

Grindon, L., & Sadowski, D. (2021). *Catholic campaign for human development turns 50.* National Catholic Reported: The Independent News Source.

Hackley, D. (2022). *Understanding podcast users: Consumption motives and behaviors.* University of Florida: College of Journalism and Communications. www.jou.ufl.edu/insights/understanding-podcast-users-consumption-motives-and-behaviors/

Hodges, T. L., Rowland, M. L., & Isaac-Savage, E. P. (2016). Black males in Black churches. *New Directions for Adult & Continuing Education, 150,* 47–57. https://doi.org/10.1002/ace.20185

Isaac, E. P. (2014). Lyceum guild: A ministry on a mission. *The Journal of Traditions & Beliefs, 1*(4), 21–32.

Isaac, E. P., & Rowland, M. L. (2002). Institutional barriers to participation in adult education among African Americans within religious institutions. *Journal of Research on Christian Education, 11*(2), 101. https://doi.org/10.1080/10656210209484935

Johnsen, S. (2014). Where's the 'faith' in faith-based organizations? The evolution and practice of faith-based homelessness services in the UK. *Journal of Social Policy, 43*(2), 413–430.

Knowles, M. S., Holton (III), E. F., Swanson, R. A., & Robinson, P. A. (2020). *The adult learner: The definitive classic in adult education and human resource development* (9th ed). Routledge.

Maemonah, M., Purnama, S., Rohinah, R., 'Aziz, H., Bastian, A. B., & Syafii, A. (2022). The shift in the authority of Islamic religious education: A qualitative content analysis on online religious teaching. *The Qualitative Report, 27*(9), 1830–1846. https://doi.org/10.46743/2160-3715/2022.5325

Masruri, M., Ismail, F., Kirin, A., Ibrahim, A., & Misbah, M. (2022). Reciting the Quran and friendship online as a method of post-COVID-19 soul and mental care. *Journal for the Study of Religions and Ideologies, 21*(62), 84–99.

Mayombe, C. (2020). Adult learners' perception on the use of constructivist principles in teaching and learning in non-formal education centers in South Africa. *International Journal of Lifelong Education, 39*(4), 402–418. https://doi.org/10.1080/02601370.2020.1796834

Merriam, S. B., & Brockett, R. G. (2007). *The profession and practice of adult education: An introduction.* Jossey-Bass.

Muslim Women's Organization. (n.d.). www.mwo-orlando.org

O*NET OnLine. (2021). *Director, religious activities and education.* www.onetonline.org/link/summary/21-2021.00

R'boul, H. (2021). Alternative theorizing of multicultural education: An Islamic perspective on interculturality and social justice. *Journal for Multicultural Education, 15*(2), 213–224.

Salvation Army. (n.d.) *Adult & senior education.* www.kroccda.org/kroc-cda/communityed/

Zippia: The career expert. (n.d.). *What is a community organizer?* www.zippia.com/community-organizer-jobs/

Chapter 23

Workforce Development Careers

Yvonne Hunter-Johnson

Workforce education and development, like adult education, lacks one conclusive definition. Rather, it is a concept that describes a wide community range of activities, policies, and programs (Jacobs, 2002). Workforce education and development includes a myriad of training programs dedicated to developing employees and sustaining their careers. The concept encompasses the process of obtaining the knowledge, skills, and abilities (KSAs) that improve an individual's overall performance in their respective workplace. Workforce education and development includes not only skill-based training for limited professions but also numerous training programs, apprenticeships, internships, and on-the-job training across many professions. Equally important is the understanding that employees are not the sole recipients of the investment in workforce education and development. This investment has a long-lasting impact on the employers and organizations, local communities, and the economy. Additionally, investment in employee development includes collaborative efforts from community organizations, private and government funding, and international opportunities. This chapter provides an overview of workforce education and development, aligns workforce education with adult learning, and prepares the reader for a career in this field.

Benefits of Workforce Education and Development

The many benefits associated with workforce education and development are visible across the employee, organizational, and societal levels. At the employee level it includes recruitment and career advancement. Organizations benefit from improved competitiveness and training programs that make a real difference. Society's main benefit is economic growth and development. This next section details these and other benefits.

Employee Level

Benefits at this level reach all areas of employee engagement, including career advancement, performance improvement, job satisfaction, and the recruitment of new employees. Examples are provided below.

Career Advancement. Investment in continued training and development of employees can aid their upward mobility resulting from their enhanced qualifications and specialized skills. Additionally, obtaining new KSAs can prepare employees for leadership positions.

Enhanced Job Performance. Participation in workforce education and development equips employees with specialized skills that improve performance and increase productivity at both an individual and an organizational level. According to the Organization for Economic Cooperation and Development (2019), organizations that focused on and continuously invested in education and training initiatives were associated with higher productivity.

DOI: 10.4324/9781003259602-26

Job Satisfaction, Retention, and Turnover. Providing recognition, training, and development opportunities shows a sense of investment and commitment from the employer to the employee. This investment can have a rippling impact on employee job satisfaction (i.e., being equipped with relevant training to perform duties and responsibilities) and cement a sense of belonging to the organization, ultimately reducing employee turnover. According to the Society of Human Resource Management (Grensing-Pophal, 2023), organizations that emphasized workforce education and development initiatives showed improved employee job satisfaction and retention rates. Hence, happy employees are more inclined to stay with their employers.

Recruitment. Workplace training and development can be used as a navigational tool for career advancement in an organization. The organization can communicate these opportunities for growth and development during the recruitment and hiring process.

Organizational Level

Organizational improvements achieved from an effective education and workforce development program include improved competitiveness, innovation and creativity, effective problem solving, viable intellectual capital, and transfer of training. This is discussed in more detail in this section.

Improved Competitiveness. The continued investment of workforce education and development at an organizational level will yield a skilled or specialized workforce. It creates opportunities to be on the cutting edge regarding trends and issues in a continuously changing industry. Further, organizations learn to adapt modern technologies, work processes, and market trends. All of this leads to improved competitiveness for the organization.

Promoting Innovation and Creativity. A culture of continuous learning and development benefits an organization's overall performance and promotes a work environment where learning, innovation, and creativity are celebrated. Hence, employees may be more apt to engage in professional development activities to benefit their careers.

Proactive Problem Solving. Workforce education is best used as a proactive problem-solving measure rather than a reactive one, which can be detrimental to an organization resulting in loss of profit and market space. Continuous training and development in the workplace are also tools to promote critical thinking. Proactive employees are equipped with the skills and abilities to address, predict, or overcome organizational and industry challenges.

Intellectual Capital. Intellectual capital is closely entwined with workforce education and development and is directly associated with an organization's success. Organizations must be equipped to use intellectual capital as a strategy to promote a competitive advantage.

Transfer of Training. "Transfer of training is the extent to which trainees are able to apply the knowledge, skills, and attitudes acquired in training to the job context" (Noe, 2017, p. 283). At an organizational level, effectively designed workforce education and training programs can ensure that transfer of training and learning enhances overall organizational productivity. Additionally, it reduces job-related accidents, measures the effectiveness of training, and promotes an organizational culture of learning and development.

Societal Level

Large-scale benefits resulting from effective education and workforce development programs include economic development and a greater pool of qualified candidates for important organizational positions. For this reason, federal, state, and local governments are often willing to fund workforce development programs.

Economic Growth and Development. Organizations equipped with skilled and productive employees can have a direct correlation to economic growth and development at a societal level. The National Bureau of Economic Research reported that investments in education and training correlate with an increase in productivity and economic growth (Acemoglu & Autor, 2012).

Lower Unemployment Rates. Organizations, vocational schools, community colleges, and universities focused on workforce education and development initiatives contribute to building the talent pool of skilled workers to fill important job openings. A study by the Organization for Economic Cooperation and Development (2019) found that higher levels of education and training were associated with lower unemployment rates.

History of Workforce Education and Development

The historical roots of workforce education and development are grounded in the industrial revolution from the 18th and early 19th centuries. During this era, machines began to replace manual labor (Gonzalez, 2009). Consequently, a demand arose for specialized workers with the knowledge and skills to effectively operate these new technologies in the workplace. To ensure the workers were equipped to be successful during this transition, the first vocational schools and trade apprenticeships were born (National Center for History in the Schools, n.d.). These educational institutions served as the foundation for developing the workforce of the time and emphasized teaching practical skills along with basic literacy and numeracy aimed at the skill-based professions.

Vocational education was formalized in the U.S. in the early 20th century with the introduction of the Smith-Hughes Act in 1917. This Act was the ultimate source of federal funding for vocational education programs in secondary education. Its goal was to flood the workforce with skilled employees using secondary education as a funnel that prepared and transitioned students to the career of their choice, specifically in the fields of agriculture, trade, and industry. Hence, this birthed the vocational education system, which was originally offered through the U.S. public school system and continues to evolve in the 21st century.

The Second World War brought a paradigm shift to the workforce. The KSAs of workers skilled in agriculture, trades, and industry molded into new skills that accommodated the defense industry. Government training initiatives and programs equipped workers with new skill sets needed to support the war. These government training initiatives continued after the war. During this era, a lack of equity regarding fair dispersal and access to education and training programs also became evident. Marginalized populations such as women, minorities, and individuals with lower social-economic status were not privy to education and training until the 1960s and 70s. The Civil Rights Act of 1964 and the Vocational Education Act of 1963 provided a gateway for disadvantaged groups to receive education and training by expanding training opportunities. See Gordon and Schultz (2020), the School-to-Work Opportunities Act (1993), and the Workforce Investment Partnership Act (1997) for a more extensive list of important legislation related to workforce education in the United States.

Workforce education and development continues to evolve to address the needs of a changing and complex society. These education and training initiatives have been extended to include a broad range of programs including on-the-job training and professional development, along with college and university degree programs. Workforce education and development is critical for economic growth and competitiveness in the United States and around the globe. It has become a priority on a global perspective for governments, employers, and educational institutions worldwide.

Workforce education and development also continues to advance as a discipline in response to economic conditions and the growing needs of the workforce. New evolving topics include technology and digital skills, diversity and inclusion, human-centric work, global perspectives, and remote workforce, among others. Skills needed for today's workforce include, but are not limited to, creativity, innovation, critical thinking skills, digital upskilling, and flexibility. Furthermore, workforce education and development programs continue to receive funding from a multitude of federal and state government agencies, colleges, and the private sector.

My Experience Connecting Workforce Education and Development and Adult Education

My introduction to workforce education was unique and unexpected. My background is in law enforcement in the Royal Bahamas Police Force, The Bahamas. I served 18 years and resigned as a sergeant to pursue my passion for workforce education and development using adult education as my navigational tool. My career in law enforcement began as a station officer before transitioning into policing the streets of Nassau, Bahamas. I later transferred to the Criminal Investigations Department, responsible for investigating major crimes such as murder, armed robbery, kidnapping, burglary, suicides, aggravated assaults, and manslaughter. My specialization, however, was investigating sexual offenses.

After approximately 10 years of investigating such criminal activities and obtaining a master's degree, I became a trainer at the Police Training Academy. My responsibilities included professional development of law enforcement officers and officers of other essential services (Royal Bahamas Defense Force, Her Majesty's Prisons, Bahamas Customs, and Bahamas Immigration). As a training specialist, I oversaw curriculum design and development, assessment, evaluation of peer teaching, and many other duties.

As a training specialist with a master's degree, it was paramount that I was equipped with the KSAs to provide the best learning environment for my trainees. Equally important to me was that the KSAs received in the learning environment were transferable to the work environment. To this end, I pursued a diploma in education from the University of The Bahamas. While the information gleaned from this diploma was essential as it related to understanding the concept of learning, instructional methods, classroom management, and theories of education, the perspective focused on K-12 and I still experienced a void regarding the adult learners in my courses and my responsibility for workforce education and training at the Royal Bahamas Police Force. While the diploma in education was a great foundation for teaching and learning, I needed much more to ensure the delivery of effective learning environments for nontraditional learners which truly met their unique needs. I needed to understand how nontraditional learners learned, what impacted their learning, how to be more effective as an adult educator, and what strategies to utilize to promote learning and development. I wanted to understand the educational theories that guided educating adults and to make sure I was properly preparing the trainees for the workforce.

To this end, I enrolled in an adult education doctoral program. Pursuing this degree created a new zeal in my passion for workforce education and development. I now understood the guiding principles of adult education and how they influence me as a workforce education and development professional. New concepts and strategies entered my sphere of knowledge, such as best practices and strategies related to promoting culturally relevant learning environments while demonstrating culturally relevant pedagogy. I comprehended and valued incorporating the experience of my learners in the learning environment and how to make the connection to the theory or concept being taught more effectively. I could now emulate all the theories and concepts of adult education in my learning environment to enhance it and promote transfer of training from the learning to the workplace. This was my "ah ha" moment of the connection between adult education and workforce education. More specifically, I recognized how adult education serves as an effective foundational platform in the field of workforce education despite the professional setting.

Making the Connection: Adult Education and Workforce Education

This section clarifies the theoretical and practical links between the fields of adult education and workforce education. Among other points, adult learning and the connection between adult education and workforce education are explored.

Adult Learning

The concept of adult learning cannot be encapsulated in one authoritative definition. Instead, various overarching definitions abound, though common key themes and concepts emerge. These varied definitions are important, considering the multifaceted concept of adult learning and the different perspectives adults bring to the learning environment. According to the National Center for Education Statistics (2020), adult education refers most directly to the activities purposefully created to maximize the learning taking place for adults regardless of who they are or what their barriers may be. In this iteration of adult education, emphasis is placed on activities that promote adult learning which eliminate any perceived deterrent that may arise from one's social role or age. However, the definition of adult learning provided by the American Association for Adult and Continuing Education (n.d.) focused on the systematic processes of learner engagement to bring about new knowledge and skills in the learning environment. Here, emphasis is placed on the process of engaging adults in a learning experience classified as meaningful and relevant while still addressing the adult learner's specific needs and interests. Merriam and Bierema (2014) defined adult learning as the process of acquiring KSAs through intentional and self-directed learning experiences that occur after the completion of formal education. Similarly, the American Psychological Association (2022) also supports the notion of adult learning as a process of intentional, self-regulated, and self-motivated learning by adults. The common ideas threaded within these various perspectives describe adult learning accordingly: it involves adults in a formal or informal setting, engaged in a lifelong process that requires the adult to be motivated, self-directed, and autonomous. See Chapter 1 which elaborates further on adult learning.

Aligning Workforce Education to Adult Education

Workforce education and development programs, like adult learning, generate a myriad of definitions. According to the U.S. Department of Labor Employment & Training Administration (2022), adult learning is a comprehensive approach to the delivery of education and training services for individuals aged 18 and over, "which includes a range of activities designed to help individuals achieve their employment and education goals, and acquire the skills necessary to enter and succeed in the workforce" (p. 1). With this point of reference, this section demonstrates the alignment of adult learning to workforce education and discusses how theories in the field of adult education support and enhance adult learning in organizations and promote workforce education and development.

What is the Connection? Adult Learning and Workforce Education

There is a friendly relationship and close connection between the fields of adult learning and workforce education and development. The two entities naturally support each other. In the workplace, many (adult) employees participate in and benefit from workforce education and development. Motivation for this involvement in education and training may derive from a desire for personal development, career advancement, financial compensation, career change, or numerous other reasons. (See Chapter 11 for more information on organizational employee development.)

The focus of workforce education and development programs is on the adult learner, who may be a traditional or a nontraditional learner. In whatever circumstance, the aim of workforce education and development is to provide employees (now understood and perceived as adult learners) with the relevant KSAs to be successful in their workplace. Education and training in the workplace can mirror various initiatives that include on-the-job training, technological training, soft skills training, industry-specific training, managerial and leadership training, team building, and many other offerings.

Adult Learning Theories Applied to Workforce Education and Development

The field of adult education includes many underlying theories. Emphasis here is placed on a selected set of theories and how they are effectively applied to workforce education and development. See Chapter 2 for additional information on these concepts.

Transformative Learning. Transformative learning was originally developed by Mezirow (1991), who believed that adults are able to transform their perspectives and beliefs through a process of critical reflection and dialogue with others. Based on this premise, adult learners in workforce education and training learning environments should receive opportunities for critical reflection and continuous dialogue with others. This approach can be facilitated in both a virtual and face-to-face setting. Examples include blogs, journal entries, prompted critical reflections, discussion forums, in-class discussions, group discussions, case studies, presentations, and other interactive activities.

Experiential Learning. Developed by Kolb (1984), the idea of experiential learning maintains that adults learn best when able to reflect on experiences and apply what they have learned to new situations (Kolb & Kolb, 2005). In a training environment, this happens when trainees are given the opportunity to apply the content being learned to real-world experiences. Additionally, trainees can engage in hands-on activities or scenarios that reflect real-world experiences. The learners are then asked to apply content learned to these experiences.

Prior Learning Experience. According to the Canadian Information Centre for International Credentials (2011), prior learning experience encompasses the KSAs and competencies obtained from formal or informal means to gain experiences prior to enrolling in a program, training, or learning environment. In workforce education and development, the experiences and knowledge base of the learners are of critical importance related to course content. Instructors can incorporate strategies such as standardized tests, portfolio assessments, and interviews (Boud & Falchikov, 2007). Instructors should also incorporate tools such as flexibility and competency-based learning in the learning environment.

Andragogy. Originally coined by Alexander Kapp, a German philosopher, in 1861, andragogy was introduced into the United States by Malcolm Knowles, who described it as the process of teaching adults (Merriam et al., 2007). Andragogy assumes that the needs of adults in a learning environment differ from those of children. Hence, the approach to learning by instructors should reflect this (Knowles et al., 2020). See Chapter 21, which expands on the concept of andragogy. In a training environment, this theory is applied by allowing active learner involvement in the learning process, ensuring that learning is relevant to the learner and is immediately applicable. It is of utmost importance that the learning environment reflects the needs of the learners specific to their workplace, both professionally and personally. The inclusion of the learner's experience is critical regarding content in the training environment and self-directed learning should also be emphasized.

Self-Directed Learning. Self-directed learning emphasizes the importance of adult learners to take responsibility for their own learning and to direct their own learning process (Caffarella, 2000). In a training environment, this is demonstrated by trainers allowing learners to take ownership of their learning process. Hence, trainers can provide opportunities for self-paced training, self-assessment tools, reflection, feedback, and incorporation of learning contracts in the training environment.

Social Learning Theory. Originally developed by Bandura (1977), social learning theory emphasizes how observation and modeling contribute to adult learning, along with the consequences of this behavior. In a training environment, this theory is facilitated by trainers modeling expected behavior in the work environment. Social learning theory is most effective for training that focuses on developing soft skills and behavior modification. Group assignments, activities, and projects are highly recommended, as well as peer mentoring and social learning networks focused on collaboration and knowledge learning.

Preparing for a Career in Workforce Education and Development

In the previous section, the various theories of adult learning that inform workforce development were explained. In the following section, the elements needed for a successful career in workforce development are discussed.

Qualifying for a Career in Workforce Education

To become properly equipped for a career in workforce education and development, there are many considerations. These include education and training, certificates, experience, communication skills, principles of adult learning, technology and research skills, and professional development.

Education and Training. Most positions in the field of workforce education and development require a bachelor's or master's degree. The degree level will vary depending on the position title. Degrees in fields such as adult education, workforce education, organization learning, or human resource development provide the greatest resources for adult learning. See similar jobs on O*Net for further explanations, including sample salaries, job descriptions, and potential job opportunities.

Certificates/Licensure. Depending on the focus in workforce education and development, specific certifications or licenses may be required. Many of the professional associations listed at the end of this chapter can provide valuable information regarding available certificates and licensure.

Experience. For all workforce education and development professionals, at least 3–5 years of experience is recommended in that field. This can include positions from entry level to more advanced levels. Of course, it is also beneficial to demonstrate industry experience in the field for which the educators will be facilitating the courses and programs of education and training.

Communication Skills. It is critical that individuals working within the field of workforce education and development exhibit effective communication skills. These include verbal, nonverbal, written, presentation, research, listening, negotiation, interpersonal, and conflict resolution skills.

Applying Principles of Adult Learning. As a workforce education and development specialist, it is important to understand and apply the concepts and principles of adult learning. These include course design and development, instructional methods, the learning environment, and the roles of adult learners and adult educators.

Technology/Research Skills. It is paramount that professionals in the field of workforce education and development are equipped with the technical skills to design and develop courses or programs. They also need the technology to support the desired instructional delivery methods, including both virtual and face-to-face learning environments.

Professional Development. It is vital to continuously develop your professional KSAs, and competencies to ensure that you are effective and efficient with your duties and responsibilities. Such professional development initiatives include topics related to specific industries, instructional design, adult education, and workforce education and development. These initiatives can be delivered via multiple modes such as webinars, conferences, workshops, job shadowing, certification and credentialing programs, leadership development programs, and many more.

Professional Associations

Academy of Human Resource Development (www.ahrd.org)
American Association of Adult and Continuing Education (www.aaace.org)
Association of Talent Development (www.td.org)
National Association of Workforce Development Professionals www.nawdp.org)
National Council for Workforce Education (www.ncwe.org)
Society of Human Resource Management (https://shrm.org)

Careers in Workforce Education

In the workforce, human resource development specialists, training instructors, education officers, and talent developers (see Chapter 11 for additional information) are tasked with designing, developing, and delivering to employees a set of education and training programs created specifically for adult learners. These professionals in the organization must thereby be highly knowledgeable about the concepts of adult learning and how to apply the principles of adult learning to any training being designed. Hence, it is paramount that the education and training programs (a) be flexible, considering the work and personal schedule of the employees, (b) promote self-directed learning, (c) encourage input from the experiences of the trainees, (d) provide culturally relevant pedagogy, (e) afford opportunities for the trainees to be active participants in the learning process, and (f) include discussions of the applicability of the training and training content, ensuring that trainees understand the relevance and applicability of the training either personally or in their work environment. In the field of workforce education and adult education, there are numerous careers. Some examples follow.

- Career and Technical Education (CTE) Teacher/Instructor – develops and delivers educational programs that prepare learners for specific careers and industries. They work in secondary schools, community colleges, and vocational schools.
- Workforce Development Specialist – designs and implements programs (see Chapter 4) that address the skill gaps in the workforce, with the goal of helping workers acquire new skills and knowledge that match the needs of employers and industries.
- Career Coach/Counselor – helps individuals to identify their career goals, assess their skills and interests, and develop a plan for achieving their career objectives. They may work in schools, colleges, or private organizations.
- Adult Education Instructor – provides educational programs for adult learners who may need to develop their basic literacy, numeracy, or language skills, or who seek to earn a high school diploma or an equivalency credential (see Chapter 7).

- Human Resource Development Specialist – assists with the development of employees' KSAs necessary to perform their jobs in an effective manner while advancing their careers (see Chapter 11).
- Instructional Designer – creates and develops educational materials, programs, and courses, utilizing a multiplicity of technologies and instructional design principles to ensure effective and engaging learning experiences (see Chapter 18).
- Program Manager – oversees the development and implementation of workforce education and development programs, ensuring that they align with the needs of learners, employers, and industries.
- Assessment/Evaluation Specialist – designs and conducts assessments and evaluations of educational programs to measure their effectiveness and impact, identify areas for improvement, and provide feedback to instructors and administrators (see Chapter 5).
- Curriculum Developer – creates and designs educational curricula that align with industry standards and meet the needs of learners and employers (see Chapter 11).
- Education Administrator – oversees the operations and management of educational programs and institutions, ensuring that they meet the needs of learners, comply with regulations, and achieve their educational goals.

Resources for Careers in Workforce Education

Locating Certificates: Certifications | CareerOneStop (www.careeronestop.org/FindTraining/Types/certifications.aspx)

Career Readiness: What Is Career Readiness? | naceweb.org (www.naceweb.org/career-readiness/competencies/career-readiness-defined/)

Updating Your Skillset: My Skills Are Out of Date | CareerOneStop (www.careeronestop.org/FindTraining/FindYourPath/my-skills-are-out-of-date.aspx)

Career Assessment Tools: Career Assessment Tools | Career Development | nau.edu (https://in.nau.edu/career/career-advising-2/career-assessment-tools/)

Job Hunt Strategies: Strategies | Job Centers | CDO Workforce (www.cdoworkforce.org/for-job-seekers/strategies)

Interview Tips for Non-faculty Positions: Interview Tips | Prospects.ac.uk (www.prospects.ac.uk/careers-advice/interview-tips)

Conclusion

Workforce development is an integral component of an individual's work life and by extension organization and society. It serves as a foundational platform for employee development, which has a rippling impact on the organization and society. The history of workforce development is rich and closely intertwines with adult education, which is manifested in a variety of workforce development initiatives. As a workforce development specialist, it is critical to understand theories of adult education with the view of applying them within the workforce. It is equally important as a workforce development specialist to be equipped with the knowledge, skills, and abilities as it relates to researching careers related to the field, actively engaging with professional organizations, and serving as a navigational tool for other novice professionals in the field. The intention of this chapter is to promote an understanding in these areas and to prepare individuals as workforce development specialists grounded in theories of adult education.

References

Acemoglu, D., & Autor, D. (2012). What does human capital do? A review of Goldin and Katz's The Race between Education and Technology. *Journal of Economic Literature*, 50(2), 426–463. https://doi.org/10.1257/jel.50.2.426

American Association for Adult and Continuing Education. (n.d.). *Definition of adult education*. www.aaace.org/what-is-adult-education

American Psychological Association. (2022). Adult learning. https://dictionary.apa.org/adult-learning

Bandura, A. (1977). *Social learning theory*. Prentice Hall.

Boud, D., & Falchikov, N. (2007). *Rethinking assessment in higher education: Learning for the longer term*. Routledge.

Caffarella, R. S. (2000). Goals of self-directed learning. In G. A. Straka (Ed.), *Conceptions of self-directed learning: Theoretical and conceptual considerations* (pp. 37–48). Waxmann.

Canadian Information Centre for International Credentials. (2011). *Prior learning assessment and recognition*. www.cicic.ca/docs/default-source/publications/prior-learning-assessment-and-recognition.pdf

Gonzalez, A. (2009). The history of workforce education in the United States. *The Journal of Industrial Teacher Education*, 46(2), 6–20.

Gordon, H. R. D., & Schultz, D. (2020). *The history and growth of career and technical education in America* (5th ed.). Waveland Press, Inc.

Grensing-Pophal, L. (2023, August 9). *How to retain your talent*. Society of Human Resource Management. www.shrm.org/resourcesandtools/hr-topics/people-managers/pages/how-to-retain-your-talent.aspx

Jacobs, R. L. (2002, October 17–19). *Understanding workforce development: Definition, conceptual boundaries, and future perspectives* [Paper presentation]. International Conference on Technical and Vocational Education and Training. Winnipeg, Canada. https://umanitoba.ca/unevoc/2002conference/text/papers/jacobs.pdf

Knowles, M. (1970). *The modern practice of adult education: Andragogy versus pedagogy*. Association Press.

Knowles, M. S., Holton (III), E. F., Swanson, R. A., & Robinson, P. A. (2020). *The adult learner: The definitive classic in adult education and human resource development* (9th ed.). Routledge.

Kolb, A. Y., & Kolb, D. A. (2005). Learning styles and learning spaces: Enhancing experiential learning in higher education. *Academy of Management Learning and Education*, 4(2), 193–212.

Kolb, D. A. (1984). *Experiential learning: Experience as the source of learning and development*. Prentice Hall.

Merriam, S. B., & Bierema, L. L. (2014). *Adult learning: Linking theory and practice*. Jossey-Bass.

Merriam, S. B., Caffarella, R. S., & Baumgartner, L. M. (2007). *Learning in adulthood: A comprehensive guide* (3rd ed.). Jossey-Bass.

Mezirow, J. (1991). *Transformative dimensions of adult learning*. Jossey-Bass.

National Center for Education Statistics (NCES). (2020). *Adult education*. https://nces.ed.gov/programs/coe/glossary/

National Center for History in the Schools. (n.d.). *The rise of vocational education*. https://nchs.ucla.edu/history-standards/standards-for-grades-5-12/the-rise-of-vocational-education

Noe, R. A. (2017). *Employee training and development* (7th ed.). McGraw-Hill.

Organization for Economic Cooperation and Development (OECD). (2019). *OECD employment outlook 2019: The future of work*. OECD Publishing. https://doi.org/10.1787/9ee00155-en

School-to-Work Opportunities Act of 1994, H.R. 2884, 103rd Cong. (1993). www.congress.gov/bill/103rd-congress/house-bill/2884

U.S. Bureau of Labor Statistics. (2021). *Occupational outlook handbook*. Adult Basic and Secondary Education and ESL Teachers. www.bls.gov/ooh/education-training-and-library/adult-literacy-and-ged-teachers.htm

U.S. Department of Health, Education, and Welfare. Office of Education. Bureau of Adult, Vocational, and Technical Education. (1969). *The vocational education amendments of 1968*. (ED039352). ERIC. http://files.eric.ed.gov/fulltext/ED039352.pdf

U.S. Department of Labor Employment & Training Administration. (2022). *Workforce development solutions*. www.dol.gov/agencies/eta/employers/workforce-development-solutions.

Workforce Investment Partnership Act of 1998, H.R. 1385, 105th Cong. (1997). www.congress.gov/bill/105th-congress/house-bill/1385

Conclusion

Creating a Career in Adult Education

Paul G. Putman, E. Paulette Isaac-Savage and Catherine H. Monaghan

Goal and Themes

Our overarching goal was to answer the question "What can I do with a degree in adult education?" with a specific focus on careers outside of academia. Many books exist describing how to become a faculty member or work at a college or university, but, until now, no books present readers with a sampling of the myriad of opportunities available to them with a degree in adult education. We also sought to elevate the voices of practitioners whenever possible, to hear from them directly about the day-to-day activities in which they engage, the opportunities and challenges they face, along with the competencies (also known as knowledge, skills, and abilities [KSAs]), insights, and tips needed for success. Four themes related to careers in adult education surfaced as we read chapters in both parts of this book. First, the practitioners did not experience a single career pathway. Second, the authors noted that entering the field of adult education can happen at multiple points during one's career. Third, technology is playing a significant role in adult education careers, and that role is expected to increase in the future. And finally, cultural competency is now a major skill that needs to be developed by adult educators.

No One Pathway

The practitioners in this text came to work in adult education through a multitude of pathways. The topics presented in Part I of this book explore in practical terms the primary competencies in the field; they also include short sections on the career journeys of the authors. These, along with the individual stories that appear in Part II of the book, demonstrate that there is no singular journey in a career in adult education. Several authors note the importance of early-career work outside of adult education that helped inform and enhance their paths while nurturing their sense of adult education as a vocational calling. It is our hope that readers are inspired by the stories shared throughout the book.

Never Too Late

Many authors discovered their passion for adult education during a different first career. Often a change in life circumstances ("and then life happened…") led to a shift. While learning about adult education in your twenties is great, many enter the field later in life, and in this field that is perfectly fine, and it is not unusual. Some came to adult education through moving into training positions in their previous career.

Technology

Multiple chapters point to technology as a necessary proficiency and/or trend that the authors view as important competencies as adult education moves online in many sectors.

DOI: 10.4324/9781003259602-27

This may be due at least in part to the COVID-19 pandemic quarantine during which much of this book was written and compiled, and the quarantine's role in all of us becoming immersed in the challenges and opportunities inherent in adult education mediated by technology. As Porterfield notes in Chapter 6, there are a myriad of tools along with technologies and the options continue to expand. It can be overwhelming and exciting all at once. "It is like looking at an unfinished 1,000-piece puzzle! Where do you start, and what are the connectors?" (Collins, Chapter 7).

Cultural Competency

There is one entire chapter devoted to the work of adult educators in the field of diversity, equity, and inclusion (DEI). (See Chapter 14 in this volume.) However, throughout almost all the chapters, the need to be skilled in cultural competency was emphasized. This cultural competency extends first to the adult learners, and then to the wealth of material from diverse voices. This skill allows the adult educator to create safe spaces for all learners while enriching the depth of the topics that they may be presenting in their educational spaces. The following chapters contained dynamic discussions about this topic: Chapter 2, Practical Skills for Teaching Adults; Chapter 7, Adult Basic Education/English as a Second Language/Family Literacy; Chapter 8, Adult Environmental Education; Chapter 9, Community-Based Adult Education; Chapter 16, Military Education; Chapter 19, Policy Leadership in Adult Education Reform; and Chapter 20, Professional Development with the K-12 Setting.

"But What About …?"

We compiled this book to elevate the voices of practitioners in an attempt to begin answering the question "What can I do with a degree in adult education?" This is not an exhaustive collection of every adult education career possibility, but an entry point to exploring careers within the practice of adult education. We acknowledge that there are many more careers than we had space for in this book. We hope that readers are pleased with the variety of career pathways presented, and if they did not find an exact match, that this book will spark their interest in learning about other careers in the field.

There are also many positions and careers that exist at the intersections of options presented in this text. You can combine areas to capitalize upon your strengths and interests. Albert Einstein is credited with the idea of *combinatory play*, in which two seemingly unrelated items are explored to produce some new idea. If you were inspired by more than one chapter in this book, consider exploring possibilities at the intersection of the chapters that resonate with you the most. For example, you could be a consultant (Chapter 10) in a nonprofit (Chapter 17) engaged in evaluation (Chapter 5).

As we mentioned earlier, there was not enough space to include all the career possibilities. While we realize that some may be interested in faculty or positions in higher education, we also know these areas are covered extensively by others. However, we did include an appendix for those who might want to explore the higher education possibilities in depth.

Meta-Competencies in Career Development

Career competencies "involve critical reflection on oneself and one's professional life and, as such, they are part of a continuous process of learning through experience" (Skakni et al., 2022, p. 2). These are often referred to as meta-competencies (as opposed to simply generic or transferable skills) as "they do not focus on specific skills to practice a profession or perform specific tasks but instead allow individuals to develop skills for navigating their career trajectories" (Skakni et al., 2022, p. 2). These career competencies can be categorized, and Skakni, et al. (2022) cite the work of Akkermans et al. (2013), noting that:

> career competencies can be categorised into three core dimensions, each comprising two sub-dimensions. First, the reflective dimension refers to awareness and critical thinking about one's work-related values, motivations, strengths, and weaknesses. The sub-dimensions are reflection on motivations (values, passions, and intentions concerning one's career) and reflection on qualities (strengths, shortcomings, and perceived skills concerning one's career). Second, the communication dimension relates to the ability to network professionally and promote oneself in professional contexts. The sub-dimensions are networking (ability to create and expand personal and professional networks for career-related purposes) and self-profiling (ability to promote one's knowledge, abilities, and skills in the workplace and external labour markets). Finally, the behavioural dimension refers to the active exploration of career opportunities and an ability to steer one's career. The sub-dimensions are work exploration (ability to explore and search for further education, work, and career-related opportunities) and career control (ability to influence learning and work processes related to one's career by setting goals and planning how to fulfill them). (pp. 2–3)

This categorization also echoes the Protean Career Model discussed in the Introduction to this volume as a possible model for those who are seeking to engage or are engaged in a career in adult education.

More specifically, the National Association of Colleges and Employers (NACE) identifies eight competencies for workplace and career success:

1. Career and self-development
2. Communication
3. Critical thinking
4. Equity and inclusion
5. Leadership
6. Professionalism
7. Teamwork
8. Technology

(National Association of College and Employers, 2021)

These competencies can be studied by research or observation to some extent but only strengthened through practice. Adult education learners and practitioners can seek out opportunities by working with their supervisors and employers or by volunteering with nonprofit organizations as board members or in other roles. Working with a mentor or career coach/advisor can also be useful.

Career Competencies in Adult Education

Part I of this book began with an overview of the field (Chapter 1) and then focused on the primary skills and competencies for adult educators. These include practical teaching (Chapter 2); facilitation (Chapter 3); program planning (Chapter 4); assessment, evaluation, and educational research (Chapter 5); and technology (Chapter 6). These are well-aligned with the Standards for Graduate Programs in Adult Education developed by the Commission of

Professors in Adult Education of the American Association for Adult and Continuing Education (www.aaace.org/page/CPAEStandards).

Throughout Part II of the book, practitioners highlight competencies beyond the primary ones that they see as most important for specific spheres of practice within adult education. Readers can refer to specific chapters, reference lists, and the index for additional information. Several secondary competencies were mentioned multiple times, and three of those most-often mentioned are highlighted below.

Building Partnerships. These chapters had the most robust discussion on this topic: Chapter 8, Adult Environmental Education; Chapter 12, Correctional Education; Chapter 14, Careers in Diversity, Equity, and Inclusion; and Chapter 20, Professional Development within the K-12 Setting.

Communication. The authors of these chapters provided additional information and examples: Chapter 7, Adult Basic Education/English as a Second Language/Family Literacy; Chapter 10, Consulting; and Chapter 19, Policy Leadership in Adult Education Reform.

Leadership. This topic was explored in detail in the following chapters: Chapter 11, Corporate Training, Global Learning and Talent Management; Chapter 14, Careers in Diversity, Equity, and Inclusion; and Chapter 17, The Nonprofit Sector.

There are other competencies that also cross the spectrum of the field of adult education. Some of these include budget management, critical thinking, emotional intelligence, flexibility, knowledge about the field of adult education, political savviness, project management, time management, and writing. Not every position will require experience or expertise in every competency. Also, just because a particular chapter does not explicitly mention a specific competency does not mean that it is not helpful or important to that sphere of adult education. It will be helpful for readers to take stock of their own areas of comfort and expertise, and also their desired areas for learning and growth as they consider their next positions.

General Career Advice

During the course of compiling this book, some helpful general career advice tips emerged. A few standouts for consideration for those searching for their first or next position in adult education:

Update Your Profiles and Resume

Make sure your LinkedIn and other professional online profiles are up to date and reflective of the image you want to convey for potential employers who take the time to research you online. Update your resume with an eye to positions you are seeking. Include keywords that you see often in position descriptions. Note that specific advice on how to craft the perfect resume will vary. For example, while most professionals recommend keeping your resume length to one or two pages, Hennes (Chapter 10) recommends a longer or more complete resume for certain types of positions.

There is no one perfect resume format and a lot of it is personal preference. Remember that the purpose of the profile or resume is just to get to the next conversation or stage in an organization's selection process.

Craft Your Elevator Pitch

An elevator pitch is a 30–60-second overview of who you are and what you are seeking for the next step of your career. It is called an elevator pitch as 30–60 seconds is about the amount of time you would have to talk during an elevator ride with a captive audience. You will want to be succinct and memorable. It is worth the time to write this out and memorize it so it is always at the ready should an opportunity arise to share your story and what you are seeking. You will want to have this available for networking opportunities. Aldenhuysen in Chapter 13 speaks specifically to crafting your pitch.

Explore

Considering a new career adventure? Do not sleep on the idea of a good informational interview. Do it! Most professionals are happy to spend 30 minutes talking about their career journey and answering a few questions about their day-to-day work, the joys and challenges they face, and advice that they might have for professionals wanting to do what they do. Offer to buy them a cup of coffee and if they agree to meet, come to the meeting with your elevator pitch, just a few questions, and prepare to soak in the knowledge shared. And be prepared to leave after 30 minutes. Follow up with a thank you note, an electronic copy of your resume in case they want to share it with anyone, and a LinkedIn request thanking them again for meeting with you. A month or two after your meeting, send another brief thank you note sharing how you followed up on their advice and with a brief update on your search.

If you are currently employed full time and just want to explore another career direction, consider moonlighting as a consultant (if that is not a conflict of interests) and/or volunteering. Even spending just a few hours a week in a role can often give you a good sense of whether or not that next step might be right for you.

Dig Deeper

Several authors note that position titles listed on websites do not always match the actual jobs or tell the full story, so it is important to dig deeper. Take the time to research the organization and people. A bit of internet sleuthing will often do the trick.

General Job/Career Websites

Throughout Part II of the book, authors shared websites specific to the various spheres of adult education discussed in their chapters. The following websites may be additionally helpful for expanding your search.

Glassdoor: www.glassdoor.com
Indeed: www.indeed.com/
LinkedIn: www.linkedin.com
Monster: www.monster.com
O*NET OnLine: www.onetonline.org

The Importance of Mentors

Finding a mentor in the same career field is one of the best things you can do for yourself; seek out local groups for professionals or find out who has a similar role to you (or is in a position of leadership you might like to achieve yourself one day) and reach out. These people are integral to growing as a leader and changemaker in your field and can introduce you to other influential individuals in your community. Mentorship can go both ways; you may find yourself seeking advice

> from your mentor one afternoon over coffee and fielding questions from them the next time you meet for lunch. Leveling the playing field like this and being flexible and comfortable enough in your mentor/mentee relationship to serve either role as needed will help you learn and grow in ways you never expected! When I first moved to the Midwest, I sought out individuals who had similar jobs in town and simply asked if we could meet up and talk. Six years later, we are still friends and meet up frequently for advice, support, and just to hang out!
>
> (Claire Aldenhuysen, personal communication, February 25, 2023)

Get Involved: Professional Organizations

We feel that it is important to get involved in at least one local, national, or international professional organization. Throughout the text, the contributing authors provide examples. These organizations offer a community of like-minded professionals who are often grappling with the same challenges that you are facing. Most focus on member education to help you accomplish your professional goals and add value to your work. They also provide an important opportunity for service (giving back to the field) and leadership development. We also note that often the best/least expensive time to join a professional organization is while you are a student. That said, many companies will cover membership dues and support participation in professional development and educational opportunities such as webinars, workshops, and conferences.

Other Tips to Advance Your Career

Take your career to the next level by saying yes to opportunities that expand your professional toolbox of skills, experiences, and items that grow your audience or brand.

- Volunteer with a professional organization.
- Serve in a leadership role with a professional organization.
- Write a blog post, newsletter article, or peer-reviewed journal article.
- Present or co-present at a conference.
- Offer to take on additional responsibilities while someone is on extended leave or on an interim basis while a position is being filled.

Additional Certifications: Are They a Worthwhile Investment?

Certifications are a great way to communicate that an organization (someone besides yourself) would attest that you have a particular set of skills. This is meaningful and valuable – particularly if the credential is from a well-recognized organization. This should be balanced with the knowledge that, beyond something that is entry level, certain positions tend to also want years of experience along with the certification.

Ultimately, it comes down to the individual in terms of whether or not they think it would be worth the time and money. Certifications may provide an edge in getting an interview, but do not guarantee a job. Also note that if a position were to come available, and someone saw that it required a certification, it is likely that, unless they had already been studying for it, the position would be filled before they acquired the credential.

If, for example, I wanted to become a programmer, I think my best track would be to ask my current workplace how I can take on extra duties that are programmer-related or adjacent.

> Additionally, I could pursue a credential (and I imagine rubbing elbows with programmers would aid me in that pursuit). If my job could not provide me the means to gain additional technical experience and I were set on making a career change, I think a *bootcamp* learning experience would be my next consideration. However, readers should note that bootcamps are like certifications – some are more meaningful, valuable, and reputable than others.
>
> Chris Rennison, Senior Manager, Center for Instructional Technology and Distance Learning, Cleveland State University (personal communication, March 9, 2023)

Advice for Adult Education Academic Programs and Faculty

Many program faculty in adult education work to include graduate students in scholarly endeavors such as conference presentations and co-authoring journal articles. Within the context of the professor/student relationship and graduate coursework, this is a great way for adult education learners to learn more about the field and get involved professionally. Once students graduate, it is difficult to maintain these endeavors. Faculty have new classes of students to teach and mentor, and graduates often have new jobs to navigate with new professional associations and opportunities to explore. However, just because it may take more time and/or effort to engage alumni and other adult education practitioners does not mean it is not worthwhile. On the contrary, if the field of adult education is to succeed, practitioners need to be partners and not just participants to be studied.

Faculty members may want to ask themselves how many current practitioners they know both in and out of their area of specialization; how many who are not alumni of the programs that the faculty teach in; and how are they as faculty enthusiastically seeking out their advice and expertise?

Faculty and others situated within the Academy need to actively seek out ways to include and partner with practitioners. Co-authoring articles and co-presenting both at conferences and for local organizations is one way. A quick sidebar about peer-reviewed academic journals – while we are not arguing against their importance, it is worthwhile to remember that by and large they are not easily accessible to practitioners who are not in graduate programs. And as discussed in Chapter 11, practitioners are more apt to read the publications from their professional associations.

For those leading departments or adult education programs at universities, consider developing an advisory board of practitioners. The group could meet occasionally (maybe once a year or even every three years) to review programs and suggest updates from the field. The group could be a resource for off-campus internship opportunities for students and more.

Suggestions for Course Curriculum

At the master's level, this textbook would be useful for those courses that, according to the CPAE program standards, focus on an introduction to the nature, function, and scope of adult education. At the doctoral level, a course that focuses on the historical, current, and future role of adult educators in our society would find this textbook invaluable. At both levels, the voices of the practitioners and their career journeys are useful for introductory courses.

Sample Lesson Plan. With a goal of helping learners become more knowledgeable of career possibilities within adult education, instructors could ask learners to select a chapter from Part II that is of interest to them personally. In addition to reading the chapter, learners would interview a practitioner working in that area. Learners might then present a 5–10-minute overview to the class or create a 5-minute video overview with snippets from interviews of practitioners along with the related chapter and post them online. Participating in a paired discussion or creating an online discussion post about their own adult education career aspirations could be a meaningful follow-up activity and inspire learners in new ways with the many opportunities available to them. It could potentially provide them focus as they continue to pursue their degree.

The Future of Careers in Adult Education

Practitioners in this book describe their master's and doctoral degrees as indispensable competitive advantages. They note that they often have to explain to supervisors and potential employers what exactly a degree in adult education means, but that, more importantly, they stressed how their knowledge and philosophical approach to the work (regardless of what sphere of adult education it exists within) benefits significantly from their academic study.

While the *Handbook of Adult and Continuing Education* (Rocco et al., 2021) calls for the field of adult education to continue to strengthen scholarship, we encourage scholars to also strengthen practice, and actively engage in listening to and amplifying the voices of practitioners in the field. There are many opportunities to blur the lines between scholarship and practice, and practitioners have much to offer.

As editors, we have been honored and privileged to work with outstanding contributing authors and shepherd this book into the world. Wherever your career path in adult education takes you, may you find joy and all the best kinds of challenges in this important work.

References

National Association of Colleges and Employers. (2021). *Competencies for a career-ready workforce*. www.naceweb.org/uploadedfiles/files/2021/resources/nace-career-readiness-competencies-revised-apr-2021.pdf

Rocco, T. S., Smith, M. C., Mizzi, R. C., Merriweather, L. R., & Hawley, J. D. (Eds.). (2021). *The handbook of adult and continuing education* (2020 ed.). Stylus.

Skakni, I., Maggiori, C., Masdonati, J., & Akkermans, J. (2022). Ready for careers within and beyond academia? Assessing career competencies amongst junior researchers. *Higher Education Research & Development*, 1–16.

Appendix

This section provides book resources for those seeking positions in higher education – either as a faculty member, a student affairs practitioner, or in an administration and leadership role in higher education.

Faculty

The Academic's Handbook, Fourth Edition (2020) edited by Lori Flores & Jocelyn Olcott
Advice for New Faculty Members: Nihil Nimus (2000) by Robert Boice
Becoming a Professor: A Guide to a Career in Higher Education (2015) by Marie K. Iding & R. Murray Thomas
Black Faculty in the Academy: Narratives for Negotiating Identity and Achieving Career Success (2015) edited by Fred A. Bonner II, Aretha Faye Marbley, Frank Tuitt, Petra A. Robinson, Rosa M. Banda, & Robin L. Hughes
Candid Advice for New Faculty Members: A Guide to Getting Tenure and Advancing Your Academic Career (2021) by Marybeth Gasman
The Craft of Research, Fourth Edition (Chicago Guides to Writing, Editing, and Publishing) (2016) by Wayne C. Booth, Gregory G. Colomb, Joseph M. Williams, Joseph Bizup, & William T. FitzGerald
The Handbook of Scholarly Writing and Publishing (2011) edited by Tonette S. Rocco & Timothy Gary Hatcher
How to Write a Lot: A Practical Guide to Productive Academic Writing (2018) by Paul Silvia
Mapping Your Academic Career: Charting the Course of a Professor's Life (2015) by Gary M. Burge
The Professor Is In: The Essential Guide to Turning Your Ph.D. into a Job (2015) by Karen Kelsky

Student Affairs

Beginning Your Journey: A Guide for New Professionals in Student Affairs (2015) by Marilyn J. Amey
Careers in Student Affairs: A Holistic Guide to Professional Development in Higher Education (2017) by Peggy C Holzweiss & Kelli Peck Parroott

Leadership and Administration

An Insider's Guide to University Administration (Higher Ed Leadership Essentials) (2020) by Daniel Grassian
How to Be a Dean (Higher Ed Leadership Essentials) (2019) by George Justice

Careers Outside of Academia

Building a Career Outside Academia: A Guide for Doctoral Students in the Behavioral and Social Sciences (2019) edited by Jennifer Brown Urban & Miriam R. Linver

Going Alt-Ac: A Guide to Alternative Academic Careers (2020) by Kevin Kelly, Kathryn E. Linder, & Thomas J. Tobin

General Career Advice

When Can You Start? The Only Job Search Guide You'll Ever Need (2018) by Paul Freiberger

Index

Note: *Italic* page numbers refer to *figures* and **Bold** page numbers refer to **tables**

501(c)(3) 204
501(c)(6) 204

access issues, of adult educators 16–17
accreditation 36, 54, 57, 205, 206
Accreditation Council for Continuing Medical Education (ACCME) 208
active-duty military positions 160
administration: correctional education 124; leadership and 240
Adobe Captivate 179
adult and workforce education (AWE) policy 184–187; field-related organizations **189**; future of 193–194; policy advocacy 188; policy work in 192
adult basic education (ABE): future of 76–78; job opportunities in 74; literacy programs 72; overview 71–72; professional qualifications 72–73; successful adult educator in 78–79; WIOA regulator of 74; *see also* adult foundational education
adult community/continuing education (ACE) 71
adult development 11
adult education (AE) 11–12; academic programs and faculty 238–239; activities 13; in assessment and evaluation 57; career model of 5; community-based. *see* community education; competitive advantage 210; contemporary challenges 59; and continuing education 13–14; definition 24; faculty members in 1; field 11–20; formal 12; forms 12; future of 115; Google Workspace for 63–66; graduate-level programs in 115; graduate programs 193; health professions education 146–153; informal 12, 13; knowledge of 85; master's degree in 78; museum education as 129; nonformal 13; philosophy 36; policy in 4; power dynamics 15; principles of 4; process of 12; programs 49, 72; publicly funded 12; robust 60–62; settings of 12–13; societal change and 42; teaching. *see* teaching; as technology. *see* technology; trends 171–173; workforce education and development 225–226

Adult Education Act (AEA) 186
Adult Education and Family Literacy Act of 1998 (AEFLA) 186
adult education and literacy (AEL) 71, 72
adult education theory 46
adult educators: access issues 16–17; competencies 25–27; constant of change issues 17–20; core skills needed by 14; emerging justice issues 18–19; in English as a Second Language 78–79; future opportunities 57; issues 15–20; as lifelong learners 31, 32; persistence and completion issues 16–17; power issues 15–16; professional preparation 14–15; roles of 13–14; technology self-assessment for 67
adult environmental education (AEE): career path 82–83; characteristics 81; future 87–88; historical overview of 81–82; international 84–85; organizations and agencies 88; overview 81; valued skills 83–87
adult foundational education 12, 185. *see also* adult basic education (ABE)
Adult Higher Education Alliance 19
adult learning 3, 11; adult and young 16; barriers for 73–74; concept of 2, 226; educational programs for 42; environments 26; knowledge 148; life transitions 73; social roles 11; theory-informed instruction for 27–30
Adult Learning and Development Theory 170
adult learning professionals (ALPs) 187, 192, 193
adult learning theories 16, 227–228. *see* andragogy; experiential learning; self-directed learning; transformative learning; assumptions and implications 75–76; and instructional design 174; and practice 84, 177–178
adult literacy education (ALE) 71
adult-oriented learning theory 27–30
adult secondary education (ASE) 71; WIOA regulator of 74
advising role, of adult educators 13
advocacy 18, 19, 185, 186
affirmative action 138
affirmative facilitation approach 38, 39

agile 103
Agile Learning Design (ALD) model 111, 177
Ahmed, M. 3, 4, 12
air quality monitoring 86
Aldenhuysen, Claire 3
Allen, W. C. 103
American Alliance of Museums (AAM) 134
American Association for Adult and Continuing Education (AAACE) 75, 226
American Association of Adult Education 14, 129
American Society for Association Executives (ASAE) 209, 210
Analyze, Design, Develop, Implement, Evaluate (ADDIE) model *44*, 44–45, 177; consulting 103–105; elements of 111
Anderson–Bloom Taxonomy 60
andragogical methods 35
andragogy 71, 75, 113, 143, 227; concept of 75; Knowles' theory of 46, 207
Annett, Cynthia 85–86
Army Learning Model 160
Articulate Storyline software 179
artificial intelligence (AI) 171, 172
arts education 129, 130, 134
assessment: case study 50–56; definition 49; and evaluation 49–50, **50**; future of adult education in 57; learners 73; planning for 54; practice and theory 56–57
Assessment, Evaluation, and Accountability in Adult Education (2020) 49
asset-based approach 38–39
asset-based community development 95
Association for Arts Administration Educators (AAAE) 135
Association for Talent Development (ATD) 114
association management system (AMS) 205
association professionals 210–211; roles of 205–206
authenticity 26

Bailey, J. 219
Bandura, A. 228
Barrett, Ian C. 4
Basarmak, U. 77
Beginner Teacher's Assistance Program (BTAP) 72
behavioral interview process 53
behavioral specialist 199
behaviorist learning theory 148
Bierema, L. L. 11, 226
Black Lives Matter (BLM) movement 18
Blassingame, Casandra 2
Bloom's Taxonomy 60
Blumenstyk, F. M. 17
Bohonos, J. W. 113
Bristol, Trammell L. 4
Brockett, R. G. 11
Brookfield, Stephen 20, 26, 32, 217
brownfields 83, 84
budgeting skills 55

budget management 235
budgets 197, 218
Bureau of Labor Statistics (BLS) projects 78
business acume 116, 140

Caffarella, R. S. 14, 16, 45, 161
calling 5, 30, 121, 232
career development 5, 93, 185, 210, 212
CareerHQ 212
careers, in adult education: in community education 91; competencies in 233–234; dimensions 234; exploration 35; in K-12 education 35; model 5; opportunities 114–115; overview in 1–4; workforce development 222–230
case study 50–56; Logic model for *54*, 54–55; request for proposals (RFP) 50, **51–52**, 53–56
Catholic Campaign for Human Development (CCHD) 217
Center for Faith-Based and Neighborhood Partnerships (CFBNP) 215
Center for Teaching and Learning 179
Certificate in Health Professions Education (CHPE) program 147
certification leaders 206
Certified Association Executive (CAE) 209–210
change 207, 212, 217, 219
change management 100, 102
Changing Landscape of Online Education (CHLOE) project 181
Chavis, D. 178
Cherewka, Alexis T. 4, 185
Chief Diversity Officer (CDO) 139
Chief Executive Officer (CEO) 50, 174, 206
Chief Financial Officer 174
Chief Learning Officer 113
Chief Online Officer 174
Christian educator 219
Citizen Action Groups (CAGs) 82, 83
civilian positions 157–160
Civil Rights Act of 1964 224
classroom management 47, 72, 134, 225
climate justice 88
Climate Justice Alliance 88
Clover, D. E. 81
coaching role, of adult educators 13
Coalition on Adult Basic Education (COABE) 75
coercive power 15
cognitive development 161
collaboration skills 47
College of Education and Human Development (CEHD) 147
college promise program 168
Collins, Royce Ann 3
Collins, Stephanie W. 4
combinatory play 233
Commission of Professors of Adult Education (CPAE) 83

communication 100, 102; and community building 61; skills 74
community action 93
community air monitoring 86–87
community-based approach 82
community-based programming 25
community capacity building 95
community education 3; academic training 91; career featuring 91–92; core competencies for 93–95; definition 92; opportunities in 97; in practice 91–93, 95–96; programs 75; project management 95; skills 92, 94; successful as 97–98; teachers 120–122; versatility 92
community engagement 83, 95
community foundation 165
community health workers and organizers 150
Community of Inquiry model 178
community organizing 42, 95, 217
community outreach 95
community partners 86
community stakeholders 167
competencies: for adult learners 25–27; consulting 104–105; correctional education 122; diversity, equity, and inclusion (DEI) 140–141; facilitation 39–40; museum education 132–134; nonprofit sector 168–169; professional organizations 208–209; for program planning 46–47
competency based learning 227
competency-based standardized test 74
"concept bloat" 31–32; risk of 32
conscientization process 29
constant of change 17–20
constructivism 216
constructivist learning theory 148
consulting: ADDIE model 103–104; career path 100–101; competencies 104–105; contract process 101–103; diversity 139–140; elevator pitch 106; future 105–106; program planning 103–104; self-directed learning 104; terminology 103
continuing education 207; professional development vs. 207
continuing education and training (CE/T) 35, 36, 40; adult and 1, 13–14
Coombs, P. H. 3, 4, 12
Cooper, Mary F. 71
coordination skills 151
core competency models 186–187
core values 37, 38
corporate training 109–116; Instructional Systems Design 110–111; leadership 112–113; measurement and evaluation 111–112
correctional education: administrators 124; careers in 120–125; future of 126; impact on recidivism 119; librarians 124–125; opportunities 125–126; and professional development 125; programs and settings 120; students' barriers to participation 118–119
correctional librarian 124–125
correctional officers 124
COVID-19 pandemic 59; online education 77, 181
credential 141, 209–210
credentialing 211
credibility 26, 84, 141
credible educators 26
critical consciousness: development of 31–32; framework 30–31
critical disability theory 19, 20
critical incident questionnaire 32
critical pedagogy 93
critical thinking 60, 208
Cross, K. P. 16–17
cultural competency 30–31, 149, 233
cultural institutions 128–135
cultural sensitivity 74
Cunningham, Phyllis 93
curriculum development 20, 46, 75, 124, 134, 160
customer relationship management (CRM) software 66

Daffron, S. R. 14, 16, 45, 161
Dang, N. L. T. 63
Darkenwald, G. S. 13
Day in the Life of an Instructional Technology Coach, A (Engler) 200
decision-making 103, 121, 141, 150, 184, 185
deep learning 18
demographic shifts 18–19
Department of Defense (DoD) 156
Department of Education (DoE) 176
Department of Education Office of Career, Technical, and Adult Education (OCTAE) 188
DeSimone, R. L. 44
dialogue, facilitation of 94
Diamond, R. M. 60
digital badging 18
digital inclusion 193
digital literacy 209
digital media literacy 18
Director of Christian Education (DCE) 214–215
Director of Leadership Development 112
Director of Organizational Development 113
Director of Religious Education (DRE) 217–218
Director of Talent Management 113
Dirkx, J. M. 63
"disorienting dilemma" 29
dispositional barriers 17
distance learning 110
Distributive Education Clubs of America (DECA) 35
diversity 19–20, 30–31; and equity 26–27; and inclusion 30–31; program manager 138–139; and social emotional needs coaches 201–202; trainers and experts 150

diversity consultant 139–140
diversity coordinator 138
diversity director 139
diversity, equity, and inclusion (DEI) 30–31, 54; career pathways 142–143; certifications 141–142; competencies 140–141; current and emerging trends 144; degrees and credentials 141; field of organizational 138; nonprofit sector 172; professional associations 144; roles and responsibilities 138–140
diversity, equity, inclusion, and justice (DEIJ) 95
diversity program manager 138–139
docent 133
Doctor of Pharmacy programs 24
donor development cycle 170
donor populations 166
Dweck, C. S. 31–32
dyslexia coordinator 201

economic development 84, 223
educational program 42; colleges and universities 42; workplace-based 42; *see also* program planning
educational theory 31–32
education consulting 100. *see also* consulting
Education for Sustainability (EfS) 87–89
education manager 205
education policy 185
education policy leadership 185
education services series 159
Education Technology/Media Producer 110
Einstein, Albert 233
eLearning Developer 101, 110, 174, 175
elevator pitch 106, 132
Elias, J. L. 41
emancipatory transformational learning 29
emergency remote teaching 59
emerging justice issues 18–19
emotional intelligence 209
empathy 37
employee resource groups 138, 143
engagement efforts 15–20
English as a Second Language (ESL) 11, 71, 200–201; adult educator in 78–79; future of 76–77; job opportunities in 74
English for Speakers of Other Languages (ESOL) program 71, 185
English language learners (ELLs) 72, 200
enhancement levels, of SAMR model 62
environmental issues 82, 87
environmental scans **187**
environments, psychologically safe 26
equity 26–27, 30–31
evaluation 49; assessment and 49–50, **50**; case study 50–56; definition 49; future of adult education in 57; model 112; practice and theory 56–57
evaluator 50, 51, 54, 184
evidence-based research skills 148

Exceptional Student Services (ESS) 123
executive staff 206
experiential learning 28–29, 144, 227
expert power 15

face-to-face learning 14, 59, 66, 109, 229
facilitation: adult learners' life transitions 73; affirmative 38; career opportunities 40; competencies and strategies 39–40; learning 37; method 37–39; productive dialogue 94; Rogers' theory of 36–37; skills 34–36; *see also* facilitation theory
facilitation theory 36–37
facilitative teaching. *see* facilitation theory
faculty development 147
faculty development program 161
faith-based organization (FBO) 215, 217, 218
Family and Community Partnership Liaison Program 199
family literacy programs 72; future of 76–77; job opportunities in 74
feedback 149
field-related organizations **189**
Finn, D. 76
flexibility: consulting 105; museum education 132
flipped classroom approach 148
Floyd, George 18, 217
formal adult education 3, 12
formal educational system 3
formal religious education 215–216
Fortune 500 110, 114
foundations 165; community 165
Four-Branch Model of Emotional Intelligence (1997) 209
Freire, P. 20, 29, 59, 60, 62, 66, 180
Frost, R. 67
Frye, S. 218
full-time adult education practitioners 14
funder(s) 166
funding opportunities 75, 187, 188
fundraiser 166

GED® 123
General Education Degree (GED) 71, 72, 156
General Service (GS) positions 157
Generation Xer 196
gifted coordinator 201
globalization 42
global learning 109–116
Google Classroom 63, 65
Google Workspace, for education 63–66
Gordon, H. R. D. 224
Gouthro, P. A. 76
Gracious Center for Learning and Enrichment Activities (GCLEA) 215
grant proposal writer. *see* grant writers
grant writers 166
grant writing 143, 185

Index

Great Recession 129
Green, Wendy M. 2, 24
Grenier, R. S. 129
Griswold, W. 3
Groen, J. 143
Grogan, M. 196
ground rules 38
Grow, G. 28
GuideStar 211

Hamutoglu, N. B. 77
Handbook of Adult and Continuing Education 20, 49, 239
Hannon, K. 17
"haphazard process" 43
Haskell Environmental Research Studies Center (HERS) 82, 83
Haskell Indian Nations University (Haskell) 82
hazardous substances 82
healthcare administrators 151
healthcare enterprise 149
healthcare environment 149
health information personnel 151
health/patient advocates 150
health professions education 146–153; access key resources 149; competencies 148–150; cultural competencies 149; evidence-based research skills 148; feedback 150; future of 152; healthcare environment 149; interpersonal communication skills 149; knowledge of medical/health terminology 149; learning/instructional designer 151; medical writers 151; networking 150; opportunities and responsibilities 150–151; patient care coordinators 151; program evaluation 149
Hennes, Cathryn A. 4
Higher Education Act of 1965 178
High School Equivalency (HiSET) 71
Hill, L. H. 2, 49, 149
HiSet© 123
Hite, L. M. 5
Hoffman, Alexander 2, 24
honesty 16, 178
Horton, M. 32, 88, 89
Houle, Cyril 11, 13
Houle's pyramid of leadership 14, *15*
human-centric approach 37
Human Performance Improvement (HPI) 113
Human Performance Technology (HPT) 113
human resource development 43, 45
Hunter-Johnson, Yvonne 4

Imposter Syndrome 140
individual adult learners 13
Individual Education Plan (IEP) 123
individualized transformational learning 29
Individuals with Disabilities Education Act (IDEA) 123

informal adult education 3, 12, 13
informal learning 128–130, 216, 219
informal religious education 215–216
information literacy 18
institutional barriers 17
institutional racism 140
Institutional Review Board (IRB) 84
instructional coach 198–199
instructional design. *see* online learning/instructional design
instructional designer 174
Instructional Systems Design (ISD) 110–111
instructional systems series 159–160
instructional technologist 177
instructional technology coordinator 200
integrated education and training (IET) 190
Integrated English Literacy and Civics Education 185
"integrative approach" 119
intellectual capital 223
interactive model of program planning 45
intercultural competence 85
international AEE 84–85
international exchange 84–85
International Society for Performance Improvement (ISPI) 114
interpersonal communication skills 149
intervention specialist 195
interviews, with client 102
Isaac-Savage, E. P. 18, 113

Jacobson, L. 197
Jeremic, R. 20
job description 43, 92, 105
job opportunities, for adult educators 74
job skills training 39, 106
Joint Professional Military Education (JPME) 161
journals 114–115

Kansas State University (K-State) 82, 83
Kapp, Alexander 227
Kawalilak, C. 143
K-12 education 101; behavioral specialist 199; career in 35; career opportunities 197–202; competencies 197; future of 202–203; instructional coaches 198–199; instructional technology coordinator 200; professional development in 195–202; public school systems 188
Kegan, R. 29
Kennedy, Rosary-Joyce 4
King, Martin L. 214
Kirkpatrick training evaluation model 112
knowledge of leadership theory 164, 170
knowledge, skills, and abilities (KSAs) 4, 103, 177, 222, 232; policy process **190**; policy research and analysis 190, **191**; practitioner 187, **187**
Knowles, M. S. 46, 75, 104, 113, 115, 178, 227
Knowles' theory of andragogy 207

Kolb, D. A. 46, 227
Kolb's experiential learning 46
K-State TAB Programs 84
Kurt, S. 76

Lanzo, Caryn 3, 179
large-scale expansion 17–18
leadership: and administration 240; corporate training 112–113; Houle's pyramid of 14, *15*; workshops for professional development 135
leadership skills 14, 24, 106, 113
leadership theory 170
lean Six Sigma 113
learner assessment **187**
learner-centered approach 37, 86
learning community 62–63
"learning disability" 123
learning environments 26
learning experience architect 101
learning/instructional designer 151
learning leaders 205
learning management systems (LMS) administrator 174–177, 205
learning modalities 111. *see also* face-to-face learning
learning process, and technology 59–60
Lee, H. T. 119
legacy software systems 106
legitimate power 15
Leven, Blase 84–85
LGBTQ 143
lifelong learning 31, 32, 71, 72, 125, 216
limited liability company (LLC) 101
Lindeman, Eduard 11
LinkedIn 107, 235
LinkedIn Learning 65, 179
literacy programs 72
Little Village Environmental Justice Organization (LVEJO) 86
Logic model, for case study *54,* 54–55
Lord, B. 131
Lord, G. D. 131

managerial skills 14
Marine Corps 162
Martin, F. 59
Martin, James B. 3
Martin, L. G. 54
Massive Open Online Courses (MOOCs) 18
Maxwell, Kathi 198, 200
Mayer, J. D. 209
McDonald, K. S. 5
McMillan, D. 178
McPherson, G. 78
Measurement and Evaluation (M&E) 111–112
medical writers 151
Meecha, Christina 3
memorandums of understanding (MOUs) 187

mentoring role, of adult educators 13
mentorship 236–237
Merriam, S. B. 11, 36, 41, 226
Merriam, S. G. 13
Merriweather, L. R. 18
Messmer, J. E. 121
meta-competencies 233–235
Mezirow, J. 227
Microcredentialing 212
Microsoft 365 program 209
military-affiliated learners 156
military education 3, 156–163; active-duty military positions 160; civilian positions 157–160; future 161–162; practice and theory 160–161
mindset theory 32
misinformation 18
Missouri Association for Adult Continuing and Community Education (MAACCE) 75
mixed-methods research methods 55
Monaghan, C. H. 4, 113
monitoring and evaluation 95
motivation, theories of 46
Movement Generation Justice and Ecology Project 88
muddiest point formative feedback method 32
multiple stakeholder 43, 44
Murray-Johnson, Kayon 2, 3, 20
Murray's career journey 109–110
museum education 128–135; and administration 128; as adult education 129, 131; competencies 132–134; creativity and curiosity 133; organizational levels 130–131
Museum Education Roundtable 134
"*Mwalimu*" 91
My Brother's Keeper (MBK) program 215

National Action Plan for Adult Literacy 2021 192
National Association of Colleges and Employers (NACE) 234
National Bureau of Economic Research 224
National Center for Education Statistics (2020) 226
National Literacy Act (NLA) of 1991 186
National Priorities List (NPL) 82
Native American and Other Minority Institutions (NAOMI) program 82
needs assessments 39, 46, 47
networking 107, 135
neuromyths 31, 32
New Faculty Orientation (NFO) program 148
Newman, Michael 93, 94
niche 101, 102
Nixon, Richard 138
nonformal adult education 4, 13
nonformal learning 84, 128, 216
non-profit organizations 50, 120, 204
nonprofit sector 164–173; author's experience 164; competencies and credentials 168–169;

definition of 164; diversity, equity, and inclusion (DEI) 172; fundraisers 166; future of 171–173; grant writers 166; professional associations 171; program manager 165–166; program officer 166–167; roles and responsibilities 165–168; scholarship officer 167–168; volunteer administrators 168
non-subject-matter experts (SMEs) **190**
North American Association for Environmental Education 88
Nyanungo, Hleziphi Naomie 3
Nyerere, Julius 91

Office of Career, Technical, and Adult Education (OCTAE) 188
Ohio Department of Education 201
Ohio Resident Educator Program 196
OneDrive/Google Drive 63
OneNote Class Notebook 63, 65
O*NET OnLine 216
online collaboration tools 63
online course design 178
Online Course Quality Review Rubric (OSCQR) 178
online document collaboration 63
Online Learning Consortium 174
online learning/instructional design 77, 110, 174; content and media development 175; future of 181; instructional technologist 177; LMS Administrator 176, 177; project management 175; quality assurance 175; teaching and training 175–176
online training 3
on-the-job training 224
organization 102
organizational behavior 38
organizational culture 196
organizational learning 109
organization development (OD) 38

Palloff, R. 178
participatory approaches 94
participatory learning 81
patience 74
patient care coordinators 151
Pearson, W. 17
pedagogy 85, 93
performance management 139, 141
performance support systems 113
performative activism 140, 144
personalized engagement 171
philanthropic sector 165
philanthropy 165
Phillips model 112
Pickard, A. 74
policy: in adult education 4; processes and development 188–190; research and analysis 190–192, **191;** *see also* education policy; public policy
policy advocacy 186
policy leadership 192–193; adult and workforce education 184; career paths in 185–186; core competency areas 186–187; KSAs. *see* knowledge, skills, and abilities (KSAs)
political savviness 235
popular education 81, 83, 86, 93
Porterfield, Michael 2, 3, 179–180
post-secondary education 12, 17, 125
power: dynamics in adult educators 15–16; issues 15–16; program planner 16; *see also* reward power and coercive power
power dynamics, in adult education 15
Pratt, Daniel 148
Pratt, K. 178
Precertification Workshop (PCW) 72
Preparing Adult Educators for Social Justice (Isaac-Savage and Merriweather) 18
prescriptive role, of adult educators 13
problem-based learning strategies 29
professional associations 204, 210–211
professional development (PD) 66, 192, 229; for adult educators 77; *vs.* continuing education 207; correctional education and 125; education and 206; in K-12 education 195–202; leadership workshops for 135
professional educator 12
professional organizations 75, 114, 180, 202, 204–213, 237–238; adult learners 207; association professional 210–211; association, roles of 205–206; certification leaders 206; competencies 208–209; competitive advantage 210; executives 206; job listings 212; learning leaders 205; overview 204–205; practice and theory 206–208; professional development *vs.* continuing education 207; salaries and benefits 211
professional preparation, adult educators 14–15
professional qualifications 72–73
professional societies 204
program assessment 13
program developer/administrator 13
program evaluation 54–55, 149; *see also* evaluation
program evaluator 54–55
Program for the Accreditation of Joint Military Education (PAJE) 161
program manager 165–166
program officer 166–167
program planner 16
program planning: adult education theory 46; collaboration skills 47; competencies for 46–47; consulting 103–104; and delivering programs 94–95; evaluation skills 46–47; interactive model of 45, 161; job 43; models for 44–46, 53; overview 42–43; process 43–44; project management 47; *see also* educational programs

program planning theory 169–170
project management 47, 175; community education 95
prospects populations 166
Protean Career Model 234
psychologically safe environments 26
publicly funded adult education 12
public policy: adult and workforce education 184; career in 185–186; Cherewka, Alexis 185; core competency areas 186–187; education policy 185; Reyna, Aaron J. 185; Roumell, Liz 184; *see also* policy; policy leadership
Puentedura, R. R. 61, 62
Putman, P. G. 170

qualitative research 55
Quality Matters (QM) 174, 181
quantitative research 55

Ragan, T. J. 178
Ramdeholl, D. 20
Rao, N. J. 60
recidivism 119
recruiters, consultant 102
reducing recidivism 126
referent power 15
refugees 167
regional museum associations 134
religious activities 217–218
religious education (RE): community organizations 215; competencies 216–218; formal and informal 215–216; philosophical approach 216; technology in 218–219
request for proposals (RFP) 2, 50, **51–52**, 53–56; program evaluator 54–55
research skills 228, 229
resourcefulness 74
restorative justice 126
restored citizenship 120–122, 124
resumes 107, 235
retention 60, 168, 223
Revised Bloom's Taxonomy (RBT) 60–62; "coupling" of 62; and SAMR model 61–62
reward power 15
Reyna, Aaron J. 4, 185
Rhodes, Christy M. 2
robust adult education 60–62
Rocco, T. S. 19
Roessger, K. 54
Rogers, Carl 36–37
Rogers, D. L. 77
roles, of adult educators 13–14
Rose, A. D. 24
Rosenberg, M. B. 40
Ross-Gordon, Jovita M. 2, 3, 20
Roumell, Elizabeth A. 4, 184

safety training 120

Salovey, P. 209
SAMR model of technology 60–62
Schmidt, Steven W. 2
scholarship donors 167–168
scholarship officers 167–168
School-to-Work Opportunities Act (1993) 224
Schultz, D. 224
Schwarz, R. 38
self-directed learning (SDL) 28, 32, 75, 143, 228; consulting 104
self-directedness 207–208
self-help groups 13
sense of community 178
significant learning 174
situational barriers 16–17
skilled facilitator approach 37–38
slacktivism 140
"smile sheets" 112
Smith-Hughes Act in 1917 224
Smith, P. L. 178
social constructivism 177–178
social emotional needs coaches 201–202
social justice 18, 30
social learning theory 228
social media 32; platforms 18; sites 107, 212
Society for Human Resource Management (SHRM) 114
soft skills 100, 104, 227, 228
Software Development Life Cycle (SDLC) 103
Sork, T. J. 16
Staged Self-Directed Learning (SSDL) model 28
stakeholder 16, 43, 201
standardized tests 123
standards development 36, 206
State University of New York (SUNY) 178
Steinert, Y. 147
stewardship 166, 170
stories 79
storytelling 79
strategic planning 160
Strickland, Shawna L. 4
structural barriers 139
subject matter experts (SMEs) 36, 63, 139, 175
Sumner, J. 81
sustainability education 81

talent management 109–116
tangible assets 34
teacher-centered approach 37
Teachers of English to Speakers of Other Languages (TESOL) 201
teaching: authentic and credible educators 26; critical consciousness 30–31; cultural competence 30–31; diversity and equity 26–27; educator competencies for 25–27; learning environments 25–26; literacy 72;

psychologically safe environments 26; theory-informed instruction 27–30
Teaching English to Speakers of Other Languages (TESOL) 73
Technical Assistance to Brownfields (TAB) Program 83
technical writer 100–102
technology 232–233; Bloom's Taxonomy and critical thinking 60; integration 76–77; learning community 62–63; learning process and 59–60; professional development 66; in religious education 218–219; SAMR model of 60–62; self-assessment for adult educators 67; skills 66; strategies for using 67; for teaching and learning 77
technology acuity **190**
technology-based learning 18
technology training 100, 102
TEDEd 65
TEFL 73
Temporary Assistance for Needy Families (TANF) 39
TESL 73
test facilitator 122
Test of Adult Basic Education (TABE) 72, 123
Test of English as a Foreign Language (TOEFL) 73
third sector. *see* nonprofit sector
Thomas, R. R. 138
1700 occupational group 157; series 158–160
time management 104
tokenism 140
total quality management 113
training: corporate 109–116; instruction series 159; occupational series 158; transfer of 223
training specialist 72, 110, 225
transformational learning 29–30
transformation levels, of SAMR model 62
transformative learning 85, 144, 227
transitional education 122

United Nations Educational, Scientific and Cultural Organization (UNESCO) 82
United States: adult education programs in 118; Doctor of Pharmacy programs in 24; incarceration rate in 118; Office of Personnel Management (OPM) 157–158; postsecondary education programs 17
Universal Design for Learning (UDL) 19, 27

University of Missouri–St. Louis (UMSL) 71
U.S. Agency for International Development 83
U.S. Climate Action Network 88
U.S. Environmental Protection Agency (EPA) 82
U.S. Office of Personnel Management (OPM) 157–158

Van Der Werff, J. 161
Vella, Jane 88
Verner, C. 11
video conferencing 63
virtual facilitators 40
virtual reality 18
vocation 121, 186
vocational education 224
Vocational Education Act of 1963 224
volunteer administrators 168
volunteer management 143
VP of Learning and Organizational Development 112
Vygotsky, L. S. 178

Walter, P. 81, 82
Wasserman, Kim 86
Werner, J. M. 44
white privilege 140
Winland, Murray 4
Wolpert-Gawron, H. 198
workforce development 40, 96, 222–230; *see also* workforce education
workforce education 222–224; and adult education 225–226; benefits 222–224; career in 228–229; employee level 222–223; history of 224–225; on-the-job training 224; organizational level 223; societal level 223–224
Workforce Innovation and Opportunity Act (WIOA) 74, 185, 186, 188
Workforce Investment Act (WIA) of 1998 185, 186
Workforce Investment Partnership Act (1997) 224
workplace-based educational program 42
workplace training and development 13
writing skills 39, 55, 193

Xie, K. 59

Zacharakis, J. 161